D0141270

Reader in Archaeological Theory

Post-Processual and Cognitive Approaches

Archaeologists are increasingly concerned with how artifacts and sites can be interpreted, and what they may reveal about the past. They face perplexing questions about their work: can we discover a "real" past, or do we simply create the past in the present? And can we reconstruct the thoughts and emotions of prehistoric peoples, or are we limited to studying their diet, economy and technology? This *Reader in Archaeological Theory: Post-Processual and Cognitive Approaches* presents sixteen articles addressing these and other key theoretical issues using a format which makes this notoriously complex subject easy for students to understand. This volume:

- provides an intellectual history of different approaches to archaeology, contextualizing post-processual and cognitive archaeologies in terms of academic trends within and outside the discipline
- organizes these important papers into clear sections which deal with: constructing approaches to archaeology; the meanings of things; the prehistoric mind and cognition; gender; ideology and social theory; and archaeology's relationship to today's society and politics
- includes lucid section introductions contextualizing each topic, explaining why the papers included are important and what they imply about archaeological practice, and summarizing the key points of each
- emphasizes research from the New World, making these advances in archaeological theory especially relevant to North American students.

David S. Whitley is the US representative of the ICOMOS rock art committee and lectures at UCLA. He is an internationally acclaimed expert on rock art, on which he has published widely.

ROUTLEDGE READERS IN ARCHAEOLOGY

Series editor: David S. Whitley

Reader in Gender Archaeology
Edited by Kelley Hays-Gilpin and David S. Whitley

Reader in Archaeological Theory

Post-Processual and Cognitive Approaches

edited by
David S. Whitley

London and New York

First published 1998
by Routledge
11 New Fetter Lane, London EC4P 4EE

Simultaneously published in the USA
and Canada by Routledge
29 West 35th Street, New York,
NY 10001

Typeset in Bell Gothic and Perpetua by
Florencetype Ltd, Stoodleigh, Devon

Printed and bound in Great Britain by
TJ International Ltd,
Padstow, Cornwall

British Library Cataloguing in Publication Data

A catalogue record for this book is available from the
British Library

Library of Congress Cataloguing in Publication Data

Reader in archaeological theory: post-processual and
cognitive approaches/[edited by] David S. Whitley.

(Routledge readers in archaeology)

Includes bibliographical references and index.

1. Archaeology–Philosophy.
2. Archaeology–Methodology.   3. Cognition and
culture. I. Whitley, David S. II. Series.

CC72.R4 1998

930.1'01–dc21   97–30384

ISBN 0–415–14159–1 (hbk)
ISBN 0–415–14160–5 (pbk)

Contents

CONTENTS

Contributors

Persis B. Clarkson, University of Winnipeg, Department of Anthropology, 515 Portage Ave, Winnipeg, MB R3B-2E9, Canada.

Charles R. Cobb, SUNY, Department of Anthropology, PO Box 6000, Binghampton, NY 13902-6000, USA.

Kent V. Flannery, University of Michigan, Museum of Anthropology, Ann Arbor, MI 48109-1076, USA.

Ian Hodder, Cambridge University, Department of Archaeology, Cambridge, CB2 3DZ England.

Dorothy Hosler, Massachusetts Institute of Technology, 8-138 MIT, Cambridge, MA 02139, USA.

Mary C. Kennedy, Washington University, Department of Anthropology, CB 1114, St. Louis, MO 63130-4899, USA.

A. Bernard Knapp, University of Glasgow, Department of Archaeology, Glasgow, G12-8QQ, Scotland.

Mark P. Leone, University of Maryland, Department of Anthropology, College Park, MD 20742, USA.

J. David Lewis-Williams, Archaeology Department, University of the Witwatersrand, Johannesburg, 2050, South Africa.

Joyce Marcus, University of Michigan, Museum of Anthropology, Ann Arbor, MI 48109-1076, USA.

Randall H. McGuire, SUNY, Department of Anthropology, PO Box 6000, Binghampton, NY 13902-6000, USA.

Steven Mithen, University of Reading, Department of Archaeology, Reading RG6 2AA England.

Christopher S. Peebles, Indiana University, Glenn A. Black Lab, 9th & Fess Sts, Bloomington, IN 47405, USA.

Dean Saitta, University of Denver, Department of Anthropology, 2130 S. Race St, Denver, CO 80208-0174, USA.

Michael Shanks, University of Wales, Department of Archaeology, Lampeter SA48 7ED, Wales.

Christopher Tilley, University College Lond, Department of Anthropology, Gower St, London WC1E 6BT, England.

Patty Jo Watson, Washington University, Department of Anthropology, CB 1114, St. Louis, MO 63130-4899, USA.

Gary White Deer, Route 5, Box 308P, Ada, OK 74820, USA.

David S. Whitley, ICOMOS Rock Art Committee, 447 Third St, Fillmore, CA 93015, USA.

PREFACE

Archaeological method and theory have changed dramatically since about 1980. What had previously been a discipline marked by only a couple of different approaches has changed into a field with numerous perspectives and commitments, some of which have evolved rapidly in name, substance and method over the course of only a few years. This no doubt is healthy for the discipline. But it is difficult for the student who must wend his or her way through conflicting and often polarized points of view, in an effort to find their own sense of what archaeology is, and how it can and should be practiced.

This reader is a compilation of articles intended to help the student understand the diversity and main trends in cognitive and post-processual archaeologies. Its purpose is to introduce the primary philosophical and methodological problems that these approaches attempt to resolve, and the kinds of substantive archaeological issues that they address. As is to be expected, it reflects my own views of and concerns about the nature of these approaches, and my own agenda in promoting them. Let me briefly explain these at the outset.

A primary concern in preparing this reader results from my take on the general perception of cognitive and post-processual archaeologies that are maintained by my fellow American colleagues. This is not entirely a seat-of-the-pants perception of these views: it is based on a series of commentaries formally expressed at regional and national meetings over the last few years. Although necessarily a generalization, the rank-and-file viewpoint, judging from these commentaries, seems to turn on a few key points. Each of these contributes to the sense that cognitive and post-processual archaeologies are somewhat irrelevant to the Americanist archaeologist. What is worse, the feeling exists that, if ignored long enough, these approaches will eventually go away.

1   Cognitive and post-processual archaeologies are a foreign (primarily English) phenomena. This distances them from Americanist research geographically and, thereby, conceptually, diminishing their importance to American archaeologists.

2   Cognitive and post-processual archaeologies are all armchair theorizing. The impli-
        cation here is that, while they might sound good on paper, they have little value
        to empirical archaeological research and an interest in actually understanding the
        past, as opposed to just talking about how one might understand it.
3   Cognitive and post-processual archaeologies are interesting but the reason that
        American archaeologists have retained their processual approach is because it has
        worked so well in their region. This is the ultimate argument for maintaining the
        status quo.
4   The challenge to processual archaeology is exclusively from the most extreme brand
        of post-processual archaeology, and this is taken to comprise an extreme form of
        relativism.

A main purpose in preparing and organizing this reader is to counter these positions, because each of them is, in my view, false. I have intentionally emphasized American contributions to the literature in an attempt to break the view that cognitive and post-processual archaeologies were invented by, and are now primarily practiced by, English archaeologists. A review of the history of recent archaeological research shows, for example, that a number of American archaeologists were conducting cognitive and post-processual studies during the 1970s and early 1980s (e.g., Lathrap 1973; Flannery and Marcus 1976; Hall 1976, 1977; Deetz 1977; Davis 1978; Fritz 1978; Wynn 1979, 1981), as were archaeologists in other countries (e.g., Lewis-Williams 1980, 1981, 1982; Huffman 1981). The point here is not to claim some false pride of place for American (or other) archaeologist as the inventors of these approaches. It is to empha-size instead that they are developments within western archaeology as a whole, including American. Likewise, my emphasis on American approaches and applications is intended to demonstrate that cognitive and post-processual archaeologies are not solely or even predominantly an English practise today.

In part this perception of who is doing what where, and what exactly they are doing, has resulted due to a general tendency in the way this work is being conducted. Much (but by no means all) of the emphasis by English archaeologists associated with Cambridge University has been theoretical. This is because they recognize that theory is important. The American contributions, in contrast, have tended to be more empiri-cally oriented. The theoretical statements are, of course, the most widely read, because they are broadly applicable. A statement about the fundamental relationship of archae-ology to science is relevant to all archaeologists, regardless of their region of interest. Yet an empirically-grounded, ideological study of Maya epigraphy and iconography (e.g., Freidel and Schele 1988) is primarily of interest to Mayanists, and is only read by them. The combination of these two tendencies, an English emphasis on theory and an American emphasis on empirical studies, matched against the nature of the way that the profes-sion reads the literature, leads to a false conclusion: that cognitive and post-processual archaeologies are primarily English, and that they are exclusively theoretical statements. Yet as these papers show, there is substantial empirical research being conducted within the broad constraints of these approaches, and a significant amount of it is occurring in the Americas.

The third perspective, that processual archaeology should be retained regionally because of its empirical success, is ultimately anti-intellectual. It assumes that archaeologists can ignore any critique that they do not like, as long as they are self-satisfied in what they are doing. As a number of contributions in this volume show, processualism may have been successful in some of its endeavors, but this has only been in terms of certain problem-domains. Regardless of one's commitment to scientific methods and goals, the positivism of processual archaeology entails a series of problematic implications and philosophical views. A commitment to good science and/or archaeology – which I assume all archaeologists and students aspire to – necessitates, fundamentally, that these problems be resolved. This cannot occur through arguments that appeal to special conditions on a region-by-region basis – an exceptionalist argument, I might add, that precisely contradicts some of the positivist tenets that it purports to support, especially the positivist view of a unified science, applicable to all disciplines.

Finally, there is a widespread and self-serving perception in American processual archaeology that the only alternative to it is the most extreme form of post-processualism. This is a convenient debating strategy: it is much easier to dismiss an extremist point of view than one that is closer to your own. Yet this is ultimately a false characterization on two counts. First, much research has been conducted that has sought to expand the scientific investigation of the past into new areas, using new kinds of data and new theoretical models. This has the potential to improve scientific archaeology – hardly contradictory to the wishes of processualists – yet this has been ignored, or grossly misunderstood, due to guilt by association. Here, no middle ground is allowed to exist. Second, even the more extreme positions of certain post-processualists have been caricatured as much more extreme than, in fact, they are. Post-processualists, for example, have been careful to draw distinctions between their positions and extreme forms of relativism, where "anything goes". These distinctions may be subtle to the processualists, but to ignore them is to misrepresent these post-processualist positions in fundamental ways. Some post-processualists, of course, are likewise guilty of critiquing a caricatured view of positivist science. But the important point is that, in either case, all this does is to create straw men, the knocking over of which serves no real purpose.

My goal in organizing this volume is partly to point to a middle ground in the recent debates. It is intended to provide a sense of the real continuum of approaches that has developed over the last two decades. I believe that this will give you a better view of recent trends in archaeological method and theory than may be obtained from reading a few works that establish the polarized views of a couple of key voices. These voices are important, but they are not the only ones that need to be heard.

David S. Whitley
Fillmore, California
"The Postmodernist Capital of Ventura County"

■ ■ ■

References

Davis, E.L. (ed.) (1978) *The Ancient Californians: Rancholabrean Hunters of the Mojave Lakes Country*, Los Angeles: Natural History Museum of Los Angeles County.

Deetz, J.F. (1977) *In Small Things Forgotten*, New York: Doubleday Anchor.

Flannery, K. and J. Marcus (1976) "Formative Oaxaca and the Zapotec Cosmos", *American Scientist* 64: 374–83.

Freidel, D. and L. Schele (1988) "Kingship in the Late Preclassic Maya Lowlands: The Instruments and Places of Ritual Power", *American Anthropologist* 90: 547–67.

Fritz, J. (1978) "Paleopsychology Today: Ideational Systems and Human Adaptation in Prehistory", in C. Redman *et al.* (eds) *Social Archaeology: Beyond Subsistence and Dating*, New York: Academic.

Hall, R. (1976) "Ghosts, Water Barriers, Corn and Sacred Enclosures in the Eastern Woodlands", *American Antiquity* 41: 360–64.

——(1977) "An Anthropocentric Perspective for Eastern Woodlands Prehistory", *American Antiquity* 42: 499–518.

Huffman, T.N. (1981) "Snakes and Birds: Expressive Space at Great Zimbabwe", *African Studies* 40: 131–50.

Lathrap, D.W. (1973) "The Gift of the Cayman: Some Thoughts on the Subsistence Basis of Chavin", in D.W. Lathrap and J. Douglas (eds) *Variation in Anthropology*, Ubrana, Illinois Archaeological Survey.

Lewis-Williams J.D. (1980) "Ethnography and Iconography: Aspects of Southern San Thought and Art", *Man*, n.s., 15: 467–82.

——(1981) *Believing and Seeing: Symbolic Meaning in Southern San Rock Paintings*, London, Academic.

——(1982) "The Economic and Social Contexts of Southern San Rock Art", *Current Anthropology*, 23: 429–49.

Wynn, T. (1979) "The Intelligence of Later Acheulean Hominids", *Man* 14: 371–91.

——(1981) "The Intelligence of the Oldowan Hominids", *Journal of Human Evolution* 10: 529–41.

ACKNOWLEDGEMENTS

I have incurred debts to a number of people in preparing this volume. It originally got under way through the support of Andrew Wheatcroft and has been ably pushed along by Victoria Peters, both at Routledge. I thank them for their assistance and patience. Patricia Stankiewicz, Janet Goss and especially Nadia Jacobson have also provided tremendous support in producing the volume. I owe a special debt to the authors included here, whose research is the real point of all of this. Chris Peebles, Kelley Hays-Gilpin, Persis Clarkson, Mitch Allen, Jim Pearson, Bob Elston and Mary Lou Larson have graciously assisted me in various ways during the preparation of this volume. And, of course I owe considerable thanks to Tamara and Carmen Whitley who, once again, have put up with my odd schedule of writing hours, and my tendency to cover all horizontal surfaces in the house with piles of books and papers.

The papers in this volume have been reprinted through the kind permission of their authors and publishers, from the following original sources:

Flannery, K.V. and J. Marcus (1993) Cognitive Archaeology. *Cambridge Archaeological Journal* 3:260–67.

Leone, M.P., (1986) Symbolic, Structural, and Critical Archaeology. In *American Archaeology: Past and Future*, edited by D.J. Meltzer, D.D. Fowler and J.A. Sabloff, pp. 415–33.

Shanks M. and Hodder I. (1995) Processual, Postprocessual and Interpretive Archaeologies. In *Interpreting Archaeology: Finding Meaning in the Past*, edited by I. Hodder, M. Shanks, A. Alexandri, V. Buchli, J. Carman, J. Last and G. Lucas, pp. 3–28. London: Routledge.

Hosler, D. (1995) Sound, Color and Meaning in the Metallurgy of Ancient West Mexico. *World Archaeology* 27:100–115.

Clarkson, P.B. (1996) Archaeological Imaginings: Contextualization of Images. To appear in *Proceedings of the 1996 Chacmool Conference*. University of Calgary.

Mithen, S. (1994) From Domain Specific to Generalized Intelligence: A Cognitive Interpretation of the Middle/Upper Paleolithic Transition. In *The Ancient Mind: Elements of Cognitive Archaeology*, edited by C. Renfrew and E.B.W. Zubrow, pp. 29–36. London: Cambridge University Press.

Lewis-Williams, J.D. (1991) Wrestling with Analogy: A Methodological Dilemma in Upper Paleolithic Art Research. *Proceedings of the Prehistoric Society*, 57 Pt. 1:149–60.

Peebles, C.S. (1991) *Annalistes*, Hermeneutics and Positivists: Squaring Circles or Dissolving Problems. In *The Annales School and Archaeology*, edited by J. Bintliff, pp. 108–24. Leicester: Leicester University Press.

Cobb, C.R. (1991) Social Reproduction and the *Long Durée* in the Prehistory of the Midcontinental United States. In *Processual and Postprocessual Archaeologies: Multiple Ways of Knowing the Past*, edited by R.W. Preucel, pp. 168–82. Carbondale: Center for Archaeological Investigations, Occasional Paper N. 10.

Watson, P.J. and Kennedy, M.C. (1991) The Development of Horticulture in the Eastern Woodlands of North Armerica: Women's Role. In *Engendering Archaeology: Woman and Prehistory*, edited by J.M. Gero and M.W. Conkey. pp. 255–69. Oxford: Blackwell.

Knapp, B. (1998) Boys Will Be Boys: Masculinist Approaches to a Gendered Archaeology. Third Australian Women in Archaeology Conference edited by J. Hope, M. Casey, D. Donlan and S. Wellfare. Canberra: ANH Publications, RSPAS, The Australian National University.

Whitley, D.S. (1994) By the Hunter, For the Gatherer: Art, Social Relations and Subsistence Change in the Prehistoric Great Basin. *World Archaeology* 25:356–72.

McGuire, R.H. and Saitta, D. (1996) Although They Have Petty Captains, They Obey Them Badly: The Dialectics of Prehispanic Western Pueblo Social Organization. *American Antiquity* 61: 197–213.

Tilley, C. (1989) Archaeology as Socio-Political Action in the Present. In *Critical Traditions in Contemporary Archaeology: Essays in the Philosophy, History and Socio-politics of Archaeology*, edited by V. Pinsky and A. Wylie, pp. 104–15.

White Deer, G. (1997) Return of the Sacred: Spirituality and the Scientific Imperative. In *Native Americans and Archaeologists: Stepping Stones to Common Ground*, edited by N. Swidler, K.E. Dongoske, R. Anyon and A.S. Downer, pp. 37–43. Walnut Creek: AltaMira Press.

Chapter 1

NEW APPROACHES TO OLD PROBLEMS
Archaeology in Search of an Ever Elusive Past

David S. Whitley

Introduction

Can we use stone tools to reconstruct the evolution of language
in early hominids? Does knowledge of the past require an empathic
understanding of the feelings and emotions of prehistoric peoples?
Are relationships between prehistoric social groups characterized
by dominance and conflict, or cooperation and integration? What
place did art and symbolism play in the workings of prehistoric
societies? And is archaeology a science that can reconstruct some
objective view of the past or, instead, merely a reflection of the
present, used to satisfy our own (often unrecognized) ideological
needs?

These and similar questions have coursed through Anglo-
American archaeology since about 1980. They have challenged the
intellectual dominance and academic complacency of the archaeology of the 1970s, in the process contesting its philosophical basis,
substantive interests and explanatory capabilities. Hardly unique to
archaeology, similar intellectual movements are visible in other
academic fields, including social sciences such as geography and
sociology, and disciplines in the humanities like history and literature.

Yet for all the widespreadness of this intellectual upheaval, in
archaeology (at least) it is far from settled. For some archaeologists, this challenge to the *status quo* has served to further entrench
the rationale and approach of the 1970s, variously labeled new,
processual or settlement-subsistence archaeology. Perhaps blind-
sided by these intellectual changes by not having seen them coming
on the horizon, in some cases these archaeologists have been put

in the position of either defending their last thirty years of hard work, or conceding that their research careers are now irrelevant due to the writings of some French social critic whose name they cannot even pronounce. Entirely aside from the intellectual issues involved, their resistance to change is understandable, if not predictable. Other, typically younger, archaeologists have committed to the new ways of viewing and studying the past. Their work has gone by various names, ranging from contextual, to radical, to interpretive, to post-modernist, but the main strands are most commonly called post-processual and cognitive archaeology – terms that are used here. And other archaeologists – probably the majority – fall somewhere in between. They wonder whether these new approaches are anything more than armchair theorizing. They are uncertain of the relevance of French literary theory to the stone artifacts from the Archaic site they have been excavating. They doubt that we can reconstruct the minds of prehistoric peoples in any scientific way. And they are confused by the assertion that archaeologists create the past in the present and, therefore, that there is no objective past to reconstruct or know. If this is so, they ask, then how can archaeology be relevant, or worth doing at all?

This reader has been prepared with this last group of archaeologists in mind. Its purpose is to provide an overview of some of the main themes and trends in cognitive and post-processual approaches that have appeared and been elaborated in Anglo-American archaeology since about 1980. This is no easy task because these new approaches are, by their very nature, diverse and quickly evolving. Unlike the change from traditional to new archaeology during the 1960s, the development of cognitive and post-processual approaches has involved a movement away from a single point of view towards multiplicity. Cognitive and especially post-processual archaeology involve shifting perspectives on theory, methods, and sources of theoretical inspiration, making them something of a moving target. Yet it is precisely the difficulty in defining cognitive and post-processual archaeologies and outlining their research agendas in simple terms that makes a reader like this so necessary.

Origins and similarities

What are cognitive and post-processual archaeologies? How do they differ from the processual archaeology of the 1970s, and from each other? What implications do they have for the archaeology of the twenty-first century? These and others like them are the larger questions that are brought by a student to a volume of this nature. For this reason, it is worth starting with some definitions and an outline of some of the major tenets of these approaches, before turning to the authors and papers included here.

The term "post-processual" is, by its very nature, relational. It implies the antecedent "processual"; in this case *processual archaeology* – the definition of which is a good place for us to begin. This is not so much because processual archaeology

is poorly understood but because its intellectual history has some important implications for our main subject, cognitive and post-processual archaeologies. In broad
terms the new or processual archaeology reflected an effort to make traditional
archaeology, which was primarily descriptive and concerned with defining culture-
history, into a scientific anthropology. The model of science adopted by processual
archaeology was the one current in the 1950s and, to a lesser extent, during the
1960s. It is referred to, by archaeologists, as *positivism*. Its main points included an
interest in explaining empirical observations about human behavior through cross-
cultural generalizations or laws; a belief that these empirical observations (our
archaeological data) are independent of our theories, that these data can be used
to test theories, and that the result will be an objective knowledge about the past;
and the idea that a logical structure for scientific testing and explanation could be
found in the natural sciences (such as physics or chemistry). Indeed, as with many
sciences in the post-World War II era, the methods and philosophical commitments
of the positivist natural sciences were thought to be universally applicable to all
sciences, natural and social, including archaeology.

Processual archaeology also maintained a "systemic view of culture", which served
as its link to scientific anthropology. This sees cultures as systems of socially transmitted behavior patterns that relate human communities to their ecological settings.
Culture change is then primarily a process of adaptation to the environment and
natural selection. Technology, subsistence and elements of social organization most
directly tied to production (such as economy) are the most important aspects of
culture to analyze, from this perspective, because they are the most strongly linked
to adaptation. The corollary of this last point is that cultural phenomena such as
religion, ritual and art are epiphenomenal – derivative or secondary in nature
and thus analytically irrelevant (see Keesing 1974:75–76).

Processual archaeology was of course a historical product of its time. One important implication of this fact results because positivism (assumed to be the "true"
and "only" science) was itself in a state of intellectual upheaval at the same time
that it was being adopted by archaeologists (Toulmin 1977; Alexander 1982a;
Gardner 1985; Giddens and Turner 1987a; Manicas 1987; Shanks and Tilley 1987a;
Kelley and Hanen 1988). Anthropology, reflecting wider shifts in the sciences, was
also changing (D'Andrade 1984; Ortner 1984), even though a segment of it has
retained the concern with systems and adaptation seen in archaeology. Processual
archaeology, in other words, undertook the adoption of a model of science and an
anthropological approach exactly when these were in the process of being replaced
in the social sciences more generally, and within anthropology specifically. This is
important and is the first point that needs to be made about cognitive and post-
processual archaeologies. *At the simplest level, cognitive and postprocessual archaeologies
can both be understood as efforts to "update" archaeology and bring it back in-line with
ongoing trends in science and philosophy* (Hodder 1987a:xv).

Why processual archaeology adopted (and in many cases still retains) an
approach that was on the way out in other disciplines is open to debate. Doctrinaire

processualists argue that the loyalty to this approach results from its empirical success. Although processual archaeology has largely abandoned its original goal of defining law-like explanations for human behavior in favor of middle-range theorizing, it still has been productive, and there is some truth to this assertion. But another factor results from the nature of the specific scientific model that processualism adopted. Because positivism was thought to represent a kind of "unified science" applicable to all disciplines, processual archaeologists perceived their primary methodological task to be examining and adopting the logic of the natural sciences, the model upon which positivism was based. They also assumed that positivism was the only form of science – it was literally "positivism or else" – and that this kind of science entailed no philosophical contradictions or problems. In this view, philosophical issues as well as intellectual debates in other social sciences (including anthropology) could be – and were – ignored (see Alexander 1982a:7; Giddens and Turner 1987a:2). The danger of such a circumstance is well expressed by Reed (1981:477) for a parallel but archaeologically relevant case in psychology: "Attempts to remove all philosophizing from a domain are likely to remove only explicit, potentially improvable ideas at the expense of embedding tacit, potentially damaging, ideas into the fabric of a field" (see also Toulmin 1977:152). The unified science view of positivism allowed archaeologists to ignore intellectual debates in other disciplines just as one of these debates, within philosophy, was undermining this very same positivist science (see Alexander 1982a).

Reed's comment about psychology is particularly relevant to archaeology because it was directed towards one of the major intellectual movements of the twentieth century, one that was implicitly but widely adopted in processual archaeology: *behaviorism* (Peebles 1992; Whitley 1992). Processual archaeologists are not alone in having implicitly adopted behaviorism. Sociologist (and self-avowed behaviorist) George Homans (1987:65) has noted that "many social scientists who in fact use behaviorism do not realize that they are doing so". This is because many take behaviorism as "just common sense", based on the fact that crude general characteristics of our own behavior are what we tend to know best, and most easily apply to our analyses (*ibid*:66). Our impressionistic views of the way we behave serve as analogies and models that we project on to past behavior.

Behaviorism is an intellectual position that is allied with positivism. It holds that people and the things that they create can be understood best in terms of stimulus and response relationships (D'Andrade 1984:88). It thereby incorporates a strong belief in the "supremacy and determining power of the environment" (Gardner 1985:11): individuals are passive reflectors of the forces and factors in their surrounding environments, not individuals acting out their own ideas or intentions. Human behavior, in other words, is caused by external events and forces. Behaviorists also typically maintain that research should be restricted to the directly observable (behavioral responses), and that the explanation of these observables rests in observable phenomena (external stimuli). As cognitive scientist Howard Gardner notes, behaviorists:

eschew such topics as mind, thinking, or imagination and such concepts as plans, desires, or intentions. Nor ought they to countenance hypothetical mental constructs like symbols, ideas, schemas, or other possible forms of mental representation . . . . According to behaviorists, all psychological activity can be adequately explained without resorting to these mysterious mentalistic entities.

(Gardner 1985:11)

The direct link between behaviorism and processualism's "systemic view of culture" should be obvious. Culture change, one of the primary intellectual interests of processual archaeology, starts with changes in the environment (the external cause), necessitating shifts in adaptation (human behavior), yielding a new form of culture (a social phenomenon). For archaeologists, all of these are seen in the directly observable material aspects of the archaeological record: artifacts, monuments, sites, and their distributions and environmental associations.

The results of these perspectives in archaeology have been manifest in different ways. One is a variant of "behavioral archaeology" (Earle and Preucel 1987; Earle 1991) that has the advantage of explicitly recognizing and building on its connections with behaviorist theory. Another is the concern with site formation processes and middle-range theory (e.g., Schiffer 1976; Binford 1977). This seeks, in general terms, a better understanding of the way the archaeological record reflects past behavior – in essence, to make our archaeological "observables" more objectively so. But the most important if not pervasive link with behaviorism is the ecological – adaptationist perspective that is a foundation of processual archaeology. From this perspective explanation of past human events is sought in external factors and events such as environmental change. This makes the human mind and cognition largely irrelevant.

It is the behaviorism of processualism (or, more precisely, its rejection) that unites cognitive and postprocessual archaeologies. At the risk of coining an additional term, both are, in essence, "post-behaviorist" approaches to prehistory. This is the second point that is necessary to understand these approaches.

Cognitive and postprocessual archaeologies, then, challenge the behaviorism of processual archaeology. They do this by tacitly recognizing that human mind and cognition were key factors in the creation of the archaeological record, and they must be invoked if an adequate explanation or interpretation of past behavior is to be achieved. They do this because they view processual archaeology, at a minimum, as inadequate or, in the more extreme views, as fatally flawed, in scientific, philosophical and/or ideological terms. Examples of why this is so, expressed in theoretical terms and by empirical case studies, are provided in the papers included in this volume; there is no need to outline them here. More important, at this point, is a formal, even if provisional, sense of what cognitive and post-processual archaeologies are, and how they differ.

Although there is widespread consensus about the general nature of processual archaeology, much less agreement exists over any single definition of cognitive or post-processual archaeologies. Contrasting definitions and interpretations have been presented by Leone (1982), Trigger (1984), Hodder (1985, 1991), Patterson (1990), Preucel (1991), Yoffee and Sherratt (1993), authors in the *Norwegian Archaeological View*, 22, 1989, and the Viewpoint section of the *Cambridge Archaeological Journal* 3[2], 1993, among others, as well as in some of the papers included here. Without claiming that it is a consensus view, I define *cognitive archaeology* as an approach that seeks explanations of human behavior at least in part by explicit reference to the human mind. Cognitive archaeologists, in this view, retain a commitment to science and scientific method, although not necessarily to the positivism of processualism. This enables some of them to perceive their cognitive archaeological approach as an outgrowth of processual archaeology. Cognitive archaeology is a rejection of behaviorism, but not a repudiation of all things processual. I include *structuralist archaeology* as a variant of cognitive archaeology. Derived from French anthropologist Claude Lévi-Strauss' structuralism, this approach is predicated on a universal theory of the way the mind operates, and is part of an effort to develop a science of the mind. (A fundamental principle of this theory is the notion that the mind structures the world in terms of binary oppositions, such as good and bad, black and white, and so on). *Post-processual archaeology* maintains an interest in the human mind and especially the importance of intentional human actions (products of thinking rather than simply reacting individuals) in creating the past. Typically, post-processual archaeologists disavow scientific method and explanation in favor of interpretations of the past. Post-processualists also foreground ideological factors in the reconstruction and use the past, and sometimes maintain political commitments in the modern world that are explicitly stated in their archaeological writing.

There are, of course, a number of approaches that fall somewhere in between these extremes. These will become evident in the papers included here, as well as the discussion below.

Summary

Processual archaeology developed at the start of a period of intellectual change in philosophy, science and the humanities. It primarily incorporated the older ideas and approaches that were even then being questioned and replaced in other disciplines. Cognitive and post-processual archaeologies represent efforts to update archaeology by incorporating many of these new ideas, theories and approaches. Cognitive and post-processual archaeologies differ in a number of ways (below) but share a rejection of the behaviorism that is fundamental to processual archaeology. Tacit in this rejection of behaviorism is the importance of mind and cognition both in the creation of the archaeological record, and in its explanation or interpretation. The existence of cognitive and post-processual archaeologies as challenges to processual archaeology demonstrate that the latter's belief that there could be a single unified science, appropriate for all disciplines, is false. Not only is there no single approach (scientific or otherwise) applicable to all disciplines, but there does not even seem to be just one for archaeology, taken alone.

Major themes and major differences

Once beyond the general similarities outlined above, any typology of cognitive and post-processual archaeologies would be hard if not impossible to construct. Many post-processualists, in fact, would consider such an effort counter-productive, because heterogeneity in approaches and perspectives is one of their goals. In the following discussion, I outline instead some of the key themes and issues that are discussed or implied by these disparate approaches. As the articles in this reader make clear, different archaeologists combine these themes and accept or reject these issues in different and sometimes unexpected ways.

Archaeology and science

The most fundamental issues in cognitive and post-processual archaeologies, of course, are philosophical ones (as they must be for all disciplines). A key theme then is the philosophical basis for archaeology and archaeological research, with particular attention focused on the nature of "science". The related question is whether archaeological research can be conducted "scientifically". In this context I use "science" in the loose, general sense in which it is commonly employed by non-philosophers: some reasonably systematic approach that yields repeatable conclusions with wide ranging applicability, and knowledge that is objective. This definition of science is intentionally more general than the one I have given for positivism (above).

The theoretical and philosophical issues raised by cognitive and post-processual archaeologies and their implications for archaeology are complex and not easily summarized. More detailed discussions of some of them, from various archaeological perspectives, are provided by Hodder (1982, 1986), Wylie (1982, 1985a, 1985b), Shanks and Tilley (1987a, 1987b), Preucel (1991), and Whitley (1992). Another good overview is provided by Jeffrey C. Alexander (1982a). Alexander's discussion is advantaged because it addresses these issues from a sociological perspective, making it easier for us to relax the archaeological commitments, biases, and emotions that we bring to a review of the matter. As he shows, sociology confronted these issues before archaeology. And it survived.

The primary contention in the philosophical debate concerns the question of whether an objective reconstruction of the past can occur. By objective here is meant a reconstruction that is true to the actual events in the past, rather than one that is influenced or biased by the scientist making the reconstruction, due to his or her values, or by the social and cultural context within which he or she conducts this research. If no such objective past can be reconstructed, then obviously any claims to objective knowledge (in a general sense, "truth") must be false.

This calls into question the ability to conduct science at all, inasmuch as some degree of objective knowledge is the scientific goal.

This issue turns on a technical point that concerns the relationship between empirical facts (our archaeological data) and our theories. By theories here I mean the larger philosophical, ideological and metaphysical beliefs and attitudes that we hold, more than the specific hypotheses that we may be investigating archaeologically, although these count too. Positivists maintain that a radical break exists between facts and theories; that empirical facts are "theory-free". This is important because if this is not so, and if facts depend somehow on theories, then the facts cannot rightly be used to test or prove theories in any conclusive sense (because the two are intrinsically related). The theory-free nature of facts is essential for the positivist claim of obtaining objective knowledge.

Postpositivism is a reaction against positivism, including its theory-free view of facts. Like post-processualism, it represents a range of views, but as a general rule post-positivist philosophies of science claim that facts and theory are inherently related. The reason for this is straightforward. Without a guiding theory, we do not know what our facts are, or should be. Potentially, they could be any empirical phenomena in the universe. Certainly, we do have a "common sense" view of what archaeological facts are, allowing us to eliminate many phenomena as irrelevant and keeping some that are not. But this is based on our knowledge of the history of archaeological practise, as well as on our implicit assumptions and biases. It is not the result of a situation in which facts are some kind of "givens" that exist, independent of our theories and our selves, as positivism supposed.

Projectile points provide a good, if trivial, example of this circumstance. We all recognize them as archaeological "facts", regardless of whether we are processual, post-processual, or cognitive archaeologists. We also all recognize that certain attributes of projectile points are inferentially useful and serve as facts in their own rights. Basal shape is used in typologies, and helps us establish age and cultural affiliation. Lithic material may be indicative of trade relations. And flaking patterns may be used to reconstruct a tool production sequence. But let us consider a hypothetical case: what about color? Is the color of a projectile point an archaeological "fact", or should it be?

To my knowledge projectile point color is not typically considered an archaeological fact. This is because most archaeologists lack theories about prehistory indicating that stone tool color has any inferential value. Yet it is possible, using ethnographic data, to construct a plausible ethnographic argument for just such a view in the region where I conduct my research, the Great Basin. Color here had symbolic meaning: black was associated with males, the direction east and controlled and positive supernatural power; red with women, west and dangerous and uncontrolled supernatural power. Projectile points were used for hunting, but they were also part of shamanic rituals, where color symbolism was important (Whitley 1998a). They are also found in ceremonial contexts: as burial offerings. If projectile points were used ceremonially, and color symbolism was incorporated into ritual, it follows that the color of these artifacts may have some inferential meaning, and thus that color should be an attribute of projectile points we record, and treat as a "fact".

This suggestion appears even more reasonable when two other circumstances are raised. This first concerns one of the historic Numic bands, known as the White-Knife Shoshone (see Steward 1938:161–163) who lived in this region. In this case it is precisely the color of a stone tool that was used ethnographically as the identifying characteristic of this particular band, indicating that stone tool color had meaning pertaining to band membership. The second circumstance concerns the sexual division of labor. Bow hunting was a male activity; arrows were therefore male artifacts (one Numic term for them is synonymous with "penis"); and black was the color associated with males. It might reasonably be inferred that (all things being equal, relative to available lithic materials) black would be the preferred color for projectile points. (If this seems implausible, consider the fact that no professional football teams use pink as their team color, reflecting pervasive gender – color symbolism in our own culture). Projectile point color can then plausibly be argued to have the potential to inform us about symbolic, social and political dimensions of the material culture record.

Again, this is not intended as a plea to treat the color of stone tools as an archaeological fact. It is just meant to illustrate that our "common sense" view of facts is based on experience and biases, and that facts do not have some independent and objective existence outside of our theories, as positivism supposed. We ignore the color of stone tools because we have no widely known example of a study showing how this attribute might be useful in archaeological interpretations. And color is ignored in more general terms because processual archaeology assumed that symbolism and other such mental constructs are epiphenomenal, and therefore play little part in archaeological explanations.

The putative theory-free nature of facts is one of the most problematic postulates of positivism, and it was attacked in some of the earliest critiques of this model of science. Even in positivist processual archaeology the difficulty in objectively understanding empirical facts has been recognized, resulting in efforts to develop middle-range theory (e.g., Binford 1977). This was thought necessary because of unique problems presented by the nature of our archaeological facts: the archaeological record is an indirect reflection of behavior, and cannot give us direct behavioral observations. Actually, other social sciences had similar difficulties with their facts too (even though they do not derive them from the archaeological record), so the problem is not solely archaeological. The best example is sociology, which has a long history of concern with middle-range theory, preceding that in archaeology by a few decades (e.g., Merton 1949). It is for this reason that philosophers sometimes call middle-range theory an attempt to develop an "observation language". It is also for this reason that the positivism of processual archaeology has been widely rejected as a model of science in most disciplines. While philosophy is a contentious field, there does seem to be widespread (though

I'm sure not universal) agreement that positivism's radical distinction between theory and fact is unsupportable. *The belief that fact and theory are independent is a core postulate of positivism. The widespread rejection of this belief is one of the key justifications for cognitive and post-processual archaeologies.* As should be clear, it involves a fundamental philosophical problem for science, and therefore should not be ignored.

Unfortunately, there is no single, widely accepted solution to the fact–theory problem, with a continuum of positions having developed. The extreme philosophical position, known as *relativism*, is that fact and theory are fully equivalent. All knowledge is then based on the knower, and there is no independent way of verifying anything. Everything is subjective, including the past, and since there can be no objective past there can be no objective reconstruction of it. Often there is a strong ideological and moral commitment that accompanies this position. This claims that the knowledge that we create (in our research) is a reflection of existing structures of dominance and subordination in our society. Our efforts to create and promote this knowledge are *de facto* efforts to support the (unjust) social *status quo*. In this view, science is a kind of political and moral action. The role of the aware and critical scientist is to fight these structures of dominance. This is done by creating knowledge in the form of critical interpretations that expose social injustice. This position is a rejection of science, as such.

The moderate postpositivist view (moderate because it represents less of a move away from positivism) holds that even though fact and theory are interrelated we still should (and can) maintain a categorical distinction between them. This is partly based on the commonsense observation that different individuals can share the same perspective or knowledge, and therefore that some degree of objectivity is attainable. A good example of this is provided by our language skills: the fact that one language can be intelligibly translated into another is evidence that objectivity exists at some level, and that knowledge is more than entirely personalized (Laudan 1981:184; Newton-Smith 1982). Another example derives from the projectile points noted above. Although archaeologists do not view projectile point color as a fact, they all at least share a recognition of projectile points themselves as facts.

Incidentally, after thinking up the example of color as a potentially meaningful fact pertaining to projectile points, I decided to check this idea with Bob Elston. He is a lithic archaeologist who has worked in the White-Knife Shoshone region, including at some of their chert quarries. Although he was aware of additional ethnographic support (in Great Basin mythology) for the plausibility of this hypothesis, the only patterning in the color of projectile points he was aware of is related to distance from lithic source: more white projectile points are found near sources of white chert, and more black ones near obsidian quarries. Color, in other words, is only a pertinent fact about projectile points in so far as it is correlated with lithic material type. Since we already record material type as a fact, we are then justified in ignoring the color of these stone tools in our analyses. This suggests that our shared view of what pertinent facts are may not be so bad, after all. Archaeologists in this case cannot be accused of overlooking something of great importance due to their theoretical bias. This indicates that there are a set of core "facts" shared within a discipline that exist outside our individual ideological biases and philosophical commitments, further supporting the moderate position. Moreover, the moderate position is necessary because of a massively debilitating problem with extreme relativism: since there are no independent means to verify anything, according to relativism, there can be no sure way for relativism to uphold precisely this same contention. Relativism, here, defeats itself.

The moderate position also maintains that there is a true and objective past, although we may not be able to recognize it (in the sense of developing singular scientific tests that will reveal it). The point of science is then not necessarily to discover truth (an objective past), but to attempt to move increasingly closer to it. The way this is done is not through the critical tests of positivism (processual archaeology emphasized falsification as the preferred means of testing theories). Instead, it is with a procedure that Kelley and Hanen (1988) have labeled "inference to the best hypothesis": using empirical evidence to select the best among a series of competing hypotheses. This is an effort to employ a method of science that is more sophisticated than positivism, not a rejection of science in the general sense. *It is then possible to accept this important critique of positivism – that fact and theory are not independent but are related – without rejecting science. A rejection of processual archaeology therefore does not require a rejection of science.*

It is important to note that there are different dimensions to each of these positions, and that there are a continuum of potential commitments along each of the dimensions. The ideological and moral dimension of relativism, for example, could be incorporated into a moderate postpositivist scientific perspective. This implies a recognition that our modern ideological views do influence our perspectives on the past, and that we need to recognize and remove this bias if we wish to improve our scientific reconstructions. *Critical archaeology*, which is discussed by Mark Leone in this volume, is one of the strains of post-processual archaeology that adopts this position. In his formulation, critical archaeology does not reject science. But it does make the entirely reasonable request that archaeologists examine, and eliminate, their ideological biases before they interpret the past. This hardly seems contentious, in my view.

On the other hand, some relativists seem to have adopted a posture of moral authority, resulting from their belief that ideology and social research are entirely inseparable (see Bernstein 1976). They imply that their approach to research is better than others because it is oriented towards recognizing and correcting social inequalities. In this view anyone who disagrees about how research should be conducted is, in essence, implied to be immoral. This is because such researchers perpetuate a social system that has been identified (by the accuser) as wrong. Whether or not individual researchers kick their dogs, abuse their significant others, or contribute to the subordination of the Third World is not my concern here although, obviously, these are bad things. I emphasize, instead, that while the ideological and methodological dimensions of social research, including archaeology, are linked, whether they can be reduced to a single dimension is, at best, a contentious issue. It is related to the fact–theory problem (above) because values (and thus moral judgments) are kinds of biases that we bring to our research (and that influence our facts). The moderate position is that these dimensions are related but that we can and need to make categorical distinctions between them. As Alexander (1981:281) has noted: "Social science is inherently ideological, but it is not only so".

This raises the larger issue of where the different strains of cognitive and post-processual archaeologies fall on the post-positivist continuum. I view the cognitive archaeologists as falling near the moderate position sketched above (see Whitley 1992). Some of them may believe (and perhaps even claim) that they are still practising positivism, but I suspect that their actual scientific approach is more along post-positivist lines. But what is most important is that cognitive archaeology is at least an implicit rejection of behaviorism (above), yet it still maintains a commitment to scientific knowledge in one form or another.

Post-processualists, on the other hand, tend towards the other end of the continuum. It is very important to note, however, that none of them (to my knowledge) advocates a position of extreme relativism, even though they are widely believed to do so. My suspicion is that some of the post-processualists are perceived this way because they have broadcast strong ideological commitments. In this case their critics (processualists) are guilty of the same conflation as these post-processualists: equating ideology and methodology. Most post-processualists, in fact, stop short of extreme relativism by claiming that knowledge of the past is socially constructed, not that it is entirely subjective. This allows them to avoid the nihilism of extreme relativism, advocate the importance of modern ideological beliefs in the creation of knowledge, and adopt a reconstruction of the past based on humanistic rather than scientific principles.

One final point can be made about archaeology and philosophy in light of the debate over science and the "proper" approach to follow in archaeology. This is a rather sage comment made by Jane Kelley and Marsha Hanen (1988:6), and it is that arguments by philosophers are always controversial. Appeals to the authority of a particular philosopher (or school of philosophy) cannot then be taken, alone, as justification for adopting a particular position about the relationship between science and archaeology. This is because it is almost always possible to find another philosopher supporting a position to the contrary.

Archaeology and humanism

Some archaeologists, primarily post-processualists, reject science and scientific explanation for some of the reasons discussed above, as well as due to other problems they see in processual archaeology (see Hodder 1982, 1986). They adopt, in its place, a humanistic perspective which, in general terms, foregrounds the importance of the individual in any analysis or interpretation. Although there are many variant expressions, humanistic approaches tend to favor a focus on the particular rather than the general; historical contingency and context in place of scientific causality; the individual instead of the group; and interpretation and meaning, not explanation. Many of these issues are discussed in the papers included here, but I would like to raise one of these at this juncture. This concerns an aspect of hermeneutics, because this is a primary method followed by many post-processual archaeologists.

Interpretation and understanding may be generally subsumed under the term *hermeneutics* (see Taylor 1971). This is the method (or art) and philosophy of interpreting and understanding, central to which is the concept of meaning. Although we all have a commonsense feel for what is implied by "meaning", in fact it is a very difficult concept to define (even for philosophers). It implies an understanding of historical and cultural context. It requires a perspective on individual motivations and intentions. And it may also suggest an empathic cognizance of whomever we aim to study, such as prehistoric peoples. To construct fully and adequately an understanding of the past, a humanist position might hold, it must include some sense of the feelings of those who lived in the past. It is this issue that I wish to address.

The belief that "feelings matter" is viewed by most people as the exact opposite of science. Going back to Plato, Descartes, and Kant, the argument has been made that rationality (and ultimately science) is based on formal logic, with emotion entirely removed. I suspect it is this belief that so strongly sets many processual archaeologists against post-processualist hermeneutics. Scientific reason is opposed to emotion, a processualist might say, and so any concern with emotions – or even with an "understanding" that implies some degree of empathic awareness – is a rejection of science. I suspect that many post-processualists might make the same argument because processualists and post-processualists are largely united on this point. They just differ on which is better: explanation or understanding. But I would like to show that the distinction between rationality and emotion is a false one. Perhaps surprisingly to many, this position may be supported by scientific rather than humanistic arguments, including the interesting medical case of Phineas Gage.

My contention is based on increasing neurophysiological and experimental evidence showing that reason and emotion are inextricably linked (DeSousa 1991; Johnson-Laird and Oatley 1992; Damasio 1994; LeDoux 1994). "Emotions" are mental states in the sense that they occur within our minds. (In fact, they are actually physical, because they involve specific neurochemical states). "Emotional feelings", like anxiety or elation, are our bodily reactions to emotions. ("Tactile feelings" of course derive from external stimuli). Emotional feelings include such observable phenomena as changes in blood pressure, heart rate, skin color ("blushing"), and so on. Emotions, then, are observable; they are not entirely mentalistic phenomena. Indeed, we have a common saying to describe our "intuition", which is itself an emotion: it is "our gut feeling". We use this expression because we do feel emotions throughout our viscera, including in our stomach (Klivington 1989).

Emotions are tied to reason partly based on the fact that these faculties are situated in the same general area of the brain, the prefrontal cortices. Evidence for this fact was first brought to the attention of scientists in the last century as a result of an accident experienced by Phineas Gage (Damasio 1994). Gage had the great misfortune of having had a bar of steel rammed through his left cheek and out of the top of his head on the right side. Surprisingly, he survived this railroad accident, but he was no longer the same man. By all accounts, an industrious, courteous and hard-working young man was transformed, by brain damage, into a social deviant who could not make appropriate personal and social decisions, or plan for the future. This was despite the fact that he did not lose his intellectual capacities in the strict sense.

Based on this and similar cases, damage to specific parts of the prefrontal area is now argued to result in an elimination of emotions and to thereby yield an inability to make proper decisions concerning social and personal matters ("social knowledge"). This occurs even though the injury does not affect performance on standard intelligence tests, memory, or problem-solving in the abstract sense. Emotional capabilities are required for the proper and complete functioning of human reasoning, especially involving decision-making. Neurophysiology tells us that Plato, Descartes and Kant were wrong. As you will see, so does Gary White Deer (below).

Moreover, emotions are widely understood, at least in part, as originating in adaptive instincts, something that Charles Darwin first noted in 1872 (see Darwin 1965). The "fight or flight" instinct – flee or defend yourself when confronted by an aggressor – is perhaps one of the most basic of these, and it engenders fear. But hunger (and therefore subsistence), and the reproductive drive (and therefore affective pair-bonding and population growth), are also instincts. They too result in emotions that lead to patterns of human behavior that archaeologists have always assumed are both adaptive and rational. From this perspective rational behavior in part requires emotions. It follows that explaining rational behavior implies some consideration of human emotions, even if only implicitly.

In my view, derived from recent cognitive neurosciences research, the hermeneutic perspective of many post-processualists is correct: some consideration of emotions is required to adequately interpret the past. But unlike what most of the processual and post-processual archaeologists both seem to assume, this does not imply that understanding, the humanist's goal, and scientific explanation, the aim of science, are necessarily opposed. As a number of social theorists and researchers have contended (e.g., Popper 1972; Weber 1975; Huff 1982:91), explanation and understanding are not antithetical, but must be used together, if adequate interpretations of social phenomena are desired. Neurophysiology supports this view.

Here then is the critical point. *Processual and post-processual archaeologists alike have perceived a series of unbridgeable or near-unbridgeable intellectual and philosophical positions, setting themselves distinctively apart.* Fact and theory is one of these; science and humanism is another; and emotion and reason a third. It is true that the philosophical commitments that some archaeologists make do lead to polarization, but this is not necessarily required. *Moderate positions also exist that accommodate both the critiques of processualism, and its scientific agenda.*

One final point is important here. It concerns the relevance of this largely theoretical discussion to empirical matters. While we might concede that emotion is inextricably tied to reason, it is perhaps another matter to argue that we can reconstruct prehistoric emotion archaeologically. It cannot be done, at least scientifically, many might contend. I argue, in fact, that we can reconstruct archaeological incidents of emotion, at least in a limited sense (see Whitley 1998b). Moreover, these reconstructions can improve our scientific understanding of the past. My argument for this is too detailed to be reviewed here, and I do not ask that this assertion be accepted on faith at this time. I suggest, instead, that the idea not be rejected out of hand due to pre-existing biases and beliefs. As I have attempted to show here, many of these biases and beliefs have been wrong. Others may be as well.

Archaeology, social theory and culture theory

A third important theme in cognitive and post-processual archaeologies involves an explicit concern with *social theory* and (more implicitly) *culture theory*. Social theory is a theory or model of the structure and operation of society, which is a group of humans living together in some fashion. Social theory contrasts with culture theory, which (as the name implies) is a theory about the nature of culture. A given culture may be linked to a society, but culture is something different than society, and the two may not perfectly overlap. Culture comprises the worldview, symbols, beliefs and/or norms of behavior that people share. In southern California, where I live, all of the residents of this region are part of a single American society, but not everyone shares the same culture. The culture of many legal and illegal immigrant farm workers, for example, is Hispanic, in part reflecting their recent arrival from Latin America.

Although there are some exceptions, the social theory underlying processual archaeology was predominantly *structural-functionalism*. This is particularly characteristic of research where social theory was never discussed – the majority of the cases – and this is another of the intellectual problems with processual archaeology. This problem results because structural-functionalism is a model of society that was derived, inductively, to explain the structure and workings of modern Protestant Euro-American society. As should be immediately apparent, the unrecognized use of our own form of modern society as a model for prehistoric ones is problematic. Cognitive and post-processual archaeologists are certainly not the first to recognize the potential problems of such an implicit analogy guiding archaeological research. Much earlier archaeologists, including V. Gordon Childe, considered alternative social theories, such as Marxism (see Kohl 1981). But *the emergence of cognitive and post-processual archaeologies represents a much more widespread rejection of structural-functionalism*, with a number of different models replacing this theory of society. The result is that explicit discussions of social theory are common in this literature. Equally importantly for the student, this literature presupposes a familiarity with the specialized jargon of social theory, which is formidable.

This is not the place for a detailed discussion of different social theories (see Strasser and Randall 1981; and Giddens and Turner 1987b, for reviews), but a few summary points are in order, starting with a brief description and critique of structural-functionalism. This is necessary to explain why many cognitive and post-processual archaeologists have sought alternatives. In structural-functionalism society is considered structured or organized in a fashion analogous to an organism: all parts (like the organs in your body) work together towards the good of the whole. (This so-called "organismic metaphor" for society was eventually replaced by a systems metaphor. The terms were changed but the model was largely the same). While this seems reasonable enough (or at least debatable), the real problems for the archaeologist studying non-western, traditional societies result from two other characteristics of structural-functionalism. First, because change is caused by factors external to a body or a system, the same view was applied to their analog, a society. Hence there is an emphasis on environmental change as the cause for social change in processualism. This serves to rob individual humans of any control over their own destiny: change is a condition imposed on societies by outside forces, not created within. Second, the functions of modern western society are institutions such as politics, religion, economics, and so on. Because we intuitively know that our society functions along the lines of these institutions, these were assumed to apply to the past. The problem here is that traditional non-western societies in fact may not be structured in such terms at all.

The best example of this concerns the separation of politics from religion, as two distinct institutions. Certainly such as separation exists in modern American society. This is because it is a central tenet of our political ideology, guaranteed by our Constitution. But historically this separation was not even a traditional western European one: the Protestant Reformation was all about establishing this break, and making secular political power distinct from the religious. (Hence the need to explicitly establish separation of church and state in our constitution). Nor is this separation, to this day, even a uniformly European one. Grimes (1976), for example, has shown that some Hispanic Catholic communities easily accommodate a structure of authority that combines politics and religion, and see no contradiction in doing so. Structural-functionalism, then, is a dubious model for the kinds of societies that are most commonly studied by archaeologists. When this model of society was applied implicitly to the past by processual archaeologists they had all the problems that it creates, combined with the added problem of not recognizing that these problems existed.

There have been two primary concerns in conceptualizing alternatives to structural-functionalism. The first is the need to avoid the problematic, implicit analogy with western Protestant societies. The second is the desire to foreground the importance of individual human actions, intentions and agency in creating societies, past and present. The dominant alternative has been historical-materialism. This is partly because of its long tradition of intellectual development, which extends back to the writings of Karl Marx in the mid-nineteenth century. It has many variants (Marxism, dialectics, structural Marxism, class analysis, critical theory, etc.), making difficult if not impossible any effort to provide a quick summary (see Friedman 1974; Bonte 1979; Kohl 1981; 108–112; Krysmanski and Tjaden 1981; Alexander 1982b; Honneth 1987; Miliband 1987; and McGuire 1992, for reviews of various approaches).

Four points may be emphasized about historical-materialism in general terms. The first, which often isn't obvious to American students, is that it is a social and not a political theory, and thus that it need not entail any particular political commitments. Second, it models societies based on a series of functions, not institutions, with the purpose of analysis precisely being to define these functions and their interrelationships. This makes it more easily applicable to traditional societies that may have differed, in fundamental ways, from post-Reformation Euro-American Protestant societies. Historical-materialism is, therefore, a social theory that does not presuppose an equivalence between past and present societies. Third, it views social change as primarily resulting from internal conflicts between groups within a society, rather than due to external influences. This opens the door for human actors consciously to make their own lives and history. Fourth, it can accommodate the view that beliefs and ideology are more than epiphenomenal; that beliefs and ideologies are actively created and employed by individual humans, and thus are important in social stability and change.

This last point, which implies "mental phenomena" like beliefs, raises the issue of culture theory in archaeology. Culture theory was undeveloped and very implicit in processual archaeology but, at base, it was behaviorist (above): culture is a set of behavioral norms or mental templates transmitted from one individual to the next. One irony of processual archaeology is the fact that it attempted to eliminate the normative assumptions of traditional archaeology embedded in the notion that artifact types result from mental templates, yet these normative views were retained in its behaviorist model of culture. This logical contradiction appears to have been largely implicit, but it was not entirely unrecognized. In a circumlocution, processual archaeologists relatively early on "eliminated" this contradiction by expunging culture from any explicit archaeological consideration (Whitley 1992:62–63). Again, this compounded the problems implied by the culture concept with the added problem of assuming that they had been eliminated.

The recognition of the importance of culture is another major theme of cognitive and post-processual archaeologies. For some, primarily the American-trained anthropological archaeologists like Mark Leone (included here), James Deetz (1977, 1988a), and Tom Huffman (e.g., 1986, 1996), this concern is explicit. For others, notably English post-processualists whose exposure presumably has been to British social anthropology where culture is less a central concern, it is more implicit. Still, it is revealed in the central importance these archaeologists place on symbolism, meaning and worldview. In a cognitive formulation, this is what a culture is: a shared system of symbols, values, meanings and beliefs. Yet these are not norms, the mental templates and prescribed patterns of behavior implicit in processual archaeology. They are instead actively created, used and changed by individuals as they live out their lives. This ties the concept of culture in a general way to the historical-materialist concern with beliefs and especially ideology. And it shows that it is possible to employ a developed culture theory and a social theory in an integrated fashion, unlike the circumstance in processual archaeology, where the two were contradictory, and one had to be dropped from analysis to make the program coherent.

A number of the papers included here explain and explore how something as seemingly intangible as culture can be reconstructed archaeologically, and so I leave that job to them. But one final clarification needs to be made about culture and culture theory. This concerns a question that I suspect many might ask: how can systems of symbols and meaning at once have been created, used and manipulated by individual humans, yet still have been sufficiently shared and patterned to allow their identification and study – especially by late-coming outsiders such as archaeologists?

The assumption underlying this question is that mental entities like beliefs and symbols are either "fixed" norms that are shared by everyone, and therefore potentially easy to identify and study, or they are entirely idiosyncratic and, in essence, unstudiable. A commonsense examination of our own cultural use of symbols tells us, correctly in this case, that both of these extremes are wrong. As cognitive culture theorists have been careful to explain (e.g., Schneider 1972:38), the key difference here is the one between constitutive and regulative rules. Constitutive rules are norms; they are like the algorithms that underlie computer programs. Once a program is started it will run precisely as specified, with no room for deviation. Hence the need to debug newly written programs: they do what we tell them to do, which is sometimes not what we want them to do. Regulative rules, in contrast, are general guidelines or frameworks. They are like the rules to the game of chess. These specify how a game must be played, but they do not determine how a specific game will turn out, or who will win.

This is how culture works; why it can be manipulated and used actively in the past and present; and why it can be studied. Culture is a shared system of beliefs, customs, values, and so on – mental constructs all. Like behaviorism's norms, culture influences behavior but, unlike these norms, it doesn't fully determine our physical actions. This is because people think, decide to change things and, often enough, do things "wrong". "Rules are made to be broken", some say. So too is culture.

And anyone who doesn't believe this obviously hasn't raised children, or themselves ever been a teenager.

Postmodernism and poststructuralism

The final perspective that is seen in some cognitive and post-processual archaeological approaches that warrants discussion concerns postmodernism and poststructuralism. What are they? How do they differ (if at all)? And, most importantly, what do they imply for archaeology? They have slightly different intellectual histo-ries, one primarily French, the other originating in America. These require brief explanation, before moving on to their implications of these positions for archae-ology.

We can begin with *postmodernism*. This originated in American literary criticism during the late 1950s and 1960s, and it comprises three related issues: an artistic and aesthetic movement; a critique of modernism; and a social and political movement (Seidman 1990; Hyussen 1990; Downey and Rogers 1995). Like "post-processual", postmodernism is a relational concept raising the question: what is the *modernism* that postmodernism claims to replace? In this context modernism is seen as the pervasive American worldview for the majority of the twentieth century. It too involved the three issues noted above, including the Modernist artistic and aesthetic styles, and the modernization movements in economic development, technology and science. Tied to these is the third component, the rise of capitalism as a liberating economic system and political ideology. Postmodernism challenges each of these.

The postmodernist break with modern art, for example, was said to begin with Andy Warhol and pop art, and everything that followed. In architecture it involves the replacement of the "high-modernist" designs of architects like Mies van der Rohe – rectangular high-rises with rigid glass "curtains" for walls – by the histor-ical eclecticism of architects such as Phillip Johnson (combinations of Roman colonnades, Chippendale pediments, etc., on a single facade). Postmodernism's social and political movement is also said to have begun during the 1960s, with the "counter-culture" and political activism that developed at that time. The counter-culture movement explicitly challenged the prevailing social and culture order of the mid-century, most importantly in terms of issues like life-style choices, and mores and morals. Right or wrong, it caused people to critically examine their lives in ways that had not been common, to so many, previously. The "meaning of life" has become an issue of common social concern, rather than simply a meta-physical problem interesting to only a select few (Seidman 1990).

One of the more prominent spokesmen for the postmodernist movement, Jean-François Lyotard (1984), has characterized it as "incredulity towards metanar-ratives". By this he means skepticism toward (if not rejection of) our predominant social, political and intellectual theories and beliefs. Obviously this includes a chal-lenge to science as our pre-eminent means of obtaining knowledge. While many American archaeologists then tend to see postmodernism primarily as an intellec-tual debate about the validity of science, the implications of the cultural movement are also important. Moreover, these influence archaeology in a series of often unrec-ognized ways. Processual archaeologists may feel certain that postmodernism will never replace scientific archaeology. But what they may not realize is that it has already profoundly affected their lives and work.

"Incredulity towards metanarratives", though typical of the opaque writing style of postmodernism, for example, calls for a series of things. Prominent among these is an elimination of male, WASP ("white anglo-saxon protestant") social and cultural dominance. One obvious archaeological result is the appearance of gendered/feminist and Third World archaeologies (e.g., Conkey and Spector 1984). These are intellectual reactions reflecting a recognition that western science has been biased towards a white, European male perspective. As I think even processualists will agree, archaeology can be engendered without endangering it, because a gendered perspective does not in and of itself require a rejection of science. Postmodernism, then, has helped us to recognize implicit biases in our research, and this can only be considered a good outcome of it.

But even more fundamentally, the postmodernist cultural movement can be at least partly credited with the appearance of cultural resource management, which itself reflects a wider societal acceptance of the importance of non-white, non-WASP, multicultural history and prehistory. Recall that, in America, we had archaeological protection laws as early as 1906. While archaeological salvage was certainly conducted in earlier times, the large majority of our laws and regulations still have been developed since the early 1970s – fully in step with other postmodernist social expressions, like the broad-based environmental movement (Hyussens 1990). Since roughly 60–75 per cent of all American archaeologists are now employed in some aspect of cultural resource management, the impact of this postmodernist trend on our profession can hardly be ignored.

A closely related postmodernist impact on American archaeology involves Native Americans (see Leone 1991). This is most widely seen in NAGPRA, the Native American Graves Protection and Repatriation Act of 1990. This law reflects society's development of a respect for Native Americans and Native American concerns, and an empowering of non-western history and religion. One result of the tension between archaeologists and Native Americans due to NAGPRA is an often-stated archaeological belief that "archaeologists need to get-their-act-together concerning the Indians". Actually, I think this misses the main message of NAGPRA, which involves more than archaeologist–Native American relations. Archaeologists need to get-their-act-together concerning society as a whole. Postmodernist American society supports archaeology because it favors multiculturalism; because it has developed an interest in non-western religions and history; and because, at some widely-felt level, there is a sense of collective guilt over the way that Native Americans have been treated historically. This is not say that society has fully rejected science and scientific knowledge (as some postmodernists would like to believe). But if American society is given the choice between empowering Native American religious beliefs (which processual archaeology claims are not worth studying) and optimal foraging theory, the choice is obvious. Processual archaeology loses, hands down.

Postmodernism then is an inductive categorization of our modern worldview and society. By this I mean that the concept has been developed, after the fact, to describe and unify a series of observable cultural and social phenomena in terms of a whole. This implies that we can argue about whether or not postmodernism is a true break with or an evolution out of modernism; we can debate whether it is an adequate classification of our existing "condition"; and we can contest how ultimately important it may be. But we cannot really argue against the fact that we exist in a culture and society that do manifest these phenomena that social critics describe by the term "postmodern" (except, of course, at some rarified philosophical level). Americans now do consume more salsa per year than ketchup; sushi bars are common in most cities; we drink more wine than the traditional American liquors, whiskey and beer; and more people work at home, and live in single-parent families. Similarly, tract houses are being built to incorporate historical architectural styles, and aware developers recognize that environmental sensitivity can be a selling point for their developments. All of these are "postmodernist" trends. Even the small, old-fashioned farming town where I live has been remade in a postmodernist image. Originally graced by early twentieth-century architecture, due to an odd geophysical quirk it was destroyed in the 1994 Northridge earthquake (we are over twenty miles from the epicenter). The rebuilding effort was intended to be historically faithful, to recapture the original flavor and style of the town. But what we have gotten instead is historical kitsch: Federalist cupolas, Romanesque colonnades, and Rococo and Moderne pediments and embellishments, all combined in a postmodernist melange. This fools all of our town politicians, most of the townspeople, and some of our tourists. But historical it is not. It is postmodernist to its core. "Fillmore – Postmodernist capital of Ventura County" is the new motto I have suggested for the town. And this points to the fact that, *whether we like it or not, we are all postmodernist archaeologists. Arguments to the contrary are simply quibbles about definitions.* This may surprise many archaeologists, much like Monsieur Jordan in Moliere's *Le Bourgeois Gentilhomme*, who discovers, after forty years, that he has always been speaking prose.

This is not to imply that there is no, and potentially should not be, contested terrain between processual and postmodernist approaches. The more challenging aspect of postmodernism to archaeology (as if NAGPRA is not enough) involves its intellectual opposition to science, technology, and development. This is where the battlelines are drawn. Many postmodernist social critics contend that modernism incorporated the belief that societies were on the road to emancipation due to scientific progress; that technology, industry and capitalism would provide the basis for rational and just societies, marked by increasing wealth and personal freedom for everyone. This belief served to legitimize the scientific endeavor, thereby making the acquisition of scientific knowledge a necessary step for human progress (Downey and Rogers 1995).

Postmodernists claim that the promises of modernism have not been met. Instead, science has promoted hegemony (dominance) rather than emancipation. They point to the failure of regional economic modernization theories and programs in the Third World, and the rapid exploitation of the world's natural resources, as evidence for the hegemony of science and the Euro-American world. They conclude that science and the west have not freed but instead have dominated and exploited the rest of the world. Because science has failed as a social force, and because its knowledge has been a source of oppression, its grand theories and methods need to be questioned, if not rejected outright. Anthropology and archaeology are considered particularly guilty in the service of oppressive science. This is because of their direct relationships with non-western peoples and culture (living and dead). One real outcome is that ethnic studies programs and departments have proliferated at universities even as anthropology budgets have been cut, and departments downsized. This reflects the conclusion that alternative modes of knowledge, and means for gaining knowledge, should be explored and adopted, to replace those of a morally bankrupt western science (Seidman 1990).

So far I have emphasized postmodernism. Aside from the historical logic of this presentation, I did this for a purpose. This is to counter the prevailing American archaeological view that postmodernism is a European, primarily French, phenomenon. As should now be evident, postmodernism *per se* derives largely from America. The French contribution has a different origin, though the French and American positions have, belatedly, come together. The French contribution is *poststructuralism*. This reflects the general "linguistic turn" in theorizing that the social sciences have taken during the last few decades (Giddens 1987; Hyussen 1990).

Poststructuralism is a reaction against and move beyond structuralism, the binary theory of mind associated with Lévi-Strauss (above). Poststructuralism primarily originated among a group of French social philosophers and semioticians, including Roland Barthes, Jacques Derrida, and Michel Foucault, working during the late 1960s and 1970s. (Poststructuralism was, at least initially, less influential in the United States due to an alternative American reaction against the structural linguistic base of Lévi-Strauss' work: Noam Chomsky's transformational grammar. The early appearance of Chomsky's work impeded the widespread acceptance of Levi-Strauss' approach in America, and thereby made less relevant the subsequent French critiques of it). Although different poststructuralists have expressed diverse views, three key facets of the poststructuralist perspectives are the following.

First, poststructuralism builds on structuralism's concept of "decentering the subject". For structuralists, this meant that the meaning of communication lies in the structure of a message (e.g., an oral myth), because this structure reflects a binary structure of the mind that the myth-teller is unaware of. For poststructuralists this same decentering is taken to imply that the author or originator of any kind of communication is separated from its message. Communication occurs regardless of, and sometimes in opposition to, the ostensible intent of the person instigating the message. This serves to delegitimize the authority and position of the author, and the idea that there are single meanings in communication in general.

Second, all communication is taken as a text analog. Since all human phenomena (speech, behavior, ritual, and material culture) communicate messages in some way, a "textual analysis" approach to material culture has developed; hence, "reading the past" (Hodder 1986).

Third, "deconstruction" has been adopted as a primary method of analysis. This is a method of discourse analysis, and it reflects two beliefs. The more fundamental is that existing theories, interpretations and explanations are based on underlying assumptions and presuppositions that are so basically wrong that they cannot be rehabilitated and *reconstructed*. Instead, they must be *deconstructed*, starting at the very beginning. The additional belief is in the fundamental ambiguity of communication. Truth and meaning are created internal to a text, and do not exist outside it. Since everything is a "text", a "reading" or interpretation of a text creates another text, the reader's understanding of the reading, the meaning of which is *another* text, and so on (in a self-perpetuating spiral). There is no truth, authority or even rational and essential self, in this view, because all has dissipated into the context of text. Text is, by its nature, fragmented and characterized by a plurality of meanings. Texts are dynamic processes, and so too then is the process of their interpretation (Staton 1987). From this view of fundamental ambiguity, postmodernism's "incredulity of metanarratives" (above) derives. The political implications of the rejection of the "metanarratives" of science and of scientific knowledge also derive from belief.

The relationship of poststructuralism and postmodernism was, at least initially, ambiguous. What appears to be most important, at this point, is that since the late 1970s poststructuralism and postmodernism have been melded, particularly in American intellectuals' minds. From this perspective postmodernism, *per se*, is the aesthetic, cultural and social movement, with poststructuralism its intellectual rationale. (It is essentially this melded view that I presented above as "postmodernism"). But Andreas Hyussen (1990) has noted a common misconception in this view. As he carefully shows, poststructuralism is really just a theory and critique of modernism. It explains what modernism is and has been; criticizes this; and calls for political and social action. But this call for action actually is a call for rejection: a rejection of modernism, its values and its approaches (including progressive science). Little else is elaborated, and so it is hard to know where postmodernism leads, beyond rejection and critique.

The intellectual implications of postmodernism for archaeology are then somewhat unclear (here I use the term in the synthetic American sense to include poststructuralism). Although there have been some archaeological treatments of these approaches (see authors in Tilley 1990; and Tilley 1991), it is not yet certain where they will go, beyond an aesthetic and intellectual celebration of multiculturalism. On the other hand, the social implications of postmodernism are quite obvious, and have already profoundly affected archaeology. Even the most dyed in the wool processual archaeologist cannot ignore the importance of postmodernism to our profession. This is because postmodernism is, itself, a prime rationale for archaeology, even if it is an archaeology that is partly motivated and controlled by Native American concerns. We study the past but we cannot live in it, and postmodernism is, truly, the current condition of our lives. My view is that we ignore postmodernism at the risk of losing our profession, regardless of whether our intellectual commitment is to processualism or its alternatives.

But – hey – my view may be unique. After all, I live in a postmodernist town.

Summary

Cognitive and post-processual archaeologies are unified in their efforts to move beyond positivism. Still, there are many different positions that have emerged from the rejection of this main tenet of processual archaeology. One of these involves a rejection of the positivist model of science. This rejection is endorsed by post-processualists and by many cognitive archaeologists. Post-processualists tend to take it as a rejection of all science, however, while certain cognitive archaeologists view it more narrowly. They seek alternative models of science that resolve the problems of positivism but that allow them to retain general scientific goals. Some post-processualists also view the general rejection of science as a call for humanism, and its concern with the particular, the historical and the empathic. Some cognitive archaeologists recognize the importance of these humanistic concerns, but feel that they too can be accommodated within an improved model of science.

Cognitive and post-processual archaeologies have also incorporated an explicit reconsideration of the social and cultural theories that underlie all social sciences. They view the dominant social theory of processual archaeology, structural-functionalism, as an inappropriate model for non-western prehistoric societies, and look to a variety of different social models to replace it. Likewise, cognitive and post-processual archaeologists have explicitly or implicitly adopted a cognitive culture theory, to replace the behaviorist theory of processual archaeology. Many processual archaeologists, finally, seem to view the cognitive and post-processual movements as a widespread call for postmodernism, viewing this as a challenge to western science and scientific knowledge. With regard to some dimensions of postmodernism this may be so. But postmodernism also pertains to the nature of the current social and cultural world that we live in. This social and cultural context has already profoundly influenced archaeology. It is for this reason that we cannot ignore postmodernism, regardless of how hard we might try, because we live in it.

One final point can be made about the development and meaning of cognitive and post-processual archaeologies. This involves an analogy with physics, and pertains to the shift from Newtonian to Einsteinian physics. One result of this fundamental change in our understanding of the nature of the universe has involved our sense of time and space. These have been relativized, moving them away from a Newtonian sense of absolutism. This has made them much more complex but, in the process, also better able to explain the empirical world as we know it. I do not want to imply here that cognitive and post-processual archaeologies are as important an intellectual development as Einstein's theory of relativity; such a contention would be silly. What I emphasize, instead, is simply that they too serve to "relativize" our understanding of the past. They imply that knowledge is much less absolute and certain, and that the world is more complex, than positivism would have us believe. But they also promise, to varying degrees, that the accommodation of this relativity, and a recognition of the world's complexity, will aid our understanding of the past in fundamental ways. And this can only be seen, by all archaeologists, as a good goal.

References

Alexander, J.C. (1981) "Looking for Theory: 'Facts' and 'Values' as the Intellectual Legacy of the 1970s", *Theory and Society* 10:279–292

—— (1982a) *Positivism, Presuppositions and Current Controversies: Theoretical Logic in Sociology, Volume 1*, Berkeley: University of California.

—— (1982b) *The Antinomies of Classical Thought: Marx and Durkheim: Theoretical Logic in Sociology, Volume 2*, Berkeley: University of California.

Bernstein, R.J. (1976) *The Restructuring of Social and Political Theory*, Philadelphia: University of Pennsylvania.

Binford, L.R. (1977) "General Introduction". In L.R. Binford (ed.) *For Theory Building in Archaeology: Essays on Faunal Remains, Aquatic Resources, Spatial Analyses, and Systemic Modeling*, New York: Academic Press.

Bonte, P. (1979) "Marxist Analyses and Social Anthropology: A Review Article", *Critique of Anthropology* 13 and 14 (vol. 4):145–163.

Conkey, M.W. and J. Spector (1984) "Archaeology and the Study of Gender", *Advances in Archaeological Method and Theory* 7:1–38, New York: Academic.

Damasio, A. (1994) *Descartes' Error: Emotion, Reason and the Human Brain*, New York: G.P. Putnam.

D'Andrade, R.G. (1984) "Cultural meaning systems", In R.A. Shweder and R.G. D'Andrade (eds) *Culture Theory: Essays on Mind, Self and Emotion*, Cambridge: Cambridge University.

Darwin, C. (1965) *The Expression of Emotions in Man and Animals*, Chicago: University of Chicago (Original publication, 1872).

Deetz, J.F. (1977) *In Small Things Forgotten*. New York: Doubleday Anchor.

—— (1988a) "Material Culture and Worldview in Colonial Anglo-America", In M.P. Leone and P.B. Potter, Jr. (eds) *The Recovery of Meaning: Historical Archaeology in the Eastern United States*, Washington, D.C.: Smithsonian Institution.

DeSousa, R. (1991) *The Rationality of Emotion*, Cambridge: MIT Press.

Downey, G.L. and J.D. Rogers (1995) "On the Politics of Theorizing in a Postmodern Academy", *American Anthropologist* 97:269–281.

Earle, T.K. (1991) "Toward a Behavioral Archaeology", In R. Preucel (ed.), *Processual and Postprocessual Archaeologies: Multiple Ways of Knowing the Past*, Center for Archaeological Investigations, Southern Illinois University at Carbondale, Occasional Paper No. 10.

Earle, T.K. and R. Preucel (1987) "Processual Archaeology and the Radical Critique". *Current Anthropology* 28:501–538.

Friedman, J. (1974) "Marxism, Structuralism and Vulgar Materialism", *Man* (NS) 9:444–469.

Gardner, H. (1985) *The Mind's New Science: A History of the Cognitive Revolution* (second edition), New York: Basic Books.

Giddens, A. (1987) "Structuralism, Post-structuralism and the Production of Culture". In A. Giddens and J.H. Turner (eds) *Social Theory Today*, Stanford: Stanford University.

Giddens, A. and J.H. Turner (1987a) "Introduction", In A. Giddens and J.H. Turner (eds) *Social Theory Today*, Stanford: Stanford University.

——(eds) (1987b) *Social Theory Today*, Stanford: Stanford University.

Grimes. R.L. (1976) *Symbol and Conquest. Public Ritual and Drama in Santa Fe, New Mexico*, Ithaca: Cornell University.

Hodder, I. (1982) "Theoretical Archaeology: A Reactionary View", In I. Hodder (ed.) *Symbolic and Structural Archaeology*, Cambridge: Cambridge University.

——(1985) "Post-Processual Archaeology", *Advances in Archaeological Method and Theory* 8:1–26, New York: Academic Press.

——(1986) *Reading the Past: Current Approaches to Interpretation in Archaeology*. Cambridge: Cambridge University.

——(1987b) "Foreword". In *Re-Constructing Archaeology: Theory and Practice*, by M. Shanks and C. Tilley, Cambridge: Cambridge University.

——(1991) "Interpretive Archaeology and Its Role", *American Antiquity* 56:7–18.

Homans, G.C. (1987) "Behaviorism and After". In A. Giddens and J.H. Turner (eds) *Social Theory Today*, Stanford: Stanford University.

Honneth, A. (1987) "Critical Theory". In A. Giddens and J.H. Turner (eds) *Social Theory Today*, Stanford: Stanford University.

Huff, T.E. (1982) "On the Methodology of the Social Sciences: A Review Essay, Part II", *Philosophy of the Social Sciences* 12:81 94.

Huffman, T.N. (1986) "Cognitive Studies of the Iron Age in Southern Africa", *World Archaeology* 18:84–95.

——(1996) *Snakes and Crocodiles: Power and Symbolism in Ancient Zimbabwe*, Johannesburg: Witwatersrand University.

Hyussen, A. (1990) "Mapping the Postmodern". In J.C. Alexander and S. Seidman (eds) *Culture and Society: Contemporary Debates*, Cambridge: Cambridge University.

Johnson-Laird, P.N. and K. Oatley (1992) "Basic emotions, rationality and folk theory", *Cognition and Emotions* 6:201–223.

Keesing, R. (1974) "Theories of Culture", *Annual Review of Anthropology* 3:73–97.

Kelley, J.H. and M.P. Hanen (1988) *Archaeology and the Methodology of Science*, Albuquerque: University of New Mexico.

Klivington, K. (1989) "Emotions: A Gut Feeling". In K. Klivington (ed.) *The Science of the Mind*, Cambridge: MIT.

Kohl, P.L. (1981) "Materialist Approaches in Prehistory", *Annual Review of Anthropology* 10:89–118.

Kosslyn, S.M. and O. Koenig (1992) *Wet Mind: The New Cognitive Neurosciences*, New York: Free Press.

Krysmanski, H.J. and K.H. Tjaden (1981) "The historic-materialistic theory of societal development". In H. Strasser and S.C. Randall (eds) *An Introduction to Theories of Social Change*, London: Routledge and Kegan Paul.

Laudan, L. (1981) "The Pseudo-Science of Science?", *Philosophy of the Social Sciences* 11:173–198.

LeDoux, J. (1994) "Emotion, Memory and the Brain", *Scientific American* 270:50–57.

Lee, R.B. and I. DeVore (eds) (1968) *Man the Hunter*, Chicago: Aldine.

Leone, M.P. (1982) "Some Opinions About Recovering Mind", *American Antiquity* 47:742–760.

——(1991) "Materialist Theory and the Formation of Questions in Archaeology", In R. Preucel (ed.) *Processual and Postprocessual Archaeologies: Multiple Ways of Knowing the Past*, Center for Archaeological Investigations, Southern Illinois University at Carbondale, Occasional Paper No. 10.

Lyotard, J.F. (1984) *The Postmodern Condition*, Minneapolis: University of Minnesota.

Manicas, P.T. (1987) *A History and Philosophy of the Social Sciences*, Oxford: Basil Blackwell.

McGuire, R.H. (1992) *A Marxist Archaeology*, Orlando: Academic.

Merton, R. (1949) "On Sociological Theories of the Middle Range", *American Sociological Review* 13:164–168.

Miliband. R. (1987) "Class Analysis". In A. Giddens and J.H. Turner (eds) *Social Theory Today*, Stanford: Stanford University.

Newton-Smith, W. (1982) "Relativism and the Possibility of Interpretation". In M. Hollis and S. Lukes (eds) *Rationality and Relativism*, Oxford: Basil-Blackwell.

Ortner, S.B. (1984) "Theory in Anthropology since the Sixties", *Comparative Studies of Society and History* 26:126–166.

Patterson, T.C. (1990) "Some Theoretical Tensions within and between the Processual and Postprocessual Archaeologies", *Journal of Anthropological Archaeology* 9:189–200.

Peebles, C.S. (1992) "Rooting Out Latent Behaviorism in Prehistory". In J.-C. Gardin and C.S. Peebles (eds) *Representations in Archaeology*, Bloomington: Indiana University.

Popper, K. (1972) *Objective Knowledge: An Evolutionary Approach*, Oxford: Clarendon.

Preucel, R. (1991) "The Philosophy of Archaeology". In R. Preucel (ed.) *Processual and Postprocessual Archaeologies: Multiple Ways of Knowing the Past*, Center for Archaeological Investigations, Southern Illinois University at Carbondale, Occasional Paper No. 10.

Reed, E.S. (1981) "Behaviorism, Consciousness and the Philosophy of Psychology", *Philosophy of the Social Sciences* 11:477–484.

Schiffer, M.B. (1976) *Behavioral Archaeology*, New York: Academic.

Schmidt, P. (ed.) (1996) *The Culture and Technology of African Iron Production*, Gainesville: University Press of Florida.

Schneider, D.M. (1972) "What is Kinship All About?", In P. Reinig (ed.) *Kinship Studies in the Morgan Centenniel Year*, Washington, D.C.: Anthropological Society of Washington.

Seidman, S. (1990) "Substantive Debates: Moral Order and Social Crisis – Perspectives on Modern Culture". In J.C. Alexander and S. Seidman (eds) *Culture and Society: Contemporary Debates*, Cambridge: Cambridge University.

Shanks, M. and C. Tilley (1987a) *Re-Constructing Archaeology: Theory and Practice*, Cambridge: Cambridge University.

—— (1987b) *Social Theory and Archaeology*, Cambridge: Polity.

Staton, D.F. (1987) "Pre-Text, Con-Text and Sub-Text". In D.F. Staton (ed.) *Literary Theories in Praxis*, Philadelphia: University of Pennsylvania.

Steward, J.H. (1938) *Basin-Plateau Aboriginal Sociopolitical Groups*, Smithsonian Institution, Bureau of American Ethnology, Bulletin 120.

Strasser, H. and S.C. Randall (eds) (1981) *An Introduction to Theories of Social Change*, London: Routledge and Kegan Paul.

Taylor, C. (1971) "Interpretation and the Sciences of Man", *The Review of Metaphysics* 25:3–51.

Tilley, C. (ed.) (1990) *Reading Material Culture: Structuralism, Hermeneutics and Post-Structuralism*, Oxford: Basil Blackwell.

—— (1991) *Material Culture and Text: The Art of Ambiguity*, London: Routledge.

Toulmin, S. (1977) "From Form to Function: Philosophy and History of Science in the 1950s and Now", *Daedalus* 106(3):143–162.

Trigger, B. (1984) "Archaeology at the Crossroads: What's New?", *Annual Review of Anthropology* 13:275–300.

Weber, M. (1975) *Roscher and Kries: The Logical Problems of Historical Economics*, transl. G. Oakes, New York: Free Press.

Whitley, D.S. (1992) "Prehistory and Post-Positivist Science: A Prolegomenon to Cognitive Archaeology", *Archaeological Method and Theory* 4: 57–100. Tucson: University of Arizona.

—— (1998a) *Art Rupestre en Californie: L'art du chamanes*, Paris: Editions du Seuil.

—— (1998b) "Cognitive Neurosciences, Shamanism and the Rock Art of Native California", *Anthropology of Consciousness* (forthcoming).

Wylie, A. (1982) "Epistemological Issues Raised by a Structuralist Archaeology". In I. Hodder (ed.) *Symbolic and Structural Archaeology*, Cambridge: Cambridge University.

—— (1985a) "Between Philosophy and Archaeology", *American Antiquity* 50:478–490.

—— (1985b) "Putting Shaker Town Back Together: Critical Theory in Archaeology", *Journal of Anthropological Archaeology* 4:133–147.

Yoffee, N. and A. Sherratt (eds) (1993) *Archaeological Theory: Who Sets the Agenda?*, Cambridge: Cambridge University.

PART ONE

Theoretical Viewpoints

INTRODUCTION

Cognitive and post-processual archaeologies represent a series of radical theoretical breaks with processual archaeology, with major disagreements over the philosophy and methodology of the discipline resulting. Or do they? Our attention typically focuses on extreme positions. These stand out more from the plethora of archaeological publications that are generated in any given year. Yet how representative are the more extreme statements of the real currents in the ongoing changes in archaeological method and theory? A careful examination of the literature shows both that more moderate positions exist than is sometimes acknowledged, and that even those archaeologists espousing the more radical views are, in fact, not as extreme as they are sometimes made out to be.

The three chapters in this section start with a paper by Kent Flannery and Joyce Marcus, both of whom have long-standing credentials in the processualist camp. They provide their definition of cognitive archaeology and review its place in the discipline, contending in the process that it is an outgrowth of processual archaeology. Indeed, their view is that the addition of cognitive analyses to archaeological research is a logical step that is necessary to attain the kind of holistic archaeology that processualism initially sought as its goal.

Flannery and Marcus make three related and particularly important points in light of the larger debate about processualism and its cognitive and post-processual alternatives. The first involves their explicit concern with prehistoric culture, which they define cognitively rather than by reference to behaviorist theory. By foregrounding this emphasis they direct archaeology back towards anthropology, and away from a unidirectional emphasis on behaviorist–ecological concerns that is common in much processual archaeology. As with the initial statements of new archaeology, the cognitive approach in this formulation is truly a kind of anthropological archaeology.

The second important point is their emphasis on the use of ethnohistorical sources in reconstructing cognitive aspects of the past. This is a methodological principle used by a number of the authors in this volume. A common criticism of it is that such an approach simply projects the recent past on to the prehistoric. The corollary of this criticism is that we cannot know whether the prehistoric past was like the recent past. Africanist Tom Huffman, another cognitive archaeologist, has offered two key responses to these criticisms. The first is that change of any kind is an empirical problem in archaeology, so if change has occurred between the recent and the prehistoric pasts it should be archaeologically recognizable (Huffman 1986:85). The second and related point is that the combination of ethnohistorical with archaeological research can, literally, allow us to rewrite or improve ethnohistory and ethnography (Huffman 1996). Like historical archaeology, which augments the study of historical records with archaeological research, we are then justified in using ethnohistorical data in prehistoric archaeological work. This is because such an approach recognizes that archaeological and ethnohistorical sources provide different but complementary kinds of data, both of which are useful for a full reconstruction of the past.

A third key point that comes out of Flannery and Marcus' chapter is implicit but fundamentally profound, especially in light of the tacit attitude of many that prehistoric cognitive systems simply cannot be reconstructed. As they show through a series of examples, the symbolic, religious, ideological and cosmological systems of the past can be reconstructed and interpreted, and this can be done scientifically. This counters the view of many processualists who insist that such efforts simply create "just-so" stories.

Since 1982, when he published the article "Some Opinions About Recovering Mind", Mark Leone has served as a major American voice supporting new approaches and methods in archaeological research. In his contribution to this reader he tackles the difficult problem of trying to synthesize some of the divergent intellectual trends that have developed in the last few decades. Leone divides these into three areas: symbolic archaeology, which he associates with Ian Hodder; structural archaeology, exemplified by James Deetz, Henry Glassie and David Freidel; and critical archaeology, of which he is a key proponent. Yet even within this tripartite division, Leone recognizes a series of unifying characteristics and emphases. Two of these are the recursive nature of culture – the fact that culture is not passive but instead is actively created, used, modified and manipulated – and the concern with meaning. Both of these emphases could, in essence, be subsumed under a cognitive culture theory that recognizes the importance of human agency and motivation in social life. This further emphasizes the connection between many practitioners of cognitive and post-processual archaeologies and anthropology, the study of culture.

Leone's discussion of critical archaeology introduces another important concern of these alternative approaches. This is the fact that the practice of archaeology is itself a social phenomenon; that in our practice of the discipline we bring ideological biases and prejudices to our work; and that these biases structure and influence our reconstructions of prehistory. The past, in essence, is an interpretation that we create in the present and, as the history of archaeological research has shown, any given "created past" may change over time. This being so, a common reaction is that archaeology is, therefore, irrelevant. What is the point of archaeology if it simply serves to create a reflection of our present social biases? But, as Leone (1991) has pointed out elsewhere, this fact makes archaeology all the more relevant, rather than irrelevant. This is because a critical archaeology, one that is self-reflexive and aims to uncover and expose its ideological commitments, can help us achieve a social critique of our own place in society. Not only is archaeology relevant for studying the past, it is also relevant for understanding the present.

The third contribution to this section is by Michael Shanks and Ian Hodder. Both authors have been major voices in the "post-processual debate", as it has sometimes been termed. The positions of both, too, have in certain cases been unfairly caricatured by some processualists as extremely radical and nihilistic. Certainly, Shanks and Hodder have proposed major changes in the ways we think about and conduct archaeology. But they have also been careful to draw important distinctions between their propositions and untrammelled relativism – the position suggesting "anything goes". This is well illustrated in this chapter, which provides a detailed outline for "interpretive archaeology". Their chapter serves as a synthesis of many of the suggestions they have made over the years for the way archaeology should be conducted. Although I have not adopted the term "interpretive archaeology" here as a replacement for "post-processual archaeology" (simply because it is not yet in widespread circulation), their use of this change in terminology is important. It points to the fact that interpretive archaeology is more than just a critique of processualism, and that it proposes a series of specific philosophical commitments, methods and orientations in the study of the past that are entirely distinct from processualism.

Two points are made by these authors that are worth noting, if only because they counter the common view that postprocessual/interpretive archaeology is terminally relativistic. The first is their acknowledgement of the importance of generalization, indicating that interpretive archaeology is not entirely particularistic. Indeed, they point out that the ability to generalize is required for archaeology, yet this generalization necessarily must be tied to context if it is to yield meaningful interpretations of the past. They also make a key distinction concerning relativism. They distinguish epistemic from judgmental relativism, and opt for the former. This maintains that knowledge is constructed relative to a particular social and cultural context, whereas judgmental relativism maintains that all knowledge is of equal value. Again, epistemic relativism emphasizes the importance rather than irrelevance of archaeological practice.

Do cognitive and post-processual archaeologies represent a radical break from previous archaeological approaches? Perhaps. But your views on this question are as much a reflection of your perspective of the nature of processual archaeology as they are your opinions about the various alternatives. There appears to be room for movement on both sides of this question.

■ ■ ■

Further reading

Hodder 1986
Deetz 1988a
Renfrew and Zubrow 1994
Shanks and Tilley 1987a, 1987b
Leone, Potter and Shackel 1987

■ ■ ■

References

Deetz, J.F. (1988a) "Material Culture and Worldview in Colonial Anglo-America", in M.P. Leone and P.B. Potter, Jr. (eds) *The Recovery of Meaning: Historical Archaeology in the Eastern United States*, Washington, D.C.: Smithsonian Institution.

Hodder, I. (1986) *Reading the Past: Current Approaches to Interpretation in Archaeology*. Cambridge: Cambridge University Press.

Huffman, T.N. (1986) "Cognitive Studies of the Iron Age in Southern Africa", *World Archaeology*, 18:84–95.

—— (1996) *Snakes and Crocodiles: Power and Symbolish in Ancient Zimbabwe*, Johannesburg: Witwatersrand University.

Leone, M.P. (1991) "Materialist Theory and the Formation of Questions in Archaeology", in R. Preucel (ed.) *Processual and Postprocessual Archaeologies: Multiple Ways of Knowing the Past*, Center for Archaeological Investigations, Southern Illinois University at Carbondale, Occasional Paper No. 10.

Leone, M.P., Potter, P.B., Jr. and Shackel P.A. (1987) "Toward a Critical Archaeology", *Current Anthropology* 28: 283–302.

Renfrew, C. and Zubrow, E.B.W. (eds) (1994) *The Ancient Mind: Elements of Cognitive Archaeology*, Cambridge: Cambridge University Press.

Shanks M. and Tilley, C. (1987a) *Re-Constructing Archaeology: Theory and Practice*, Cambridge: Cambridge University.

—— (1987b) *Social Theory and Archaeology*, Cambridge: Polity.

Chapter 2

COGNITIVE ARCHAEOLOGY

Kent V. Flannery and Joyce Marcus

Praised by some and dismissed by others, "cognitive archaeology" has become one of the latest archaeological approaches to be labelled without ever having been defined. Now comes a belated effort to define it, and to decide whether it was born of inspiration or just antipathy toward other approaches.

The decade of the 1960s saw a great upsurge in what has been called "subsistence-settlement archaeology" – studies of prehistoric demography and changing settlement patterns, the origins of agriculture and irrigation, the human use of soils, plants and animals (Ucko & Dimbleby 1969; Ucko *et al.* 1972). The archaeological approaches associated with this upsurge were philosophically positivist and methodologically rigorous, with a heavy emphasis on material remains and a commitment to the notion that subsistence behaviour was the infrastructure of cultural systems.

It was to be expected that not all archaeologists would share this commitment, or leap upon the subsistence-settlement bandwagon. Some complained that the materialist focus of the 1960s dehumanized history, and that ways should be sought to include more of the values, ideas, beliefs, and cognitive processes that make the human species unique. By the early 1970s, one could search the American Anthropological Association's guide to anthropology departments and find occasional archaeologists who, like John Fritz and Robert Hall, listed "cognitive archaeology" among their research interests.

Many subsistence-settlement archaeologists were distinctly lukewarm toward the notion of cognitive archaeology (Sanders 1974, 119). For some, the realm of "ideas" was so nebulous and undocumented in the archaeological record that it could not be studied

scientifically. For others, such cognitive areas as religion and ideology were epiphenomena, dependent variables so far removed from the primary variables of the
subsistence economy as to be trivial and unworthy of study. Such attitudes slowed
the growth of cognitive archaeology but could not prevent it entirely.

By the mid-1970s articles involving some aspect of cognition were appearing
regularly in the archaeological literature. Our own first effort (Flannery & Marcus
1976) was an attempt to understand the ancient Zapotec Indians more fully by
combining their cosmological beliefs with a more traditional analysis of their
subsistence and settlement. We did not see ourselves as "cognitive archaeologists",
what ever that might be. We simply tried to show that one could explain a higher
proportion of ancient Zapotec subsistence behaviour if, instead of restricting oneself
to a study of agricultural plants and irrigation canals, one took into account
what was known of Zapotec notions about the relationship of lightning, rain, blood
sacrifice, and the "satisfizing ethic". We also stressed that we could only do so
because the sixteenth-century Spanish eyewitness accounts of the Zapotec were
so rich.

Despite the reservations of mainstream subsistence-settlement archaeologists,
interest in cognitive archaeology continued to grow throughout the 1980s. Like
Topsy in *Uncle Tom's Cabin*, however, it just "growed" in a haphazard, unsystematic
way, undefined as an area of study and clearly meaning different things to different
people. To some, including the present authors, it was merely an opportunity to
make mainstream archaeology more holistic whenever possible (Flannery & Marcus
1976, 383). For others, it was a reaction against what they saw as the "vulgar materialism" of subsistence-settlement archaeology. For a third group of archaeologists,
however, it took what we believe is a direction to be discouraged: it was seen as
the shortcut to a kind of "armchair archaeology" that requires no fieldwork or
rigorous analysis of any kind. As a result of this shortcut, many of the worst fears
of materialists have been realized; any fanciful mentalist speculation is allowed, so
long as it is called "cognitive archaeology".

The search for a definition

Ironically, despite the support of a foundation, a journal, and a growing number
of enthusiasts, cognitive archaeology has yet to be defined. What, in fact, is it?
What subject matter does it cover? Should it be considered a separate branch of
archaeology, or simply a set of topics within holistic archaeology? Is cognitive archaeology the study of epiphenomena, as many subsistence-settlement archaeologists
would claim? Can it in fact be done, and if so, is it even worth doing?

Let us propose a tentative definition of the subject, one our colleagues can expand
or modify as they wish. Cognitive archaeology is the study of all those aspects of
ancient culture that are the product of the human mind: the perception, description, and classification of the universe (cosmology); the nature of the supernatural

(religion); the principles, philosophies, ethics, and values by which human societies are governed (ideology); the ways in which aspects of the world, the supernatural, or human values are conveyed in art (iconography); and all other forms of human intellectual and symbolic behaviour that survive in the archaeological record. Note that this definition makes no mention of such common subsistence-settlement behaviours as hunting, fishing, farming, plant collecting, tool-making, and so on, although it acknowledges that human intelligence is employed in all of them. They are omitted because their inclusion would inevitably make it difficult to distinguish between "cognitive archaeology" and "archaeology".

What we do in this article is restrict ourselves to four major topics listed in the paragraph above: cosmology, religion, ideology, and iconography. We begin with a definition of each, because we have noted tremendous confusion in the literature about where one topic ends and the other begins. In particular, we note confusion between cosmology and religion, and between religion and ideology. The fact that there is an interface between any two of these topics does not justify blurring their definitions.

We next attempt to refute the materialist notion that any of these topics is an "epiphenomenon". In refutation we offer a series of studies, drawn from the literature, that suggest otherwise. These studies indicate that there may be rigorous ways to approach cognitive questions about archaeology. At the same time, we argue that such cognitive approaches can only be used when conditions are appropriate; that is, when the body of supporting data is sufficiently rich. When it is not so rich, cognitive archaeology becomes little more than speculation, a kind of bungee jump into the Land of Fantasy.

Finally, we will argue that cognitive archaeology should never become a separate branch of archaeology. If it is to be rigorous and scientific it must remain part of mainstream archaeology, something that subsistence-settlement archaeologists do to make their work more holisitic, and something that they do only when the data are sufficient. Were it to be seen as a separate branch of archaeology, it would become an instant magnet for dilettantes and charlatans. When well done, cognitive archaeology makes archaeology broader and more well-rounded; poorly done, it results in some of the worst archaeology on record.

Cosmology

All cultures have a theory of the universe, or cosmos, and the rules by which it works; even twentieth-century astronomers are said to be doing cosmology when they describe "the Big Bang". For many cultures, of course, the cosmos includes supernatural beings which provide the linkup between cosmology and religion.

Cosmology can be defined as a theory or philosophy of the origin and general structure of the universe, its components, elements, and laws, especially those

relating to such variables as space, time, and causality. How the cosmos is structured affects both religion and ideology.

Understandably, many subsistence-settlement archaeologists think that cosmology
can be conveniently left to the humanists. Who cares how some ancient culture
conceived of the universe? Isn't the important thing the way they used soil, water,
plants, and animals to their advantage?

One answer is that the way cultures conceive of the cosmos strongly influences
subsistence and settlement. Two of the clearest examples of that fact can be drawn
from J.D. Hughes' contrast between Greek and Roman attitudes toward the environment (Hughes 1975).

The Greeks, according to Hughes (1975, 48) "saw the natural environment as
the sphere of activity of the gods". Because various gods and goddesses made their
homes in the wilderness, there existed the widespread practice of setting aside a
grove of trees, called an *also*, as a sacred area of land; alternatively, a grove called
a *tenemos*, the abode of a deity, could be set aside only for worship. Hunting in
such sacred groves was forbidden.

As a result of this conception of the forest's place in the cosmos, forestry in
ancient Greece became the concern of the government of each *polis*. Inscriptions
show that Greek states "controlled the cutting of timber on their own territory
and required replanting in some cases" (Hughes 1975, 71). To be sure, these practices were insufficient to prevent some areas of Greece from being converted
to second-growth *maquis or garrigue*. They do, however, indicate a cosmology
in which some forests were seen as an appropriate, necessary, even sacred part of
the universe.

Hughes contrasts this cosmology with that of the Romans, whose attitudes toward
nature he calls "distinctly utilitarian". He describes the Romans as "avaricious and
practical" in their use of the environment; in their cosmology "the world [was] here
for human use" (Hughes 1975, 87). Like the Greeks, the Romans had set aside
some groves of trees as sacred. Unlike the Greeks, they were willing to cut down
trees in such groves, sacrificing a pig and saying a prayer "to smooth the ruffled
feelings of the god or goddess . . . who lived there" (Hughes 1975, 88).

The long-term effects of a cosmology in which all plants and animals exist for
human use are not hard to imagine. The Romans significantly deforested Italy and
were forced to look elsewhere for timber, importing pines from the Black Sea,
cedars from Lebanon, larch from the Alps, and citrus trees from North Africa. In
spite of the growing shortage of local timber, state forests continued to be rented
out to private exploiters (Hughes 1975, 101).

Hughes' study shows that when enough is known about the cosmology of an
ancient people, one is in a better position to interpret their use of the environment. When little or nothing is known, however, as in the case of many nonliterate
ancient cultures – caution is advisable. It is not likely that we will be able to "reconstruct" ancient cosmologies for such cultures based solely on an examination of
their plant and animal remains.

Religion

A religion can be defined as a specific set of beliefs in a divine or superhuman power or powers, to be obeyed and worshipped as the creator(s) and/or ruler(s) of the universe. Religions usually involve a philosophy and a code of ethics, both related to the quest for the values of an ideal life. That quest has three phases: (a) the ideal itself; (b) a set of practices for attaining the values of the ideal; and (c) a theology or world view relating that quest to the universe. It is this world view that lies at the interface between religion and cosmology.

Anyone who regards religion as an epiphenomenon should read Paul Wheatley's illuminating study of overseas trade between India and Southeast Asia in the early centuries of the Christian era (Wheatley 1975). Not only does it contrast the ideals of Hinduism and Buddhism, it also shows the penetration of religion into economics and challenges the supremacy of the law of supply and demand.

According to Wheatley, the Roman emperor Vespasian (AD 69–79) prohibited the export of precious metals from the Roman Empire, aggravating a perceived shortage of gold in India. This shortage was all the more keenly felt because nomadic disturbances along the Bactrian trade route had cut off India's access to Siberian gold (Wheatley 1975, 233).

The Indians heard that gold was available on the surface of the ground in the Malay Peninsula, Java, and the lands of the South China Sea. Here lay potential for great trade, in the formalist sense of a "demand" (in India) and a "supply" (in Malaysia). That trade could not be realized, however, because it would have involved long ocean voyages which would bring devout Hindus into contact with *mleccha* – foreigners who, because of their different religion, were a source of pollution.

Under Hindu religion, contact with heathens was considered contaminating, especially for those of the Brahmin caste. "The old Brahmanism had paid heed to the laws of Manu which totally prohibited such voyages [to distant areas]" and prescribed a three-year penance if the prohibition was violated (Wheatley 1975, 234). Thus it was neither a lack of sailing technology nor the presence of unfavourable economic conditions that prevented India from getting at Southeast Asia's gold; it was the Brahmin notion of ethnic purity through avoiding contact with *mleccha*.

Significantly, what turned the tide was the expansion of Buddhism, a rival religion that rejected Brahmin notions of ethnic purity and the concept of pollution through contact with foreigners. The spread of Buddhism into India thus "did much to dispel the Hindu repugnance to travel" (Wheatley 1975, 234), opening up the sea lanes to Southeast Asia. Within a few centuries, wealthy Indian merchants were plying those lanes, bringing back to their subcontinent much more than gold.

Perhaps equally important was the impact of Indian civilization on Southeast Asia, a region that had previously been organized at the chiefdom level. Colonies of Indian traders began to spring up in Malaysia, Burma, and Java, introducing Indian concepts of kingship and nobility. What resulted was a period of "Indianization" (Wheatley 1975, 249) during which Southeast Asian chiefdoms evolved into kingdoms whose governance was based on Indian conceptions of social order. As high-caste Indian entrepreneurs raised the level of sociopolitical complexity in Southeast Asia, the temple cities of that region became centres for the diffusion of Indian customs and beliefs.

Wheatley's study clearly shows religion's power to interfere with laws of supply and demand or "rational" economic behaviour. It also shows how religion can provide the catalyst by which a new political ideology enters a region and guides cultural evolution. High-caste Indian merchants gained their "gold route" and changed the course of Southeast Asian history forever; but the change might never have taken place without Buddhism's conquest of the Brahmin's fear of foreigners.

To be sure it is easier to demonstrate religion's central role through a study like Wheatley's than to provide a rigorous method for studying religion archaeologically. In another article (Marcus & Flannery 1994), we outline such a method for ethnohistorically-documented cultures like the Zapotec of ancient Mexico.

The method consists of (a) constructing a model of the ancient religion by analyzing the ethnohistoric documents; (b) isolating those elements, such as temple structures and ritual artefacts, that are likely to be preserved archaeologically (Marcus 1978); (c) undertaking an analysis of ancient temple plans and a "contextual analysis" of ritual paraphernalia (Flannery 1976); and finally (d) comparing and contrasting the observed archaeological remains with the expected pattern derived from ethnohistory. Once again we stress that when the ethnohistoric record is lacking, far less success should be anticipated.

Ideology

Among our four categories of cognitive investigation, ideology is perhaps the most frequently confused with one of the others – often, in fact, with *all* of the others. It is useful to remind oneself that Marxism, fascism, and American democracy are all ideologies. Thus ideology falls within society and politics, not religion (although, to be sure, the lines between the three may be blurred by political movements such as Islamic Fundamentalism). Ideology may be defined as the body of doctrine, myth, and symbolism of a social movement, institution, class, or group of individuals, often with reference to some political or cultural plan, along with the strategies for putting the doctrine into operation. The point at which symbolism is used serves as an interface with iconography.

To give just one example, every archaeologist who works on the transition from egalitarian society to rank society is dealing with a change in ideology. Egalitarian societies do not simply remain egalitarian because they are poor, marginal, or underdeveloped; most have "levelling mechanisms" that work to prevent the emergence of rank. Such societies may have numerous *acquired* differences in status, but their egalitarian ideology counteracts any tendency for such status differences to become *hereditary*, or "institutionalized". The emergence of hereditary ranking requires the adoption of a new ideology in which institutional élites are rationalized.

In the ethnographic literature, one of the classic treatments of the emergence of ranking is Leach's (1954) study of highland Burma. For many decades, the Kachin hill people oscillated between *gumlao* (egalitarian) and *gumsa* (rank) organization, with much of their paradigm for rank behaviour drawn from the Shan aristocracy of the nearby lowlands. Their periodic reversion to egalitarian society shows that, at least for the Kachin, the emergence of rank was not an irreversible process.

Some 25 years later Jonathan Friedman, drawing on Leach's research but adding a great deal of his own, presented an analysis of the ideological changes involved in the evolution of such "Asiatic social formations" (Friedman 1979). His reconstruction of the ideological shift in Burmese societies is worth considering in some detail.

In the egalitarian groups considered by Friedman, society is composed of a series of lineages of equal prestige. Each local lineage has its own set of ancestor spirits, arranged in comparatively short genealogies of three or four generations (Friedman 1979, 41). There is also a village spirit, called a *nat*, which represents the local territory and is regarded as its "owner". This "village *nat*" is conceived of as a remote ancestor of all local lineages. On a higher, more remote plane lie a series of "celestial *nats*" which, at this egalitarian stage, can be approached by any lineage through the mediation of its own ancestors.

During the transition to rank society, the "single most important transformation" is the monopolization of the village *nat* by a particular local lineage (Friedman 1979, 41). That local lineage is thereby converted into a chiefly lineage whose ancestors are descended from the spirit who controls all lands belonging to the community. Furthermore, the celestial *nats* are transformed as well; they are now ranked by age (following earthly rules of succession), and the chiefly lineage can now be traced back to the chief celestial *nat*, to whom it is affinally related. The head of this one élite lineage, since he is genealogically related to the spirits who control the well-being of the community, becomes a chief who serves as a mediator between the community and the supernatural. His favoured genealogical status entitles him to special privileges, which are tolerated because the old egalitarian ideology has now been superseded by an ideology of hereditary inequality.

Friedman (1979, 42) even provides us with one of the possible mechanisms by which the new ideology is made palatable to the commoner lineages of society. Under the egalitarian system, all lineages took turns in sponsoring the ritual feasts to which members of other communities were invited, and which brought acquired prestige to the hosts. During the transition to chieftainship, the emerging élite lineage – which before had only represented its community when it took its turn to play host – gradually begins to take over the job of host on a permanent basis. This élite lineage's ability to give more generous feasts is interpreted by other lineages as evidence for a closer association with the *nats*, and hence as evidence that its members are genealogically descended from higher spirits. Ironically, this "evidence" makes use of one of the theorems of the old egalitarian ideology, namely the notion that a lineage could only afford a truly spectacular feast if smiled upon by the *nats*.

Friedman's scheme is shown in diagrammatic form in Figure 1. In his model of the original egalitarian ideology (left) there are five lineages, all equal, living on land "owned" by a village *nat;* the celestial *nats* hover above. What happens next (right) is an ideological change in which the village *nat* is redefined as the direct ancestor of one of the five lineages. That lineage is elevated to the status of a "chiefly lineage", and the former village *nat* becomes the "chief's ancestor". Hereditary inequality emerges because one lineage's ancestors are powerful spirits, while everyone else's ancestors are mere mortals. The chief, rather than the village *nat*, then becomes the mediator with the supernatural, and the four "commoner" lineages derive their status from their relationship with the chief rather than from a supernatural being.

Friedman's model is an ethnographic one, but we consider it relevant to an archaeological case, namely the rise of hereditary inequality among the Zapotec of Oaxaca, Mexico (Marcus 1989). Between 1400 and 1150 BC there is no evidence for hereditary inequality in the early villages of that region. Between 1150 and 850 BC one begins to see the artistic depiction of what may be supernatural lineage ancestors equivalent to those in Friedman's model. One appears to represent "earth" in the form of "earthquake" or were-jaguar; the other appears to represent "sky" in the form "lightning" or fire-serpent. Some degree of hereditary ranking appears during this period (documented more fully in Flannery and Marcus 1983; Marcus 1989).

As the Zapotec state formed (during the centuries leading up to 150 BC), depictions of sky and lightning became increasingly associated with the élite, while depictions of the were-jaguar faded into oblivion; "earthquake" survived mainly as

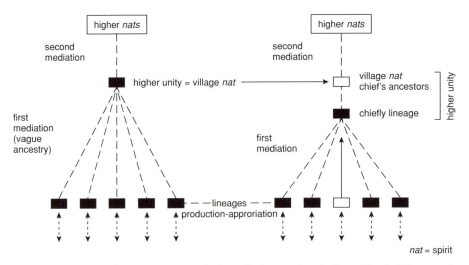

Figure 1   Friedman's model for the ideological changes that facilitate the shift from egalitarian society (left) to rank society (right) in Southeast Asia. (Redrawn from Friedman 1979, 44.)

a hieroglyph in the ritual calendar. It would seem that an ideological shift, like that proposed by Friedman, accompanied the elevation of lightning's descendants to a position of pre-eminence in the Zapotec political system.

Iconography

Iconography is a subject whose definition has drifted somewhat over the years. It can refer either to the making of an icon by carving or drawing, or to the analysis of the icons themselves; today it most often refers to the analysis. (Once thought of mainly as a religious image, statue, bust painting or engraving, an "icon" has also had its meaning broadened recently to include professional athletes and rock musicians.)

When archaeologists use the term "iconography" today, they are usually referring to an analysis of the way ancient peoples represented religious, political, ideological, or cosmological objects or concepts in their art. Unfortunately, the quality of analysis is highly variable. In cases where a great deal is known about the cosmology, religion, or ideology of an ancient people – as for example, through history or ethnohistory – iconography can be a truly scientific analysis. In cases where no such background information is available, "iconography" can turn out to be little more than science fiction. In such cases, the art of an ancient culture merely serves as a kind of neutral Rorschach blot onto which the author projects his or her own personality. The literature in Mesoamerica includes hundreds of such idiosyncratic fantasies, each of which tells us far more about the author than about the ancient culture. Almost inevitably, the authors of such studies ask us to trust their "highly-developed intuition" in lieu of any acceptable supporting evidence for their interpretation.

Ironically, one of the best iconographic analyses of a body of Precolumbian art was done by a subsistence-settlement archaeologist, Olga Linares (1977). That is because Linares brought to her study the same kind of rigour she uses in her survey, excavation, and analysis; she relied on actual evidence rather than the "unusually refined aesthetic sense" claimed by so many of the worst iconographers.

For her study, Linares chose decorated burial vessels from high-status cemeteries at a series of chiefly sites in the central Panamanian provinces (Veraguas, Coclé; Herrera, Los Santos). These cemetery sites spanned the period AD 500–1500, with the latest of them falling at the time of the Spaniards' arrival in Panama (Lothrop 1937; 1942). Linares was therefore able to use eyewitness accounts of sixteenth-century Panamanian chiefdoms in her analysis, including documents by Gonzalo Badajoz (in Andagoya 1865), Gaspar de Espinosa (1864; 1873), Bartolomé de Las Casas (1951), and Gonzalo Fernández de Oviedo y Valdés (1851–1855).

Many cemetery vessels are painted in a flamboyant, polychrome style, with naturalistic animal representations. Their open shapes and their placement in the ground suggest that the motifs were meant to be seen from above by funeral participants or graveside mourners. The great intrinsic value of the vessels is suggested by the fact that some were later removed from one grave to be placed in another, or even deliberately destroyed in what could be acts of status competition.

Four main lines of information were used in Linares' study: (1) ethnohistoric accounts of sixteenth-century Panamanian chiefdoms; (2) knowledge of animal species diversity in the Panamanian tropics; (3) primary archaeological data on the context of the graves and the burials they contain; and (4) the range of themes and/or motifs painted on the pottery vessels.

Ethnohistory tells us that sixteenth-century Panamanian chiefdoms featured a high level of warfare or raiding, with intense competition for positions of leadership. Painted motifs and special tattooing were applied to the body of important individuals as badges of rank and bravery. Warriors fighting under a single chief wore a special motif to distinguish them from warriors fighting under rival chiefs. Such warriors were also buried with helmets, a wide range of weapons, and other military paraphernalia.

The central Panamanian art style was based on a rich symbolic system, using animal motifs as metaphors to express the qualities of bravery and aggression desired in both chiefs and warriors. Linares noted that plants were rarely depicted, and reasoned that the attributes of certain animals were being used to communicate the rank and bravery of the buried warriors. She pointed out that species diversity in the humid tropics is significantly higher than in temperate zones, facilitating an artist's selection of animal species thought to have the desired qualities while ignoring others. Tropical species have evolved complex and varied interspecific and intraspecific patterns of interaction, including predation, commensalism, mimicry, and elaborate signalling systems. Such animal behaviour mirrors the complexity of human behaviour, providing abundant raw material for symbolism and its iconographic expression.

Once Linares turned to the specific animals uses on the burial vessels of the Panamanian chiefdoms, she noted that there had been careful selection of those which reflect the aggressive values of the warrior. Some are man-eaters, some predators, some belligerent fighters, while others bite, sting, or have toxic defences. For example, Parita Polychrome designs often feature a predator and its prey — the hammerhead shark and the stingray — with the former known to feed on the latter. Pottery from Sitio Conte and other sites in Coclé, Herrera, Veraguas, and the Azuero Peninsula featured not only sharks and rays, but also crocodiles, raptorial birds, and crabs. Some of the most common birds were guans and/or curassows, large gallinaceous birds which are notoriously ill-tempered and whose males often fight furiously among themselves (Table 1). The artistic depiction of each animal emphasizes precisely those organs or body parts involved in predatory or defensive activities such as biting, clawing, stinging, and so forth.

As significant as those animals depicted on funerary vessels were those not represented. Prey species and animals with soft body parts, such as agoutis, pacas, rabbits, sloths, monkeys, opossums, iguanas, and most fish were essentially ignored by the

Table 1 Behavioural qualities of animals depicted in the funerary art of Panamanian chiefdoms. (Adapted from Linares 1977.)

Category of animal	Significant attributes
Crocodiles	Potentially man-eating
Large felines (puma, jaguar)	Potentially man-eating
Sharks	Potentially man-eating
Stingrays	Potentially dangerous
Needlefish	Potentially dangerous
Scorpions	Capable of stinging
Crabs	Capable of pinching
Guans/Curassows	Notably belligerent
Hawks	Predatory
Turtles	Defended by a hard shell
Armadillos	Defended by a hard shell
Squid	Defend themselves with ink
Poisonous snakes	Potentially dangerous
Poisonous toads/frogs	Potentially dangerous
Toxic marine worms	Potentially dangerous

artist, even though they were among the animals commonly eaten (and present in middens). These animals, despite their economic importance to the Panamanian chiefdoms, simply did not reinforce the values of bravery, fighting ability, rank, or warrior status desired by the painters of funerary vessels. Moreover, body parts of many of the aggressive animals depicted iconographically – such as shark's teeth and stingray spines – were themselves included in the same graves. Linares concluded that in the cognized world of the Panamanian chiefdom, animals had been carefully chosen from the diversity of tropical species in order to communicate those qualities most admired in the chief and his warriors.

We have chosen Linares' study as our example of how archaeological iconography should be done for several reasons. Among other things, it demonstrates that iconography is not some esoteric skill that must be employed by a group of investigators different from those who do subsistence-settlement archaeology. Iconography works just fine when it is analytical and draws on a wide range of social and natural sciences. In turn, this suggests that the "special gifts" claimed by many iconographers may be no more than a smokescreen designed to discourage closer examination of their reasoning.

Summary and conclusions

In this paper we have considered four categories of human intellectual activity – cosmology, religion, ideology, and iconography – that could be considered appropriate subjects for cognitive archaeology. Those four categories do not by any means exhaust the subject matter of the field. We do think, however, that our four chosen topics cover a great deal of what passes today for cognitive archaeology.

Do we really believe that archaeologists can work on these topics? Yes, but only under the appropriate circumstances and with the appropriate rigour. When a great deal of background information is available — as, for example, among the sixteenth-century Aztec or New Kingdom Egyptians — it makes sense to reconstruct the cosmology and religion of those people. When almost no background knowledge is available, as for the aceramic Neolithic, such reconstruction can border on science fiction. That is when every figurine becomes a "fertility goddess" and every misshapen boulder a "cult stone".

Are cosmology, religion, ideology, and iconography mere epiphenomena, unworthy of scientific study? We hope we have shown the opposite. We hope we have shown that cosmology affects the way the natural environment is used, that religion can promote or inhibit commerce with foreigners, that ideology must change before rank society can evolve, and that iconography can be used to reinforce the militaristic values of competing chiefdoms. Those topics cannot be dismissed out of hand by subsistence-settlement archaeologists.

On the other hand, we understand why many subsistence-settlement archaeologists are sceptical of cognitive archaeology. No approach has greater potential for dilettantism, flights of fancy, charlatanism, and intellectual laziness. No one is likely to make up a fictitious plant assemblage from a site, but we see fictitious religions, ideologies, and cosmologies made up on the spot in both the New and Old Worlds.

Subsistence-settlement archaeology requires a lot of work, much of it tedious and time-consuming: strenuous surveys, careful and extensive excavations, fine screening and flotation, painstaking identification of plant and animal remains, and so on. If cognitive archaeology can be done with the same careful, painstaking effort as subsistence-settlement archaeology, few will have any doubts about it.

Unfortunately, the cognitive route is frequently chosen by those who, while wishing to call themselves archaeologists, do not have the patience for the work described above. Searching for a way around the rigour and tedium, they have seized upon cognitive archaeology as a shortcut. Worse still, they often see it as a prestigious shortcut, one that relies on "brilliance", "insight", or "intuition" rather than hard work. They would like us to believe that they don't have to survey, dig, or analyze archaeological remains because they have "special gifts" denied the rest of us. We, on the other hand, suspect that they don't survey, dig, or analyze because they aren't concerned with what actually happened in prehistory.

When we see cosmology derived solely from the alleged orientation of a building to a particular star, when we see an entire ideology reconstructed from the style of a carving, and when we see ancient religion reconstructed from a handful of figurines or the red dado painting on the wall of a shrine, we have a right to be sceptical. Equally troubling is the notion — clearly subscribed to by some self-styled "cognitive archaeologists" — that the quality of a theory is to be measured by its style and flair, rather than the extent to which it is grounded in evidence.

It is for all these reasons that we believe cognitive archaeology should not be a separate branch of archaeology. The study of cosmology, religion, ideology, and iconography, and other products of the ancient mind, should simply be a task that the well-rounded archaeologist takes on as a matter of course – when it is appropriate.

Do we then need cognitive archaeology? Yes, but as a way of making mainstream archaeology more holistic, rather than creating an esoteric subdiscipline. The biggest challenge facing cognitive archaeology is to become anchored as firmly in the ethnographic, historic, ethnohistoric, and archaeological records as the more subsistence- and settlement-based aspects of archaeology. Like the New Archaeologists of 25 years ago, aspiring cognitive archaeologists should heed the advice of Jesse D. Jennings (1968, 329): "At all costs, all archaeologists need to remember that, like Antaeus, they must continue to 'touch the earth' or they will lose their strength."

■ ■ ■

References

Andagoya, P., (1865). *Narrative of the Proceedings of the Pedrarias Davila in the Provinces of Tierra Firme or Castilla del Oro, and the Discovery of the South Sea and the Coasts of Peru and Nicaragua*, trans. C.R. Markham. (Hakluyt Society 34.) London: Hakluyt Society.

Espinosa, G. de, (1864). Relación hecha por Gaspar de Espinosa, Alcalde Mayor de Castilla del Oro, dada a Pedrarias de Avila . . ., in *Colección de Documentos del Archivo de Indias*, Tomo II. Madrid: Imprenta Española, 467–522.

Espinosa, G. de, (1873). Relación e proceso quel Lic. Gaspar Despinosa, Alcalde mayor, hizo en el viaje . . ., in *Colección de Documentos Inéditos del Archivo de Indias*, Tomo XX. Madrid: Imprenta del Hospicio, 5–119.

Fernández de Oviedo y Valdés, G., (1851–55). *Historia general y natural de Las Indias, Islas y Tierra Firme del Mar Océano*. 4 vols. Madrid: Imprenta de la Real Academia de la Historia.

Flannery, K.V., (1976). Contextual analysis of ritual paraphernalia from formative Oaxaca, in *The Early Mesoamerican Village*, ed. K.V. Flannery. New York (NY): Academic Press, 333–45.

Flannery, K.V., and J. Marcus, (1976). Formative Oaxaca and the Zapotec cosmos. *American Scientist* 64, 374–83.

Flannery, K.V. and J. Marcus (eds.), (1983). *The Cloud People, Divergent Evolution of the Zapotec and Mixtec Civilizations*. New York (NY) & San Diego (CA): Academic Press.

Friedman, J., (1979). *System, Structure and Contradiction: The Evolution of "Asiatic" Social Formations*. (Social Studies in Oceania and South East Asia 2.) Copenhagen: The National Museum of Denmark.

Hughes, J.D., (1975). *Ecology in Ancient Civilizations*. Albuquerque (NM): University of New Mexico Press.

Jennings, J.D., (1968). *Prehistory of North America*. New York (NY): McGraw-Hill Book Company.

Las Casas, B. de, (1951). *Historia de las Indias*. 3 vols. Mexico: Fondo de Cultura Económica.

Leach, E.R., (1954). *Political Systems of Highland Burma*. London: G. Bell & Sons.

Linares, O.F., (1977). *Ecology and the Arts in Ancient Panama: On the Development of Social Rank and Symbolism in the Central Provinces*. (Studies in Pre-Columbian Art & Archaeology 17.) Washington (DC): Dumbarton Oaks.

Lothrop, S.K., (1937). *Coclé: An Archaeological Study of Central Panama*. Part I. (Memoirs of the Peabody Museum of Archaeology and Ethnology, Harvard University VII.) Cambridge (MA): Peabody Museum.

—— (1942). *Coclé: An Archaeological Study of Central Panama*. Part II. (Memoirs of the Peabody Museum of Archaeology and Ethnology, Harvard University VII.) Cambridge (MA): Peabody Museum.

Marcus, J., (1978). Archaeology and religion: a comparison of the Zapotec and Maya. *World Archaeology* 10, 172–91.

—— (1989). Zapotec chiefdoms and the nature of formative religions, in *Regional Perspectives on the Olmec*, eds. R.J. Sharer and D.C. Grove. (School of American Research Advanced Seminar Series.) Cambridge: Cambridge University Press, 148–97.

Marcus, J. & K.V. Flannery, (1994). Zapotec ritual and religion: an application of the direct historical approach, in *The Ancient Mind*, eds C. Renfrew & E.B.W. Zubrow. Cambridge: Cambridge University Press.

Sanders, W.T., (1974). Chiefdom to state: political evolution at Kaminaljuyu, Guatemala, in *Reconstructing Complex Societies: An Archaeological Colloquium*, ed. C.B. Moore. Cambridge (MA): MIT Press, 97–121.

Ucko, P.J. & G.W. Dimbleby (eds), (1969). *The Domestication and Exploitation of Plants and Animals*. London: Duckworth.

Ucko, P.J., R. Tringham & G.W. Dimbleby (eds), (1972). *Man, Settlement and Urbanism*. London: Duckworth.

Wheatley, P., (1975). Satyanrta in Suvarnadvipa: from reciprocity to redistribution in ancient southeast Asia, in *Ancient Civilization and Trade*, eds J.A. Sabloff & C.C. Lamberg-Karlovsky. Albuquerque (NM): University of New Mexico Press, 227–65.

Chapter 3

SYMBOLIC, STRUCTURAL, AND CRITICAL ARCHAEOLOGY

Mark P. Leone

Leone

Introduction

What are symbolic archaeology, structural archaeology, and critical archaeology? Given that they are different approaches to archaeology, what do they share? And given that these two approaches do not compose a uniform movement, what are the currents and crosscurrents between them and mainstream archaeology?

Symbolic archaeology, structural archaeology, and critical archaeology are three quite different approaches to archaeological data. None of them is completely defined as yet. None grows directly out of either traditional (Leach 1973) or the new archaeology (Clarke 1973) and yet all three have drawn significant attention. The archaeologists involved in them appear to be involved in the same issues and operate with the same assumptions (Hodder 1982a, Spriggs 1984; Miller 1982b; Moore and Keene 1983). As these approaches are being defined it is becoming clear that they are not necessarily headed for similar analyses (Bender 1985, Patterson 1984). It is, however, clear to anyone who reads the archaeological literature today, that many archaeologists are concerned with meaning (Hodder 1982a, 1983), ideology (Kristiansen 1984; Paynter 1985; Handsman 1980, 1981, 1982), structure (Friedman and Rowlands 1977; Glassie 1975; Freidel 1981), and cognition (Deetz 1967) in past societies. In order to approach such areas through the archaeological record, ideas, models, and theories have been borrowed and explored from structuralism, cognitive anthropology, symbolic analysis, and Marxism (Baudrillard 1975, Gledhill 1981; Godelier 1977, 1978; Meillassoux 1972; Wallerstein 1976).

Symbolic, structural, and critical archaeology are chosen in this essay because their spokespersons are increasingly vocal and widely read, and because their differences are not as clear within the field as they should be. The point of this essay is not to address the origins of these approaches, whether they are mainly American or British, nor to identify schools of thought associated with universities or with particular scholars. The point is to identify the basic assumptions and to see how they are expressed in the five illustrations discussed and quoted below.

Four issues

These three initiatives in archaeology can be understood by reference to four issues. The first one is the interactive or recursive quality of culture. Rather than supposing that culture, including the rules, behavior, and things produced, is borne by people in a fairly passive and unaware fashion, the assumption is that people create, use, modify, and manipulate their symbolic capabilities, making and remaking the world they live in. This does not necessarily mean the capacity to dominate, control, or even to change culture in directive or politically forceful ways. It is, however, an effort to see that, like language, its use shapes our lives, and our lives would be shapeless without it. The major impact in archaeology of this viewpoint comes in regarding material culture as an instrument in creating meaning and order in the world (Conkey 1982; Donley 1982; Kus 1982; Moore 1982; Parker Pearson 1982), and not solely as the reflection of economics, social organization, or ideology.

The importance of this point is well developed by John Barrett who attempts to adapt Giddens (1979, 1981, 1982a, 1982b) to archaeology.

> One attempt to break with functionalism involves shifting the focus of analysis from the consequences of human action to the intentions and motivations of that action. . . . In the theory of structuration, Giddens employs an analytical frame of the "time-space continuum" within which the actions of knowledgeable human subjects reproduce the institutional conditions of their own existence. Giddens means . . . discursive knowledge (which) encompass[es] the practical knowledge of "how to go on" . . . it is knowledge which is drawn upon for, and reproduced in, human action. Here the subjects draw upon their reflexive experience of an objective world, which appears constituted as a meaningful cultural resource, and act upon those same external conditions to reproduce and transform them, bequeathing the results of that action as the conditions for future action.
>
> (Barrett 1988:5–9)

This is the recursive quality of culture, which sees people as actors, symbols as central to human existence, and material culture in context as analogous to language in its capacity to order human life.

The second crucial issue behind symbolic, structural, and critical archaeology is an emphasis on meaning. All approaches deny the kind of materialism which has over the years come to be associated with the new archaeology. As materialism was inherited from Leslie White, Julian Steward, reinterpreted through Marvin Harris and A. P. Vayda, and a host of other, largely American, scholars, it became a form of determinism that has been avoided by most British social anthropologists and all American symbolic anthropologists. The materialism which has been rejected by symbolic (Hodder 1985) and critical archaeology is that which is seen as a hierarchy of factors going from ecological, technological, and demographic considerations to social organization, and to a vaguely defined ideological or religious organization.

In a concrete historical sense in archaeology, the last twenty years' progress has revolved around the remarkably productive studies of the natural environment, domesticated plant and animal foods, and the tools, shelters, and techniques used to supply, support, reproduce, and control a population, society, and a whole culture. While sometimes taking potshots at these achievements, symbolic archaeology rejects the materialism that ignores meaning, the context of daily life, deliberate attempts to manipulate social relations, and the whole world of thought. On the other hand, the sources (Habermas 1971, 1981) of critical archaeology, which are here separate from the others, do not renounce a materialist tradition. Such archaeology argues that in any society where there are contradictions, conflict, or exploitation, to expect smooth functioning or adaptation as the new archaeology did, is to miss a major part of the culture. Ideology is the mechanism, the part of a cultural system that hides or masks the contradictions, and thus prevents active conflict from occurring (Althusser 1971; Barnett and Silverman 1979). Ideology has, until recently, never been defined in archaeology in any coherent or operational way.

How is culture conceived by these approaches to archaeology? Is it levels, a system, or like language? What interacts and where is cause? Barrett (1988) and the symbolic archaeologists (Miller 1982a; Tilley 1982, 1984) avoid the notion of levels in preference for a picture of people using symbols to negotiate reality on a moment by moment basis. Structuralists see a coherent set of symbols (oppositions) shaping daily life, but in the examples used below from Freidel and Schele (1988) and Deetz (1977; 1983) we can see they are not so concerned with how the oppositions are affected by use. For their part, critical archaeologists do conceive of levels in the Marxist sense, but see ideology as powerful in maintaining society, its coherence, and its continuity: ideology is what reproduces society intact.

The third issue that helps to define both symbolic and critical archaeology is a critique of the function of the past and scientific knowledge of it in society. Symbolic (Shanks and Tilley 1987a) and critical archaeology (Gero et al. 1983; Leone 1981a, 1981b; Meltzer 1981) assert the active role of the past in the society that is interested in it. Both approaches assert that the past, whether it be known through the sciences of the past, the vernacular media, myth, or through museums, is an active vehicle for communicating and composing meanings. Neither position will allow archaeology to assert scientific neutrality, or its role as the objective producer of accurate knowledge about the past (Wylie 1981, 1985a), or even as a socially irrelevant pursuit. Symbolic archaeology asserts that since the past is a social creation, and that because it exists in most societies in endless variations, and further, that because archaeology produces one of these variations, the priviliged status of archaelogy must be examined for its own good. Where does its right to dominate come from? Why is the archaeological interpretation considered the only correct one?

Critical archaeology forcefully asserts with Marx that history is always produced in the service of class interests (Bloch 1977; Gero 1983; Wobst 1983). Furthermore, it asserts that appeals to scientific objectivity are likely to obfuscate discussion of the assumption of objectivity. Thus, an exploration of the political function of archaeology may produce both a consciousness of the social function of archaeology as well as a set of questions for archaeology to address that may be of greater social benefit. Thus, while symbolic archaeology on the one hand is aware that the past is a social construct and is just as dynamic a part of culture as language, critical archaeology, on the other hand, sees history as ideology, and likely to be pernicious if ignored. Therefore, attention to archaeology's ideological status may produce important, archaeologically answerable questions.

Fourth, from within symbolic archaeology has come a serious denial of the place of positivism in archaeological science (Hodder 1982a; Miller and Tilley 1984). Within critical archaeology the critique is less severe in its implications and more hopeful of sustaining the tradition of the later sixties and seventies. Symbolic archaeology is not willing to grant a culture-free status to the self-proclaimed self-watching abilities of Western scientific logic. There are two points: an unaware science is ignorant of its own culture. Further, since method is itself of cultural origin, it may ultimately not be possible to create or depend on a science of the past to produce any more than a strong interpretation. This does not imply that all pasts are equal, but it does imply that any science that believes itself to be active in the cross-cultural tradition or in the law-searching tradition, or in the tradition that regards an examination of its connection with modern society as mere social philosophy is blinding itself to the fundamental proposition of anthropology: we and our institutions are cultural creations, and we do not exist outside culture.

Critical archaeology has not divorced itself so completely from the emphasis on scientific method developed over the last twenty years in archaeology. The word "critical" in any scholarly context means that the relations between the assumptions and discoveries of the discipline and their ties to modern life are a central concern and are subject to examination (Habermas 1971). Such examination automatically subjects the questions, methods, and discoveries of a science or discipline to questions which ask how the scientist's surroundings dictate the questions, influence the method, and predetermine either the results or, more usually, their meaning and interpretation. Nonetheless, critical studies do not hope for or cause the impoverishment of a science or discipline. The point is to produce neither a debilitating skepticism nor a pointless relativism.

The most prominent work done by British symbolic archaeologists is with different aspects of the Bronze Age of Northwest Europe. Hodder (1982b), Shanks and Tilley (1982) Tilley (1984), Shennan (1982), Kristiansen (1984), and Parker Pearson (1984) have taken a stratified society in which there were marked differences in access to wealth, and asked how was power justified, used, and perpetuated. Their analyses of the standard remains of the Bronze Age suggest that the rituals associated with burials, barrows, and utensils were used by the powerful to convince the less powerful of the existence of equality when that relationship was actually diminishing. The basic assumptions in these analyses are that stratification was based on unequal access to power, or goods, but is always tentative and must be justified or masked. Stratification is a dynamic, not a stable, relationship. The second assumption is that some material items, like those associated with burial, can be used, probably in ritual contexts, to convince all involved of the justice of the situation and thus to neutralize potential conflict, and so to continue society intact. This precis of the argument distills too much, however, to see the difference between a symbolic and a critical interpretation.

Hodder's (1982b) argument shows cogently what he is after. In the Dutch Neolithic there are a series of well-known phases marked by different settlement, subsistence, and ceramic patterns. Early on, settlements were nucleated, agriculture was intensive, and pottery was decorated in clearly bounded areas. Later, pottery decorations are related to each other (Hodder 1982b:165).

> The pottery designs of [phases] A to E has been described as incorporating increasing numbers of contrasts and oppositions. Complex communal burial and associated ritual are known throughout the early . . . phases. But in phases F and G . . . megaliths cease to be constructed. . . . The construction of tombs in the early [phases] argues for the presence of corporate groups and . . . the use of communal burial mounds and monuments . . . symbolize local competing groups and lineages in north and west Europe. . . . The tombs, and an ideology related to ancestors, may have functioned not only to legitimate dominant groups, but also to legitimate their traditional rights tied to one place.

> (Hodder 1982b:170)

> [Given change to dispersed settlement, contradictions emerge between] dominant and subordinate groups to emphasize traditional, stable ties to ancestors, in the context of shorter term, expanding settlement. . . . [Consequently] the decrease in identifiable contrasts and categorical oppositions in the pottery forms and decoration of the late [phases] could have acted to deny the earlier social distinctions, and to emphasize connections and interrelationships. By expressing a decreased concern with categorization and by drawing less attention to the boundaries between these categories, a new pattern of social and economic relationships could be set up.

> (Hodder 1982b:171)

> The material culture [burial, pots, axes] is organized into a complex series
> of categories and oppositions so that the associated activities can play a part
> in drawing attention to and legitimating individual rights in a context in which
> there is increasing potential for the disruption of those rights. ". . . On the
> North European plain . . . groups manipulated burial, pottery and the symbols
> . . . in order to maintain traditional rights. . . . The new process of legit-
> imization resolved the earlier contradictions . . . [as did the] symbolic
> distinction in pottery and . . . the daily activities associated with . . . its use."
> (Hodder 1982b:175, 176)

Material culture was used by people in institutional settings to negotiate the
change from stable, closely settled hierarchical groups to unstable, widely scattered,
also hierarchical groups. The groups changed and so did people's places in and
among them. Thus there had to be negotiation over place, which means that meaning
changed and this was facilitated through the use of many items of material culture.
This particular illustration of Hodder's work is important because of its emphasis
on meaning and context, its emphasis on the recursive quality of material culture,
which in turn allows us to see that people as individuals, not as population aggre-
gates, die, are buried, take part in rituals which are genuinely significant in their
lives, make, use, and rely on pottery vessels to help define their lives, resolve
conflicts within them, and furthermore, that this is an interpretation of elements
of the archaeological record. The validity of this interpretation outside a small part
of Europe is irrelevant; its strength lies in its ability to take normally separated
aspects of archaeological data, and to articulate the relationships that produced
them. Consideration of burial, subsistence, ritual, settlement, and their changes
over time in terms of the stresses, conflicts, and contradictions is not at all normal
behavior among conventional archaeologists. Also, there is obviously a hypothesis
behind the article. Hodder is opposed to variable testing of the kind that shreds
the fabric of the past for an accuracy that has limited value in the present. Hodder's
piece does not offer a conclusion with a stated degree of veracity; it offers an
ending which is plausible, which can be expanded or changed by other archaeologists just as easily as could be done by using strict positivist procedures.

A case of structural archaeology

In isolating symbolic archaeology as a topic, we have the benefit of discussing a
form of archaeology that is being elaborated continually. Its major contributions
involve an integration of the massive data on the Northwest European Neolithic.
Its ethnoarchaeology (Donley 1982; Kus 1982; Moore 1982; Parker Pearson 1982)
and its critique of the new archaeology are also, obviously, important. Upon examination, it is clear that symbolic archaeology's achievements cannot be isolated from
the progress made by cognitive or structural archaeology.

Since symbolic archaeology exists as a movement contemporaneously with structural analyses, it is reasonable to ask what is its relationship to reconstructions of the New England mind set (Deetz 1977), the cognitive rules of folk housing in Virginia (Glassie 1975), Olmec cosmology (Furst 1968), or Maya cosmology (Freidel 1981)? A number of American archaeologists have been concerned with symbolic, or in a Parsonian framework, cultural issues for some time. For many, indeed most, culture is a level of meaning or thought that includes values, cosmology, patterns held unawares, or structures composed of oppositions. Such a reality exists alongside and is independent of social organization. Culture facilitates social reality. Further, these archaeologists do not find cause for change or stability in any one level of reality, but rather reinforcement between them. Most would agree with the recursive quality of material culture, but as an afterthought not as a basic operation to start with. For these archaeologists, it is culture or symbols that are recursive with changes in politics, settlement expansion, dynastic or govern-mental shift, or subsistence. Structural and cognitive scholars also would find a recursive relationship between archaeological constructions and the society of the archaeologists inevitable. Except for Kehoe (1984a, 1984b) none seems to have pursued it yet as a research strategy. All these archaeologists favor interpretation over the testing of precisely arranged variables, hypothesis fashion, as suggested by an approach from positivism.

When one reads Deetz, Glassie, Freidel, Furst, Hall, or some of the others, there is a horde of data, and tremendous emphasis on an idea of complex dimensions to fit all the archaeological pieces together. Such authors attempt to produce a whole that either corrects a previous error of archaeological fragmentation or because it replaces overly simple explanations of social change.

David Freidel's work on Maya cosmology is a useful example. He has been working for years on Maya iconographic images and, along with Linda Schele (Freidel and Schele 1988), has tried to understand their meaning and textual place in terms of the changes in Maya society from the Preclassic to Classic to Postclassic, or for about a thousand years (roughly 200 BC-AD 800). Freidel and Schele begin by using changes in iconography to trace changes in the meaning of the symbols that are associated with political power.

> The Late Pre-classic symbolic model was based on the passage of Venus as Morning and Evening Star with the rising and setting of the sun. . . . They developed an amazingly effective cosmogram . . . which the community could verify by simply observing the sky. As the model was expanded and adapted . . . two processes of change stand out. The historical identities of Late Pre-classic rulers have not been found recorded in public space, suggesting that personal and historical identity of rulers did not require permanent verification in the form of public monuments. Exactly the opposite is true of the Classic period. The legitimation of individual rulers through genealogy and supernatural charter and in public space with public participation seems to

have been the prime motivation for the erection of public art in the Classic period. Those [later] rulers legitimized their positions by claiming identity as the gods of the cosmogram.

(Freidel and Schele 1988: 27–29)

This innovation in the Late Pre-classic period occurs in the context of a rapid and profound reorganization of Maya society in which a heretofore *de facto* elite becomes legitimate and acceptable to the general populace. The result is a greatly expanded access to labor and goods celebrated in the construction of massive centers.

(Freidel and Schele 1988: 31)

. . . the Lowland Maya were not in a position . . . to reverse strategies of production and trade, population growth and other indigenous factors reinforcing the trend towards increased social complexity and inequality. In the face of these dynamic social conditions, an ideal of social equality became increasingly untenable and finally underwent transformation to a model of reality which made elitism both rational and necessary. The social result was the explosive release of energy invested in central places celebrating the new order.

(Freidel and Schele 1988: 36)

[Freidel and Schele finish off with establishing the power of the symbols whose political use they have so effectively described.] As metaphor, the twin ancestors [Sun and Venus] provide a potent image for lateral blood ties between lineages, communities, and peoples adhering to the same myth cycle. As twins are of the same womb and blood, so all Maya are of the same ancestry and blood. Brotherhood lends itself to egalitarian values and their kinship sanctions. [In the Classic period they became ranked, and] this positioning provides a celestially correct cosmic model, with Morning and Evening Star above the rising and setting sun. . . . By asserting that time had passed between the birth of the twins, as given in the hieroglyphic texts at Palenque, the Maya displayed the principle of ranking, of inequality, in their icon and concept.

(Freidel and Schele 1988: 37)

The mass of data on the elements showing the iconography is not included in the excerpts. Were they presented, the clear use of structuralism to highlight oppositions would be unmistakable. Freidel proposes a social as well as a cultural revolution among the Lowland Maya; these are independent but simultaneous, mutually supporting, with neither causing the other. He insists that there is no need to depend on invasion or environmental disturbance on which to base the changes. Thus, along with the symbolic archaeologists, Freidel sees people thinking order into their world through the use of central, powerful, and pliable symbols. These symbols initiate behavior and rationalize it as well.

In Freidel and Schele's treatment of material culture is the understanding that material objects are recursive or forming. Friedel can be and is more clear than Hodder, Shanks, Tilley or Sheenan about how ritual life and shrines and temple structures shaped people's lives. He can be, since ethnohistoric texts exist to give a good idea of what Mayan cosmology was and what its manifestations were. No such help is available from the Neolithic of Northwest Europe. We have long had the evidence from linguistics, semiotics, and from structural and symbolic anthropology that cultural materials form; they are active ingredients in thought and behavior. Nonetheless, when the material record was defined as reflective of all aspects of behavior, the recursive quality of culture, including material culture, tended to be ignored or considered second, when at all.

Cognitive archaeology

"Ignored" may be a better way to characterize how theory within the new archaeology handled material culture, and, indeed, culture as a whole. Even so, Binford's early and central move of defining material culture as being shaped by all levels of culture, and thus of reflecting all its components is an essential step in allowing Freidel to take Preclassic cylinders and Classic pyramids and postulate a cosmogram. True, the method Freidel employs is structuralist and its assumptions about what material culture encodes may simply coincide with the new archaeology's. They may be independent, but they are not contradictory. Yet, the recursive quality of the items is clearly seen by the symbolic and structural archaeologists, and it is not employed by materialist archaeologists.

The contrast in Freidel's position with Deetz (1977) and Glassie (1975), who are quite concerned with thought, is important because the latter do not explore the impact of symbolically constituted behavior back on the symbolic structure. Both Deetz and Glassie, one an archaeologist and the other a folklorist, are concerned with reconstructing the rules or cognitive patterns behind expressions of folk material culture. Their method is structuralist and they take the recursive quality of material culture more as a given, than as a topic for detailed description. Since Deetz employs Glassie, and uses archaeological data from New England in the 17th, 18th, and 19th centuries, he is a useful illustration of the two points they share with the symbolic archaeologists. Deetz is occupied with the consistency of thought (its power) that finds expression in a vast array of material items. He is committed to building a case strong enough to link large and diverse ranges of functionally unrelated items. He is willing to attempt this approach, using logic that takes a culturally specific opposition and finds replication in other cultural domains as evidence of accuracy. Deetz is no less scientific than Hodder, Freidel, or Lévi-Strauss. He is less concerned with defining tests, but quite concerned with generality, which is just as much a part of science as measurement.

Deetz, Glassie, and Freidel, unlike the symbolic archaeologists, are unconcerned with the origins of their questions. Insofar as Deetz and Glassie are concerned with early American culture they are concerned with American society today. But they are not concerned with systematic examination of research categories, the locus of the oppositions found in the data, or the social function of the interpretation which they create. Indeed, there is no particular concern with why the American patterns they so cogently describe ceased, or why today is, or is not, their product.

Deetz begins his analysis by using Glassie (1975: 189–190) to say that in Anglo-America when "the social, economic, political and religious conditions . . . changed . . . people adapted . . ., developing new modes of thought, and [then] the things they did, the artifacts they made, manifested the changes that had taken place in their minds" (Deetz 1981: 14).

In Virginia, in New England, and throughout Anglo-America in the late 18th and 19th centuries, "individualism signals 'the point at which the face-to-face community dies' [Glassie 1975: 190]. This important statement is based on observed changes in vernacular housing. This shift from corporate communal organization to lonely individualism is reflected in many aspects of the material world" (Deetz 1981: 13).

> The shift from extensive to intensive structures [appearing to be random vs. symmetrically ordered] that accounts for shrinking chimneys, lowering ceilings and roofs, and tucking behind of ells and sheds in Virginia appears in New England not only in similar architectural changes but also in the disappearance of shared seating at meals, shared utensils, and the appearance of the very impersonal, private urn and willow design, which is profoundly different from both the earlier death's heads and cherubs, both of which extensively related the individual to the community by portraying a part of him or her as it passed by. Simple forms replace complex forms in the rapid change from multicolored ceramics to those predominantly white and blue. In foodways, complex pottages and stews give way to discrete foodstuffs, served separate one from another. Like ceramics, gravestones, earlier made from slates, schists, and sandstones in a range of colors – blue, red, green, black and buff – also become uniformly white, carved from low grade local marbles. The disappearance of borders on louvres, doors and windows in houses is paralleled by the reduction in size and complexity of borders on gravestones, and at least a change in the average width and decorative elaboration of the marleys (edges) of plates and saucers toward less framed, more open forms. And the shift to symmetry reflected in central hall houses – tripartite and severely symmetrical – in all of the Anglo-American world is paralleled by the emergence of a symmetrical relationship between the individual and his or her material culture, utensils, foodstuffs, and burial pits.
>
> (Deetz 1983: 33)

To arrive at the synthesis of the profound conceptual changes that occurred in America during the 18th century and that peaked before 1800, Deetz used oppositions employed by Glassie to describe Middle Virginia folk housing, and applied them to ceramics, foodways, mortuary remains, and music. The oppositions are intellect/emotion, private/public, artificial/natural substance, scattered/clustered, extensive/intensive, complex/simple, framed/open, and nonsymmetry/symmetry. All these fall under Lévi-Strauss' larger opposition order/chaos or culture/nature

Deetz has taken an interpretation, which one could call legitimately a hypothesis, and tried it on data from New England, where he showed it has a strong ability to fit wide ranges of vernacular material culture. As the idea assumes generality, both in domains covered and in space, it becomes less particularistic but does not lose its ability to include local context. Deetz's current work in the historical archaeology of South Africa will provide a place to extend the idea. Once outside the American context, Deetz will, or may, face the worldwide impact of an organizational form for everyday life that stems from England and Holland, or from the colonial process. Dealing with our direct ancestors leads, naturally enough, to the tie to ourselves, which is one of the central issues in archaeology.

Critical archaeology

As soon as any archaeologist assumes the recursive quality of culture and the active quality of material culture, it follows logically that archaeology may have some active impact on our own society. Just as myths about ancestors are verified through astronomical prognostication in the Bronze Age (Thorpe 1981) and in the Classic Maya, and were used to support local power structures, it may follow that our reconstructions of the past, which are verified through archaeological data, have a social function analogous to the ones we are postulating for ancient societies. Archaeology thus, may be more than a neutral and objective science.

How does an archaeologist explore the relationship just mentioned? And what will we know as a result? Such an exploration is known either as phenomenological self-reflection, or critical analysis, depending on the assumptions used. The assumption behind the first is that knowledge of another culture is always constituted through categories and methods that can never be freed from the scholar's culture. Thus, ethnographic, and, logically, archaeological, knowledge is always contingent. This produces the skeptical position which implies that if the distant other cannot be known independently, the effort at knowing is always going to be questionable. A critical analysis stems from a Marxist position and does not deny the possibility of knowing the other, ethnographic or archaeological. Rather, the position argues that all knowledge is class-based and histories are composed for class purposes. Science is a politically contingent enterprise. It is not just that science is part of its own culture, which is obvious with anthropology, but that it is subject to political and economic aims. An examination of those aims leads to knowledge of the political uses of science, and of the sources of the questions, methods, and results which the

science produces. Stemming from this argument is the unwillingness of both symbolic and critical archaeologists to allow an unreflective positivism to assert the
degrees of certainty with which its methods relate the past.

Critical archaeology, based on the work of Habermas (1971) and Lukacs (1971),
does not join symbolic archaeology in such severe doubts about understanding the
past. Its concern is with understanding pasts that are more relevant to its theoretical concerns. What are the pasts of those who have been denied a history:
women, blacks, the Third World, workers? What is the past of ideology?

Two initial efforts that stem more from hermeneutical reading than from critical analysis have been made to disentangle deep prehistory from myth. They (Perper
and Schrire 1977 and Landau 1984) illustrate why we should be concerned with
the cultural basis of our work and what the results of disentanglement can be.

> These [myths] allow us to see the hunting model for what it is: a mixture of
> biological facts and evolutionary concepts entangled in the constricting threads
> of western myth [the Genesis stories of eating of the tree of knowledge, and
> eating meat after the flood]. It is these mythic notions that distinguish the visions
> of human evolution . . . from those of modern ecologists and evolutionists for
> whom human behavior is not dominated by irrevocable actions, but is above
> all, a matter of constant adaptation, flexibility, and plasticity. . . . The most
> plausible ecological strategy would have been to avoid depending on only one
> foodstuff and to adapt a flexible, mixed diet. In truth, there need have been
> no single act, no primal trigger, no expulsion from Eden to set off an
> irreversible series of evolutionary changes. We need not have been shot into
> existence by one major dietary change.
>
> (Perper and Schrire 1977:458)

> [The myth entangled point of view,] that hunting transformed the ancestral
> primate into man is found in the seminal essay by Washburn and Avis. . . .
> [They argue that] a combination of tool-using and meat-eating were there-
> fore key factors in producing man. . . . Ardrey finally says explicitly what
> Washburn, Campbell, and others only imply. He lays bare the essence of
> hunting for the anthropologist, by stating unequivocally that it lies at the
> center of human behavior today and that its effects were not only powerful
> but irreversible. In his terms, we hunted because we were human, but more
> important, we are human because we hunted. The hunting model is the coun-
> terpart of [the Genesis] myth. . . .
>
> (Perper and Schrire 1977:454)

In a more technically exhaustive analysis, Landau (1983; 1984:262–268) shows
that:

> accounts of human evolution usually feature four important episodes: terres-
> triality, bipedalism, encephalization, or the development of the brain, intelli-
> gence, and language; and civilization, the emergence of technology, morals,

and society. . . . [The order of these episodes] may vary between paleo-anthropological accounts [but] they tend to fall into a common narrative structure [which] can also describe traditional literary forms such as the folktale or hero myth.

(Landau 1984:266–267]

[One part of the structure which produces the uniform narrative] is that history can be seen as a meaningful totality. Behind this lies the idea that scattered events of the past can be linked with the present in an overall continuous series . . .; a sequence of events . . . organized into an intelligible story with a beginning, a middle, and an end.

[Landau 1984:267]

[A second part of narrative structure] is that history can be seen as a series of critical moments and transitions. . . . This is especially true of Darwinian narratives, which, owing to their emphasis on natural selection, are often cast in terms of transformation through struggle. Events are not inherently crises, however, nor are they transitions, they acquire such value only in relation to other events in a series

[Landau 1984:267]

[A third part of the narrative structure] is that history can be explained by arranging events into a sequence. Selecting events and arranging them sequentially involves considerations of causality . . .; what happens next often cannot be answered separately from the questions of how and why it happened and how it all turns out. Thus, although scientific explanations may invoke specific laws to account for events . . ., such explanations must be distinguished from explanatory effects produced simply by the sequential ordering of events. In other words, the task is to determine whether scientific explanations apparently based on natural laws are actually a function of narrative procedures.

(Landau 1984:267)

In turning to critical archaeology now, two changes are apparent in the analyses produced within a reflexive context (Wylie 1985b). The first is that the relationship between the present and interpretations of the past is assumed to be a political and economic one. And, second, it is also assumed that a past can be discovered or interpreted archaeologically that can comment on the origins and impact of that tie so that the ideological and class-centered nature of history is illuminated.

The two steps are well illustrated in the research of Handsman (1980, 1981, 1982) working on the historical archaeology of western Connecticut. He begins with a series of modern towns like Canaan and Litchfield, which from their outward appearance look like perfect 18th century New England villages, right out of stereotypes from Norman Rockwell, Grandma Moses, and traditional calendar scenes.

The New England urban village as a complex social place appeared around 1800 and "is marked by an increase in the disparity of the distribution of wealth within

many villages, as well as the appearance of commercial and professional specialization" (Handsman 1981:5). The classic New England village replaced an earlier
landscape made up of scattered farms with a few wide places in the road where
there were nucleated settlements. Why then was the New England village defined
as agrarian and used to hide the industrial process which accompanied it and why
has that use continued? Why is "the modern system . . . constituted so as to segre-
gate itself from what appeared before" (Handsman 1981:16)?

Handsman proceeds to argue that "modern America's past is not a more simplified version of itself but an entirely different [noncapitalist] world. . . . Thus the
history of the village of Canaan is capable of being written . . . to reveal the structural discontinuities and then to explore the missing pieces" (Handsman 1981:18).
To do so Handsman has isolated the classes of artifacts that show the processes of
industrially based urbanization. These processes are explored because they are the
origins of daily life today and because they sustain exploitation and are hidden
behind an ideology that says the processes have existed since colonial times.

These industrial processes are recoverable archaeologically in a tavern midden
(1750–1850) by reasoning that:

> during the first century of its use, when the center village of Canaan did not
> exist between 1750 and 1850, the everyday lives of the inhabitants of the
> Lawrence Farmstead [the earlier use of the tavern] did not differ from one
> year to the next. The range of activities which took place, the equipment
> and facilities which were used during these activities, and the deposited activ-
> ities from them will tend to be homogeneous from one analytical unit to the
> next.
>
> Once the process of settlement growth, socio-economic differentiation,
> and commercial and professional specialization begin, this principle of redun-
> dancy will disappear, to be replaced by everyday lives which are variable and
> non-redundant from one moment to the next. The associated archaeological
> record of everyday life at the tavern [a later use of the farmstead] should
> become more individuated . . . whether specific [archaeological] units are
> compared to one another or to units . . . of the earlier period.
>
> (Handsman 1981:13–14)

Handsman (1981:14) reasons that undifferentiated deposits of ceramics, bottle
glass, window glass, nails and construction hardware represent a homogeneous way
of life, and that a greater degree of dispersion represents greater differentiation.
And indeed "the earlier midden displays a coarse-grained structure while the later
midden, reflective of a period of urbanization, is characterized by a fine-grained
. . . individuated . . . highly differentiated . . . deposit" (Handsman 1981:13–14).

A critical archaeologist has taken a living environment, in this case the well-known
New England village, and has shown that it was constructed to be and remains
a mask. That makes it ideology in the Marxist sense. The center villages so commonly assumed to be unaltered since the 18th century are indeed 19th century

representations created by an industrializing elite to ground itself and its large variation in wealth in an earlier agrarian era which valued independence, equality, and
family. By extension, it may also be the case that many of the museum villages, historic houses, living farms, media presentations of the past, and virtually all popular
uses of archaeology and history in this country are ideological. A critical archaeologist's task is to examine such environments that have an archaeological component
and show which political and economic factors in the present have created them.
Furthermore such a study should show how those factors are disguised within the
setting from the past. Such economic or political factors are usually not well understood in the present and to illuminate them, is to give them a history through archaeology as Handsman has tried to do. He has established the switch to an industrial
existence through archaeology, which was an existence the society had to deny by
the use of settlement pattern and architecture. The denial was necessary because of
the contradiction between the ideal of equality and the reality of substantial disparity in wealth and power. That denial prevents knowledge of shifting family relations,
gender definition, wage relations, and property holdings. These factors, when given
a history by a critical archaeologist, in turn contribute to an awareness of the role
of capitalism in producing histories that disguise but do not educate (Lukacs 1971).
The point in a critical archaeology is to understand the past in order to create a
consciousness of modern society.

   The question of consciousness is a central one in symbolic archaeology and in
critical archaeology. The question stems from the problematic relationship between
present and past. Awareness of the range of possibilities for influence of the present
on interpreting the past, and of the recursiveness of history, makes apparent the
problem of the appropriation of the past. Sensitivity to this problem has led Hodder
(1984:25–32, 1985:1–26) to the position that all pasts are culturally constituted.
If one of them is more accurately interpreted because it was derived from more
rigorous methodology, then the practice that produces rigor must also be seen as
culturally constituted and that such a basis for accuracy may be a bogus basis for
authority. This is a paradoxical situation, which leads logically to suggesting that
other peoples and classes develop their own pasts. Critical archaeology, on the
other hand, presents an equally difficult course: to write the history of domination and resistance, which must by definition include the use of archaeology itself.

   There is no question that symbolic, structural, and critical archaeologists feel
that there are two developments in the new archaeology that are unfortunate. One
is that it has become so rational it is dehumanized, and, as a result, it has diminished its ability to situate itself in its own society and has thus left archaeology
vulnerable to a political critique. By "rational" is meant concern with the degree
of certainty over conclusions, a concern which has tended in the 1970s and 1980s
to restrict conclusions to subsistence, numbers of people, and numbers of things,
and away from social relations, symbolic relations, and the role of humans and of
tradition. Much of the best of archaeology has become not only mechanical but
almost devoid of cultural context.

The unintended consequence of such heavy emphasis on a strict epistemology has been a deepening of the chasm between archaeology and its own society. There has been no concern within the materialist tradition in archaeology with how society shapes its own past. This is true too for more traditional Marxist archaeologists in Europe and America. When Trigger (1984a; 1984b) pointed out obvious misuses of the past, he also implied that there is no dominant conceptual apparatus within any kind of archaeology on which archaeologists can formulate a response to his descriptions. There is nothing in materialist theory that would tell us what to do in the face of the scandalous passivity toward our own society which characterizes archaeology today.

Thus, we can understand Hodder's assertion (1984) that hands are to be kept off other people's pasts, for our own epistemologies are so deadening. An analysis of the role of epistemology is the basis for the claim by critical archaeologists that teaching is political action. These two assumptions are behind an attempt to reach the public with an understanding of how a past is constructed, and of the history of the central economic relations of modern society. The utter irrelevance of most of historical archaeology today is taken to stand as witness to the power of capitalism to disguise its own history. Consequently, excavations have been opened to the public in several places in the United States on the East Coast (Leone 1983; Potter and Leone 1987) and in Arizona, not just to satisfy public curiosity, or to justify spending public money on archaeology, but explicitly to show that the past is not dug up; we think up and with the past. Such an ideological quality is the basis for understanding that the past can be interpreted in a multitude of ways, including some that are quite manipulative.

The idea of awareness invites professionals or practitioners to ask themselves to see that in celebrating fifty years of the SAA, the celebration has to consist of decisions derived from current social practices. These are then used, largely unintentionally, to shape the celebration of the past. This celebration gives present reality a depth it may not have, and acts to perpetuate current relations into the future and inevitably must preclude challenges from those so excluded. We all know culture works this way, but we also know that it is our business to know this actively. And in the active consciousness is presumably greater choice as to whether simple duplication is our fate.

■   ■   ■

References

Althusser, Louis (1971) Ideology and Ideological State Apparatuses. In *Lenin and Philosophy*, translated from the French by Ben Brewster, pages 127–186. Monthly Review Press, New York.

Barnett, Steve and Martin G. Silverman (1979) *Ideology and Everyday Life*. University of Michigan Press, Ann Arbor.

Barrett, John C. (1988) "The Field of Discourse: Reconstituting a Social Archaeology", *Critique of Anthropology*, 7:5–16.

Baudrillard, J. (1975) *The Mirror of Production*. Telos Press, St. Louis.

Bender, Barbara (1985) Emergent Tribal Formation in the American Midcontinent. *American Antiquity* 50(1):52–62.

Bloch, Maurice (1977) The Past and the Present in the Present. *Man* 12(2):278–292.

Clarke, David L. (1973) Archaeology: The Loss of Innocence. *Antiquity* 47(1):6–18.

Conkey, Margaret W. (1982) Boundedness in Art and Society. In *Symbolic and Structural Archaeology*, edited by Ian Hodder, pages 115–128. Cambridge University Press, Cambridge.

Deetz, James (1967) *Invitation to Archaeology*. The Natural History Press, Garden City, New York.

—— (1977) *In Small Things Forgotten*. Anchor Books, Garden City, New York.

—— (1981) Material Culture and World View in Colonial Anglo-America. Paper presented in Millersville, Pennsylvania.

—— (1983) Scientific Humanism and Humanities Science: A Plea for Paradigmatic Pluralism in Historical Archaeology. *Geoscience and Man* 23 (April) 29: 27–34.

Donley, Linda Wiley (1982) House Power: Swahili Space and Symbolic Markers. In *Symbolic and Structural Archaeology*, edited by Ian Hodder, pages 63–73. Cambridge University Press, Cambridge.

Freidel, David A. (1981) Civilization as a State of Mind. In *Transformations to Statehood*, edited by Gordon Jones and Robert Kautz, pages 188–227. Cambridge University Press, Cambridge.

Freidel, David A., and Linda Schele (1988) Symbol and Power: A History of the Lowland Maya Cosmogram. In *Maya Iconography*, edited by Elizabeth P. Benson and Gillette Griffin, pages 44–93. Princeton University Press, Princeton.

Freidman, J., and Michael Rowlands (editors) (1977) *The Evolution of Social Systems*. Duckworth, London.

Furst, Peter T. (1968) The Olmec Were-Jaguar Motif in the Light of Ethnographic Reality. In *Dumbarton Oaks Conference on the Olmec*, edited by Elizabeth P. Benson, pages 143–174. Dumbarton Oaks, Washington, D.C.

Gero, Joan M. (1985) Gender Bias in Archaeology: A Cross-Cultural Perspective. *In* The Socio-politics of Archaeology, edited by Joan M. Gero, David M. Lacy, and Michael L. Blakey. *University of Massachusetts, Department of Anthropology, Research Report* 23:51–57. Amherst.

Gero, Joan M., David M. Lacy, Michael L. Blakey (editors) (1983) The Socio-politics of Archaeology. *University of Massachusetts, Department of Anthropology, Research Report* 23. Amherst.

Giddens, Anthony (1979) *Central Problems in Social Theory*. Macmillan, London.

—— (1981) *A Contemporary Critique of Historical Materialism*. Macmillan, London.

—— (1982a) *Profiles and Critiques in Social Theory*. Macmillan, London.

—— (1982b) *Sociology: A Brief but Critical Introduction*. Macmillan, London.

Glassie, Henry (1975) *Folk Housing in Middle Virginia*. University of Tennessee Press, Knoxville.

Gledhill, J. (1981) Time's Arrow: Anthropology, History, Social Evolution, and Marxist Theory. *Critique of Anthropology* 16:3–30.

Godelier, Maurice (1977) *Perspectives on Marxist Anthropology*. Cambridge University Press, Cambridge.

—— (1978) The Object and Method of Anthropology. In *Relations of Production: Marxist Approaches to Economic Anthropology,* edited by D. Seddon, pages 49–126. Frank Cass, London.

Habermas, Jurgen (1971) *Knowledge and Human Interests*. Beacon Press, Boston.

—— (1981) *The Theory of Communicative Action, Volume 1: Reason and the Rationalization of Society*. Beacon Press, Boston.

Handsman, Russell G. (1980) The Domains of Kinship and Settlement in Historic Goshen: Signs of a Past Cultural Order. *Artifacts* 9:2–7.

—— (1981) Early Capitalism and the Center Village of Canaan, Connecticut: A Study of Transformations and Separations. *Artifacts* 9:1–21.

—— (1982) The Hot and Cold of Goshen's History. *Artifacts* 3:11–20.

Hodder, Ian (1982a) (editor) *Symbolic and Structural Archaeology*. Cambridge University Press, Cambridge.

—— (1982b) Sequences of Structural Change in the Dutch Neolithic. In *Symbolic and Structural Archaeology*, edited by Ian Hodder, pages 162–177. Cambridge University Press, Cambridge.

—— (1983) *The Present Past: An Introduction to Anthropology for Archaeologists*. New York: Pica Press.

—— (1984) Archaeology in 1984. *Antiquity* 58:25–32.

—— (1985) Postprocessual Archaeology. In *Advances in Archaeological Method and Theory*, edited by Michael B. Schiffer, 8:1–26. Academic Press, Orlando, Florida.

Kehoe, Alice B. (1984a) The Myth of the Given. Paper presented to the Society for American Archaeology, Portland, Oregon, April 1984.

—— (1984b) The Ideological Paradigm in Traditional American Ethnology. Paper presented to the American Ethnological Society, Asilomar, California, April 1984.

Kristiansen, Kristian (1984) Ideology and Material Culture: An Archaeological Perspective. In *Marxist Perspectives in Archaeology*, edited by Matthew Spriggs, pages 72–100. Cambridge University Press, Cambridge.

Kus, Susan (1982) Matters Material and Ideal. In *Symbolic and Structural Archaeology*, edited by Ian Hodder, pages 47–62. Cambridge University Press, Cambridge.

Landau, Misia (1983) The Anthropogenic: Paleoanthropological Writing as a Genre of Literature. University Microfilms, Ann Arbor, Michigan.

—— (1984) Human Evolutions as Narrative. *American Scientist* 72:262–268.

Leach, Edmund (1973) [Concluding Address] In *The Explanation of Culture Change*, edited by Colin Renfrew, pages 761–771. University of Pittsburgh Press, Pittsburgh.

Leone, Mark P. (1981a) Archaeology's Material Relationship to the Present and the Past. In *Modern Material Culture*, edited by Richard A. Gould and Michael B. Schiffer, pages 5–14. Academic Press, New York.

—— (1981b) The Relationship between Artifacts and the Public in Outdoor History Museums. In *The Research Potential of Anthropological Museum Collections*, edited by A.M. Cantwell, Nan Rothschild, and James B. Griffin, pages 301–313. New York Academy of Sciences, New York.

—— (1983) Method as Message. *Museum News* 62(1):35–41.

Lukacs, Georg (1971) Reification and the Consciousness of the Proletariat. In *History and*

Class Consciousness, translated by Rodney Livingstone, pages 83–222. M.I.T. Press, Cambridge.

Meillassoux, C. (1972) From Reproduction to Production. *Economy and Society* 1:93–105.

Meltzer, David (1981) Ideology and Material Culture. In *Modern Material Culture*, edited by Richard A. Gould and Michael B. Schiffer, pages 113–125. Academic Press, New York.

Miller, Daniel (1982a) Artifacts as Products of Human Categorisation Processes. In *Symbolic and Structural Archaeology*, edited by Ian Hodder, pages 84–98. Cambridge University Press, Cambridge.

—— (1982b) Explanation and Social Theory in Archaeological Practice. In *Theory and Explanation in Archaeology*, edited by Colin Renfrew, Michael J. Rowlands, Barbara Abbott Segraves. Academic Press, New York.

—— (1985) Ideology and the Harappan Civilization. *Journal of Anthropological Anthropology* 4:1–38.

Miller, Daniel, and Christopher Tilley (editors) (1984) *Ideology, Power and Prehistory*. Cambridge University Press, Cambridge.

Moore, Henrietta (1982) The Interpretation of Spatial Patterning in Settlement Residues. In *Symbolic and Structural Archaeology*, edited by Ian Hodder, pages 74–79. Cambridge University Press, Cambridge.

Moore, James A., and Arthur S. Keene (editors) (1983) *Archaeological Hammers and Theories*. Academic Press, New York.

Parker Pearson, Michael (1982) Mortuary Practices, Society and Ideology: An Ethnoarcheological Study. In *Symbolic and Structural Archaeology*, edited by Ian Hodder, pages 99–113. Cambridge University Press, Cambridge.

—— (1984) Economic and Ideological Change: Cyclical Growth in the Pre-state Societies of Jutland. In *Ideology, Power, and Prehistory*, edited by Daniel Miller and Christopher Tilley, pages 69–92. Cambridge University Press, Cambridge.

Patterson, Thomas C. (1984) Exploitation and Class Formation in the Inca State. Paper presented at the May 1984 meeting of the Canadian Ethnological Society, Montreal.

Paynter, Robert (1985) Models of Technological Change in Historical Archaeology. Paper read at the Council on Northeast Historical Archaeology, SUNY-Binghamton, October 19–21.

Perper, Timothy, and Carmel Schrire (1977) The Nimrod Connection: Myth and Science in the Hunting Model. In *The Chemical Senses and Nutrition*, edited by Morley Kare and Owen Maller, pages 447–459. Academic Press, New York.

Potter, Parker B., Jr., and Mark P. Leone (1987) Archaeology in Public in Annapolis: The Four Seasons, Six Sites, Seven Tours, and 32,000 Visitors. *American Archaeologist*. 6:51–61.

Schrire, Carmel (1984) Wild Surmises on Savage Thoughts. In *Past and Present in Hunter Gatherer Societies*, edited by Carmel Schrire. Academic Press, Orlando.

Shanks, Micheal, and Christopher Tilley (1982) Ideology, Symbolic Power and Ritual Communication: A Reinterpretation of Neolithic Mortuary Practices. In *Symbolic and Structural Archaeology*, edited by Ian Hodder, pages 129–154, Cambridge University Press, Cambridge.

—— (1987a) *Reconstructing Archaeology: Theory and Practice*. Cambridge University Press. Cambridge.

Shennan, Stephen (1982) Ideology, Change, and the European Early Bronze Age. In *Symbolic and Structural Archaeology*, edited by Ian Hodder, pages 155–161. Cambridge University Press, Cambridge.

Spriggs, Matthew (1984) *Marxist Perspectives in Archaeology*. Cambridge University Press, Cambridge.

Thorpe, I.J. (1981) Anthropological Orientations on Astronomy in Complex Societies. Paper read at the third Theoretical Archaeology Group Conference, Reading, U.K.

Tilley, Christopher (1982) Social Formation, Social Structures and Social Change. In *Symbolic and Structural Archaeology*, edited by Ian Hodder, pages 26–38. Cambridge University Press, Cambridge.

—— (1984) Ideology and the Legitimation of Power in the Middle Neolithic of Southern Sweden. In *Ideology, Power and Prehistory*, edited by Daniel Miller and Christopher Tilley, pages 111–146. Cambridge University Press, Cambridge.

Trigger, Bruce (1984a) Alternative Archaeologies: Nationalist, Colonialist, Imperialist. *Man* 19(3): 335–370.

—— (1984b) Archaeology at the Crossroads: What's New? *Annual Review of Anthropology* 13: 275–300.

Wallerstein, I. (1976) A World-System Perspective on the Social Sciences. *British Journal of Sociology* 27: 343–352.

Wobst, H. Martin, and Arthur S. Keene (1983) Archaeological Explanation as Political Economy. In *The Socio-politics of Archaeology*, edited by Joan M. Gero, David M. Lacy, Michael L. Blakey. *University of Massachusetts, Department of Anthropology, Research Report* 23: 79–88. Amherst.

Wylie, Alison (1981) Epistemological Issues Raised by a Structuralist Archaeology. In *Symbolic and Structural Archaeology*, edited by Ian Hodder, pages 39–46. Cambridge University Press, Cambridge.

—— (1985a) The Reaction against Analogy. In *Advances in Archaeological Method and Theory*, edited by Michael B. Schiffer, 8: 63–111. Academic Press, New York.

—— (1985b) Putting Shakertown Back Together: Critical Theory in Archaeology. *Journal of Anthropological Archaeology*. 4: 133–147.

Chapter 4

PROCESSUAL, POSTPROCESSUAL AND INTERPRETIVE ARCHAEOLOGIES

Michael Shanks and Ian Hodder

Post-processual archaeology, as the label implies, is something of a reaction and supercession of this processual framework (especially after Hodder, ed., 1982; see also Hodder 1985, 1986). Since the late 1970s issue has been taken with most of these tenets of processual archaeology: the character of science and aims of objective explanation; the character of society; and the place of values in archaeology, the sociopolitics of the discipline, its contemporary location as a mode of cultural production of knowledges.

Doubt, from theoretical and empirical argument, has been thrown on the possibility of an anthropological science, based upon observation of residues of patterned behaviours, detached from the present and aspiring to value-freedom (as positive knowledge). So the processual–post-processual debate has centred upon the forms of knowledge appropriate to a *social* science, how society may be conceived (reconciling both patterning or structure and individual action, intention and agency), and upon the workings of the discipline of archaeology, its ideologies and cultural politics, its place in the (post) modern present.

The debate has tended towards a polarisation of positions, and it is this which has led to an obscuring of the issues. Post-processual has come to be seen by some as anti-science, celebrating subjectivity, the historical particular in place of generalisation: the cultural politics of the present displacing positive knowledge of the past. Above all, the authority of a scientific and professional knowledge of the past is posited against particular and subjective constructions, a pluralism of pasts appropriate each to their own contemporary constituency: science is pitted against relativism (Yoffee and Sherratt (eds) 1993, Trigger 1989b, Watson 1990).

We refer to an obscuring of the issues because this polarisation is unnecessary indeed, damaging. We are proposing that a consideration of the character and scope of interpretation may help overcome the polarisations. And, to begin, a renaming may be appropriate. The label "post-processual" says nothing about what it stands for, other than a relative position in respect of processual archaeology. If we are to use interpretation as an epithet, *interpretive archaeologies* may be used as a more positive label, perhaps, for many of those approaches which have been called postprocessual. These are archaeologies (the plural is important, as will become clear) which work through interpretation. And we hope it will become clear that a careful consideration of interpretation entails abandoning the caricatures of science versus relativism, generalisation versus the historical particular, and the objective past versus the subjective present.

The main aspects of archaeologies termed interpretive might be summarised as follows.

- Foregrounded is the person and work of the interpreter. Interpretation is practice which requires that the interpreter does not so much hide behind rules and procedures predefined elsewhere, but takes responsibility for their actions, their interpretations.
- Archaeology is hereby conceived as a material practice in the present, making things (knowledges, narratives, books, reports, etc.) from the material traces of the past – constructions which are no less real, truthful or authentic for being constructed.
- Social practices, archaeology included, are to do with meanings, making sense of things. Working, doing, acting, making are interpretive.
- The interpretive practice that is archaeology is an ongoing process: there is no final and definitive account of the past as it was.
- Interpretations of the social are less concerned with causal explanation (accounts such as "this is the way it was" and "it happened because of this") than with *understanding or making sense* of things which never were certain or sure.
- Interpretation is consequently multivocal: different interpretations of the same field are quite possible.
- We can therefore expect a plurality of archaeological interpretations suited to different purposes, needs, desires.
- Interpretation is thereby a creative but none the less critical attention and response to the interests, needs and desires of different constituencies (those people, groups or communities who have or express such interests in the material past).

To interpret, the act of interpretation: what do the words mean and imply?

We particularly stress the active character of interpretation: one is an intrepreter by virtue of performing the act or practice of interpreting. An interpreter is a translator, an interlocutor, guide or go-between.

Meaning

To interpret something is to figure out what it means. A translator conveys the sense or meaning of something which is in a different language or medium. In this way interpretation is fundamentally about meaning. Note, however, that translation is not a simple and mechanical act but involves careful judgement as to appropriate shades of meaning, often taking account of context, idiom and gesture which can seriously affect the meaning of words taken on their own.

Dialogue

A translator may be an interlocutor or go-between. Interpretation contains the idea of mediation, of conveying meaning from one party to another. An interpreter aims to provide a reciprocity of understanding, overcoming the lack of understanding or semantic distance between two parties who speak different languages or belong to different cultures. Interpretation is concerned with dialogue, facilitating and making easier.

In a good dialogue or conversation one listens to what the other says and tries to work out what they mean, tries to understand, to make sense. Translation may be essential to this, performed either by a separate interpreter or by the parties of the dialogue themselves. Further questions might be asked and points put forward based on what has already been heard and understood. The idea is that dialogue moves forward to a consensus (of sorts) which is more than the sum of the initial positions. This *fusion of horizons* (a term taken from hermeneutics, the philosophy of interpretation, discussed below) is potentially a learning experience in which one takes account of the other, their objections and views, even if neither is won over.

It is not a good and open dialogue if one party simply imposes its previous ideas, categories and understandings upon the other. Preconceptions are simply confirmed. It is not good if the interpreter does not recognise the independence of the interpreted, their resistance to control and definition. A good conversation is one perhaps which never ends: there is always more to discover.

What might be a dialogue with the past? One where the outcome resides wholly in neither side but is a product of *both* the past and the present. Archaeological interpretation here resides in the gap between past and present. Such a dialogue is also ongoing. We will take up these points again below.

Uncertainty

Interpretation involves a perceived gap between the known and the unknown, desire and a result, which is to be bridged somehow. There is thus uncertainty, both at the outset of interpretation (what does this mean?) and at the end of the act of interpretation. It could always have been construed in a different way, with perhaps a different aspect stressed or disregarded. Although we might be quite convinced by an understanding we have managed to achieve, it is good to accept fallibility and not to become complacent. Is this not indeed the character of reason? Rationality is not an abstract absolute for which we can formulate rules and procedures, but is better conceived as the willingness to recognise our partiality, that our knowledge and reasoning are open to challenge and modification. Final and definitive interpretation is a closure which is to be avoided, suspected at the least.

Exploration and making connections

Interpretation implies an extension or building from what there is here to something beyond. We have already mentioned that interpretation should aspire to being open to change, exploring possibility. Exploration of meanings is often about making different connections.

Here can be mentioned the structuralist argument that meaning, if it is to be found at all, resides in the gaps between things, in their interrelationships. A lone signifier seems empty. But once connected through relations of similarity and difference with other signifiers it makes sense. In deciphering a code different permutations of connections between the particles of the code are explored until meaning is unlocked.

Judgement

A sculptor or woodcarver might examine their chosen material, interpret its form and substance, taking note of grain and knots of wood, flaws and patterning in stone, and then judge and choose how to work with or against the material. An archaeologist may examine a potsherd, pick out certain diagnostic traits and judge that these warrant an identification of the sherd as of a particular type: they choose an identification from various possibilities. Interpretation involves judgement and choice: drawing sense, meaning and possibility from what began as uncertainty.

Performance

In this way interpretation may refer to something like dramatic performance, where a particular interpretation of a dramatic text is offered according to the judgement of performers and director. The text is worked with and upon. Focus is drawn to certain connections within the characters and plot which are judged to be significant. Interpretation is here again reading for significance, where significance is literally making something a sign.

Dramatic interpretation has further dimensions. A text is read for significance and courses of action inferred. A past work (the text of a play) is acted out and in so doing it is given intelligible life. Now, there is no need here to take a literal line and think that archaeological interpretation involves those experimental reconstructions of past ways of life that are familiar from television programmes and heritage parks (though there is here a serious argument for experimental archae-ology). We would rather stress that interpretation is in performance an *active apprehension*. Something produced in the past is made a presence to us now. It is worked upon actively. If it were not, it would have no life. An unread and unper-formed play is dead and gone. Analogously an archaeological site which is not actively apprehended, worked on, incorporated into archaeological projects, simply lies under the ground and decays. The questions facing the actor-interpreters are these: How are the characters to be portrayed? What settings are to be used? What form of stage design? What lighting, sound and ambience? Simply, what is to be made of the play? (Pearson 1994).

Courses of action inferred, projects designed: these are conditions of interpre-tation.

Critique

Judgement here involves taking a position, choosing how to perform, what to do, which meanings to enact or incorporate. Involved is a commitment to one perfor-mance rather than another. Any interpretation is always thus immediately critical of other interpretations. Performance is both analytic commentary on its source, the written play, but also critical in its choice of some meanings and modes and not others.

The ubiquity of interpretation forgotten in black boxes

Interpretation is insidiously ubiquitous. There are always choices and judgements being made even in the most mundane and apparently empirical activities. Describing and measuring an artefact, for example, always involves acts of inter-pretation and judgement. Which parts of a stone axe-blade are to be measured, for example, and from where to where?

But some interpretation is often overlooked when people accept certain inter-pretive conventions. So, for example, plants are most often described according to scientific species lists. But these species lists are not "natural": they are the result of scientific interpretation concerning the definition and classification of plants and creatures. Such interpretation may have occurred a while ago now, and be more of interest to historians of science, but it should be recognised that the choice or judgement is made to accept that interpretation. Interpretations such as this concerning the classification of plants are often worth following simply because so much work would be required, starting almost from first principles, to redesign natural history. The idea of a species is tied in to so many other things: evolu-tionary theory and ecology, botany and zoology, etc.

When an interpretation or set of interpretations is accepted, treated as uncon-troversial and no longer even seen for what it is, the term *black-boxed* can be used. Interpretation is made, accepted and then put away, out of sight and often out of mind, in a black box. It allows us to live with the world more easily; we would otherwise be as infants, asking whether this thing in front of us really could be interpreted as a table with a box upon it which is most difficult to interpret, a computer.

Indeed, all archaeology is hereby interpretive, concerned intimately with the interpretation of things. However, some archaeologists refuse to accept this, or choose to overlook or black-box acts of interpretation. Excavation, for example, is so thoroughly interpretive. Many students on their first dig find the uncertainty very disturbing. Where does one layer end and another begin? How can you tell? How can it be ascertained that this scatter of traces of holes in the ground was once a wooden house? Yet this pervasive interpretive uncertainty is the construction of "hard" facts about the past.

Hermeneutics

The theoretical and philosophical field of interpretation, the clarification of meaning and achievement of sense and understanding, is covered by *hermeneutics*. Hermeneutics addresses the relationship between interpreter and interpreted when that which is to be interpreted is not just raw material to be defined and brought under technical control, but *means* something. The term traditionally applied to the reading of texts and the understanding of historical sources – Is the source authentic? What does it mean? What were the author's intentions? We do not propose a simple import of hermeneutic principles into archaeology, but will be noting their relevance.

Having unpacked the idea of interpretation, we will now develop some of the observations.

Uncertainty

Interpretation is rooted in a world which cannot be tied down to definitive categories and processes. Consider classification. Articles are grouped or a group divided according to their similarities. Each class or taxon contains those articles judged the same. There are two fields of remaindering or possible foci of uncertainty where judgement is required. First, it may not be absolutely clear where a particular article belongs, particularly if the criteria for inclusion in a class are not specific, if an article is approaching the edges, the margins of a taxon, or if it is somehow incomplete. Second, there is always a remainder after classification. Classification never completely summarises. There are always aspects or attributes of an article which are disregarded and which remain outside taxa, embarrassing classification.

Classification operates under a "rule of the same". Taxa are characterised by relative *homogeneity*. This is a legitimate strategy for coping with the immense empirical variety and particularity that archaeologists have to deal with. However, we should be clear that classification does not give the *general* picture; it gives the *average*. It is not a general picture because there is no provision in classification for assessing the norm, the taxa (where do they come from; they are supplemental or external to the classification), nor the variations within a class, nor the variability of variability. Classification is less interested in coping with particularity: why are the members of a class of pots all in fact slightly different?

Things are equivocal. A pot can be classified according to its shape and decoration as of a particular type. But thin-sectioned under a polarising microscope it explodes into another world of micro-particles and mineral inclusions. The pot is not just one thing which can be captured in a single all-encompassing definition. There is always more than can be said or done with the pot. A single pot is also multiple. It depends on the trials we make of it, what we do with it, how we experience it – whether we attend to surface and shape or slice it and magnify it.

Instead of smoothing over, we can also attend to that which does not fit, to the rough and irregular, to the texture of things. Everyday life is not neat and tidy. History is a mess. We can attend to the equivocal, to the absences in our understanding, focus on the gaps in neat orders of explanation. Conspicuously in archaeology there can be no final account of the past – because it is now an equivocal and ruined mess, but also because even when the past was its present it was to a considerable extent incomprehensible. So much has been lost and forgotten of what never was particularly clear. Social living is immersion in equivocality, everyday uncertainty. What really is happening now? There are no possible final answers.

Uncertainty and equivocality refer to the difference of things: they can be understood according to a rule of the same, but difference escapes this rule, escapes homogeneity. Because an attention to texture which escapes classification is outside of qualities of sameness (the homogeneity of what is contained within the class), the term *heterogeneity* may be used. To attend to difference is to attend to heterogeneity – the way things escape formalisation, always holding something back.

Nietzsche's and Foucault's projects of *genealogy* involves revealing the difference and discontinuity, the heterogeneity in what was taken to be homogeneous and continuous. Nietzsche reveals the "uncertain" origins of morality (1967). Sexuality is shown to be far from a biological constant by Foucault (1979, 1984a, 1984b).

The social world is thoroughly *polysemous*. This is another concept which can be related to uncertainty. That a social act or product is polysemous means that it can always be interpreted in various ways. Meanings are usually negotiated: that is, related to the interpersonal practices, aspirations, strategies of people. We repeat the classic example of the safety pin, the meaning of which was radically renegotiated by punk subculture in the 1970s (Hebdige 1979).

The forms of social life are constituted as meaningful by the human subjects who live those forms. People try to make sense of their lives. This ranges from interpreting the possible meanings of a politician's speeches and actions to trying to make sense of the fact that you have been made redundant and may never work again even though you are highly skilled.

Giddens (1982, 1984, p. 374) has related this characteristic of the social world (that it is to do with interpretation and meaning) to the hermeneutic task of the sociologist. He describes the difficult *double hermeneutic* of sociology. First, it aims to understand a world of meanings and interpretations (society). Second, sociologists themselves form a social community with its own practices, procedures, assumptions, skills, institutions, all of which in turn need to be understood.

Shanks and Tilley (1987a, ch. 5 especially pp. 107–8) have described a fourfold hermeneutic in archaeology, four levels of interpretation and the need to develop understanding: understanding the relation between past and present; understanding other societies and cultures; understanding contemporary society, the site of archaeological interpretations; and understanding the communities of archaeologists who are performing interpretations. Thus, not only do archaeologists translate between "their" and "our" world, but they also have to deal with worlds separated in space and time. But it is difficult to argue that sociologists deal with a double hermeneutic, anthropologists with a threefold hermeneutic and archaeologists with a fourfold. Certainly the societies with which prehistoric archaeologists deal are often remote, and there are many social and cultural layers that have to be bridged. But a palaeolithic archaeologist is not dealing with more hermeneutic layers than a historical archaeologist, and it is inadequate to assume that some cultures in space and time are more "like us" than others. It is better to assert with Giddens that all the social sciences can be contrasted with the natural sciences in that they face a double rather than a single hermeneutic. Certainly at the methodological level the problem is always one of fusing two horizons, the scientific and the past society. Other information from Western and other ethnographic contexts may be brought into the argument, but always through the scientific community. The archaeologist faces the distant past in the same way that any social scientist faces "the other", even if the scanty nature of the evidence and the great spans of time involved greatly increase the uncertainty of interpretation.

When the uncertainty of an interpretation declines it is black-boxed and need no longer be subject to suspicion and negotiation. The controversy over an interpretation is settled and closed. What allows one interpretation to prevail over another? Archaeological cultures, for example, are no longer interpreted by many as racial groups; it is not something now usually entertained as a possible interpretation. What allows or brought about the closure? A common answer might be reason and the facts. Close examination of empirical examples shows that ethnicity is not reflected in what archaeologists call cultures. But the history and philosophy of science indicate that such an explanation for the closure of scientific controversy is not enough. The central principle is that of *underdetermination*. This is the Duhem-Quine principle which holds that no single factor is enough to explain the closure of a controversy or the certainty acquired by scientists. It is the philosophical basis of most contemporary history and sociology of science. Theory is never fully determined by the facts or by logic. There is always something which sets off doubts about the certainty, always something missing to close the black box for ever. David

Clarke (1968) was very willing to relate material culture patterning to ethnicity after his ethnographic investigations. Cultural and, by extension, racial identity are clearly established with reference to material culture, though perhaps not in the precise terms of the archaeological culture concept (Conkey and Hastorf, eds, 1990).

Creativity and the technology that is archeology

The equivocality, heterogeneity or multiplicity of the material world means that choices must be made in perception and to what we attend. The archaeological record is an infinity in terms of the things that may be done with it and in terms of how it may be perceived. Which measurements are to be made? Are some aspects of an artefact to be disregarded in coming to an understanding? How is justice to be done to the empirical richness of the past? How is an archaeological monument such as a castle to be represented? Measured plans may be prepared and descriptions made of masonry and sequence of construction from observations of structural additions and alterations. Here attention is focused upon certain aspects of the architecture deemed worthy by conventional archaeology. But what of other experiences and perceptions of such a monument? This is hardly an exhaustive treatment of architecture. A technical line drawing may direct attention essentially and almost wholly to the edges of masonry – a subjective choice. Turner, in his sequence of picturesque renderings of castles in the early nineteenth century, focuses upon situation in landscape and attempts to convey the passage of light across monumental features. Both approaches are selective; but both also, we suggest, attend accurately to the empirical, albeit in different ways.

Archaeological interpretation requires that some things be connected with others in order to make sense of what remains of the past. Circular features in earth of contrasting colour are associated with removed wooden stakes, and then in turn associated with other post-holes to trace the structural members of a building. To interpret is in this way a creative act: putting things together and so creating sense, meaning or knowledge.

We are concerned to emphasise that the person of the archaeologist is essential in coming to understand the past. The past is not simply under the ground waiting to be discovered. It will not simply appear, of course, but requires work. Consider discovery. Discovery is invention. The archaeologist uncovers or discovers something, coming upon it. An inventor may be conceived to have come upon a discovery. Discovery and invention are united in their etymology: *invenire* in Latin means to come upon, to find or invent. Invention is both finding and creative power. The logic of invention, poetry and the imaginary is one of conjunction, making connections. It is both/and, between self and other; not either/or. The pot found by the archaeologist is both this and that (surface decoration and mineral inclusions). A castle is both technical drawing and romantic painting. It is there in the landscape and here in a painting. It is both of the past and of the present. Archaeology's poetry is to negotiate these equivocations and make connections. It is the work of imagination.

This is to deny the radical distinction of subjectivity and objectivity in that the subjective is simply the form that the objective takes.

Foregrounding the creativity of the interpreting archaeologist is to hold that archaeology is a mode of production of the past (Shanks and McGuire 1991, Shanks 1992). This would seem to be recognised by those many archaelogists and text-books which talk at length of archaeological techniques – archaeology seen as technology. The past has left remains, and they decay in the ground. According to their interest an archaeologist works on the material remains to make something of them. So excavation is invention/discovery or sculpture where archaeologists craft remains of the past into forms which are meaningful. The archaeological "record" is, concomitantly, not a record at all, not given, "data", but made. "The past" is gone and lost, and *a fortiori*, through the equivocality of things and the character of society as constituted through meaning, never existed as a definitive entity "the present" anyway. An archaeologist has a raw material, the remains of the past, and turns it into something – data, a report, set of drawings, a museum exhibition, an archive, a television programme, evidence in an academic contro-versy, and perhaps that which is termed "knowledge of the past". This is a mode of production.

To hold that archaeology is a mode of production of the past does not mean that anything can be made. A potter cannot make anything out of clay. Clay has properties, weight, plasticity, viscosity, tensile strength after firing, etc., which will not allow certain constructions. The technical skill of the potter involves working with these properties while designing and making. So there is no idealism here which would have archaeology as inventing whatever pasts they might wish.

To realise archaeology as cultural production does introduce a series of impor-tant illuminations. Technical interest in the empirical properties of raw material, the viability of a project, is but one aspect of production. Other essential consid-erations include purpose, interest, expression and taste.

Purpose and interest: products always attend needs and interests, serving purpose. Here is an argument for engaging with and answering a community's interests in the archaeological past, because a discipline which simply responds to its own perceived needs and interests, as in an academic archaeology existing for its own sake ("disinterested knowledge"), can be criticised as a decadent indul-gence. Different archaeologies, different interpretations of the material past, can be produced. We suggest that a valuable and edifying archaeology attends to the needs and interests of a community, interpreting these in a way which answers purpose while giving something more, enhancing knowledges and experiences of the past and of the material world. A strong political argument is that archaeology should attend to the interests of the diversity of communities and groups that it studies, works and lives among, and draws funding from (Potter 1990).

Expression and taste

The expressive, aesthetic and emotive qualities of archaeological projects have been largely down-played or even denigrated over the last three decades as archaeologists have sought an objective scientific practice. In popular imagination the archaeological is far more than a neutral acquisition of knowledge; the material presence of the past is an emotive field of cultural interest and political dispute. The practice of archaeology also is an emotive, aesthetic and expressive experience. This affective component of archaeological labour is social as well as personal, relating to the social experiences of archaeological practice, of belonging to the archaeological community and a discipline or academic discourse. Of course such experiences are immediately political (Shanks 1992, *Archaeological Review from Cambridge*, 9:2).

The essentially creative character of production is also one of expression: taking purpose, assessing viability, working with material, and expressing interpretation to create the product that retains traces of all these stages. This expressive dimension is also about pleasure (or displeasure) and is certainly not restricted to the intellectual or the cognitive. Pleasure is perhaps not a very common word in academic archaeology, but an interpretive archaeology should recognise the role of pleasure and embody it in the product made. This means addressing seriously and with imagination the questions of how we write the past, our activities as archaeologists and how we communicate with others.

In archaeological interpretation the past is designed, yet is no less real or objective. (We can expect some to dispute the reality of a past produced by such an interpretive archaeology which realises the subjective and creative component of the present: such a product cannot be the "real" past, it might be said, because it has been tainted by the present and by the person of the archaeologist. This is precisely like disputing the "reality" of a television set. Here is a technological product which looks like a television set. To ask whether it is real is a silly question. A far better question, and one that applies to the product of archaeological interpretation, is: does it do what is required of it – does it work?) The question of archaeological design is: what kind of archaeology do we want?

A product of technology is both critique and affirmation; it embodies its creation, speaks of style, gives pleasure (or displeasure) in its use, solves a problem perhaps, performs a function, provides experiences, signifies and resonates. It may also be pretentious, ugly or kitsch, useless, or untrue to its materials and creation. In the same way each archaeology has a style; the set of decisions made in producing an archaeological product involves conformity with some interests, percepts or norms, and not with others. As with an artefact, the judgement of an archaeological style involves multiple considerations, many summarised by the term "taste". We need to consider its eloquence: that is, how effective and productive it is. We should also make an ethical appraisal of its aims and purposes and possible functions. Technical matters are implicated, of course, including how true it has been to the material past, the reality and techniques of observation that it uses to construct facts. Judgement refers to all these aspects of archaeological production: purpose, viability and expression.

Projects and networks

The "objective past" will not present itself. The remains of a prehistoric hut circle will not excavate themselves. A pot will not thin-section itself and appear upon a microscope slide beneath the gaze of a cataplectic archaeologist. Work has to be done in the sense that the remains of the past have to be incorporated into *projects*. An archaeological project has a temporality of presencing (Heidegger 1972, p. 14): the past is taken up in the work of the present which is projecting forward into the future, planning investigation, publications, knowledge, whatever. There is here no hard and fast line between the past as it was and the present. This temporality also refers us back to the character of dialogue. On the basis of what one already knows, and on the basis of prejudgement, questions are put, answers received which draw the interpreter into further prejudged questions. This is an ongoing *hermeneutic circle* (Gadamer 1975) better termed, perhaps, a spiral as it draws forward the partners in dialogue.

Archaeological projects are about connecting past, present and future, but what empirical or concrete form do they take? An archaeological project involves the mobilisation of many different things or resources. Landowners are approached, funding needs to be found, labour hired, tools and materials convened, skills operated to dig, draw and photograph, computers programmed and fed with data, finds washed and bagged, workforce kept happy, wandering cows chased off site. This is a great and rich assemblage of people, things and energies which achieve what are conventionally termed data. An archaeological project is a *heterogeneous network*. A network because different elements are mobilised and connected, but unlike a bounded system there are no necessary or given limits to the network; it is quite possible to follow chains of connection far beyond what are conceived as the conventional limits of archaeology (in pragmatic terms think of the ramifications of funding; in institutional terms the relations with the education system; in affective terms all the associations of "working in the field" (Shanks 1992)). These networks are heterogeneous because connected are entities, actors and resources of different kinds: interests, moneys, academics, career trajectories, volunteers, landowners, wheelbarrows, JCB mechanical diggers, cornfields, decayed subsurface "features", laboratories.

All these are brought together in an archaeological project which constitutes the reality of the past, makes it what it is. It is within such contingent (there is nothing necessary about them) assemblages that the past comes to be perceived and known. If we were to report objectively the detail of an excavation, all the resonances and associations, all the thoughts, materials and events, the result would be very confusing and of perhaps infinite length. This is again the paradox that specificity of detail brings into doubt the validity of sensory evidence, and points to the necessity of creative choice.

That data are constructed or crafted in (social) practices is the central contention of "constructivist" philosophy of science. Anthropological attention has been focused on communities of scientists and how they work with the physical world. In archaeology Joan Gero has recently considered the role of recording forms (basic now to excavation practice) in constructing archaeological facts.

Context and dialogue

A pot without provenance is of limited value to archaeological interpretation. It has long been recognised that placing things in context is fundamental to understanding the past. Much of conventional archaeological technique is about establishing empirically rich contexts of things.

A "contextual archaeology" makes much of the associations of things from the past (Hodder (ed.) 1987, Hodder 1986). Meanings of things can only be approached if contexts of use are considered, if similarities and differences between things are taken into account. It is often argued that, since the meanings of things are arbitrary, archaeologists cannot reconstruct past symbolism. There are two ways in which archaeologists avoid this impasse. First, artefacts are not like words in that they have to work in a material way and are subject to universal material processes. Thus, an axe used to cut down a tree must be made of rock of a certain hardness and the cutting action will leave wear-traces. An axe made of soft chalk and without wear-traces can thus be identified, on universal criteria, to be of no use for tree-cutting – an aspect of its meaning has been inferred. Archaeologists routinely think through why prehistoric actors built this wall, dug this trench, using common-sense arguments based on universal criteria. In all such work universal characteristics of materials are linked to specific contexts to see if they are relevant. Interpretation and uncertainty are involved in deciding which aspects of the materials are useful in determining meaning. Hence, and second, the archaeologist turns not to universal characteristics of materials but to internal similarities and differences. Thus, perhaps the chalk axes are found in burials with female skeletons, while the hard stone axes are found in male burials. Such internal patterning not only supports the idea that stone hardness is relevant to meaning in this case, but it also adds another level of meaning – gender. The task of the archaeologist is to go round and round the data in a hermeneutic spiral, looking for relationships, fitting pieces of the jigsaw together. Does the patterning of faunal remains correlate with the two axe types or with male and female burials? Is there any difference in axe-type deposition in different parts of the settlement system? And so on. The more of the evidence that can be brought together in this way, the more likely is one able to make statements about meaning – for example, that chalk axes were of high value and were associated with women in ritual contexts.

It is important to recognise that a contextual emphasis does not mean that archaeologists can interpret without generalisation. It is impossible to approach the data without prejudice and without some general theory. But the interpretive challenge is to evaluate such generality in relation to the contextual data. So much of what archaeologists assume in a general way is "black-boxed". But even terms like "pit", or "ditch" or "wall" or "post-hole" should be open to scrutiny to see if they are relevant in each specific context. Archaeologists always have to evaluate relevance – are there aspects of this context which make this general theory relevant? However well defined the theory, some contextual judgement has to be made.

The same or similar things have different meanings in different contexts. It is context which allows a sensitivity to diversity and to local challenges to social meanings. But, if context is so important, is not each context, each pit different with different meanings? Certainly, at a precise level this is probably true. But most contexts are grouped together in larger contexts – a group or type of pit, a site, a region and so on. The problem then becomes one of defining the context relevant for each question. Context itself is a matter of interpretation, based on defining similarities and differences. Thus a group of pits might be described as a context because of their spatial clustering, or because they are a distinctive type, or because they have similar contents. By searching for similarities and differences some contextual variation can be identified as more relevant than others, but context and content are always intertwined in a complex hermeneutic spiral. The meaning of an artefact can change the context, but the context can change the meaning.

Thus, archaeologists, working in their own contexts, are likely to pick out certain types of context in the past and look for patterning in relation to them. There can be no context-free definitions of context. A pit, ditch or post-hole is not a "natural" context. As already stated, archaeologists have to evaluate such general assumptions in relation to specific similarities and differences in the data.

Interpretation, in its concern with context, can also be described as being to do with *relationality* – exploring connections in the way we have been describing. However, an important point to re-emphasise is that context cannot only refer to the things of the past. They are inevitably bound up in archaeological projects. We will clarify with some points from hermeneutics.

Involved here is the context (historical, social, ethical, disciplinary, whatever) of interpretation itself. In coming to understand we always begin with presuppositions. There can be no pure reception of a raw object of interpretation. We begin an interrogation of an historical source with an awareness of its historical context – we view it with hindsight; the flows and commixtures of earths, silts and rubbles in the archaeological site are understood as layers. As interpreters we have to start from somewhere; what we wish to interpret is always already understood *as* something. This is prejudgement or prejudice. And it is essential to understanding. Prejudgement and prejudice are legitimate in that they furnish the conditions for any real understanding.

Another aspect of this is that the acts of looking, sensing and posing questions of things always involve intentional acts of giving meanings. These meanings (rubble as layers, for example) derive from the situation of the interpreter. So the archaeological past is always *for* something. At the least an archaeological site under excavation is part of an archaeological project, and, as we have just argued, *would not exist* for us if it were not. It is understood in terms of its possible applications and relevances in the present. So the "prejudice" of the interpreting archaeologist's position (ranging from social and cultural location to disciplinary organisation to personal disposition) is not a barrier to understanding, contaminating factors to be screened out; prejudice is the very medium of understanding – indeed, *objective* understanding.

Prejudgement and prejudiced assumptions regarding what it is we seek to understand bring us again to the hermeneutic circle introduced above. Realising that interpretation is about establishing connections and contexts involves realising interpretation as dialogic in character.

This is partly recognised by the idea of *problem orientation*, strongly supported by processual methodology. This maintains that research projects, archaeological observation and study should be designed around meaningful questions to be posed of the past. The correct methodological context is one of question and answer. Questions are considered meaningful if they fit into an acceptable (research) context. So, rather than digging a site simply to find out what was there, archaeological projects should be organised around questions which fit into a disciplinary context of progressive question-and-answer. Theory: complex society can be observed in settlement hierarchy. Hypothesis: region R has a settlement hierarchy at time T. Question: does site S display features correspondent with a level of the supposed hierarchy. Investigate. Do the data require modification of the hypothesis? This is indeed a dialogue of sorts with the archaeological past: the archaeologist questions the past in relation to their accompanying "assumptions" of theory and hypothesis; the response of the past may demand the archaeologist thinks and questions again.

But we hope that the notion of interpretation as dialogue suggests a more sensitive treatment and awareness of the relationship between interpreter and interpreted. There is much more to interpretive context. First, the interpreted past is more than something which exists to supply responses to questions deemed meaningful by male and middle-class academics of twentieth-century Western nation states (as most processual archaeologists are). The past has an independence of research design, procedures of question-and-answer (this independence is accommodated in the notion of heterogeneity). It overflows the questions put to it by archaeologists. It may be recognised that strict problem orientation may miss a great deal, and that simply being open to what may happen to turn up in an excavation is a quite legitimate research strategy. There is nothing wrong with sensitive exploration, being open to finding out.

Second, the past is constituted by meanings. By this is meant that the past is not just a set of data. Some archaeologists have responded to the Native American request for respect for the spiritual meanings of their material pasts with a cry "They are taking away our database."

This relates closely to our third and most important point: a dialogue with the material past is situated in far more than *methodological* context. The means of archaeological understanding include everything that the interpreting archaeologist brings to the encounter with the past. The context includes method, yes; but also the interests which brought the archaeologist to the past, the organisation of the discipline, cultural dispositions and meanings which make it reasonable to carry out the investigations, institutional structures and ideologies. We repeat that the archaeological past simply could not exist without all this, the heterogeneous networking of archaeological projects.

Meaning and making sense

Interpretation may suggest meanings for things from the past. A sociological argument is that social practice is to do with interpreting the meanings of things and actions; society is constituted through meanings ascribed and negotiated by social agents (Giddens 1984). So an understanding of the past presupposes that interpretation is given of past meanings of things.

Meaning is a term which requires examination. For example, archaeologists have tried to distinguish functional from symbolic meanings, primary from secondary, denotative from connotative (Shanks and Tilley 1987a, ch. 7, Conkey 1990). In practice, however, it is difficult to separate functional, technological meanings from the symbolic realm, and conversely symbols clearly have pragmatic social functions. In the material world function contributes to abstract symbolic meaning. Much symbolism is entirely ingrained in the practices of daily life, in the rhythms of the body and the seasons, and in the punctuated experience of time. The notion of abstract symbolic code, arbitrarily divorced from practice, has little role to play in current understanding of meaning and its interpretation. There has been a gradual shift in archaeology from a consideration of material culture as language, to a concern with material culture as text and then to an emphasis on practice.

It thus often becomes difficult to ask "What does this pot mean?", since it may not "mean" in a language-type way. There may be no signifieds tied to the signifier in a code. Rather it may be the case that, even if people cannot answer what the pot means, they can use the pot very effectively in social life. This practical knowledge of "how to go on" may be entirely ingrained in practices so that the meanings cannot be discussed verbally with any readiness – the meanings are *non-discursive*. This does not, of course, preclude verbal meanings being construed by an outside interpreter. And at other times – for example, in conflicts over uses and meanings – non-discursive meanings may be brought into "discursive consciousness", although in doing so actors often embellish and transform.

The meanings that archaeologists reconstruct must on the whole be assumed to be general social and public meanings. Archaeologists have sufficient data to identify repeated patterning within large contexts (sites over many decades, regions over centuries or even millennia). The meanings reconstructed must be public and social in nature. Individual variation may be expressed in variability in the archaeological record, but it is rare that the data allow repeated patterning in an individual's action to be identified. Nevertheless it is important at the theoretical level to include the dialectic between individual and social meanings since it is in such terms that the negotiation of change is conducted (Barrett 1988, Johnson 1989).

There is also the question: Whose meanings? We have argued for a fusion of horizons as being characteristic of effective interpretation. A fourfold hermeneutic places great distance and interpretive problems between past and present.

Archaeological interpretation deals with the meanings of the past for the present, so it is perhaps better to think of *making sense*. Emphasis is again placed on the practice of interpretation. As a go-between, guide or interlocutor, the archaeologist makes sense of the past, providing orientations, significances, knowledges and, yes, meanings, relevant to understanding the past. The question of whose meanings is superseded.

Pluralism and authority

A guide interpreting a map and the land can follow equally feasible paths which may offer different returns or benefits, different vistas. There are different ways of achieving the same ends. Interpretations may vary according to context, purpose, interest or project. Interpretation, we have argued, implies a sensitivity to context. With the equivocality and heterogeneity of things and the underdetermination of interpretation, there are many arguments for pluralism.

But pluralism introduces the problem of authority. On what grounds are different interpretations of the same field to be judged? The problem arises because finality and objectivity (residing in and with the past itself) have been abandoned for an attention to the *practice* of interpretation (making sense of the past as it presents itself to us now). Charges of relativism have been made (Trigger, 1980). Relativism is usually held not to be a good thing. If interpretations of the past depend on present interests and not on objectivity, then there is no way of distinguishing a professional archaeological explanation from the crazed views of cranks who may interpret archaeological remains as traces of alien visitors (Renfrew 1989).

The real issue in the debate over pluralism and relativism is that of *absolutes*. Truth and objectivity are not abstract principles inherent in the past, but have to be worked for. That Anglo-Saxon cemetery in the countryside will not excavate itself. It needs the archaeologist's interest, efforts, managements skills, excavation teams, finds-laboratories and publisher to be made into what we come to call the objective past.

There are very important issues here to do with the value of interpretation in relation to what science is commonly taken to be. Relativism has not been adequately dealt with, so we present some possible lines which can be taken regarding judgement, authority, objectivity and science.

Objectivity

It is argued that objectivity is not an absolute or abstract quality towards which we strive. Objectivity is constructed. This is not to deny objectivity, but rather, ironically, to make it more concrete. So let it be agreed that an objective statement is one which is, at the least, strong; and that, indeed, we would wish our interpretations to be full of such strong statements. What makes a statement strong? The conventional answers are that strength comes from logical coherence, or because the statement corresponds with something out there, external to the statement, or because of some inherent quality called objectivity. But who decides on how coherent a statement must be? How exact must correspondence be? And in historical and sociological studies of scientific controversies there appear many other sources of strength such as government or religious support, good rhetoric in convincing others, even financial backing.

We have been arguing that the archaeological past will not excavate itself but needs to be worked for. If objectivity is an abstract quality or principle held by reality, how does it argue for itself, how does it display its strength? No, people are needed, their projects. Gravity does not appear to all and everyone on its own. Microbes needed the likes of Pasteur (Latour 1988). So a statement about the archaeological past is not strong because it is true or objective. But because it holds together when interrogated it is described as objective. What, then, does a statement hold on to, whence does it derive strength, if not from objectivity? There is no necessary answer. It can be many things. An objective statement is one that is connected to anything more solid than itself, so that, if it is challenged, all that it is connected to threatens also to fall.

An archaeological report usually aims to present data as objectively as possible – a strong basis for subsequent inference. Its strength comes from all those diagrams and photographs, the many words of detailed description, the references to comparative sites and materials which give further context to the findings. These all attest to the actual happening of the excavation and to the trustworthiness of the excavation team. Where otherwise is the quality of objectivity? Because the report is coherent and reads well (no contradictions betraying lies and artifice), and the photographs witness things actually being found, because its style and rhetoric are found acceptable, because it delivers what is required (from format to types of information), it is described as sound. Objectivity is what is held together. If a report holds together, it is considered objective.

Challenge a fact in the report and you have to argue with all of this, with the happening of the excavation, that great heterogeneous assemblage of people, things and energies. Ultimately the only way to shake its strength is to excavate another similar site, mobilising another army of resources and people. The skill of crafting objectivity is heterogeneous networking – tying as many things together as possible.

Relativism

If the abstract and independent principle of objectivity is denied, relativism is held to result. Here an important distinction is between *epistemic* and *judgemental* relativism (Bhaskar 1979). Epistemic relativism, which we follow, holds that knowledge is rooted in a particular time and culture. Knowledge does not just mimic things. Facts and objectivity are constructed. Judgemental relativism makes the *additional* claim that all forms of knowledge are equally valid. But judgemental relativism does not follow from epistemic relativism. To hold that objectivity is constructed does not entail that all forms of supposed knowledge will be equally successful in solving particular problems. Epistemic relativism simply directs attention to the reasons why a statement is held to be objective or strong; it directs attention to the heterogeneous assemblages of people and things and interests and feelings, etc., mobilised in particular projects. To argue a relativism which maintains objectivity is socially constructed is to argue simply for *relationality*.

But on what grounds is judgement to be made? If objectivity is constructed, are different interpretations of the past to be judged according to their place in the present? Constructed objectivity would seem to imply that there is no real past. Common sense says that it is silly to think that the distance between survey transects is something to do with society or politics (Bintliff 1992). Is an archaeological interpretation to be explained not by the past but by the politics of the Council for British Archaeology or the Smithsonian?

The reality of the past

But what is the *real* past? Reality is what resists, and trials test its resistance. Kick a megalith and it hurts – it is very real. But you cannot conclude that if you used a bulldozer it would have the same result. This is not to deny reality at all, but it has to be specified which trial has been used to define a resistance and hence a *specific* reality. Look at a ceramic thin section down a microscope and there is a reality different from that of its surface decoration. Reality is plural; the artefact is a multiplicity. It depends on what "work" is done upon and with it.

So what are the conditions of trials of resistance which define reality? Interpretive encounters: they are those heterogeneous networks or projects described above – mobilised mixtures of people and things.

But there is still the problem of the authority of academic science. What is to be done about those cranks who purvey what are clearly mystical untruths about the archaeological past? It has been argued that objectivity is to be sought when the term refers to a strong statement which is held together. Relativism of the sort described here does, indeed, cherish a sense of reality when the real past is conceived as that which resists *specific* trials of resistance.

Introducing an abstract and absolute objectivity into this comparison of academic and fringe archaeology confuses things because thereby trials of resistance are made incommensurable.

Consider the opinion that scientific archaeology is objective and people who believe in ley-lines are cranks. Archaeologists have objectivity on their side; they are clever and professional. What do ley-liners have? Stupidity? Science and pseudo-science are here incommensurable; they cannot be compared. This takes us nowhere and, most important, it makes impossible an understanding of scientific controversy. Does the truth always win? What force does it have? How is it that ideas which are now totally discredited, such as the presence of phlogiston in combustible materials, were once held to be objective truths? Were people stupid then, or at least not as critical as later?

Maintaining an absolute objectivity makes it impossible to understand the reasons for there being different versions of the past. So it seems reasonable to abandon abstract objectivity and make trials of resistance commensurable. This means treating, at the outset, objectivity and "falsity", science and "pseudo-science" as equal (many scientific ideas began as cranky ideas). Trials of resistance are perfectly in order. Talk to people, understand them, persuade if necessary; instead of patronising them by playing the expert. Maintain an open and reasoned dialogue. Test what holds the respective objectivities together.

But can fringe archaeologies ever be treated in such a way? Surely there is no controversy? The general point is that it is not possible to argue with the independent reality of the past. It happened. It is not possible to argue with the laws of nature. The environment, for example, sets immovable constraints on what people can do. How can a relativist argue with this?

What were constraints in the past are often not constraints now – nature has a historical relationship with people. Indeed, it is not possible to negotiate with gravity while falling out of a tenth-storey window. But neither is it easy to negotiate with an IRA bomber. These circumstances do not often occur, however. "Hard" reality does not often suddenly impose itself. It is usually more gradual, during which time "society" may negotiate and change its practices: consider environmental change. Gravity is not so much a constraint upon an engineer as a resource used, for example, in the building of a bridge. Clay is a very real resource used by potters, but of course many things cannot be made with it. Why be obsessed with the things that cannot be done? Why not try to understand the creativity?

There still remains the issue that the past happened when it did. If it is argued that archaeology is a mode of cultural production of the past, does this mean that things did not exist before they were so constructed? Was the Bronze Age hut circle not there before being excavated? And, conversely, were prehistoric stone tools once thunderbolts?

Here it is important not to confuse existence and essence. Existence is when you specify times and settings; it is local and historical. Essence makes no reference to time and space. If something exists at time 1 (the excavated cemetery), can we conclude that it always existed, even at time 2 (i.e., in essence)? Conversely, can we conclude from the fact that something existed between time 1 and time 2 (a stone thunderbolt) that it never existed (i.e., never had an essential quality)? The same questions can be set with regard to space.

The dualism between existence and essence corresponds with the following:

existence	essence
history	nature
society	objectivity

Why should the object world be credited with essence while people only have subjectivity and historical existence? Deny the dualisms. Society then becomes more than just people, receiving objective materiality, and is no longer opposed to the natural world of objects, and nature becomes truly natural history with things having a history which is often tied to that of people. The specific realities of the past are now historically connected with those of archaeologists in particular projects – heterogeneous and historical mixtures of real people and things. If timeless essences and abstract qualities such as objectivity are put to one side as products of theology, we do not lose the solidity of archaeological facts. They are still real and important; but so, too, are archaeologists, volunteers, publishers, television companies, photographers, feelings, interests, tools, instruments and laboratories which gather and bring to historical reality those facts. There is no necessary monopoly of one particular archaeological mobilisation of people and things which is tied to objectivity. We are hereby more attuned to different archaeological projects. Reburial issues, treasure hunting, landscape art and fringe archaeology become commensurable with professional archaeology: they are but different assemblages of resources (things, practices, people, aspirations, projects, etc.).

It may be objected that this leads to the apparent nonsense that Thomsen "happened" to stone and metal tools. But this is indeed the case, because the object world is now credited with a history. Grahame Clark did happen to the settlement at Star Carr.

How could Star Carr be defined and pictured before Clark? Perhaps we should apply Clark's excavation retrospectively and suppose that the site was there all along. It is quite legitimate to believe this, but how could it be proved? There is no time machine to take archaeologists back to 1182 or 431 to check that Star Carr was there then, albeit perhaps less decayed. Rather than jumping to conclusions about total existence or non-existence – essences – why not stick with reality defined as that which resists particular trials made of it? The confusion of existence and essence is a damaging one.

A site such as Star Carr does not have an abstract essence or timeless objectivity. We argue that its objective existence has a history. Clark is part of the reality of Star Carr, just as the excavations at Star Carr are part of the biography of Grahame Clark. The reality of Star Carr includes the excavation team, the tools, the whole project.

Are we otherwise to project Clark's and our present back into the past? It is good to remember that Nazi archaeologists find their political realities in the past, projecting back from their present, tinkering with *real* history.

If objectivity is accepted as constructed, a criticism may be voiced that thereby is subjectivity unleashed. This may be countered with the argument that if objectivity is denied as an essence, so, too, must be subjectivity. The opposition between objectivity sticking to the facts and subjectivity giving way to mystical and personal feelings is a false one. Why deny that it is people who do archaeology, and that people are indeed constituted as subjectivities in historical dealings with others and with things? If objectivity is denied as an essence, subjectivity becomes the form that the object world takes – through the looking, digging, thinking, feeling, the projects, those heterogeneous mobilisations of people.

If it is accepted that archaeology is a technology, a mode of cultural construction of the past, reality, objectivity and the past are not lost. Troublesome essences and dichotomies are, however, discarded. The solidity, beauty, originality of archaeological facts are still there and may be described with terms of "fact", "reality" and "objectivity". But present also are archaeologists, volunteers, publishers, film makers, television companies, photographers, feelings and desires, instruments and laboratories which make these facts live and hold together.

Critique

Another aspect of judging the relative value and worth of different interpretations of the same field is critique.

Awareness of the dialogues at the heart of interpretation requires self-reflexivity regarding the situated and contextualised interpreters and interpretands. Vital here is the project of ideology critique, now well established in archaeology. Ideology may hinder or make impossible the project of making good sense of the past.

Another dimension of critique is rooted in the heterogeneity, otherness and consequent independence of the material past. The past may become grounds for a critique of the present in that its forms and meanings may defamiliarise and throw into contingency what is taken in the present to be natural or unchanging.

The terms "equivocality" and "heterogeneity" were introduced above to describe how something always escapes its classification, there always being more to say and consider. The old pot found by an archaeologist is equivocal also because it belongs both to the past and to the present. This is its history; it has survived. And the equivocality confers upon the pot an autonomy because it is not limited to the moment of its making or use, or to the intentions of the potter. It goes beyond. The archaeologist can look back with hindsight and see the pot in its context, so time reveals meanings which are accessible *without* a knowledge of the time and conditions of its making. The pot transcends. In this it has qualities which may be called timeless.

Here also historicism (understanding in historical context) must be denied, otherwise we would only be able to understand a Greek pot by reliving the reality of the potter, a reality which anyway was indeterminate and equivocal. We would be fooling ourselves in thinking that we were appreciating and understanding the art and works of other cultures.

Pots are often used as a means to an end by archaeologists. They are used for dating a context; they may be conceived as telling of the past in different ways. Historicist interpretation reduces the significance of a cultural work to voluntary or involuntary *expression*: the pot expresses the society, or the potter, or the date. This is quite legitimate. But there is also the pot itself, its equivocal materiality, its mystery and uncertainty, which open it to interpretation.

The pot does indeed preserve aspects of its time and it can be interpreted to reveal things about the past. So the integrity and independence of the pot does not mean that it does not refer outside of itself. It means that no interpretation or explanation of a pot can ever be attached to the pot for ever, claiming to be integral or a necessary condition of experiencing that pot. The autonomy of the pot is the basis of opposition to totalising systematics: systems of explanation or understanding which would claim closure, completeness, a validity for all time. We must always turn back to the pot and its particularity. This autonomy brings a source of authority to interpretation, if it is respected.

The autonomy of the past is also the reason why archaeological method has no monopoly on the creation of knowledges and truths about the material past. Does a painting of a castle by Turner reveal no truths of its object in comparison with archaeological treatment? Were there no truths about the material past before the formalisations of archaeological method from the late nineteenth century onwards?

There is a gap between the autonomy and dependency of the pot. If we were back in the workshop where the pot was made, we might have a good awareness of its meaning. If we were the one who actually made the pot, then it would very much be dependent upon us. But its materiality, equivocality, heterogeneity always withhold a complete understanding: the clay is always other than its maker; the pot is always more than its classification. People may interpret it in all sorts of different ways. The material world provides food for thought, for negotiation of meaning, as we have already indicated.

So the tension within the pot between dependency and autonomy is a tension between its expressive (or significative) character and its materiality. It is a gap between, for example, an image (which has an autonomous existence) and its meanings. Or between the sound of a word and its meaning to which it cannot be reduced. To bridge these gaps requires effort, work, the time of interpretation. This work is one of reconstruction and connection, putting back together the pieces which have been separated.

When a pot becomes part of the ruin of time, when a site decays into ruin, revealed is the essential character of a material artefact – its duality of autonomy and dependency. The ruined fragment invites us to reconstruct, to exercise the work of imagination, making connections within and beyond the remnants. In this way the post-history of a pot is as indispensable as its pre-history. And the task is not to revive the dead (they are rotten and gone) or the original conditions from whose decay the pot remained, but to understand the pot as ruined fragment. This is the fascination of archaeological interpretation.

Commentary and critique

The tension within the (temporality of an) artefact between past and present, between autonomy and dependence upon its conditions of making, corresponds to the complementarity of critique and commentary. Commentary is interpretation which teases out the remnants of the time of the artefact, places it in historical context. Critique is interpretation which works on the autonomy of the artefact, building references that shift far beyond its time of making. It may be compared artistically with artefacts from other times and cultures in critical art history. Critique may consider different understandings of the artefact in our present. Critique may use the integrity of the artefact as a lever against totalising systems, undermining their claims to universality. Both are necessary. Commentary without critique is empty and trivial information with no necessary relation to the present. Critique without commentary may be a baseless and self-indulgent appreciation of the aesthetic achievements of the past, or a dogmatic ideology, an unedifying emanation of present interests.

Commentary is made on the dependency of things upon their time of making, fleshing out information of times past. But the flesh needs to be brought to life, and this is the task of critique: revealing heterogeneity, yoking incongruity, showing the gaps in the neat orders of explanation, revealing the impossibility of any final account of things. This is a living reality because it is one of process rather than of arrest. It is the ongoing dialogue that is reasoned interpretation.

Designed pasts: discourse and writing

The archaeological past is written or told. It is translated into other forms.

Archaeology is a practice in which language plays a dominant part. The archaeologist comes literally to the site with a coding sheet, labelled with words, to be filled in. In addition there is a large implicit "black-box" coding sheet, never discussed, which defines walls, pits, sections, layers and so on. If the excavation process starts with language, so, too, it finishes with language. The events which take place in practice on an archaeological excavation are contingent and they are experienced differently by different participants. Interpretations are continually changed and contested. But in the end a report has to be written, the diversity and contingency subsumed within an ordered text. A story has to be told which not only describes what happened on the site (usually a minor part of the report) but also describes how the layers built up, when and perhaps why the walls were constructed, and so on. The story has to be coherent, with a beginning, a middle and an end. The site has to be moulded into a narrative using rhetoric which makes the story persuasive. A practice has been translated into words and narrative.

Archaeology, like any other discipline, constructs its object past through the workings of *discourse*. This is a key concept in directing attention not so much to

the content, but to the way something is written or told, and the social and historical conditions surrounding writing and telling. Discourse can be treated as
heterogeneous networkings, technologies of cultural production (of a particular
kind) which enable and are the conditions within which statements may be made,
texts constituted, interpretations made, knowledges developed, even people constituted as subjectivities. Discourse may consist of people, buildings, institutions,
rules, values, desires, concepts, machines and instruments. These are arranged
according to systems and criteria of inclusion and exclusion, whereby some people
are admitted, others excluded, some statements qualified as legitimate candidates
for assessment, others judged as not worthy of comment. There are patterns of
authority (committees and hierarchies, for example) and systems of sanctioning,
accreditation and legitimation (degrees, procedures of reference and refereeing,
personal experiences, career paths). Discourses include media of dissemination and
involve forms of rhetoric. Archives (physical or memory-based) are built up
providing reference and precedents. Metanarratives, grand systems of narrative,
theory or explanation, often approaching myth, lie in the background and provide
general orientation, framework and legitimation.

Discourses may vary and clash in close proximity. In a factory the discourse of
the workforce may differ considerably from that of the management. Academic
archaeology probably includes several discourses: Near Eastern and classical archaeology being distinct from Anglo-American processual archaeology. The discourse
of commercial excavation is different again. Fowler (1995) considers aspects of
discourses on the countryside, though he focuses as much on the content of the
writing. The notion of the English countryside and landscape, its development and
relation to national identity could be termed part of a metanarrative. J. Thomas
(1991a) has challenged the metanarrative of earlier British prehistory, that it was
then just as it always has been – hearty peasants in the English countryside. Other
metanarratives include the stories of cultural diffusion from centres of excellence
accompanied by conquest and population movement: an explanatory scheme based
on nineteenth-century experiences of imperialism. Larsen (1989) has related Near
Eastern archaeology to an ideology of orientalism (Said 1978). Evolutionary theories, when treated uncritically, often also form neat formulae for bringing the past
to order (Shanks and Tilley 1987b, ch. 6), which is a function of metanarrative.

Tilley (1993) has remarked upon the paradox that what we now term interpretive archaeology hardly exists, yet all archaeology is interpretive. The number
of empirical studies which are self-consciously postprocessual or interpretive
(in the senses outlined here) is growing, and the range of issues discussed in this
volume attests to the wide applicability of the concept of interpretation, but it is
less important that archaeologists adopt the label. We are simply proposing that
archaeologists, whatever their claims, always have done and can do no other than
interpret the past. This places archaeology in symmetry with those in the past who
are studied, and with those who are not archaeologists but who try to make sense
of the material past. They, too, interpreted and interpret their world, engaging in

cultural production. Foregrounding the interpretive character of archaeology deprives archaeologists of an authority which would lie in their restricted access to scientific method, abstract truth and the objectivity of the past. But they can potentially offer to others their skill in crafting and interpreting material pasts, cherishing their creative responsibilities.

References

Barrett, J. (1988) "Fields of discourse: reconstituting a social archaeology", *Critique of Anthropology*, 7:5–16.

Bhaskar, R. (1979) *The Possibility of Naturalism*, Hassocks: Harvester Press.

Bintliff, J. (1992) Comment on Thomas and Tilley, *Antiquity*, 66:111–14.

Clarke, D. (1968) *Analytical Archaeology*, London: Methuen.

Conkey, M. (1990) "Experimenting with style in archaeology: some historical and theo-retical issues", in M. Conkey and C. Hastorf (eds) *The Uses of Style in Archaeology*, Cambridge: Cambridge University Press.

Conkey, M. and Hastorf, C. (eds) (1990) *The Uses of Style in Archaeology*, Cambridge: Cambridge University Press.

Foucault, M. (1979) *The History of Sexuality, Vol. 1, An Introduction*, trans. R. Hurley, Harmondsworth: Penguin.

Foucault, M. (1984a) *Histoire de la sexualité, Vol. 2, L'Usage des plaisirs*, Paris: Gallimard.

Foucault, M. (1984b) *Histoire de la sexualité, Vol. 3, Le Souci de soi*, Paris: Gallimard.

Fowler, P.J. (1995) "Writing on the countryside," in I. Hodder, M. Shanks, A. Alexandri, V. Buchli, J. Carman, J. Last and G. Lucas (eds) *Interpreting Archaeology: Finding meaning in the past*, London, Routledge.

Gadamer, H.-G. (1975) *Truth and Method*, New York: Seabury.

Giddens, A. (1982) *Profiles and Critiques in Social Theory*, London: Macmillan.

Giddens, A. (1984) *The Constitution of Society: Outline of the Theory of Structuration*, Cambridge: Polity Press.

Hebdige, D. (1979) *Subculture: The Meaning of Style*, London: Methuen.

Heidegger, M. (1972) *On Time and Being*, New York: Harper & Row.

Hodder, I. (1985) "Postprocessual archaeology", in M. Schiffer (ed.) *Advances in Archaeological Method and Theory* 8: 1–26, London: Academic Press.

Hodder, I. (1986) *Reading the Past; Current Approaches to Interpretation in Archaeology*, Cambridge: Cambridge University Press.

Hodder, I. (ed.) (1982) *Symbolic and Structural Archaeology*, Cambridge: Cambridge University Press.

Hodder, I. (ed.) (1987) *The Archaeology of Contextual Meanings*, Cambridge: Cambridge University Press.

Johnson, M. (1989) "Conceptions of agency in archaeological interpretation", *Journal of Anthropological Archaeology*, 8:189–211.

Larsen, M.T. (1989) "Orientalism and Near Eastern archaeology", in D. Miller, M. Rowlands and C. Tilley (eds) *Domination and Resistance*, London: Unwin Hyman.

Latour, B. (1988) *The Pasteurization of France*, trans. A. Sheridan and J. Law, Cambridge, Mass.: Harvard University Press.

Nietzsche, F. (1967) *The Genealogy of Morals*, trans. W. Kaufmann, New York: Random House.

Pearson, M. (1994) "Theatre/archaeology", *The Drama Review*, Summer.

Potter, P.B. (1990) "The 'what' and 'why' of public relations for archaeology: a postscript to DeCicco's Public Relations Primer", *American Antiquity*, 55:608–13.

Renfrew, C. (1989) Comments on "Archaeology into the 1990s", *Norwegian Archaeological Review*, 22:33–41.

Said, E. (1978) *Orientalism*, London: Routledge & Kegan Paul.

Shanks, M. (1992) *Experiencing the Past: On the Character of Archaeology*, London: Routledge.

Shanks, M. and McGuire, R. (1991) "The craft of archaeology", paper delivered at the Society for American Archaeology Meetings, New Orleans.

Shanks, M. and Tilley, C. (1987a) *Re-Constructing Archaeology*, Cambridge: Cambridge University Press.

Shanks, M. and Tilley, C. (1987b) *Social Theory and Archaeology*, Oxford: Polity Press.

Thomas, J. (1991) *Rethinking the Neolithic*, Cambridge: Cambridge University Press.

Tilley, C. (1993) "Interpretative archaeology and an archaeological poetics", in C. Tilley (ed.) *Interpretative Archaeology*, London: Berg.

Trigger, B. (1980) "Archaeology and the Image of the American Indian", *American Antiquity*, 45: 662–76.

Trigger, B. (1989) "Hyperrelativism, responsibility and the social sciences", *Canadian Review of Sociology and Anthropology*, 26:776–97.

Watson, P. (1990) "The razor's edge: symbolic–structuralist archaeology and the expansion of archaeological inference", *American Anthropologist*, 92:613–21.

Yoffee, N. and Sherratt, A. (eds) (1993) *Archaeological Theory: Who Sets the Agenda?*, Cambridge: Cambridge University Press.

PART TWO

Meanings of things

INTRODUCTION

What do artifacts mean? The traditional "technocentric" archaeological view is that artifacts are simply tools, used in some overt utilitarian fashion, and then set aside once the task at hand is completed. Here, meaning lies entirely in functional performance: a hammer is what a hammer does – hammer things. One outcome of this perspective has been the development of a catch-all grouping for artifacts with no obvious or common-sense functionality: "ceremonial objects". This term has served as a kind of archaeological code for the unknowable and, presumably, intellectually irrelevant. This reinforces the technocentric belief that it is functional, workman-like behavior, as opposed to the mental realm of beliefs and rituals, that we should study in the past. Yet is technical function the sum of an artifact's meaning?

In the same vein, we can also ask: what is the meaning of an archaeological interpretation? Is it an objective reconstruction of past reality or, instead, something more akin to literature – a hermeneutic interpretation, or a scientific explanation? Both of these issues are fundamental to archaeology, and both have played a prominent part in the development of cognitive and post-processual archaeologies.

One key point about meaning is that there are always multiple levels of it – there is no single meaning embedded in any symbol, act of communication or, by extension, artifact. The kind of long trousers that I am wearing as I write this provides a good illustration of this fact. Pants are an obvious example of a mundane, utilitarian object that we use, and see others use, daily. The overt function of my pants is to keep me warm, albeit the need for warmth as I sit in my office on a summer day in southern California is debatable (I will turn on the air conditioner shortly). This points to an alternative function – another level of meaning, if you will – of my pants, which is to provide a body covering for purposes of modesty. This "meaning" implies beliefs and customs because the importance of modesty, in this sense of the term, is far from a cross-cultural universal. Yet there are other potential levels of meaning, beyond these two functional ones, that can also be inferred from my blue jeans, especially if viewed in recent historical contexts. Fifty years ago, for example, the wearing of pants would have been taken as a sign of my gender: males wore pants, females wore dresses. When I was brought up, shorts were normally worn by children and long pants by adults, so the length of pants signalled something about the wearer's age. Blue jeans were worn by laborers, while educated, white-collar folk wore slacks, so pant type served as a kind of socioeconomic indicator. (This is why many photos of early archaeologists show them in suit and tie, even while in the field). Even today, many people still view different brands of jeans as social indicators (although the economic inferences are no longer valid). Wrangler brand jeans are worn by the country music industry, rodeo cowboys, and western riders; Levi brand jeans are favored by "yuppies" – at least, according to my friends in the first group. And, regardless of brand, the daily wearing of blue jeans also serves to distinguish their wearers from another social segment of society, "The Suits" (corporate employees, as opposed to artists and writers); again, according to the music industry. But which, of all these potential meanings, is the most important? If an archaeologist wished to study blue jeans, which kind of meaning should be emphasized in an analysis, and which ones could be ignored? These are fundamental problems that all archaeological analyses confront. It is the recognition of the wide potential range of meanings in material culture that is a key facet of cognitive and post-processual archaeologies.

The two chapters in this section address this fundamental archaeological problem of meaning at two different levels. The first, by Dorothy Hosler, is ultimately derived from one of the most technological kinds of analyses performed in archaeology: metallurgical studies of bronze artifacts. Metal is a particularly good example for our consideration because we use metal constantly in our daily lives. This daily use has given us a very strong (even if implicit) common-sense view of the functional meaning of different metal alloys. Cast iron is inexpensive, brittle and breaks easily, and we use it for cheap implements where strength is not a concern. Stainless steel is expensive to produce and does not tarnish, so we use it sparingly in hospitals and kitchens. Tungsten alloys are particularly strong and relatively light but also expensive, and so they are most commonly used in airplanes and race cars. In each case structural and economic characteristics of these alloys are the determinants of their function, and this is taken to be their "meaning". Because this seems such a common-sense perspective on metal, it is easy to project this kind of view point on to prehistoric metal artifacts.

Yet in her analysis of West Mexican metallurgy, Hosler reveals two circumstances that contradict this common sense, technocentric view. Rather than showing a primary concern with overt structural and economic characteristics of alloys, ancient West Mexican metal workers were apparently more concerned with regulating the qualities of color and sound in their alloys, because these qualities were used to create and recreate the experience of the sacred. In part this emphasis resulted from the second circumstance that Hosler's analysis establishes: West Mexican metal working was primarily oriented towards the production of elite and ceremonial objects, rather than "tools" such as weapons and farming implements. In this case symbolic and ideological factors, not economic and adaptive concerns, shaped the development of technology – which is exactly the opposite of our "common sense" archaeological view of these matters.

Some might wonder whether this circumstance is unique or rare. In fact, it is not, even if archaeologists are unaccustomed to thinking in such terms. The heavily symbolic nature of another example of non-western metallurgy, for example, can be observed in Africa. Throughout the sub-Saharan region the process of iron working was (and continues to be) much more than simply "functional technology" (see papers in Schmidt 1996). Technology, again, is more than just a question of overt tool-working construction and functionability. Another example of such matters derives from Australia, where Taçon (1991) has shown that the visual quality of "brilliance" in lithics constrained changes in stone tools, and signaled alterations in regional power networks. Lithic choices may then be more than simply questions of availability and distance from source. Huffman (1986, 1996), similarly, has demonstrated how African Iron Age settlement lay-out is organized to reflect worldview, rather than for economic or defensive purposes. At the level of the individual building, Shafer (1995) has also shown how worldview can be expressed in the arrangement of individual architectural features. Each case reveals different kinds of meaning than those that have traditionally been taken for granted in processual archaeological analyses. And each of these cases, like Hosler's, shows why these different kinds of meaning are central to understanding the archaeological record.

In the second paper Persis Clarkson addresses the problem of meaning at a different level. Her concern is the meaning of our archaeological reconstructions. Her goal is to move these closer to an insider's perspective, towards the meaning that a prehistoric inhabitant of the Nazca Valley, Peru, may have held about the famous Nazca lines. She starts by raising a basic question about our interpretations: what counts? By deconstructing existing archaeological practice, Clarkson reveals what she sees as a series of problematic perceptions and commitments in the ways that archaeologists traditionally view the past. These problems she sees as inherent to our western technocentric view of the world, our foregrounding of content over process, our emphasis on dualistic perceptions of society, and ultimately on the creation of positivist texts emphasizing a few functional parts of a culture and society as representative of the complex whole.

Recognizing that our sense of the geoglyphs is based on static images produced by maps and photos, Clarkson opts instead for contextualizing the Nazca lines within their landscape. They are, in this view, texts created and used by the ancient Nazqueños interactively. This being so, the meaning of them both is and was unstable: it is fluid and changeable, just as the creation, perception and use of them varied prehistorically, and just as our western interpretations of them also have varied.

Both papers at least implicitly challenge the traditional belief of processual archaeology that our "common sense" view of the meaning of things-archaeological is adequate to understand the past. This is unsettling, perhaps, because it implies a complexity to culture and society that archaeology heretofore has been unwilling to admit. Yet this circumstance poses an important question to us: do we continue with our traditional technocentric approach to the past, even though we know it is extremely simplistic, or do we instead raise our intellectual efforts to the challenge posed by a realistic perspective on the meanings of things?

■ ■ ■

Further reading

Huffman 1996
Lechtmann 1984
Tilley 1990

■ ■ ■

References

Huffman, T.N. (1986) "Cognitive Studies of the Iron Age in Southern Africa", *World Archaeology* 18:84–95.

—— (1996) *Snakes and Crocodiles: Power and Symbolism in Ancient Zimbabwe*, Johannesburg: Witwatersrand University.

Lechtmann, H. (1984) "Andean Value Systems and the Development of Prehistoric Metallurgy", *Technology and Culture* 25:1–36.

Schmidt, P. (ed.) *The Culture and Technology of African Iron Production*, Gainesville: University Press of Florida.

Shafer, H.J. (1995) "Architecture and Symbolism in Transitional Pueblo Development in the Mimbres Valey, SW New Mexico", *Journal of Field Archaeology* 22:23–47.

Taçon, P.S.C. (1991) "The Power of Stone: Symbolic Aspects of Stone Tool Use and Tool Development in Western Arnhem Land, Australia", *Antiquity*, 65:192–207.

Tilley, C. (ed.) (1990) *Reading Material Culture: Structuralism, Hermeneutics and Post-Structuralism*, Oxford: Basil Blackwell.

Chapter 5

SOUND, COLOR AND MEANING IN THE METALLURGY OF ANCIENT WEST MEXICO

Dorothy Hosler

West Mexican metallurgy developed between AD 600 and the Spanish invasion in 1521 in a region I have designated the West Mexican metalworking zone (Hosler 1994) (Fig. 1). Metalworkers in certain sectors of this zone eventually used a host of metals and alloys, including the bronzes – copper-arsenic and copper-tin – a ternary copper-arsenic-tin alloy, alloys of copper and silver, and others to craft a variety of object classes, from tools to élite-status items. Some of these were cold worked from an initial cast blank, others were worked hot, and still others were lost-wax cast. Laboratory analytical studies demonstrate these metalworkers' technical versatility (see Hosler 1986, 1988a, 1988b; Hosler, Lechtman and Holm 1990; Hosler and Stresser-Péan 1992). The studies further reveal that the artisans were most consistently interested in elaborating two physical properties of metal, its sound and its color. Lost-wax-cast bells and, much less frequently, other sorts of metallic rattling artifacts comprise the sounding instruments. The focus on color, especially the colors of gold and silver, is apparent in bells and in other status items such as large ornamental tweezers, rings and ornamental shields fashioned from copper alloys by hot or cold work. When made from bronze, these artifacts contain the alloying element, tin or arsenic, in concentrations between 5 and 23 weight per cent, levels which laboratory studies (Hosler 1986) have shown are far higher than necessary solely to optimize artifact design and mechanical function. These levels of tin or arsenic dramatically alter the color of copper metal, however, from red to increasingly golden or silvery hues.

Artisans also used copper alloys, especially the bronzes, for utilitarian objects, such as axes, needles and awls. These contain tin

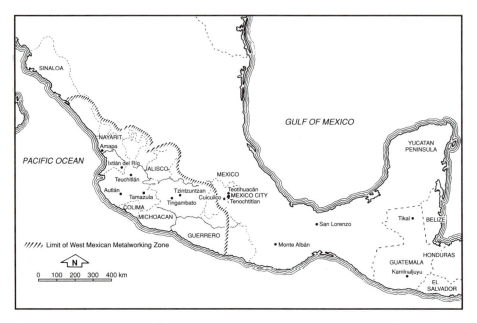

Figure 1 Map of Mesoamerica showing archaeological sites, the state boundaries in western Mexico and the limits of the West Mexican metal-working zone. Courtesy of MIT Press

and arsenic in concentrations between approximately 2 and 5 weight per cent. At these levels, alloy concentration is sufficient to confer the increased strength required to improve performance and design without appreciably affecting color.

Technical developments of this sort are especially compelling when we consider that the geological, metallurgical and chemical analytical data (Hosler 1986, 1988a, 1988c, 1994; Hosler and Stresser-Péan 1992) indicate metalworkers in this zone had a range of other options available to them. Surveys of regional geology show that the area contains abundant deposits of native metals and ore minerals. The data also show that these artisans fully understood and managed alloy properties, especially of the bronzes, and could have employed metal extensively or perhaps exclusively for tools, weapons, armor and other utilitarian objectives. Yet needles, punches, fishhooks and other tools are small in number relative to the numbers of status items in metal (see Hosler 1986, 1994). The most original technical experiments of these smiths and the bulk of their technical energies were devoted to developing sound and specific colors in objects worn by élites and nobles and used in ritual.

Here I explore the meaning of bell sounds and the colors of gold and silver in an effort to explain why these sounds and these colors played such key roles in shaping this prehistoric metallurgy. The importance of metallic colors, especially of gold and silver, in myth, shamanistic performance, cosmological schema and political ideology has been demonstrated for the central Andes and Colombia (for example, see Lechtman 1979, 1993). The West Mexican experiment is unique in that artisans achieved these culturally required golden and silvery colors through the unusual technical expedient of using the high-arsenic and high-tin bronzes. Although the mechanical properties of these alloys were required by the design characteristics of the objects, their colors were a matter of choice, accomplished by adding the alloying element in high concentrations. By generating metallic sound and these metallic colors, this ancient technology served primarily as a visual and auditory system that symbolically defined élite and sacred spheres of activity.

An overview of West Mexican metallurgy

Metallurgy emerged late in ancient Mesoamerica, appearing after AD 600 in the mineral rich western states of Michoacan, Jalisco, Colima, Nayarit and Guerrero. The technology occurred after state-level societies had been in place in adjacent Mesoamerican regions for at least several hundred years. This western area had been occupied by smaller-scale societies; larger-scale social entities did not take shape until the Tarascan state coalesced in highland Michoacan around AD 1250.

West Mexican metallurgy developed through two technological periods, each of which had its roots in the metallurgies of Central and South America (Hosler 1988a, 1988b). Elements of both these two more southerly metallurgies were introduced via a maritime route to West Mexico. During Period 1 (AD 600–1200/1300), West Mexican smiths were particularly engaged in elaborating metals' resonant qualities, casting bells in copper in a variety of shapes and sizes using the lost-wax method. They also made various tools and ornaments by cold working them to shape, but the relative numbers of these items in collections and excavated assemblages is far lower than that of bells, which comprised the focus of these artisans' technical activities (Hosler 1994). Lost-wax casting, particularly of certain bell types, had been introduced from lower Central America and Colombia. Cold working, especially of several varieties of small hand tools (i.e. needles, tweezers, etc.), was introduced from southern Ecuador and northern Peru. During Period 1, West Mexican smiths primarily used copper, although some evidence indicates that they also used a low-arsenic copper-arsenic alloy, and occasionally made objects from silver and from gold.

During Period 2 (AD 1200/1300 to the Spanish invasion), these smiths' technical repertoire greatly expanded. Michoacan, the seat of the Tarascan empire, seems to have been the locus of Period 2 technical experiments, although the artifacts also appear at sites in adjacent regions of Guerrero, Jalisco and the State of Mexico (see Fig. 1) (Hosler 1994). Metalworkers used alloys (copper-tin, copper-arsenic, copper-arsenic-tin, copper-silver and others) to redesign some of the objects they had previously made in copper, taking advantage of the alloys' strength, toughness, fluidity and color properties. Artisans added the alloying elements, tin and arsenic, to copper in low concentrations for tools such as axes which they were able to make thinner and harder. They took advantage of the same alloy properties for status objects, using tin bronze and arsenic bronze to cast thin-walled bells with intricate designs that required improved strength and solidification characteristics, for worked objects such as thin-banded rings and for large tweezers with convex shell-design blades (Hosler 1988a). As mentioned, however, the concentration of the alloying elements in such status objects was consistently higher than necessary to achieve these designs; what it did affect was color. For silvery looking castings smiths used arsenic bronze, but they preferred the tough copper-silver alloys for sheet metal objects: discs, pendants and other ornaments. In fact, copper-silver alloy hammered into sheet-metal ornaments was so common in Michoacan that the Spaniards referred to the alloy as the "metal of Michoacan" (Warren 1985).

Certain elements of Period 2 West Mexican metallurgy also were introduced from the metallurgies of Central and South America. Knowledge of the copper-arsenic and copper-silver alloy systems and of certain artifact designs derives from the metallurgies of southern Ecuador and northern Peru. The copper-tin bronze alloy, however, was introduced from the southern highlands of Peru and Bolivia (Hosler 1988b) through the same maritime network that transmitted knowledge of this technology during Period 1.

At no time during these developments did West Mexican smiths import either artifacts or raw materials from the south. What they imported was knowledge of fabrication regimes and a few prototype artifacts that were copied locally. They also reproduced the pan-American indigenous interest in metallic color, especially of gold and silver, although they invented their own methods for achieving these colors. The laboratory investigations described here have identified not only the characteristics of the technology, but its cultural bias. The technology itself provides the point of departure for this inquiry into meaning.

The meanings of bell sounds and of the colors of gold and silver

Sources

How do we begin to understand why such a large fraction of this metallurgy was devoted to elaborating these properties? What specifically did golden and silvery metallic colors and the sounds of bells mean to these ancient peoples? Sixteenth-century documents are particularly helpful in establishing the social contexts in which metallic sound and silvery and golden metallic colors played a part, at least during Period 2. Another, complementary way of approaching the problem is through indigenous terms related to metal and sounding instruments, in these documents and in Tarascan (Purepecha) and Nahuatl, two languages spoken in the zone. Tarascan was spoken by the peoples in highland Michoacan and adjacent areas; Nahuatl was the language of the Aztec or Mexica. Nahuatl speakers occupied some areas of Guerrero lying within the metalworking zone and areas contiguous with it. Nahuatl was also spoken in some areas of Michoacan (Fig. 1), especially along the Tarascan border in certain multiethnic communities. Among sixteenth-century Nahuatl documents, Bernardo de Sahagún's encyclopedic *Florentine Codex* (1950–82) is especially helpful. Documentary sources are also available from the Tarascan region and other areas of the metalworking zone. The most useful of these is the *Relación de Michoacán* (Tudela 1977), an anonymous illustrated sixteenth-century Spanish manuscript treating preconquest Tarascan and very early colonial history.

The colors of gold and silver

Golden and silvery metallic colors achieved through alloying, or, where possible, with the pure metals, were one primary technical objective of the smiths of this zone during Period 2. Why were these peoples so interested in the colors of gold and silver? The documentary evidence suggests that Tarascan peoples considered the golden and silvery objects divine and that they associated gold with the sun and silver with the moon. The *Relación de Michoacán* recounts that Hiripan, one of three brothers responsible for preconquest Tarascan expansion, wanted to recover gold, silver and other items from conquered villages.

> "What shall we do brothers? The people of the villages run away and carry off the plumes and jewels which made them nobles in the villages we have conquered. Go get them so the gods [the gold and silver objects] come back to their villages." Seeing that yellow gold and white silver, Hiripan said, "Look brothers, this yellow [metal] must be manure which the sun casts off, and that white metal must be manure cast off by the moon".
>
> (Tudela 1977: 152)

These two metals, gold and silver, divine emissions and divine property, also validated the authority of the nobility. The citation suggests that nobility defined itself through the possession of these plumes and jewels. Linguistic data reinforce the association of the sun with gold; the root *tiripeti* means gold in Tarascan, and *Tiripeti* was also the name given to gods that were individual manifestations of the sun (Brand 1951). In fact, Tarascan state treasurers stored gold diadems and discs in chests said to honor the sun, and discs of silver in honor of Xaratanga, the goddess of the moon (Tudela 1977: 257). Tarascan kings were interred with gold shields at their back and golden bells on their ankles (Tudela 1977: 219); in battle they were protected by a shield of silver (Tudela 1977: 192). Some of these objects were made from the pure metals. Others were apparently made from copper–silver and, probably, gold–silver alloys based on sixteenth-century accounts of the variable quality of the gold and silver objects which the Spaniards demanded and received from the Tarascan ruler.

Golden and silvery metallic colors also were associated with solar and lunar deities by the Aztec or Mexica in central Mexico, and by extension by Nahuatl-speaking peoples in surrounding territories. In Nahuatl, the word for gold, *cuztic teocuitlatl*, literally means "yellow divine excretions" and is taken to mean excretions of a solar deity (Campbell 1985). According to the *Florentine Codex*, that deity was Tonatiuh. The name Tonatiuh comes from the verbal root *tona* which means to shimmer, to shine or to give off heat. When the *Florentine Codex* describes the visual effect of gold, it uses *tona*, translating it to mean "to give off rays" (Sahagún 1950–82 book 11: 234). *Tona* also means for the sun to shine; thus gold shines, shimmers and gives off rays, or heat, like the sun or like *Tonatiuh*. Metal conducts heat and it is also highly reflective and here both qualities are explicitly recognized. The origins of gold are also described in the *Florentine Codex*: the name "derives from [the fact that] sometimes, in some places, there appears in the dawn something like a little bit of diarrhea. . . . It was very yellow, very wonderful, resting like an ember, like molten gold" (Sahagún 1950–82 book 11: 233). The Nahuatl word for silver, *iztac teocuitlatl*, signifies "white divine excretions" (Campbell 1985), and could mean excretions of the moon. The terms make clear that these metals were divine substances, produced, smelted or emitted by the deities (Hosler 1994).

Golden and silvery metal objects such as discs, crowns, large tweezers and pendants made from high-tin bronze, copper-silver alloys and sometimes pure gold or silver metals thus announced status. Status resided in supernatural affiliations. The quality of brilliance and reflectiveness of these objects characterizes the Mexica (Aztec) paradise, termed a "cult of brilliance" (Burkhart 1992; Hill 1987). In Nahuatl devotional literature this sacred domain is conceived as a shimmering garden. Burkhart describes the garden.

> In this symbolic garden, one came into direct contact with the creative, life-giving forces of the universe and with the timeless world of deities and ancestors. The garden is a shimmering place filled with divine fire; the light of the sun reflects from the petals of flowers and the iridescent feathers of birds; human beings – the souls of the dead or the ritually transformed living – are themselves flowers, birds, and shimmering gems. . . . This garden is not a place of reward for the righteous, existing on some transcendent plane of reality separate from the material world. It is a metaphor for life on earth, a metaphor that ritual transforms into reality by asserting that, in fact, this is the way the world is.
>
> (Burkhart 1992: 89)

Nahuatl devotional texts present the entities that fill this world as feathers, bells, flutes and flowers. Metallic colors reflecting off these iridescent entities helped create the sacred garden. These same texts frequently describe glowing and shining golden blossoms, golden petals, leaves, birds, feathers and raindrops. The examples Burkhart discusses are predominantly drawn from two Nahuatl texts, *Psalmodia Christiana*, a hymnbook composed by Fray Bernardino de Sahagún in Nahuatl to christianize the native peoples of Mexico (Sahagún 1993) and *Cantares Mexicanos* (Bierhorst 1985), a book of Nahuatl poetry composed between 1550 and 1580 dealing with the conquest and its aftermath.

We do not yet know whether a similar sacred domain also existed in Tarascan conceptions of the divine, although it seems likely given the vast quantities of golden and silvery sheet-metal ornaments Tarascan metalworkers made and the sacred qualities ascribed to golden and silvery colors. We suspect that the concept of a brilliant shimmering paradise was held elsewhere in Mesoamerica, certainly by other Uto-Aztecan speakers (Hosler 1994), and possibly among the Maya (Burkhart personal communication 1993). Some evidence also indicates that these same concepts were present in Andean South America. The implications of an Andean South American locus for these ideas is especially intriguing in view of the Andean peoples' widespread and very early focus on producing reflective golden and silvery metallic sheet – and the fact that aspects of that same sheet-metal-oriented ritual technology were introduced from the Andean area to western Mexico.

Achieving golden and silvery metallic colors, a primary technical objective of West Mexican smiths, was a means of visually creating and recreating the sacred, the essence of these deities. The sacred was embodied in a constellation of golden and silvery looking objects such as tweezers, bells, discs, rings, plaques and ornamental shields. The objects, which were made from the sacred metals of gold and silver, or their alloys with copper, were possessed by these divinities and the kings and nobles who represented them.

Bell sounds

Bell sounds and the sounds of composite bell instruments played a significant role in several sacred contexts. One is in ritual celebrating human and agricultural fertility and regeneration. Another is in warfare, where bell sounds could protect. The third is in the sacred paradise, which was created through song and sound. One of those sounds, the sound of bells, is associated with shimmering, colorful, singing birds and with human voices that represent deities and their human transformations.

The power accorded to bell sounds also determined the course of West Mexican metallurgy. Our best information comes from central Mexican descriptions of ritual in which these instruments are played. Rites for Tlaloc, Xipe Totec and Quetzalcoatl, three central Mexican deities, invariably require bells or instruments containing them. Although not all central Mexican deities were worshipped in the Tarascan region, aspects of these three are represented by deities in the Tarascan pantheon, and Tarascan ideology shares basic principles with other Mesoamerican societies including auto-sacrifice, flaying, the ball game and heart sacrifice (Pollard 1993). Ritual surrounding these events was broadly similar, as were ritual accouterments, including bells and other percussion instruments. We also know that the musical cultures of Central Mexico (Aztec), Michoacan (Tarascan) and Oaxaca were fundamentally similar (Stanford 1966), so that the instruments and the meanings ascribed to their sounds also resemble one another.

Fertility and regeneration

Rituals for Tlaloc, Xipe Totec and Quetzalcoatl representing aspects of fertility, life and regeneration are frequently created through bell sounds and the sounds of other composite percussion instruments containing bells. Rain, water, storms, thunder, lightning, rattlesnakes and new vegetation repeatedly appear as symbols of fecundity and new life and are associated with these deities. Bells and other rattling instruments played in these rituals replicated the sounds of thunder, rain and the rattle of the rattlesnake.

In addition to bells, the percussion (rattling) instruments most frequently illustrated or described from Central Mexico and surrounding territories are the hand-held rattle, the rattlestick and the mist rattleboard. Terms for some of these instruments, at least in Nahuatl, connote fertility. The Aztec rattlestick or *chicauaztli* (Stevenson 1968), a long, pointed stick containing rattles or bells, was widely employed in agricultural rites. *Chicaua*, the verbal root of the noun *chicauaztli*, means to strengthen and fortify (Karttunen 1992:46). Seler argues that the "word and symbol obviously refer to the strengthening of the reproductive function, to fertilizing" (in Sahagún 1950–82 book 1:40, note 118). The *Codex Borgia* illustrates a rattlestick above the first human pair, who appear to be covered with a common quilt, explicitly linking the instrument with human sexuality (Neumann 1974). Neumann thinks that the *chicauaztli* serves as a symbol for sexual union. The term for mist rattleboard, *ayauhchicauaztli*, also contains *chicaua*, the same verbal root. Seler describes the instrument as a board with holes. Bells were strung in them, and the bells sounded as the person carrying it walked (in Sahagún 1950–82 book 1:17, note 53). Seler says that the sounds reproduced the thunder of Tlaloc, who, according to Pasztory (1974), is a rain deity in one aspect and a deity of the earth, caves and the underworld in another.

Rites for Tlaloc, associated with lightning, rattlesnakes and the underworld, are accompanied by instruments containing bells or rattles to attract rain and thunder. The *Florentine Codex* describes the fire priest in Tlaloc's temple when the rains break out. The images graphically link snakes, their rattling sounds and rain.

> And when the rain broke out, then he forthwith arose; he seized his incense ladle. . . . The incense ladle rattled. It was in the form of a serpent. And the serpent's head also rattled. . . . Then he offered incense; to the four directions he raised [the incense ladle]. Much did it rattle; [the incense] spilled out. . . . Thus he attended to the matter; thus he called upon the Tlalocs; thus he prayed for rain.
>
> (Sahagún 1950–82 book 2: 151)

In rites honoring Tlaloc during *Etzalqualiztli*, the sixth month of the Aztec ritual calendar which marked the end of the dry season, priests carried and shook the *ayauhchicauaztli,* the mist rattleboard.

He went bearing on his shoulders the mist rattleboard, also called the sorcerer's staff. It was wide, very wide, excessively wide; and it was long, very long. And it rattled; he went along rattling it.

(Sahagún 1950–82 book 2:81)

In describing a procession to the temple of Tlaloc, the priest:

Put on his mist jacket, his rain mask or his Tlaloc mask. . . . Thus they went to the Temple of Tlaloc. . . . And when this was done, then he scattered *yauhtli* [an herb]. And he had scattered it, then they gave him the mist rattle-board. He rattled, he shook it; he raised it in dedication [to the god].

(Sahagún 1950–82 book 2: 87)

The final verse of the song of Tlaloc makes clear that rattle sounds bring rain.

To all places go
To all places reach
To Poyauhtlan
With mist-bringing rattles [*ayauhchicauztica*]
To Tlalocan taken.

(Sahagún 1950–82 book 2: 225)

Bells and bell sounds are also associated with Quetzalcoatl (the feathered serpent). In one of Quetzalcoatl's myriad aspects of wind and storm deity, he represents fertility, wind or breath, and life (Brundage 1982; Hunt 1977). Quetzalcoatl becomes the wind storm that occurs just before the rainy season begins. Sahagún calls him the "roadsweeper" of the rain gods. According to Townsend (1992: 114) the best portrayal of Quetzalcoatl is an Aztec sculpture depicting a coiled serpent rising from the earth, with a Tlaloc mask on the bottom. Quetzalcoatl's twin, Xolotl, appears as a deified form of lightning (Hunt 1977: 126). As a snake, Quetzalcoatl is often depicted with prominent rattles; the rattles are sometimes shown as bells (Emmerich 1965: Fig. 178; I. Kelly personal communication 1981). According to Sahagún, Quetzalcoatl in human form wears ankle bells. Quetzalcoatl occasionally is depicted holding the *chicauaztli*. Mayahuel, the goddess of *pulque* with 400 breasts whom Brundage (1982: 96) calls an avatar of Quetzalcoatl, holds the *chicauaztli* as well. Tezcatzoncatl, one of the rabbit gods, is also illustrated with ankle bells. Hunt thinks that these rabbit gods and gods of *pulque* also are linked to fertility (Hunt 1977: 86–7).

Xipe Totec, patron of the metalsmiths and god of new vegetation, is another deity invariably represented with percussion and rattling instruments. The *chicauaztli* is Xipe's insignia. Xipe's origins are confusing, but one possibility is that he came from the Yope-Tlapanec area of Guerrero, a zone within the metalworking area. Xipe is the principal deity of the Aztec second month, Tlacaxipeualiztli (the flaying of people), when sacrificial victims were flayed. Flaying ceremonies are related to agriculture, fertility and prosperity (Broda 1970). The objects associated with Itztli, a deity related to Xipe, make this obvious: he is depicted grasping a digging or planting stick, wearing a flayed skin and holding a basket of corn (Heyden 1986: 40). Xipe's song, collected by Sahagún, is an "invocation for rain" and focuses on the growth of the maize plant (Broda 1970: 259). It is therefore not surprising that mist rattleboards were sounded during Tlacaxipeualiztli, the ceremonies dedicated to Xipe.

> And when it was this [time], the rattleboards were sown there at Yopico. And only they, the old men of the *calpulli* at Yopico, sat singing, sat rattling their rattleboards until the day was done.
>
> (Sahagún 1950–82 book 2: 57)

The phrase "the rattleboards are sown" refers to a dance with bells that commoners danced (Broda 1970: 229), but "sowing" rattleboards also links Xipe to rain (Hosler 1994).

In the Tarascan realm, agricultural and rain-making rites must also have been accompanied by bell sounds as these peoples shared common musical cultures and ideologies with the Aztec. Tarascan musicians and religious functionaries used two other instruments as well: hand-held rattles and some other sort of rattle. Hand-held rattles, shaken by dancers, are illustrated in the *Relación de Michoacán* (Tudela 1977: 160), and another rattle is also described among metal objects exported from Michoacan by the Spaniards.

> Further, I received in native rattles of the same metal [copper-silver alloys] 4 arrobas and 33 pounds. These rattles are put together like the breast leather of a saddle with heavy cords.
>
> (Warren 1985: 119)

Although Aztec deities and divinities in the Tarascan pantheon do not directly correspond to one another, certain Tarascan deities are associated with rain and agricultural and human fertility; the bells that were so pervasive in the region must have played a part in rites dedicated to them. The deity controlling rain and fertility is Cuerauaperi, who also controlled birth and death; she was the mother of all gods and venerated throughout the Tarascan realm. Pollard (1993) thinks that her worship was widespread by the late Preclassic or Formative period. Flaying rites, analogous to those carried out for Xipe, were dedicated to her, and she was also associated with snake imagery. Curicaueri, the sky god, was the sun's messenger, a warrior, the god of the hunt, and the patron god of the Tarascan royal dynasty. Xaratanga, the moon diety, was the wife of Curicaueri and daughter of the earth goddess; she is depicted as snake, half moon coyote and vulture. Xaratanga was associated with childbirth and fertility. Although we know something about ceremonies held for them we simply do not have the detail that is available for the Aztec (Hosler 1994).

The linguistic evidence for Tarascan is not as rich as for Nahuatl. None the less, certain terms, specifically for copper and rattlesnakes, are to some extent related and suggest that sounds made by coppery objects, most likely bells, reproduced the sound of the rattlesnake. *Shari* is a root for reddish objects, including rattlesnakes, and *charha* is one for red earth, including copper. A stronger relationship exists between the terms meaning metal and metal bell, suggesting that the purpose of metal was to make bells.

> *tiamu*: Hierro, campana, etc. [iron, bell, etc.]
> *tiamu charapeti*: Hierro, cobre. [iron, copper.]

(Anonymous 1991 vol. 2: 597)

The sounds of bells as protection

Bell and other rattling sounds not only attract rain, they also protect in warfare. The Aztec god of war Huitzilopochli wore ankle bells. In a mythic battle with his 400 brothers, Sahagún (1950–85 book 3: 3) tells us that they arrayed themselves as if for war, binding little bells to the calves of their legs. None the less Huitzilopochli quickly dispatched them. The event is commemorated in myth, translated by Léon-Portilla and discussed by Matos M. (1987).

> In vain they tried to do something against him,
> In vain they turned and faced him,
> To the sounds of their bells,
> And they slapped their shields.
> They could do nothing,
> They could achieve nothing,
> They could defend themselves with nothing.

Huitzilopochli then arrays himself with their regalia, which may explain why he is shown wearing bells.

> He took from them their finery, their adornments,
> Their destiny, put them on, appropriated them,
> Incorporated them into his destiny,
> Made of them his own insignia.

(Matos M. 1987: 53–4)

Bell and rattle sounds are also associated with warfare in the Tarascan region. For example, the *Relación de Michoucán* (Tudela 1977: 190) illustrates the chief warrior wearing an ankle band with bells attached as he and his men attack a village. It also reports that when Curatame, the son of the Tarascan leader Tariacuri, dressed for war, he hung from his temples many snake rattles that dangled by their tails (Tudela 1977: 132).

The sounds of bells: the sacred garden

Another arena in which bell sounds shaped experience of the sacred is in the Aztec divine garden that Burkhart describes. The garden, while filled with luminous beings and entities, comes to be through song or sound. Bell sounds, bird songs and the human voice singing represented the agency of creation. The quotation below illustrates the metaphorical associations among them. The key verb, *icauaca*, means also to warble, murmur or clamor (Campbell 1985: 114).

> The spirit swans are echoing me as I sing, shrilling [warbling] like bells from the Place of Good Song.
>
> (Bierhorst 1985: 141)

Birds, songs, flowers, trees and golden colors are all associated with bell sounds in the Aztec paradise.

> Hear it! He's shrilling, warbling on the branches of the flower tree. He's shaking! It's the golden flower-bell, the rattle hummingbird, the swan, Lord Monencauhtzin. Like a gorgeous troupial fan he spreads his wings and soars beside the flower drum.
>
> (Bierhorst 1985: 165–7)

Speech is also associated with birds, song and bell sounds.

> May your speech resound! May there be chattering, may your songs resonate like bells!
>
> (Burkhart 1992: 95)

Other lexical evidence also shows that rattles, bells and rattling sounds are linked to song and related to speech. A single word means a clear sound, like a bell, and metallic sounds.

> *tzilictic*: Something which has a clear sound, like a bell or something similar.
> *tzilini*: For metal to sound or ring.
> *tzilinia*: To ring a bell or something similar.
>
> (Campbell 1985: 380)

In fact, the root *nahuatl*, meaning clear sound or order, also appears in compound nominals, one of which (*nauatillalia*) means town statutes; used in derived verb forms such as *nauati* (to speak loudly, or for a bell to have a good sound, or something similar), it can mean "something that sounds good like a bell or a man who speaks well" (Campbell 1985:201). These definitions link good bell sounds, order and laws or statutes; they suggest that sound transforms, it creates (Hosler 1994).

Sound and color

The idea that metallic sound can create metallic colors appears in these texts; it is through song and sound that the sacred shimmering garden comes into being, as the following stanza from *Cantares Mexicanos* shows.

> As colors I devise them. I strew them as flowers in the Place of Good Song.
> As jewel mats, shot with jade and emerald sunray, the Green Place flower
> songs are radiating green. A flower incense, flaming all around, spreads sky
> aroma, filled with sunshot mist, as I, the singer, in this gentle rain of flowers
> sing before the Ever Present, the Ever Near.
>
> (Bierhorst 1985: 141)

The same idea appears in other metaphors. These also show, however, that sound
and color can come into being through precisely the same process, and that process
can be a metallurgical one.

> I drill my songs as though they were jades. I smelt them as gold. I mount
> these songs of mine as though they were jades.
>
> (Bierhorst 1985: 207)

Smelting, that is winning metal from its ore through heat, gives birth to sound
(and song), and it also gives birth to the golden metallic colors. Sound and golden
metallic colors come into being in the same way. The material result is metallic
sound-and-color objects: the high-tin and high-arsenic bronze bells that constituted
one of the unusual technical achievements of Period 2 smiths.

The associations of metallic sound and metallic colors also appear in relation to
Xipe, god of the metalsmiths. Xipe's name may derive from Nahuatl terms related
to foreskin, to scrape or peel, to the head of the penis (Campbell 1985) and
to layer. His insignia is the *chicauaztli*. Heyden (1986: 38) and others have noted
that the rattlestick, which initiates thunder to attract rain, is an analog to the
phallus. The rattlestick is sometimes represented as a serpent. Xipe is the god who
loses (or peels) the skin, or puts on a layer of skin. Xipe can also be the rattlesnake
that loses its skin but grows a new one. The god represents the earth that loses
its skin after the harvest, and gains a new one with new vegetation, with the new
rains. The new rains are brought about by the rattling of the rattlestick. Xipe is
also the god of metalworkers. Metals are something that comes from the earth and
the gods. They are divine emissions, powerful substances that are lost, shed
and excreted but that may also provide a new layer, such as the silvery surface
layer of copper-silver alloys.

The symbolic in West Mexican metallurgy

I have explored the question of the meaning, in ancient West Mexico, of the two
elements that shaped the development of this prehistoric technology. Both pertain
to the domain of religious ideology, and they are related to one another. Sound,
here metallic sound, created color, particularly metallic color, at least in this
partial interpretation of Nahuatl devotional poetry. In considering the varieties and
numbers of metal artifacts thus far present in the West Mexican corpus, only a

small component (certain tools) belonged to strictly utilitarian spheres. The vast majority of the items fashioned during Period 2 were either sounding objects, golden or silvery colored objects, or both.

I have argued that the sounds of rattles and bells promote human and agricultural fertility, they create order and they protect. They also create color, a glittering sacred paradise full of lustrous beings. The importance of bells is not only apparent in their variety and abundance, and the ways they are used in specific rites, but is encoded in language. The material, metal, and a kind of object made from it, bells, were inextricably associated. Metal and bells were cultural synonyms. The golden and silvery colors of some bells amplify their sacred and powerful qualities. The other golden and silvery objects that appear in the West Mexican repertoire may represent and create the shimmering sacred garden, through their reflective qualities and because gold and silver are specifically identified with the solar and lunar deities.

The West Mexican case strikingly demonstrates the ways in which symbolic and ideological factors can shape technologies. The relative weight of ideological as opposed to other factors varies with the particulars of the social and environmental circumstances. I touch on this problem for the West Mexican case elsewhere (Hosler 1994). Unfortunately we do not yet have the cross-cultural archaeological and technical data necessary to understand in a more general way how these variables interact; under what circumstances certain factors take precedence over others. What is clear from this discussion is that this ancient metallurgy emphasized certain physical properties, sound and color, which expressed fundamental religious beliefs, and that those beliefs were embedded in, and perpetuated through the technology and its products.

References

Anonymous (1991). *Diccionario Grande de la Lengua de Michoacán*, 2 vols (introduction and notes by B. Warren). Morelia: FIMAX.

Bierhorst, John (1985). *Cantares Mexicanos: Songs of the Aztecs*. Stanford, CA: Stanford University Press.

Brand, Donald D. (1951). *Quiroga: A Mexican Municipio*. Washington, DC: United States Printing Office.

Broda, Johanna (1970). Tlacxipehualiztli: a reconstruction of an Aztec calendar festival from 16th century sources. *Revista Española de Antropología Americana*, 5: 197–274.

Brundage, Burr C. (1982). *The Phoenix of the Western World: Quetzalcoatl and the Sky Religion*. Norman: University of Oklahoma Press.

Burkhart, Louise M. (1992). Flowery heaven: the aesthetic of paradise in Nahuatl devotional literature. *Res*, 21: 89–109.

Campbell, R. Joe (1985). *A Morphological Dictionary of Classical Nahuatl: A Morpheme Index to the Vocabulario en Lengua Mexicana y Castellana of Fray Alonso de Molina*. Madison: Hispanic Seminary of Medieval Studies.

Emmerich, André (1965). *Sweat of the Sun and Tears of the Moon*, Seattle: University of Washington Press.

Heyden, Doris (1986). Metaphors, *Nahualtocaitl*, and other "disguised" terms among the Aztecs. In *Symbol and Meaning Beyond the Closed Community: Essays in Mesoamerican Ideas* (ed. G.H. Gossen). Albany: Institute for Mesoamerican Studies, pp. 35–43.

Hill, Jane H. (1987). The flowery world of old Uto-Aztecan. Paper presented at the 86th Annual Meeting of the American Anthropological Association, Chicago.

Hosler, Dorothy (1986). *The Origins, Technology, and Social Construction of Ancient West Mexican Metallurgy*. PhD Dissertation, University of California, Santa Barbara.

Hosler, Dorothy (1988a). Ancient West Mexican metallurgy: a technological chronology. *Journal of Field Archaeology*, 15: 191–217.

Hosler, Dorothy (1988b). Ancient West Mexican metallurgy: South and Central American origins and West Mexican transformations. *American Anthropologist*, 90: 832–55.

Hosler, Dorothy (1988c). The metallurgy of Ancient West Mexico. In *The Beginning of the Use of Metals and Alloys* (ed. R. Maddin). Cambridge, MA: MIT Press, pp. 328–43.

Hosler, Dorothy (1994). *The Sounds and Colors of Power: The Sacred Metallurgy of Ancient West Mexico*. Cambridge, MA: MIT Press.

Hosler, Dorothy and Stresser-Péan, Guy (1992). The Huastec Region: a second locus for the production of bronze alloys in ancient Mesoamerica. *Science*, 257: 1215–20.

Hosler, Dorothy, Lechtman, Heather and Holm, Olaf (1990). *Axe-Monies and Their Relatives*. Washington, DC: Dumbarton Oaks.

Hunt, Eva (1977). *The Transformation of the Hummingbird: Cultural Roots of a Zinacantecan Mythical Poem*. Ithaca, NY: Cornell University Press.

Karttunen, Frances (1992). *An Analytical Dictionary of Nahuatl*. Norman: University of Oklahoma Press.

Lechtman, Heather (1979). Issues in Andean metallurgy. In *Pre-Columbian Metallurgy of South America* (ed. Elizabeth P. Benson). Washington, DC: Dumbarton Oaks, pp. 1–40.

Lechtman, Heather (1993). Technologies of power – the Andean case. In *Configurations of Power in Complex Society* (ed. John S. Henderson and Patricia J. Netherly). Ithaca; NY: Cornell University Press, pp. 244–80.

Matos M., Eduardo (1987). The Templo Mayor of Tenochtitlan: history and interpretation. In *The Great Temple of Tertochtitlan: Center and Periphery in the Aztec World* (ed. J. Broda, D. Carrasco and E. Matos M.). Berkeley: University of California Press, pp. 15–60.

Neumann, Frank J. (1974). The rattle-stick of Xipe Totec: a shamanic element in prehispanic Mesoamerican religion. In *41st International Congress of Americanists*, vol. 2. Mexico, pp. 243–51.

Pasztory, Esther (1974). *The Iconography of the Teotihuacan Tlaloc*. Washington, DC: Dumbarton Oaks.

Pollard, Helen P. (1993). *Taríacuri's Legacy: The Prehispanic Tarascan State*. Norman: University of Oklahoma Press.

Reichel-Dolmatoff, Gerardo (1988). *Orfebrería y chamanismo*. Medellín: Editorial Colina.

Sahagún, Fray Bernardino de (1950–82). *Florentine Codex: General History of the Things of New Spain*, 13 vols (trans. A.J.O. Anderson and C.E. Dibble). Santa Fe: School of American Research.

Sahagún, Fray Bernadino de (1993). *Psalmodia Christiana: Christian Psalmody* (trans. A.J.O. Anderson). Salt Lake City: University of Utah Press.

Stanford, E. Thomas (1966). A linguistic analysis of music and dance terms for three sixteenth-century dictionaries of Mexican Indian languages. In *Yearbook II of the Inter-American Institute for Musical Research*. New Orleans: Tulane University Press, pp. 101–59.

Stephenson, Robert (1968). *Music in Aztec and Inca Territory*. Berkeley: University of California Press.

Townsend, Richard F. (1992). *The Aztecs*. London: Thames and Hudson.

Tudela, José (transcriber) 1977. *Relation de las ceremonias y ritos y población y gobierno de los indios de la provincia de Michoacán (1541)*. Morelia: Balsal Editores.

Warren, J. Benedict (1985). *The Conquest of Michoacán: The Spanish Domination of the Tarascan Kingdom in Western Mexico, 1521–1530*. Norman: University of Oklahoma Press.

ARCHAEOLOGICAL IMAGININGS
Contextualization of Images

Persis B. Clarkson

> Landscape is a cultural process.
>
> (Ingold 1994:738)

Ever since 1926, when Alfred Kroeber, Julio Tello, and Toribio Mejia Xesspe stood on a hill outside the modern town of Nazca, Peru, and noticed straight lines etched into the desert surface, hypotheses and speculations about the origin and purpose of the geoglyphs have pervaded the literature. That these explanations have been grounded largely in the performance and discourse of contemporary scientific, anthropological, archaeological, and social theories (see Harding 1983), as well as current events, has been previously explored (Clarkson 1985, 1990). In recent years, a series of intensive studies of the geoglyphs and related phenomena have engaged researchers in inter- and multi-disciplinary textual constructions of the origin and purpose of the geoglyphs. Separately and together, the considerations of astronomical orientations, the identification and ages of the associated archaeological remains, the shape categories of the geoglyphs, the environmental parameters of the region, the modern and historic ethnographic associations and analogies, and modern and ancient pan-Andean phenomena have provided researchers with what are considered to be plausible hypotheses about the origins and purposes of these ground features. In a positivist textuality we would note that recent intensive fieldwork has further allowed us to validate, reject, or reconsider previous hypotheses based on the verification of the presence/absence of certain reported features. This paper is a critical analysis of these texts.

The Nazca geoglyph phenomenon is currently understood through the parts that comprise the whole system as currently defined: geometric and biomorphic ground drawings created upon broad flat expanses of desert pavement that cannot serve any life-sustaining "functional", i.e., subsistence or residential, purpose, and which therefore demands "ideological" explanations. These reductionist readings would have us believe that an entire phenomenon – be it mechanical or cultural – can be understood if it is reduced to its smallest components.

What I perceive to be absent from the explorations is an other [sic] side of the hermeneutic circle of understanding: in addition to understanding the whole of the Nazca geoglyph phenomenon from the parts, we also need to explore the whole in order to understand the parts. What I suggest here is a consideration of the landscape in which the geoglyphs are contained – the entire *text* which includes both the semantic units, in a metaphoric sense (geoglyphs) and the context (landscape). The geoglyphs are, of course, a transformation – an active trope of physical space – in a transformed physical space which in turn results in an ideological space, or the performance of ideology on the ground, and are thus like apparently static plays. This ideology is "grounded" in two textual fields: an insider's field of the ancient Nazca geoglyph creators whose ideology is not accessible, and an outsider's field comprised of the interpreters. It is this textuality of the interpreters that interests me.

What is a landscape? Any definition is inextricably interwoven with perception, which channels and frames experience. There is what I believe to be a mistaken impression that perception can be fit within a universally constructed and understood method of observation under the aegis of disinterested scientific objectivity (Cosgrove 1984). Science is not objective but phrased within cultural and temporal frameworks (Harding 1983).

Thus, the academic construction of "real" and "perceived" environment is highly ambiguous, personal, and fleeting; because of this ambiguity, perception is not static but is always changing (Croll and Parkin 1992). I agree with Ingold (1992:53) that "culture is a framework not for *perceiving* the world, but for *interpreting* it, to oneself and others". Perception is a transformation of deep structures onto the tangible (Hodder 1987:138), and thus perception and conception cannot be separated (Pickles 1985; Rose 1980). Phenomenology in geography is concerned with "the investigation of people's 'lived world' of experience . . . 'Space' is converted into 'place', defined as a centre of meaning or a focus of human emotional attachment" (Hodder 1987:140).

"Environmental perception" is a branch of geography that is also known by the more popular term "sacred landscapes". Ethnographic studies of landscapes rely in part upon cultural or natural markers throughout the landscape to identify areas of specific importance, such as ritual or kin-related associations. The markers may be conceptualized only by the people to whom the area is significant and not recognized by those not privy to the language of the landscape (see Strehlow 1970; Tuan 1975). As well, an example from the Gabbra of the Kenyan/Ethiopian highlands suggests that the perception of the environment is multi-directional: for the

Gabbra, the landscape has a claim on the people as well as the people having a claim on the landscape (Schlee 1992:118).

Geographers and archaeologists traditionally have tended to perceive landscapes as culturally constructed and separate from natural environment. For them, landscapes are shaped over time by human use, inevitably altering the pristine original environment; empty "space" is converted into "place" by a human connection: a name, a memory, a monument, a reshaping (Hodder 1987:140; see also Hirsch 1995). In 1941 Carl Sauer stated that the historical geographer "needs the ability to see the land with the eyes of its former inhabitants, from the standpoint of their needs and capacities" (Leighly 1963). This Jimminy Cricket model reduces the human experience to bare necessities of physical survival and constrains the social, cultural, and ideological framework within which survival functions. The indigenous perception of the environment embodies more than the scientifically describable environment.

> Western Apache conceptions of the land work in specific ways to influence Apaches' conceptions of themselves (and vice versa), and that the two together work to influence patterns of social action. To reject this possibility – or, as many ecologists would be inclined to do, to rule it out a priori as inconsequential – would have the effect of "removing" the Apache from the world as they have constructed it. This, in turn, would obliterate all aspects of their moral relationship with the land.
>
> (Basso 1984:49)

As archaeologists, we look at maps, we look at airphotos, we note the location of geographic features such as rivers, valleys, mountains, roads, water sources, and archaeological sites. This kind of "high in the sky" imaging may have been present figuratively, ideologically, or factually to the ancient inhabitants of the region, but we can neither presume nor project such a semiotic system. This concept is presented nicely in a short story by Barbara Kingsolver called "Homeland". In this story, a family is going to travel to Great Grandmother's birthplace in the Cherokee nation.

> Papa unfolded the Texaco map on the table and found where Tennessee and North Carolina and Georgia came together in three different pastel colors. Great Mam looked down at the colored lines and squinted, holding the sides of her glasses. "Is this the Hiwassee River?" she wanted to know.
>
> "No, now those lines are highways," he said. "Red is the interstate. Blue is river."
>
> "Well, what's this?"
>
> He looked. "That's the state line."
>
> "Now why would they put that on the map? You can't see it."
>
> Contrary to popular opinion, "facts" do not speak for themselves.
>
> (Wagstaff 1987)

In order to begin to construct an interpretation of the framework of the entire landscape to the ancient inhabitants of the Nazca region, a "critical" – in a semantically precise way – performance of a textual deconstruction or a deconstruction of existing texts, is necessary.

Our culture is profoundly technocentric, and as such our image of Nazca figures is based on and tied to the use of technology – airphotos, maps, etc. The "image" of Nazca geoglyphs is therefore static, frozen within a bordered distant "reality". Geographer David Lowenthal has traced the notion of literally "seeing" the past to the proliferation of book illustrations in the late 18th century that accustomed us to thinking of the past as a "visual experience" (Lowenthal 1985:257; see also Lowenthal 1982; Penning-Rowsell and Lowenthal 1986; Soja 1989). The technological advantage of photographs, wherein simulacra and durable images present a static image to the readers, encases the reading from any moving or processual context of the image. I believe that the reality of the ancient Nazqueños is grounded, metaphorically speaking, in a processual and thus interactive performance. As an example, consider Northwest coast masks as we see them in a museum as static objects versus how they are employed in performance, which is decidedly not static. We can transfer this notion to the Nazca geoglyphs: why presume that they are any less processual?

Another domain of interpretation involves ranking the superiority of content over process. When we recount dreams, we describe the characters and their actions in a setting. Yet, a colleague studying the significance of dreams in a northern Alberta native community learned that who, what, why, where, and when are irrelevant: it is how you *feel* when you awake and recall the dream. I am not suggesting that we use dreams as a key to understanding past cultural productions – I am only stating that there are alternative domains of reference and context.

Still another domain of interpretation involves our assumption and projection of a dualistic nature of society, wherein we separate the sacred and the profane. Anthropological studies have shown us that this is not necessarily the case, that the embodiment of the sacred within the secular is normal. Thus, text (ideologies) can deal with a series of interpretations at the same time.

A major impediment to interpreting geoglyphs has been the lack of ethnographic analogies and models. Lewis-Williams (1982:430) has pointed out that the often-cited "hunting magic" model applied to rock art was based on "vague and misguided notions of 'primitive mentality' rather than on reliable ethnography". There is a false perception, according to Whitley, that meaning can be obtained only by talking to informants (Whitley 1992:76; Whitley and Loendorf 1994:xiv). Lewis-Williams used an anthropological-archaeological investigation to show that recent ethnographic studies that focus on the representations produced through the hallucinations of shamans can be used to understand much earlier rock art in southern Africa (Lewis-Williams 1981, 1982). He also applied neuropsychological models to Upper Paleolithic art (Lewis-Williams 1991; Lewis-Williams and Dowson 1988).

As a person thoroughly grounded in positivist thinking, this process of thinking about ancient texts does not come easily to me: I recognize that scientific method is highly biased, but lack the faith to step to a different drummer. Yet the more I have worked on – literally and metaphorically – Nazca geoglyphs, the more I am disappointed with the parameters of positivist paradigm wherein analogies are the only legitimate means by which archaeologists can stray from the hard facts of our science. The past *is* inaccessible to us, yet, we continue to transform cultural texts according to our own needs. This is not inherently "wrong", but it does need to be explicitly acknowledged.

Postmodern applications of discourse analysis place it within the realm of reading text as an active form of text. In anthropology, this new "moment" began with Geertz (E. Silverman 1990), who moved away from a positivist (cultural-ecological) paradigm to his notions about the nature and impact of "thick description". Roy Wagner (1986) supplemented this pivotal "turn" in anthropology by applying and developing the notion of trope and tropic analysis. More recently, post-modern anthropologists have deployed the work and notions of Derrida (Yates 1990). These applications would have us see ethnographic texts as intertextual works that are mediated by the existing corpus of ethnographic studies. Some of the major/significant components of discourse analysis, as noted by Barnes and Duncan in *Writing Worlds* (1992:2) indicate three major considerations:

i   written texts do not reflect "reality": reality is a highly individualistic and culturally bounded concept. Texts and constructions, constructions that are perceived to be real. Thus, the region of Nazca geoglyphs consists of plural perceptual fields;

ii   writing is dependent upon prior interpretations and thus ought to be reflexive; we reinterpret text to make it familiar to the present state – the status quo – as a cultural product and producer of cultural performance; the result is to render readings comprehensible, as well as to justify them; and

iii   what is written about is revealing not only about the text but about the author as well – social, political, and historical context, and the genre of the writing, e.g., for an academic journal, a newspaper article, etc.

Explorations of discourse analysis within archaeology have focused upon archaeological monuments as "texts" to be "read". For example, a significant body of literature exists on discourse analysis of Neolithic monuments of western Europe (see Tilley 1994). These consider the significance of polysemous texts, wherein the production of the text can be separate from the "meaning", as explored in Wagner's (1986) *Symbols That Stand For Themselves*, wherein symbols are recursively constructed, and where the meaning derived is an appropriation by the reader to translate from what is alien to something familiar. What I find uncomfortable about many of these interpretations of Neolithic monuments is the appropriation of meaning that is heavily weighted in favour of Euro-derived textuality: they provide a veneer of empiricist construction, but they tell us much about the interpreters and their cultural and academic strictures and performance. Limits that are imposed upon interpretations appear to be uncritical to the understanding that systems of perception can and do vary greatly from those of western science.

Tilley (1991) has written an account of interpretation of rock art from Nämforsen, Sweden called *Material culture and text: The art of ambiguity*. While I disagree with many of his conclusions as well as his methodology for determining meanings of Nämforsen rock art, I am intrigued by his explicit use of theoretical structuralist, hermeneutic, and Marxist frameworks to construct meanings that are by their very nature ambiguous. Tilley admits in a somewhat tongue-in-cheek manner that it is impossible to produce a complete account of the past – although this does not stop him from creating what are for me some overzealous interpretations of the rock art. But if there are numerous meanings that can be applied to material culture, activities, and behaviours of the present, why should the past be different?

The polysemous nature of "representations" is well illustrated by examples from Australian Aboriginal groups. Morphy (1989:144) notes that art not only mediates between the ancestral past and the present, but is an extension of that past into the present: art is the means by which information is passed to succeeding generations. Among some Aboriginal groups, the art produced by men and women creates representations of different significance: for women the art refers to activities of the ancestors in generalized ways and day-to-day activities, while that of men refers to specific ancestors (Munn 1973:27, cited in Tilley 1991:166). Whitley (personal communication 1995), whose work on rock art has focused upon that of the desert western US, has noted that different kinds of rock art function within the same culture, and that the ethnographic literature indicates differences in male and female symbolism within the landscape and within rock art. As well, Loendorf (personal communication 1995) has collected much evidence to indicate that rock art in the Grand Canyon and elsewhere is used over and over again. By extension, then, any single representation can be interpreted quite differently by contemporaneous, different sexes or genders, and distinct representations may be linked within a single cultural and temporal sphere (see Ingold 1993:152).

A brief example will illustrate how landscape perception *can* vary. The anthropologist Dorothy Eggan was asked by her Hopi informant to describe from memory a particular view at the Grand Canyon. Eggan described the path as crossing and winding in and out of view, while the Hopi described the path as always there, even when he could not see it. While her informant could understand her meaning, the terminology differed, particularly on the point of description of a footpath (Tuan 1975).

The long and intensive debate over whether it is possible to reconstruct past belief systems is irrelevant to the framework proposed here. If we acknowledge, instead, that the original intention of the text – whether it is geoglyphs, rock art, textile designs, oral text, etc. – will not necessarily coincide with the meaning derived at any point in time that the text is "read", then we can appreciate that the meaning of any representation/text is unstable. This is intrinsic in the quality of text: that it is dynamic and constantly troping. We treat texts as iconographs, frozen throughout time, yet the meaning was always to be moving, always shifting. Our thinking is intrinsically linear, while Hegellian dialectics are not linear and thus there is no resolution: we move from thesis to synthesis to antithesis and continue on through the same stages over again. Exploration of texts suggests that they are never read passively but are in essence rewritten as they are read. This "distanciation" of the text (Ricoeur 1981) indicates that what was originally *produced* is not necessarily equivalent to the original or any subsequently imposed or derived *meaning*.

The implications for "reading" geoglyphs that have been viewed, read, and "edited" since their original creation suggest that singular linear positivist readings are neither necessary nor practical. Polyvalency can be inherent in the intention or the interpretation at any point, and does not necessarily reflect a lack of commitment to conclusion. Tilley (1991: 78–86) refers to the notion of "mobile space, arrested time", noting that the series of rock carvings at Nämforsen must have at some point or points in time been considered as a unified work, regardless of whether the images were made individually at different times or all created at once.

If we look at the three components of discourse analysis as mentioned earlier, we can see that historically, the textual interpretations of geoglyphs have displayed much about the nature of the researchers and very little critical or discursive insight into what constitutes "reality".

Nazca: an example

Geoglyphs are known throughout a wide region of the western American continent, and although concentrated in and around the Nazca region, there are particular stylistic configurations and concentrations within the Nazca region that have not been reported elsewhere in western deserts. Most specifically, the biomorphic figures, of which there are approximately forty, are concentrated within a small area of approximately five by eight miles/kilometers, with the exception of a few known biomorphs near the Palpa and Socos drainages (Clarkson 1990).

An early phase of interpretation encompassed global analogies relevant to the interests of the researchers or concurrent with global events, particularly with our technocentrism. The popularity of the astronomical interpretations of the Nazca geoglyphs beginning in the 1940s focused on *who* made the geoglyphs. These hypotheses came about in an era of interest in aliens from outer space (such as Orson Welles' radio drama *War of the Worlds* and von Däniken's 1969 *Chariots of the Gods*) and incipient space exploration (Sputnik launch in 1957), and proceeded directly from archaeoastronomical studies of Stonehenge. The images of the Nazca pampas from the air, facilitated by aerial photography and by LANDSAT imagery, have crystallized our image of the Nazca pampas and geoglyphs and have facilitated the alienation of the geoglyphs from any ground view. No one draws them from the ground for modern purposes of illustration, and photos from the ground of "figural geoglyphs" are meant for illustration of environment.

The geoglyphs in northern Chile (Briones and Chacama 1987; Clarkson i.p.; Núñez 1976), on the other hand, have not been subjected to the same fate. Why? There are images that are as "alien" as anything one could perceive at Nazca, and there are far more of them than are found in the Nazca region. I think that the difference lies in the "ease" with which the Chilean geoglyphs can be viewed: situated on hillsides, they require no effort and thus are mundane.

More recent positivist constructions of the history of the Nazca region indicate a desire to quantify *when* the geoglyphs were made as a means to "objectify" who made them. These studies have shown that geoglyphs were made and used in the Nazca region over many centuries, and that this span may have included more than one recognizable cultural tradition (Clarkson 1990; Isbell 1978; Silverman and Browne 1991). Diagnostic ceramics from all cultural epochs, spanning approximately two thousand years from the Early Horizon through the Late Horizon, associated with the geoglyphs indicate reuse of specific geoglyphs subsequent to their initial creation. Diagnostic iconographic elements of geoglyphs that can be tied in with specific time periods based on ceramic iconography are a third means by which repeated use in antiquity over long periods of time has been determined. Repeated use over time without any indications of time depth are evident from the numerous "overlapped" geoglyphs throughout the entire region; further use of overlapping biomorphic geoglyphs as relative time markers is inappropriate because they have been swept for decades to enhance their visibility from the air.

Thus, the *discourse* of the geoglyphs is negotiable and mutable, dependent upon the particular set of parameters brought to them by the users/readers. These varying parameters are not the result of intercultural or diachronic factors, as we know from modern experience that people who speak the same language can "talk past one another". However, this does not mean that we are free to read whatever we wish into the geoglyphs. As Stock (1990) notes, the readings must be undertaken within the conceptual framework of the cultural discourse of the original creators. The geographer Pickles notes that in the interpretation of maps

> we need a theory of writing and reading which moves beyond naive empiricism and representationalism, and which does not trivialize the tracings and inscriptions of culture or literalize them, but which integrates and reforms the modes of discourse appropriate to reading. We need a broader conception of the nature of writing.
>
> (Pickles 1992: 228)

The context of the Nazca geoglyphs is visually unique. From a stationary location on the Pampa San José in the environs of biomorphs, one sees the pampa slope away from the Andes and then level off into the southern distance. Occasional isolated hills dot the landscape, and Cerro Blanco, the most prominent peak visually and ideologically, is barely visible in the distance to the southeast; another smaller white topped peak is far more visible and closer (Is this an ideological transposition of Cerro Blanco?). From a mobile situation, one crosses washes where there is a jumble of stones, vegetation, sometimes debris and a lighter colour; one crosses undisturbed mesas of darkly varnished patinated stones; one crosses deeply cut washes that emanate from the Andes. The horizon changes slowly; as far as we know, there were no (archaeological) sites visible in antiquity, with the possible exception of Cahuachi, which may have been visible from the Pampa San José during or after its occupation. From the pampas closer to Nazca, where there are very few biomorphic figures, the Aja and Tierras Blancas branches of the Río Nazca cut into the mountains rapidly; the Río Taruga runs across the southern margins of the region through soft buff-coloured sandy alluvium. Linear geoglyphs predominate in this region, although they become scarcer as the surface becomes increasingly unstable due to slope and water run-off from the Andes.

One could reduce the parameters of where geoglyphs are inscribed to a laundry list that would include patinated desert pavements that have produced a dark and stable surface unaffectable by water. But this describes a huge area that extends beyond the Nazca region under consideration here, only some of which is known to have geoglyphs. None of these areas reproduce the concentration of biomorphs in the restricted area of pampa near the Río Ingenio. This is an area bounded and at the same time open to the presence of the Andes: the mountains come to the edge of the area, and the deeply incised Río Ingenio clearly derives from the Andes mountains. You cannot see the Ingenio from most of these geoglyphs, but the configuration of mountains leaves no doubt as to where it is from any place in this area.

Reconsideration

If some of these modernly conceptualized landscapes are invisible to those outside the "system", should we assume that landscapes in which archaeologists work were conceptualized and contextualized in ways that are different from our own, and that these conceptualizations may be beyond the realm of comprehension or discovery? These questions are no different than those with which the discipline of archaeology constantly wrestles: is the past a closed system that is unavailable to us because we cannot be ethnographers to document the interrelationships between material and behavioural culture? For purposes here I will take an optimistic stance and assume that the past is at least explorable but that we must recognize the limitations. If we don't begin to think about interpretations of imagery and text differently, we will never come to different and new interpretations or make any headway in understanding the peoples who made and "read" those texts.

References

Barnes, Trevor J. and James S. Duncan (1992). *Writing worlds: discourse, text and metaphor in the representation of landscape*. London: Routledge.

Basso, Keith. (1984). Stalking with stories: names, places, and moral narratives among the Western Apache. In *Text, play, and story: the construction and reconstruction of self and society*. Edited by Edward M. Bruner, pp. 19–55. Washington, DC: American Ethnological Society.

Briones, Luis and Juan Chacama. (1987). Arte rupestre de Ariquilda: análisis descriptivo de un sitio con geoglifos y su vinculación con la prehistoria regional. *Chungará* 18: 15–66.

Clarkson, Persis B. (1985). The archaeology and geoglyphs of Nazca, Peru. Unpublished PhD dissertation, Department of Archaeology, University of Calgary.

—— (1990). The archaeology of the Nazca pampa: environmental and cultural parameters. In *The Lines of Nazca*. Edited by Anthony F. Aveni, pp. 117–172. Philadelphia: American Philosophical Society Memoir, volume 183.

—— in press. Técnicos en la determinación de las edades cronologicas de los geoglifos. *Chungará*.

Cosgrove, Denis E. (1984). *Social formation and symbolic landscape*. London: Croom Helm.

Croll, Elisabeth and David Parkin, eds. (1992). *Bush base: forest farm: culture, environment and development*. London and New York: Routledge.

Harding, Sandra. (1983). Why has the sex/gender system become visible only now? In *Discovering reality: feminist perspectives on epistemology, metaphysics, methodology, and philosophy of science*. Edited by Sandra Harding and Merill Hintikka, pp. 311–324. Boston: D. Reidel.

Hirsch, Eric. (1995). Landscape: between place and space. In *The anthropology of landscape: perspectives on place and space*. Edited by Eric Hirsch and Michael O'Hanlon, pp. 1–30. Oxford: Clarendon Press.

Hodder, Ian. (1987). Converging traditions: the search for symbolic meanings in archaeology and geography. In *Landscape and culture: geographical and archaeological perspectives*. Edited by J.M. Wagstaff, pp. 134–145. Oxford: Basil Blackwell Ltd.

Ingold, Tim. (1992). Culture and the perception of environment. In *Bush base: forest farm: culture, environment and development*. Edited by Elisabeth Croll and David Parkin, pp. 39–56. London and New York: Routledge.

—— (1993). The temporality of the landscape. *World Archaeology* 25(2): 152–174.

—— (1994). Introduction to social life. In *Companion encyclopedia of anthropology: humanity, culture and social life*. Edited by Tim Ingold, pp. 737–755. London: Routledge.

Isbell, William. (1978). The prehistoric ground drawings of Peru. *Scientific American* 239(4): 140–153.

Kingsolver, Barbara. (1989). Homeland. *Homeland and other stories*.

Leighly, J. (ed.) (1963). *Land and Life: a selection from the writings of Carl Ortwin Sauer*. Berkeley: University of California Press.

Lewis-Williams, J.D. (1981). *Believing and seeing: symbolic meaning in southen San rock paintings*. London: Academic Press.

—— (1982). The economic and social contexts of southern San rock art. *Current Anthropology* 23: 429–450.

—— (1991). Wrestling with analogy: a methodological dilemma in Upper Palaeolithic art research. *Proceedings of the Prehistoric Society* 57(1): 149–162.

Lewis-Williams, J.D. and T.A. Dowson. (1988). The signs of all times: entopitic phenomena in Upper Paleolithic art. *Current Anthropology* 31: 80–84.

Lowenthal, David. (1982). Revisiting valued environments. In *Valued environments*. Edited by John R. Gold and Jacquelin Burgess, pp. 74–99. London: George Allen and Unwin.

—— (1985). *The past is a foreign country*. Cambridge: Cambridge University Press.

Munn, Nancy D. (1973). *Walbiri iconograhy*. Chicago: University of Chicago Press.

Morphy, Howard. (1989). On representing ancestral beings. In *Animals into art*. Edited by Howard Morphy, pp. x–x. London: Unwin-Hyman.

Núñez, Lautaro. (1976). Geoglifos y trafico de caravanas en el desierto chileno. In *Anales de la Universidad del Norte (Chile)* No. 10, *Homenaje al Dr. Gustavo le Paige, SJ*, pp. 147–201.

Penning-Rowsell, Edmund C. and David Lowenthal, eds, (1986). *Landscape meanings and values*. London: Allen and Unwin.

Pickles, John. (1985). *Phenomenology, science and geography: spatiality and the human sciences*. Cambridge: Cambridge University Press.

—— (1992). Texts, hermeneutics and propaganda maps. In *Writing worlds: discourse, text and metaphor in the representation of landscape*. Edited by Trevor Barnes and James S. Duncan, pp. 193–230. London: Routledge.

Ricoeur, Paul. (1981). *Hermeneutics and the human sciences*. Cambridge: Cambridge University Press.

Rose, Courtice. (1980). Human geography as text interpretation. In *The human experience of space and place*. Edited by Anne Buttimer and David Seamon, pp. 123–134. London: Croom Helm.

Schlee, Günther (1992). Ritual topograhy and ecological use. In *Bush base: forest farm: culture, environment and development*. Edited by Elisabeth Croll and David Parkin, pp. 110–128. London: Routledge.

Silverman, Eric Kline. (1990). Clifford Geertz: Towards a more "thick" understanding? In *Reading Material Culture*. Edited by Christopher Tilley, pp. 121–159. Oxford: Basil Blackwell.

Silverman, Helaine and David Browne. (1991). New evidence for the date of the Nazca lines. *Antiquity* 65(247): 208–220.

Soja, Edward W. (1989). *Postmodern geographies: the reassertion of space in critical social theory*. London: Verso.

Stock, Brian. (1990). *Listening for the text: on the uses of the past*. Baltimore: Johns Hopkins University Press.

Strehlow, T.G.H. (1970). Geography and the totemic landscape in central Australia: a functional study. In *Australian aboriginal anthropology: modern studies in the social anthropology of the Australian Aborigines*. Edited by Ronald M. Berndt, pp. 92–140. Nedlands: University of Western Australia Press.

Tilley, Christopher. (1991). *Material culture and text: The art of ambiguity*. London: Routledge.

—— (1994) *A phenomenology of landscape: places, paths and monuments*. Oxford: Berg.

Tuan, Yi-Fu. (1975). Images and mental maps. *Annals of the Association of American Geographers* 65: 205–213.

von Däniken, Eric. (1969). *Chariots of the gods? Unsolved mysteries of the past*. Translated by Michael Heron. London: Souvenir Press.

Wagner, Roy. (1986). *Symbols that stand for themselves*. Chicago: University of Chicago Press.

Wagstaff, J.M. (1987). Introduction. In *Landscape and culture: geographical and archaeological perspectives*. Edited by J.M. Wagstaff, pp. 1–10. Oxford: Basil Blackwell.

Whitley, David S. (1992). Prehistory and post-positivist science: a prolegomenon to cognitive archaeology. In *Archaeological method and theory*, volume 4. Edited by Michael B. Schiffer pp. 57–100, Tucson: University of Arizona Press.

Whitley, David S. and Lawrence L. Loendorf. (1994). Off the cover and into the book. In *New light on old art: recent advances in hunter-gatherer rock art research*. Edited by David S. Whitley and Lawrence L. Loendorf, pp. xi–xx. Monograph 36, Institute of Archaeology. Los Angeles: Univesity of California.

Yates, Timothy. (1990). Jacques Derrida: "There is nothing outside of the text". In *Reading Material Culture*. Edited by Christopher Tilley, pp. 206–280. Oxford: Basil Blackwell.

PART THREE

Prehistoric cognition

INTRODUCTION

Unbeknown to many people (including archaeologists), the US Congress officially proclaimed the 1990s the "Decade of the Brain". This is a reflection of (and honor for) the rapid advancement of research and knowledge in cognitive sciences, neuroanatomy, neurophysiology, neuropsychology – subdisciplines that are probably most easily subsumed under the name "cognitive neurosciences". While it would be an exaggeration to contend that we now fully understand the workings of the human brain, it is certainly true that, as a result of this research, we are much closer to an understanding of it than ever before. Indeed, cognitive neuroscientists are now using empirical evidence to address fundamental issues that, for over two thousand years, were solely the provenance of philosophers and theologians – such as defining the nature of consciousness, the relationship of brain and mind, and the basis for human temperament (e.g., Damasio 1994; Hobson 1994; Kagan 1994).

These advances are of little importance to behaviorist archaeology because, at a basic level, behaviorism dismisses the human mind in favor of external causality. Yet once the constraints of behaviorism are removed from archaeological research in favor of cognition, the importance of the advances in cognitive neurosciences research becomes immediate. Since our archaeological data are residues of human behavior, and since human intention and thinking are actively implicated in behavior, it follows that the understanding of this behavior will at least in part lie in an understanding of the workings of the human mind. This is just as an understanding of the relationship of humans to their environment requires detailed knowledge of that very same environment.

The two papers in this section reflect two different approaches to the cognitive perspective on the archaeological record. In the first, Steven J. Mithen addresses one of the most important problems in Old World stone age research: the cause of the "Upper Paleolithic revolution". The traditional, western European view of this problem was that it reflected a transition from Neanderthal to anatomically modern humans: with the appearance of modern humans, an immediate elaboration of cultural behavior ensued, shown in the appearance of art, diverse tool assemblages, and so on. As additional archaeological evidence has been collected, this simple interpretation has become increasingly untenable. This is partly seen in fossil evidence, which shows that the anatomical transition was far from immediate, and partly in stone tool assemblages, which demonstrate that Neanderthal and modern humans in fact shared the same kinds of artifacts for thousands (if not tens of thousands) of years. Skeletal anatomy, alone, does not appear to provide an adequate explanation for this phenomenon.

Mithen looks instead to a cognitive explanation; specifically, one rooted in evolutionary changes in the human brain. But he argues that this "revolution" did not solely result from anatomical changes. Nor did it arise from the development of new intellectual abilities specific to particular mental domains. The Upper Paleolithic transition in his view was the product of an increasing ability to integrate different kinds of intelligences into a form of generalized knowledge. While this ability is unique to modern humans, he argues, it is not simply a function of the neuroanatomical transition to modern anatomical forms. In essence, this suggests that the development of generalized intelligence required the anatomically modern brain, but that it was a kind of "learned behavior" that developed after the fact. The anatomically modern brain was necessary but not sufficient for this transition to occur.

I suspect that some might question this suggestion. After all, don't human brains all essentially function in the same way? Neurophysiological evidence, in fact, indicates that while we all do share a basic neural architecture that precisely determines aspects of our mental processes, there is still considerable room for development and variability (Kosslyn and Koenig 1992:412; Damasio 1994:112). This is no better illustrated than by studies of the differences between Japanese and occidental brain functions (Tsunoda 1989). In very general terms, the left hemisphere of the human brain is responsible for speech, calculation and logic, whereas the right hemisphere predominates in the processing of music, shape recognition and emotions. Yet the brain's processing of speech is also partly predicated on differences between harmonic and non-harmonic sound waves, which are processed in the right and left hemispheres, respectively. This is important because different languages are predominated by distinctive harmonic versus non-harmonic sound wave patterns, such as those that emphasize vowels – like Japanese – versus those where consonants are dominant, as in many European languages. The same also holds for musical traditions, where harmonic versus non-harmonic scales may be employed. The result is that these sound wave differences can lead to cross-cultural variations in the location where language, music and even emotion (because it is often expressed verbally) are processed in the human brain. Moreover, studies of Japanese versus occidental children show that these differences do not become fixed until about the age of nine. Thus they are environmental, not biological or genetic, in origin. Given this flexibility in the development of the brain, it then seems very plausible, if not highly likely, that the full intellectual potential of the modern human brain was not realized until sometime long after it first appeared. Indeed, perhaps it has yet to be realized.

The sub-text of this discussion is important. Understanding the human brain will help us understand human behavior. But it will not in all cases allow us to predict it. The human mind is ordered in a regular way but, within this order, there is great room for individual and cultural variability. This is important because it denies the possibility of neuroanatomical determinism.

The second paper, by David Lewis-Williams, addresses another long-lived problem in Paleolithic archaeology: the interpretation of the famous cave paintings of western Europe. His emphasis in this presentation is primarily methodological: how can we construct a scientifically plausible argument for the origin of art in "archaeological deep-time" – 10,000 to 30,000 years BP? In this case there is no directly relevant ethnographic data to guide our interpretation although, historically, crude analogs between modern hunter-gatherers and Upper Paleolithic peoples certainly were called upon. These have been widely criticized, causing many archaeologists to reject ethnographic analogy altogether. Yet does this mean that analogy has no value in archaeological interpretation? This is a key question because, as noted a number of times throughout this volume, ethnographic analogy is an important approach used by cognitive and post-processual archaeologists alike.

Drawing from the work of archaeological philosopher Alison Wylie (1985), Lewis-Williams shows that the problem is not with analogy, *per se*, but with the form of the analogies that often have been applied. Rather than basing an analogy on one or a few look-alike correspondences, he builds his model on relations of relevance, which emphasize causal or determining principles. For Paleolithic art these are found in the human neuropsychology of trance, demonstrating, again, the importance of understanding the workings of the human mind for archaeologists. Humans react to trance in broadly similar ways, due to our shared neurophysiological system. This results in general similarities in the forms of the resulting mental images ("visual hallucinations") that we experience. Using an analytical model of the characteristics of these images, Lewis-Williams "tests" the Paleolithic art to determine if it, too, shares the characteristics of the mental imagery of trance. Because he is able to conclude affirmatively – that some if not much Paleolithic art appears to portray the mental images of trance – he can then suggest that the art is shamanistic in origin. This is because shamanism is a religious system that emphasizes the importance of trance as a kind of religious experience. Note, though, that this conclusion pertains solely to the origin of this art. Nowhere in this is Lewis-Williams able to suggest what it may have meant.

Mithen's and Lewis-Williams's papers, taken together, are notable on a couple of counts. The first is simply their complementarity. Both address in some fashion the origin of art through an understanding of the human mind, albeit on slightly different scales. Since we know that animals (and of course hominids) have (or had) the capacity to hallucinate, the possibility of experiencing trance imagery is not unique to modern humans. Neanderthal could have tranced but, in so far as we know, created no art to portray this experience. Mithen suggests that the missing ingredient was the ability to attribute meaning to visual symbols; visual symbols that Lewis-Williams identifies as originating in the mental imagery of trance.

The second notable point is one alluded to above: both archaeologists use cognitive neurosciences research to aid their understanding of archaeological deep-time. This is important inasmuch as a common reaction to cognitive archaeology is incredulity: the prehistoric mind cannot be reconstructed, many archaeologists believe. Yet it is precisely with reference to our oldest archaeological remains, and some of the most fundamental problems of research, that this form of cognitive archaeology has been most successfully applied. These include problems such as the nature and evolution of hominid intelligence (Wynn 1979, 1981, 1985, 1989; Brown 1993), and the origin of language (Isaac 1976; Wynn 1991; Steele *et al.* 1995). Not only can the prehistoric mind be reconstructed, from this view, but doing so is essential to understanding human origins and evolution.

■ ■ ■

Further reading

Lewis-Williams and Dowson 1988
Mithen 1996

Noble and Davidson 1996
von Gernet 1993
Whitley 1994, 1998
Wylie 1985

■　■　■

References

Brown, K.R. (1993) "An Alternative Approach to Cognition in the Lower Palaeolithic: The Modular View", *Cambridge Archaeological Journal* 3: 231–45.

Damasio, A. (1994) *Descartes' Error: Emotion, Reason and the Human Brain*, New York: G.P. Putnam.

Hobson, J.A. (1994) *The Chemistry of Conscious States: Towards a Unified Theory of the Brain and the Mind*, Boston: Little Brown and Company.

Isaac, G.L. (1976) "Stages of Cultural Elaboration in the Pleistocene: Possible Archaeological Indicators on the Development of Language Capabilities", *Annals of the New York Academy of Sciences* 280: 275–88.

Kagan, J. (1994) *Galen's Prophecy: Temperament in Human Behavior*, New York: Basic Books.

Kosslyn, S.M. and Koenig, O. (1992) *Wet Mind: The New Cognitive Neurosciences*, New York: Free Press.

Lewis-Williams, J.D. and Dowson, T.A. (1988) "The Signs of All Times: Entopic Phenomena in Upper Paleolithic Art", *Current Anthropology*, 29: 201–45.

Mithen, S.J. (1996) *The Prehistory of the Mind: The Cognitive Origins of Art, Religion and Science*, London: Thames and Hudson.

Noble, W. and Davidson, I. (1996) *Human Evolution, Language and Mind: A Psychological and Archaeological Inquiry*, Cambridge: Cambridge University Press.

Steele, J., Quinlan, A. and Wenban-Smith, F. (1995) "Stone Tools and the Linguistic Capabilities of Earlier Hominids", *Cambridge Archaeological Journal* 5: 245–46.

Tsunoda, T. (1989) "Hemispheric Dominance in Japan and the West", in K. Klivington (ed.) *The Science of the Mind*, Cambridge: MIT.

von Gernet, A. (1993) "The Construction of Prehistoric Ideation: Exploring the Universality–Idiosyncrasy Continuum', *Cambridge Archaeological Journal* 3: 67–81.

Whitley, D.S. (1994) "Shamanism, Natural Modeling and the Rock Art of Far Western North American Hunter-Gatherers", in S. Turpin (ed.) *Shamanism and Rock Art in North America*, San Antonio: Special Publication 1, Rock Art Foundation, Inc.

—— (1998) "Cognitive Neurosciences, Shamanism and the Rock Art of Native California", *Anthropology of Consciousness* (forthcoming).

Wylie, A. (1985) "The Reaction Against Analogy", *Advances in Archaeological Method and Theory* 8: 63–111, New York: Academic.

Wynn, T. (1979) "The Intelligence of Later Acheulean Hominids", *Man* 14: 371–91.

—— (1981) "The Intelligence of the Oldowan Hominids", *Journal of Human Evolution* 10: 529–41.

—— (1985) "Piaget, Stone Tools and the Evolution of Human Intelligence", *World Archaeology* 17: 32–43.

—— (1989) *The Evolution of Spatial Competence*, Urbana: University of Illinois.

—— (1991) "Tools, Grammar and the Archaeology of Cognition", *Cambridge Archaeological Journal* 1: 191–206.

Chapter 7

FROM DOMAIN SPECIFIC TO GENERALIZED INTELLIGENCE
A Cognitive Interpretation of the Middle/Upper Palaeolithic Transition

Steven Mithen

Introduction

One of the tasks facing cognitive archaeology is to contribute towards an understanding of the nature and evolution of the human mind. We need to make explicit reference to past cognition when interpreting the archaeological record and to draw inferences from that data concerning *ancient minds*. Did, for instance, *Homo habilis* have language, *Homo erectus* self-awareness or Neanderthals the capacity for analogical reasoning? While fossil endocasts may inform about brain structure, the character of past cognition must be largely inferred from the archaeological record. And to draw such inferences archaeologists need to engage with, or rather become participants in, the cognitive sciences – just as Bloch (1991) has recently argued for anthropology. This is essential since we cannot pretend to understand the ancient mind without entering debates concerning the character of the modern mind.

In this paper I focus on one of these debates, that concerning whether the mind is a general purpose learning mechanism or composed of a series of relatively independent mental modules – psychological mechanisms dedicated to specific tasks or behavioural domains. My review of this debate suggests that a major feature of human cognitive evolution has been increased accessibility between mental modules resulting in a generalized intelligence, though one remaining within a modular architecture. I consider whether the Middle/Upper Palaeolithic transition may have constituted a phase in human evolution during which there was a significant development from domain specific to generalized intelligence.

Mental modularity

A major question facing those concerned with the modern mind is the extent to which it is a general purpose information processor/learning mechanism, as opposed to being a series of mental modules – psychological mechanisms each dedicated to a specific purpose. A trend within cognitive science has been to see the mind as the latter, although several different notions of mental modularity have been proposed. While Fodor (1983) used the term "mental modules", others have used "adaptive specializations" (Rozin 1976), "multiple intelligences" (Gardner 1983), "Darwinian algorithms" (Cosmides and Tooby 1987) and "cognitive domains" (Cheney and Seyfarth 1990). Each of these is an alternative perspective on the same basic idea – that the mind (of humans and other animals) is composed of a series of discrete psychological mechanisms, which may be based in their own neurological structures. Also at issue is the degree of accessibility – the flow of information and transference of psychological processes between mental modules.

The existence of some degree of mental modularity is well established for many non-human animal species which display remarkable cognitive feats in some areas, but are unable to apply such information processing to other tasks. For instance, bees are able to navigate over vast distances and salmon "remember" a specific river in which they spawned; yet neither of these show comparable "intelligence" in other areas of their lives. In Cosmides and Tooby's terms, they have specific Darwinian algorithms for these tasks.

Chomsky (1972) used a similar argument to propose that human language is a discrete, partly innate, cognitive module. The speed at which children acquire language implies specialized psychological mechanisms for language acquisition, rather than the use of a general purpose learning mechanism. After children have acquired complex grammatical structures and extensive vocabulary, they may still remain limited in other cognitive domains, such as the use and manipulation of numbers.

Fodor (1983) built upon Chomsky's work to argue that not only language, but all processes of perception, should be thought of as modules. He characterized these as computationally elaborate, domain-specific and informationally encapsulated. By the latter term he referred to the limited database of knowledge they have access to. The most compelling example is the persistence of optical illusions when they are "known" to be false: the visual perception module is encapsulated from such knowledge. Fodor argued that these perceptual modules typically work very quickly and without control (e.g. one cannot stop oneself hearing other than by physical means). He found support for such notions of modularity by drawing on evolutionary theory, and citing examples of cognitive pathologies which impair some mental processes but leave others intact.

Fodor drew a contrast, however, between the modularity of perception and the generalized nature of cognition, or "central processes". According to Fodor, these latter are concerned with thought, reasoning, and problem solving – more generally with the fixation of belief. In central processes the information acquired by such module of perception is integrated to create a mental model of the world.

Multiple intelligences

The "multiple intelligences" theory developed by Gardner (1983) bears both similarities and differences to Fodor's approach. It makes no distinction between perception and cognition but characterizes the mind as composed of six types of intelligence:

- Linguistic intelligence – that concerned with phonology, syntax, semantics and pragmatics.
- Musical intelligence – the ability of individuals to discern meaning and importance in sets of pitches rhythmically arranged and also to produce such metrically arranged pitch sequences as a means of communicating with individuals.
- Logical mathematical intelligence – this concerns understanding the world of objects, actions and the relationships between these.
- Spatial intelligence – the capacity to perceive the visual world accurately, to perform transformations and modifications upon one's initial perceptions, and to be able to recreate aspects of one's visual experience even in the absence of relevant physical stimulation.
- Bodily-kinesthetic intelligence – the control of one's bodily motions and capacity to handle objects skilfully.
- Personal intelligence – this has two aspects. On the one hand it concerns access to one's own thoughts and feelings, while on the other it concerns the ability to notice and make distinctions among other individuals, with particular relation to their moods, temperaments, motivations and intentions.

Gardner argued that these intelligences interact with, and build upon, each other, but at the core of each is a computational capacity or information processing device which is unique to that particular intelligence and upon which are based the more complex realizations and embodiments of that intelligence. Gardner emphasized the significance of the cultural environment as to the manner in which type of intelligence will develop in each person. He noted the stress laid in the Western world on logical-mathematical intelligence. On this basis, he criticized Piagetian approaches for their almost sole focus on this when building a supposedly general theory of cognitive development.

Social and non-social intelligence

Gardner's notion of "personal intelligence" is essentially the same as that of "social intelligence" and "social knowledge". This is likely to have arisen early in human evolution (Humphrey 1976) and recent literature concerning non-human primates and cognitive development in children has given the notion of a distinctly "social intelligence" substantial support (e.g. Byrne and Whiten 1988; Cheney and Seyfarth 1990, 1992). Social intelligence is that which enables one to interact effectively with other group members, particularly with regard to forming social alliances. This requires abilities to know and exploit the character of other individuals and their social relationships, and may involve a high degree of deception (Byrne and Whiten 1992). As such, social intelligence has been characterized as distinctly Machiavellian (Byrne and Whiten 1988). Humphrey argues that for modern humans social intelligence requires "being sensitive to other people's moods and passions, appreciative of their waywardness and stubbornness, capable of reading signs in their faces and equally the lack of signs, capable of guessing what each person's past holds hidden in the present for the future" (1984: 4–5).

Cheney and Seyfarth (1990, 1992) contrasted social knowledge with non-social knowledge – that concerning other animal species, their interactions and the physical world – i.e. both animate and inanimate objects. Some of these may be relevant to survival and non-social knowledge may be alternatively termed ecological knowledge. As a cognitive domain it appears to combine elements of Gardner's spatial, logical-mathematical and bodily-kinesthetic intelligences. Cheney and Seyfarth conducted a unique series of experiments to evaluate the relative degrees of social and non-social intelligence in vervet monkeys. They found that, as theory predicted, vervet monkeys displayed much greater intelligence when interacting with conspecifics than with the non-social world. Many of the cognitive processes they used, such as the ability to classify conspecifics with regard to abstract categories, appeared inaccessible when interacting with either inanimate objects or members of other species. For instance, although a male may have no difficulty in assessing the relative social ranks of other males, he might be unable to rank the relative amounts of water in a series of containers. In addition, while the monkeys were very able to draw inferences from the behaviour of other individuals, they were very poor at drawing inferences from secondary visual cues, even when these appeared to be of considerable ecological value. For instance, the python is a major predator of the monkeys but they seemed unable to recognize the danger inherent in a recently made python track.

Darwinian algorithms

A more extreme approach to mental modularity has been taken by Cosmides and Tooby (1987, 1989). They embed their approach more firmly in Darwinism, arguing that the study of cognition makes the essential link between evolutionary theory and behaviour. Rather than positing domains or modules, they believe that the mind is composed of a large series of psychological mechanisms each dedicated to a very specific problem, the solution of which was of benefit in the evolutionary environment of modern humans. They coined the term "Darwinian algorithms" for those innate, domain-specific processes used for tasks such as kin recognition and foraging behaviour. Consequently, they stress the need to understand the character of that evolutionary environment since it provided the selective pressures for the particular psychological mechanisms that evolved and which we possess today. As such, Darwinian algorithms are now used in environments very different from those in which they evolved. As a consequence, it is likely that many forms of modern behaviour will show no adaptive relationship to the modern environment, although they can be effectively studied from a Darwinian perspective.

Accessibility and hierarchization

Accessibility refers to the degree of contact between mental modules. Rozin and Schull (1988) have argued that a critical feature of the human mind as compared with the minds of other primates, is the high degree of accessibility. Much of our own experience suggests that this is indeed the case. As Cheney and Seyfarth (1990) note, we use analogical reasoning not only to classify different types of kinship relations but in a diverse range of activities, such as when arguing about the taxonomic relations of hominid fossils. One of the major features distinguishing the human mind from that of other primates may be our ability to extend knowledge gained in one context to new and different ones. Similarly, we routinely use one psychological mechanism, probably evolved for a specific task, for a diverse array of problems. For instance we may use those evolved for interaction with conspecifics in the interaction with other animal species, as in anthropomorphic thinking. Gardner (1983) has recognized the significance of accessibility for human intelligence. While maintaining the idea that there are core psychological processes restricted to each intelligence, he notes that "in normal human intercourse, one typically encounters complexes of intelligences functioning together smoothly, even seamlessly in order to execute intricate human activities" (1983: 279). The "central system" of Fodor (1983) is the ultimate example of accessibility; for here information from all perceptual modules is combined to create a model of the world.

As Rozin and Schull (1988) describe, the theory of accessibility suggests that the principal course of cognitive evolution and development has been from domain-specific cognitive processes to a more generalized intelligence. They suggest that his fits with the developmental phenomenon of *décalage* – the sequenced appearance of the same ability in different domains, and with aspects of the development of number concepts and language. However, Greenfield (1991) has recently described the reverse process with reference to specific neural circuits. She described increasing modularity during development of those cognitive processes which control language and tool use. These become increasingly located in separate neural circuits.

Some resolution of this conflicting evidence may be found in the notion of hierarchization of cognitive processes during development and evolution. Gibson (1983, 1990, 1991a, b) has stressed the significance of hierarchical mental construction skills. That is, the development of new mental structures, each constructed by an integration of those operating at a lower level in a cognitive hierarchy. Such hierarchization appears well-established in child development. For instance Case (1985) describes how the transition from one cognitive stage to another involves the hierarchical integration of executive structures that were assembled during the previous stage, but whose form and function were considerably different. Gibson (1983; Parker and Gibson 1979) argues that in this respect human ontogeny does recapitulate its phylogeny, challenging Gould's (1976) arguments to the contrary. The process of hierarchization may be a principal means by which accessibility between mental modules occurs. It helps explain how modularity *and* accessibility may increase with experience during development.

Summary

As described, there are several perspectives on the notion of mental modularity. Some, such as Cosmides and Tooby, take an extreme view, while others such as Fodor, consider that modularity applies to perception alone. The wide range of different views largely arises from the lack of research on domain specific intelligence, leaving it as a vague and little understood area – but nevertheless of critical importance (see Cords 1992; Cheney and Seyfarth 1992; Dugatkin and Clark 1992; Tomasello 1992).

As archaeologists wishing to engage with such work, we should not feel constrained to commit ourselves to one or other perspective at present. For some issues, the most simple distinctions, such as that between social and non-social intelligence, may be most appropriate. For others, we may wish to refer to a more complex model, such as that of Gardner's "multiple intelligences". We may feel that we should define and focus on other forms of intelligences, or make distinctions within those defined by Gardner in (1983).

One such development might be a greater concern with "technical intelligence", in relation to the working of stone. As abilities in this area are likely to have had considerable selective value in human evolution, we may follow Cosmides and Tooby (1987, 1989) in suggesting specific psychological mechanisms or Darwinian algorithms evolved to facilitate the production of stone tools. This would be making an important distinction in the domain of non-social intelligence by distinguishing between interaction with inanimate and animate objects. Similarly, in light of our interest with subsistence, it is appropriate to define a "natural history" intelligence with respect to the exploitation of animals and plants.

The important point to draw from this brief review is simply the notion of modularity – the idea that certain cognitive abilities may be dedicated to particular behavioural domains. Equally important is the notion of accessibility between mental modules. The argument that this is a particular, and indeed essential, feature of the modern human mind is persuasive. As such, we might ask whether the Middle/Upper Palaeolithic transition – regarded as marking the appearance of modern behaviour and thought – may represent a significant phase of increasing accessibility between mental modules. In this regard, the many behavioural changes associated with the transition would be largely a consequence of this development in human cognition. Consequently, I now turn to the transition and, following a brief synopsis of the major issues, consider the relative degrees of mental modularity possessed by Lower/Middle and Upper Palaeolithic hominids.

The Middle/Upper Palaeolithic transition: a cognitive event?

Changes in the archaeological record that may reflect the first appearance of fully modern cognition appear after *c* 50,000 BP with the start of the Upper Palaeolithic. Most notably, we see the introduction of bone, antler and ivory technologies, the creation of personal ornaments and art, a greater degree of form imposed onto stone tools, a more rapid turnover of artefact types, greater degrees of hunting specialization and the colonization of arid regions (Mellars 1973, 1989; White 1982; Mellars and Stringer 1989). The extent to which these mark a real break in cultural/cognitive evolution, rather than a change in the manner in which archaeologists describe and interpret their material, is hotly debated (Clark and Lindly 1989; Mellars 1989; Lindly and Clark 1990).

On a global scale, the transition to modern humans and modern patterns of behaviour present a complex spatial and temporal mosaic – the apparent correlation between hominid type and culture in southwestern France is the exception rather than the rule (Mellars 1989; Chase and Dibble 1990). In most parts of the world, including the Levant, art remains rare phenomenon during the Palaeolithic. But "modern" behaviour and thought can be inferred from other types of development. In particular, we see at 50,000 BP, or soon afterwards, the colonization of the final parts of the globe, notably Australasia, Siberia and ultimately the New World. As Whallon (1989) has argued, the colonization of such areas with low density, diversity and predictability of resources is likely to have been possible only after fully modern human cognitive capacities had evolved, possibly to allow the required social structures, such as alliance networks to develop.

The appearance of language?

In light of the magnitude of the behavioural changes at the transition, Mellars (1991: 64) has asked whether we can "identify some kind of major "threshold" in human cognitive development" associated with the transition. He suggests, along with Whallon (1989) and Binford (1989), that the transition marks the first appearance of fully modern language.

This is a very enticing argument. We cannot doubt that hominids with language will behave and leave an archaeological record very different from hominids without language. There are compelling arguments, however, that language arose considerably earlier in human evolution than at the time of the Middle/Upper Palaeolithic transition.

The repeated efforts by *H. erectus* to colonize the temperate zone of Eurasia implies developed food acquisition techniques and social alliances, which in turn imply certain linguistic abilities. Deacon (1989) has argued persuasively, on the basis of neuroanatomy, that brain development relating to language occurred early in human evolution, and no further neurological changes occurred after the appearance of archaic *Homo sapiens*.

In addition, the relationship between language and the particular behavioural changes at the transition remains ill-defined. Many of these changes relate to the performance of complex practical tasks, such as, the working of bone and antler. Anthropologists have noted the minimal role that language plays in the transmission of such skills and it is probable that the knowledge to perform them is necessarily non-linguistic in character (Bloch 1991). Indeed, if we follow the modularity arguments described above, the appearance of a linguistic intelligence may not have substantial effects on many realms of behaviour. As Donald (1991) described, people who lack linguistic capacities, whether they be prelinguistic children, the illiterate deaf mutes of history or those suffering paroxysms involving language loss, all remain competent in many cognitive areas, such as episodic memory, manual skills, knowledge of the environment and the ability to cope with complex social situations.

In light of these problems with the "language thesis" we need to explore alternative possible cognitive developments. One of these is the notion that the transition marks a substantial increase in the degree of accessibility between mental modules and the development of hierarchical cognitive processes. This finds considerable support in the archaeological record.

Mental modularity and the transition

My argument in this section will be that the archaeological record of the Lower and Middle Palaeolithic reflects the behaviour and thought of hominids with relatively high levels of mental modularity as compared to modern humans. Three cognitive domains can be considered: social, technical and natural history intelligence. In each of these we have evidence for cognitive abilities not dissimilar to those of modern humans. But with regard to technical, and especially natural history intelligence, we can also recognize that something is "missing". And I suggest that this missing element is access to cognitive abilities in the other domains.

Social intelligence

It is practically impossible to draw any direct inferences from the archaeological record concerning the character of social interaction during the Lower and Middle Palaeolithic and, consequently, the nature of social intelligence. Some broad generalizations can be proposed. For instance, to have survived in glaciated northern latitudes it is likely that hominids would have formed large groups requiring complex social interactions for their maintenance (Gamble 1987; Mithen 1994; see Dunbar 1988). Also, the high levels of morphological similarity between artefacts in many assemblages, such as handaxes (e.g. see Wynn 1989; Roe 1981), imply abilities at imitation which depend upon complex social relationships and social intelligence (Mithen 1994). While the archaeological data relating to social interaction are ambiguous or absent, we can nevertheless be confident about inferring high levels of social intelligence for Lower and Middle Palaeolithic hominids simply due to its presence among monkeys and apes, as discussed above. Byrne and Whiten (1992) have presented a provocative scenario for the evolutionary trajectory of social intelligence, proposing that by 5–8 ma the last common ancestor of human and chimpanzee had sophisticated abilities in the attribution of intention to others and the imagination of alternative possible worlds. Moreover, they argue that while modern great apes may lack language, they may possess an understanding of the concept of communication. Consequently, we are able to infer at least this level of social intelligence for Lower and Middle Pleistocene hominids; if language had appeared, the complexity of social interaction and degree of social intelligence would no doubt have been substantially greater.

Technical intelligence

As discussed above, the value of stone tools in early hominid subsistence may have provided selective pressures for the evolution of specific Darwinian algorithms concerning the knapping of stone, which we may refer to as a technical intelligence. Even within the very earliest industries considerable sensorimotor skills are evident in the manufacture of tools, implying sophisticated perceptual and cognitive abilities with respect to stone working. Essentially modern cognitive abilities at working stone are evident with the Acheulian, and may be traced in the Oldowan (Gibson 1991b). The manufacture of bifaces involved long procedural templates (Gowlett 1984). Wynn (1989) has argued that the later Acheulian bifaces exhibit the use of complex spatial concepts. These are manifest in procedures such as the removal of a flake which maintains, or creates, three dimensional symmetry for an artefact. This implies the ability to make three dimensional mental rotations. The long procedural templates and use of such advanced spatial thought testify to cognition in stone knapping not substantially different from that of modern humans.

The Levallois technologies of the Mousterian also display levels of technical intelligence no less sophisticated than those of modern humans. It is now well established that the *chaînes opératoires* used by Middle Palaeolithic flint knappers were as long and complex as those used in the Upper Palaeolithic (Boëda 1988; Geneste 1988; Bar-Yosef and Meignen 1992; Mellars 1991). Along with the evidence for the transport of raw materials and tools over as much as 60–80 km (Geneste 1985; Roebroeks *et al.* 1988) this provides substantial grounds for inferring considerable planning depth and anticipation of future needs.

In general, stone industries from the Acheulian onwards appear to reflect a high level of technical intelligence, notably involving spatial thought and motor co-ordination. While these cognitive abilities were present, they were not applied to the working of bone, antler and ivory. As Dennell (1983) argued, these require a different range of motor movement, such as cutting, grooving, sawing and grinding which may have depended upon additional cognitive processes to those used in knapping stone. But it is nevertheless remarkable that such developed technical intelligence may be present with regard to the working of stone, and to be apparently absent with regard to other materials. This may be one of the strongest indications of high degrees of mental modularity prior to the transition. Moreover, as will be discussed below, the rate of technological change during the Lower and Middle Palaeolithic was minimal, implying that stone tools were playing a very different role in the adaptations of pre-modern hominids.

Natural history intelligence

Here I am referring to the cognitive abilities used in the interaction with animals and plants, and more generally those used to track environmental variability. The detailed monitoring of environmental variability and fine-tuned adjustment of foraging behaviour is one of the most impressive features of modern hunter-gatherers. For this they use a vast array of cues from which substantial amounts of ecological information can be inferred by using a detailed understanding of animal behaviour and ecological relationships (Mithen 1990). The use of technology is critical in such adaptation and significant correlations between technical and environmental variability can be traced (Torrence 1983). Such fine grained environmental adaptation, involving long-term planning, the anticipation and prediction of animal movements, and flexible response to environmental variability can be inferred from the character of Upper Palaeolithic faunal assemblages (Mellars 1989; Mithen 1990). The degree to which this is present among Middle and Lower Palaeolithic hunter-gatherers is debatable.

Even though the interpretation of Lower and Middle Palaeolithic faunal assemblages is fraught with problems, we must nevertheless infer a relatively high level of natural history intelligence for early hominids. A specifically natural history intelligence is likely to have been essential for the colonization of northern latitudes after 1 ma and to account for the diverse range of subsistence activities evident in the archaeological record. In contrast to the vervet monkeys described above, Middle, and probably Lower, Palaeolithic hominids are most likely to have been able to use secondary visual cues, such as animal tracks, in their hunting activity. Indeed, when appropriate methodologies are applied such environmental adaptation can be directly inferred. For instance, Stiner and Kuhn (1992) have demonstrated that in West Central Italy a detailed analysis of faunal remains and lithic assemblages can monitor behavioural variability during the Middle Palaeolithic that probably relates to environmental change.

The Middle Palaeolithic of southwestern France provides the most detailed and analysed data on early Palaeolithic subsistence. In particular, the faunal assemblages from Combe Grenal have been the subject of considerable discussion. In contrast to Binford's (1985) views, these, and other Middle Palaeolithic assemblages, are likely to reflect a substantial degree of large game hunting, as opposed to scavenging (Chase 1986, 1989). However, as Mellars (1989) concluded when reviewing the faunal and settlement data, such hunting is likely to have been less systematic, less intensive and less logistically organized than that of the Upper Palaeolithic. Middle Palaeolithic hunters appear to have undertaken far less prediction and anticipation of animal movements. This would have limited the degree to which economic practices were able to track environmental change, resulting in the economic "conservatism" that Chase (1986) recognized at Combe Grenal.

He concluded that animal exploitation practices remained unchanged through all but the major environmental changes. This persistence in the undertaking of the same activities at the site, in spite of environmental change, provides a dramatic contrast to the behaviour of modern humans in which site function and economic activities are very sensitive to even minor environmental variability (e.g. Binford 1982). As Chase (1986) notes, the inferred Middle Palaeolithic behaviour is difficult to explain in terms of economic rationalism. This may indicate that while the natural history intelligence of Middle Palaeolithic hominids was clearly sufficient to allow them to survive in a range of harsh environments, it nevertheless did not allow hominids to attain such fine-tuned adaptation to environmental variability as found among modern humans.

As noted above, this fine grained turning partly derives from the use of technology. As such, the natural history and technical intelligences of modern humans are intimately intertwined. During the Upper Palaeolithic this results in the constant adaptation of technology to new environmental conditions. For instance, when temperatures in Europe fell to a minimum at *c.* 18,000 BP technology became more complex and tools specialized, forming appropriate tool kits for hunting on tundra-like environments (e.g. see Strauss 1991; Zvelebil 1984). Prior to the Upper Palaeolithic, however, technology does not appear to have played this role, suggesting a separation between technical and natural history intelligence.

The most telling evidence is the stasis in technology during the early Palaeolithic. We have evidence for *H. erectus* and archaic *H. sapiens* living in a very diverse set of environments stretching from Pontnewydd Cave in North Wales (Green 1984) to the Cape of southern Africa (Keller 1973). Yet the degree of technological variability is limited and does not appear to correlate with fine grained environmental variables (Isaac 1977: 219; Binford 1989). It seems that the technology of early Palaeolithic hominids was not used to adapt to fine grained environmental variability, let alone restructure environments in the manner of modern humans. Binford (1989) makes a perceptive characterization by describing such technology as an "aid to" rather than "means of adaptation". In sum, there appears to be limited connection between technical and natural history intelligence.

Summary: intelligence and mental modularity prior to the transition

To summarize, it is most reasonable to infer relatively high degrees of social, technical and natural history intelligence prior to the transition. In many respects these appear to be similar to those of modern humans, and consequently we find considerable evidence for continuity across the transition. However, there also appear to have been major differences. Natural history intelligence does not appear capable of achieving the same degree of fine grained environmental adaptation as found among modern humans, and to be separate from technical intelligence. Similarly the cognitive processes involved in the working of stone appear to be restricted to that material, although the working of bone or antler appears to require similar skills of manipulation and spatial thought. Overall, we might suggest that while high levels of social, technical and natural history intelligence were present, the cognitive abilities within each were restricted to that specific domain, i.e. Lower and Middle Palaeolithic hominids had high degrees of mental modularity. Their intelligence is most appropriately characterized as "domain specific".

The demise of mental modularity

If, as Mellars (1991) suggests, the transition marks a major cognitive threshold, then a dramatic increase in the degree of accessibility between mental modules appears likely. After the transition, the mind appears to possess a higher degree of generalized intelligence – though remaining within a distinctly modular architecture. Cognitive processes evolved for a very specific purpose or use in particular domains, such as stone working or social interaction, became available for other domains of behaviour. The consequences for technology are substantial, as cognitive abilities such as categorization and analogous thinking, previously restricted to social interaction, became available for the manufacture of tools and can account for many of the technological changes at the transition. Other consequences of increased accessibility can be briefly considered by examining two issues: environmental interaction and the origins of visual symbolism.

Environmental interaction after the transition

According to the model of increased accessibility, the intelligence which modern humans use when interacting with the non-social world, and particularly with animal and plant species, partly derives from that evolved with regard to other behavioural domains. The cognitive abilities present in the specialized domain of natural history intelligence became supplemented with those from other domains. The most significant source of these is likely to have been the social sphere and the most important cognitive ability the attribution of mental states – now applied to members of other animal species rather than conspecifics. From the Upper

Palaeolithic onwards, the non-social world is explored and exploited partly using thought processes which evolved for social interaction.

Some of the consequences of the use of social intelligence in non-social contexts have been discussed by Humphrey (1976). He suggests that this may account for many types of fallacious reasoning repeatedly engaged in by modern humans. For instance many people have attempted to bargain with nature, such as through prayer, sacrifice or ritual persuasion. Similarly, the use of social intelligence appears to lie at the root of anthropomorphic thinking – the attribution of mental states to animals similar to those possessed by humans. Among hunter-gatherers such anthropomorphic thinking is pervasive, and anthropomorphs in Palaeolithic art indicate it stretches back to the earliest modern societies (e.g. a standing human with a feline face from Aurignacian contexts at Hohlenstein-Stadel: Marshack 1990: fig. 17.17). The predictions of animal behaviour based on anthropomorphic models are invariably correct, or at least as effective as the predictions made by western scientists (Mithen 1990: 76–7, e.g. see Blurton-Jones and Konner 1976; Silberbauer 1981; Gubser 1965). As such, the cognitive abilities derived from social intelligence supplemented those in natural history intelligence to transform the character of human–environment interactions.

The origins of visual symbolism

A further consequence of increased accessibility is that high level cognitive processes arise. Archaeologically, the most significant is visual symbolism, and here I will briefly summarize arguments I have made in detail elsewhere (Mithen 1992). Visual symbolism first appears at the start of the Upper Palaeolithic with sculptured animals and anthropomorphic figures dating to c. 35,000 BP from Vogelherd, Geissenklösterle and Hohlenstein-Stadel in southern Germany (Hahn 1972, 1984). At a similar date, ivory beads carved to represent sea shells are found at La Souquette in southwestern France (White 1989), while a range of enigmatic "vulva" signs are also found which are likely to have had symbolic status (Delluc and Delluc 1978). While arguments have been made for symbolic images during the Lower and Middle Palaeolithic (Marshack 1990; Bednarik 1992; Duff et al. 1992) all of these can be accounted for in other terms (Chase and Dibble 1989; Davidson 1992)   though their presence is important since they indicate that the constituting elements of visual symbolic capacities were present prior to the Upper Palaeolithic.

I have argued elsewhere (Mithen 1992) that the capacity for visual symbolism is constructed from four cognitive and physical processes:

1   the making of visual images;
2   classification, in the sense of recognizing that an image belongs to a certain class of symbols or constitutes the member of a new class;
3   intentional communication; and
4   the attribution of meaning to visual images.

All of these are likely to have been present by the Middle Palaeolithic. The first three are found in the behavioural repertoires of many non-human primates. Monkeys, apes and hominids clearly have the physical ability to make marks, while intentional communication and skills at classification are found in social intelligence and arose early in human evolution (Cheney and Seyfarth 1990). The fourth element, the attribution of meaning to visual images, is likely to be restricted to hominids. As discussed above, monkeys (and probably apes) appear unable to attribute meaning to inanimate secondary visual cues, and elsewhere (Mithen 1992) I have argued that this ability evolved with respect to the use of animal tracks in foraging behaviour at least by the time of the later Middle Palaeolithic.

While all of these elements of visual symbolism are likely to have been present for many millennia prior to the Upper Palaeolithic, it was only after the transition that the capacity for visual symbolism arose. The reason is likely to be that these elements were located in different cognitive domains and hence inaccessible to each other. Intentional communication and classification are likely to have evolved as aspects of social intelligence, while mark making and the attribution of meaning, both involving inanimate material objects, were originally located in non-social intelligence. Consequently, these four elements could only have been integrated to form the high level cognitive process of visual symbolism after accessibility between the social and non-social cognitive domains had arisen.

Conclusion

The hypothesis that the behavioural changes associated with the Middle/Upper Palaeolithic transition may be due to increased accessibility between mental modules is not dependent upon a change in hominid species or population replacement. Increased accessibility may have arisen within one species or indeed one society, as people may be able to learn to access domain specific cognitive abilities (Rozin and Schull 1988). The mechanism of increased accessibility (like the notion itself) remains vague; Armstrong (1992) suggests that consciousness has a major role to play. I suspect that the demise of mental modularity was a gradual process involving change both within the cognitive architecture of archaic *H. sapiens* and the appearance of *H. sapiens sapiens* with generally lower degrees of mental modularity. Indeed, we may be dealing with a process that extended after the conventional start of the Upper Palaeolithic.

This hypothesis helps solve one of the major controversies in Palaeolithic studies – the degree of continuity or discontinuity across the transition. It has generally been assumed that when a cognitive ability is present in one behavioural domain, then it must also be present in all others. Consequently, when Binford claims a lack of planning depth in subsistence behaviour (1989), this has been taken (as Binford intended) to imply a lack of planning depth in all behavioural domains. And when planning depth is argued to be present on the basis of technology

(Roebroeks *et al.* 1988), this is taken to imply that planning depth must be generally present. From the perspective of mental modularity, however, we should *expect* to find cognitive abilities restricted to particular domains. The question we must ask as archaeologists is not whether an ability is present or absent, but whether it is present or absent in a particular behavioural domain. Hence it is quite possible for early hominids to appear very modern in certain behaviours and for us to find considerable continuity across the transition, but to find difference and discontinuity in others.

As I stressed above, there are several different perspectives on mental modularity and the notion of accessibility remains vague. My discussion of the Middle/Upper Palaeolithic transition has necessarily been brief as I have made a preliminary exploration of the possible significance of the concepts of modularity and accessibility. Irrespective of the specific hypothesis of increased accessibility at the transition that I have proposed, the aim of this paper has been to demonstrate the need for a greater interaction between archaeology and the cognitive sciences. For it will only be from an engagement between these fields that progress will be made on understanding the *ancient mind*.

References

Armstrong, D.M. (1992). Monkeys and consciousness (comment on Cheney, D.L. and R.M. Seyfarth, (1992). Précis of How monkeys see the world), *Behavioral and Brain Sciences* 15: 147–8

Bar-Yosef, O. and L. Meignen (1992). Insights into Levantine Middle Paleolithic cultural variability. In *The Middle Paleolithic: adaptation, behavior and variability*, ed. H.L. Dibble and P. Mellars, pp. 163–82. Philadelphia, University of Pennsylvania Press

Bednarik, R.G. (1992). Palaeoart and archaeological myths, *Cambridge Archaeological Journal* 2: 27–57

Binford, L.R. (1982). The archaeology of place. *Journal of Anthropological Archaeology* 1: 5–31

—— (1985). Human ancestors: changing views of their behavior. *Journal of Anthropological Archaeology* 4: 292–327.

—— (1989). Isolating the transition to cultural adaptations: an organizational approach. In *The emergence of modern humans: biocultural adaptations in the later Pleistocene* ed. E. Trinkaus, pp. 18–41. Cambridge, Cambridge University Press

Bloch, M. (1991). Language, anthropology and cognitive science. *Man* (N.S.) 26: 183–98

Blurton-Jones, H. and M.J. Konner (1976). !Kung knowledge of animal behaviour. In *Kalahari hunter-gatherers*, ed. R.B. Lee and I. DeVore, pp. 326–48. Cambridge, Mass, Harvard University Press

Boëda, E. (1988). *Approche technologique du concept Levallois et évaluation de son champ d'application: Etude de trois gisements saaliens et weichséliens de la France septentionale*. Thèse de doctorat, Université de Paris X

Byrne, R.W. and A. Whiten (eds.) (1988). *Machiavellian intelligence: social expertise and the evolution of intellect in monkeys, apes and humans*. Oxford, Clarendon Press

—— (1992). Cognitive evolution in primates: evidence from tactical deception. *Man* (N.S.) 27: 609–27

Case, R. (1985). *Intellectual development: birth to adulthood*. New York, Basic Books

Chase, P.G. (1986). *The hunters of Combe Grenal: approaches to middle paleolithic subsistence in Europe*. Oxford, British Archaeological Reports (BAR International Series 286)

—— (1989). How different was middle palaeolithic subsistence? A zooarchaeological perspective on the Middle to Upper Palaeolithic transition. In *The human revolution: behavioural and biological perspectives on the origins of modern humans*, ed. P. Mellars and C. Stringer, pp. 321–37. Edinburgh, Edinburgh University Press

Chase, P.G. and H.L. Dibble (1989). Middle palaeolithic symbolism: a review of current evidence and interpretations. *Journal of Anthropological Archaeology* 6: 263–93

—— (1990). On the emergence of modern humans. *Current Anthropology* 31: 58–9

Cheney, D.L. and R.M. Seyfarth (1990). *How monkeys see the world*. Chicago, University of Chicago Press

—— (1992). Précis of How monkeys see the world. *Behavioral and Brain Sciences* 15: 135–82

Chomsky, N. (1972). *Language and mind*. New York, Harcourt Brace, Jovanovich

Clark, G.A. and J.M. Lindly (1989). The case for continuity: observations on the biocultural transition in Europe and Western Asia. In *The human revolution: behavioural and biological perspectives on the origins of modern humans*, ed. P. Mellars and C. Stringer, pp. 626–76. Edinburgh, Edinburgh University Press

Cords, M. (1992). Social versus ecological intelligence (comment on Cheney, D.L. and R.M. Seyfarth, (1992). Précis of How monkeys see the world). *Behavioral and Brain Sciences* 15: 151

Cosmides, L. and J. Tooby (1987). From evolution to behaviour: evolutionary psychology as the missing link. In *The latest on the best: essays on evolution and optimality*, ed. J. Dupré, pp. 277–306. Cambridge, Mass., The MIT Press

—— (1989). Evolutionary psychology and the generation of culture, part I, *Ethology and Sociobiology* 10: 29–49

Davidson, I. (1992). There's no art – to find the mind's construction – in offence (reply to R. Bednarik (1992), Palaeoart and archaeological myths). *Cambridge Archaeological Journal* 2: 52–7

Deacon, T. (1989). The neural circuitry underlying primate cells and human language. *Human Evolution* 4: 367–401

Delluc, B. and G. Delluc (1978). Les manifestations graphiques aurignaciennes sur support rocheux des environs des Eyzies (Dordogne). *Gallia Préhistoire* 21: 213–438

Dennell, R. (1983). *European economic prehistory*. London, Academic Press

Donald, M. (1991). *Origins of the modern mind*. Cambridge, Mass., Harvard University Press

Duff, I.A., G.A. Clark and T.J. Chadderdon (1992). Symbolism in the early Palaeolithic: a conceptual odyssey. *Cambridge Archaeological Journal* 2(2): 211–19

Dunbar, R.I.M. (1988). *Primate social systems*. London, Croom Helm

Dugatkin L.A. and A.B. Clark (1992). Of monkeys, mechanisms and the modular mind (comment on Cheney, D.L. and R.M. Seyfarth, (1992). Précis of How monkeys see the world). *Behavioral and Brain Sciences* 15: 153–4

Fodor, J.A. (1983). *The modularity of mind*. Cambridge, Mass. MIT Press

Gamble, C. (1987). Man the shoveler: alternative models for Middle Pleistocene colonization and occupation in northern latitudes. In *The Pleistocene Old World*, ed. O.
Soffer, pp. 81–98. New York, Plenum Press

Gardner, H. (1983). *Frames of mind: the theory of multiple intelligences*. New York, Basic
Books

Geneste, J.-K. (1985). *Analyse lithique des industries moustériennes du Périgord: Une approche
technologique du comportement des groupes humains au Paléolithique moyen*. Thèse de
doctorat, Université de Bordeaux I

—— (1988). Systèmes d'approvisionnement en matières premières au Paléolithique moyen
et au Paléolithique supérieur en Aquitaine. In *L'Homme de Néandertal, vol. 8, La muta-
tion*, ed. M. Otte, pp. 61–70. Liège, Etudes et Recherches Archéologiques de
l'Université

Gibson, K.R. (1983). Comparative neurobehavioral ontogeny and the constructionist
approach to the evolution of the brain, object manipulation and language. In *Glosso-
genetics: the origin and evolution of language*, ed. E. de Grolier, pp. 37–61. Harwood
Academic Publishers

—— (1990). New perspectives on instincts and intelligence: brain size and the emergence
of hierarchical mental construction skills. In *"Language" and intelligence in monkeys and
apes*, ed. S.T. Parker and K.R. Gibson, pp. 97–128. Cambridge, Cambridge University
Press

—— (1991a). Continuity versus discontinuity theories of the evolution of human and animal
minds (comment on P.M. Greenfield, Language, tools and brain: the ontogeny and
phylogeny of hierarchically organised sequential behaviour). *Behavioral and Brain
Sciences* 14: 560–1

—— (1991b). Tools, language and intelligence: evolutionary implications. *Man* 26: 255–64

Gould, S.J. (1976). *Ontogeny and phylogeny*. Cambridge, Mass., Harvard University Press

Gowlett, J. (1984). Mental abilities of early man: a look at some hard evidence. In *Human
evolution and community ecology*, ed. R. Foley, pp. 167–92. London, Academic Press

Green, H.S. (1984). *Pontnewydd Cave: a lower palaeolithic hominid site in Wales*. Cardiff, National
Museum of Wales

Greenfield, P.M. (1991). Language, tools and brain: the ontogeny and phylogeny of hierarchically organised sequential behaviour. *Behavioral and Brain Sciences* 14: 531–95

Gubser, N.J. (1965). *The Nunamiut Eskimo: hunters of caribou*. New Haven, Yale University
Press

Hahn, J. (1972). Aurignacian signs, pendants, and rare objects in Central and Eastern
Europe. *World Archaeology* 3: 252–66

—— (1984). Recherches sur l'art paléolithique depuis 1976. In *Aurignacian et Gravettian en
Europe*, ed. J.K. Kozlowski and R. Desbrosses, vol. 3, pp. 79–82. Liège, Etudes et
Recherches Archéologiques de l'Université 13

Harrold, F.B. (1989). Mousterian, Châtelperronian and Early Aurignacian in Western
Europe: continuity or discontinuity. In *The human revolution: behavioural and biological
perspectives on the origins of modern humans*, ed. P. Mellars and C. Stringer, pp. 677–713.
Edinburgh, Edinburgh University Press

Humphrey, N. (1976). The social function of intellect. In *Growing points in ethology*, ed.
P.P.G. Bateson and R.A. Hinde, pp. 303–17. Cambridge, Cambridge University Press

—— (1984). *Consciousness regained*. Oxford, Oxford University Press

Isaac, G.I. (1977). *Olorgesaille, archaeological studies of a middle pleistocene lake basin in Kenya*. Chicago, Chicago University Press

Keller, C.M. (1973). *Montagu Cave in prehistory*. Berkeley, Anthropological Records No. 28, University of California

Lindly, J. and G. Clark (1990). On the emergence of modern humans. *Current Anthropology* 31: 59–63

Marshack, A. (1990). Early hominid symbol and evolution of the human capacity. In *The emergence of modern humans: an archaeological perspective*, ed. P. Mellars, pp. 457–98. Edinburgh, Edinburgh University Press

Mellars, P. (1973). The character of the Middle-Upper Palaeolithic transition in southwest France. In *The explanation of culture change*, ed. C. Renfrew, pp. 255–76. London, Duckworth

—— (1989). Major issues in the emergence of modern humans. *Current Anthropology* 30: 349–85

—— (1991). Cognitive changes and the emergence of modern humans. *Cambridge Archaeological Journal 1*: 63–76

Mellars, P. and C. Stringer (eds.) (1989). *The human revolution: behavioural and biological perspectives on the origins of modern humans*. Edinburgh, Edinburgh University Press.

Mithen, S.J. (1990). *Thoughtful foragers: a study of pre-historic decision making*. Cambridge, Cambridge University Press

—— (1992). The origin of art: mental modularity, ecological intelligence, and the Middle/Upper Palaeolithic transition. Paper prepared for the Second AURA congress, Cairns, Australia, September (1992)

—— (1994). Technology and society during the Middle Pleistocene: hominid group size, social learning and industrial variability. *Cambridge Archaeological Journal 4* (1): 3–32

Parker, S.T. and K. Gibson (1979). A developmental model for the evolution of language and intelligence in early hominids. *Behavioral and Brain Sciences 2*: 367–407

Roe, D. (1981). *The lower and middle palaeolithic periods in Britain*. London, Routledge and Kegan Paul

Roebroeks, W., J. Kolen and E. Rensink (1988). Planning depth, anticipation and the organization of Middle Palaeolithic technology: the "archaic natives" meet Eve's descendants. *Helinium 28*: 17–34

Rozin, P. (1976). The evolution of intelligence and access to the cognitive unconscious. In *Progress in psychobiology and physiological psychology*, ed. J.M. Sprague and A.N. Epstein, pp. 245–77. New York, Academic Press

Rozin, P. and J. Schull (1988). The adaptive-evolutionary point of view in experimental psychology. In *Stevens' handbook of experimental psychology, Vol. 1: perception and motivation*, ed. R.C. Atkinson, R.J. Herrnstein, G. Lindzey and R.D. Luce, pp. 503–46. New York, John Wiley and Sons

Silberbauer, G.B. (1981). *Hunter and habitat in the Central Kalahari Desert*. Cambridge, Cambridge University Press

Stiner, M.C. and S.L. Kuhn, (1992). Subsistence, technology and adaptive variation in Middle Palaeolithic Italy. *American Anthropologist 94*: 306–39

Straus, L. (1991). Southwestern Europe at the last glacial maximum. *Current Anthropology* 32: 189–99

Tomasello, M. (1992). Cognitive ethology comes of age (comment on Cheney, D.L. and R.M. Seyfarth, (1992). Précis of How monkeys see the world). *Behavioral and Brain Sciences* 15: 168–9

Torrence, R. (1983). Time budgeting and hunter-gatherer technology. In *Hunter-gatherer economy in prehistory*, ed. G. Bailey, pp. 57–66. Cambridge, Cambridge University Press

Whallon, R. (1989). Elements of cultural change in the Later Palaeolithic. In *The human revolution: behavioural and biological perspectives on the origins of modern humans*, ed. P. Mellars and C. Stringer, pp. 433–54. Edinburgh, Edinburgh University Press

White, R. (1982). Rethinking the Middle/Upper Paleolithic transition. *Current Anthropology* 23: 169–92

—— (1989). Production complexity and standardization in early Aurignacian bead and pendant manufacture: evolutionary implications. In *The human revolution: behavioural and biological perspectives on the origins of modern humans*, ed. P. Mellars and C. Stringer, pp. 366–90. Edinburgh, Edinburgh University Press

Wynn, T.G. (1989). *The evolution of spatial competence*. Urbana, University of Illinois Press

Zvelebil, M. (1984). Clues to recent human evolution from specialised technology. *Nature* 307: 314–15

Chapter 8

WRESTLING WITH ANALOGY
A Methodological Dilemma in
Upper Palaeolithic Art Research

J.D. Lewis-Williams

> Analogies prove nothing, this is quite true, but they can make
> one feel more at home.
>
> Freud, quoted by Copi 1982, 389

In 1902 Emile Cartailhac published his *Mea Culpa d'un Sceptique*. His
acceptance of the high antiquity of pre-historic art in western Europe
followed Capitan and Breuil's convincing discoveries in Font de
Gaume and Les Combarelles and reflected a widespread change of
opinion. Despite previous scepticism, researchers were beginning to
allow that the parietal as well as the mobile art did indeed date back
to the Upper Palaeolithic. But this swing in scientific opinion opened
up an even more baffling problem: why did Upper Palaeolithic
people make these pictures? In the year following Cartailhac's turn-
about Salomon Reinach tried to answer this question by developing
an analogical argument based on ethnographic parallels. He could
see no other way of approaching the problem: "Our only hope of
finding out *why* the troglodytes painted and sculpted lies in asking
the same question of present-day primitives with whom the ethnography reveals connections" (Reinach 1903, 259; my translation, his
emphasis). Drawing on Spencer and Gillen's reports from Australia,
Reinach argued that the facts of Upper Palaeolithic art, as then
known, supported the view that the depictions were made as part
of magical and totemic rites. Although Reinach is the best known,
he was not, as he himself pointed out, the first writer to use an
ethnographic parallel to explain Upper Palaeolithic art. In 1876
Bernardin had drawn on North American ethnography to explain
the animals carved on the so-called *bâtons de commandement* (Reinach
1903, 264). Right from the beginning ethnography has played an
important part in Upper Palaeolithic art research.

Today this kind of ethnographic analogical argument is rightly criticized, but, at the same time, many researchers recognize an uncomfortable dilemma: either they attempt, by inductive, empiricist research to infer answers from supposedly objective data or they resort to analogy of one kind or another.

Recognizing the opprobrium into which analogy has fallen, workers such as Leroi-Gourhan and Marshack have favoured the first of these two strategies, but it is flawed. No matter how "objective" a researcher tries to be or how well he or she knows the data, the method produces only an illusion of objectivity and inevitability (Chalmers 1978; Lewis-Williams 1983b; 1984a; Lewis-Williams and Loubser 1986; Lewis-Williams and Dowson 1989b). The collection of data as well as the categorization and "analysis" of data must be carried out according to some preconceived theoretical position or hypothesis: how else can a researcher discriminate between relevant and irrelevant data? It is, of course, true that an argument of impeccable logic can lead to a false conclusion if its data-content is unsound, but it is equally true that an argument that is demonstrably false in its logic can never be acceptable no matter how exact its data-content or how familiar its proponent may be with the evidence. This is the case with empiricist rock art research. It therefore seems that there is no alternative but to fall back on an analogical argument if we wish to achieve some idea of the "meaning" of the art. This is in effect what has often happened. Some writers (e.g. Gould 1980) who reject analogy allow it to creep back into their writing in disguise (Wylie 1982).

In so-called mainstream archaeology much attention has been accorded to ways of tightening up and supporting analogical arguments, but in Upper Palaeolithic rock art research scarcely any attention has been given to this crucial methodological problem (for notable exceptions see Ucko and Rosenfeld 1967, 150–58; Layton 1987; Conkey 1987). There has been a tendency for writers to accept uncritically the debilitating proposition that all analogies are intrinsically misleading or, at best, helpful in only a very general and non-specific sense. In this paper I do not review the literature on analogy in general archaeological research, for example, "argument by anomaly" and the distinction between direct historical and "new" analogies, useful as it is (see Wylie 1985 for a review); instead I concentrate on Upper Palaeolithic art research and begin by distinguishing between what I call *ethnographic precedents* and *ethnographic parallels*. I then explicate in more detail a third type of analogical argument that I believe leads towards a better understanding of Upper Palaeolithic art. This step-by-step explication shows that the use of words like "cautious", "judicious" and "tentative" to qualify analogical explanations is not enough. Caution unattended by cogency does not generate confidence.

Ethnographic precedents

In the first place, it is necessary to question simple, look-alike analogies. Breuil proposed such an analogy to explain the "comet designs" engraved in the Apse at

Lascaux. He juxtaposed a photograph of the converging engraved lines with one of a French Guinea "sorcerer clad from head to foot in a disguise of plaited fibre" (Breuil 1952, 147). This disguise was said to make him "comparable to" the engraving. Breuil concluded that the engraving "*probably* represents a Palaeolithic sorcerer clad in a disguise of grass" (*ibid.*; emphasis added).

Breuil's argument is analysed in figure 1. It starts with an association in the ethnographic source between two features, A and B (a "sorcerer" and a fibre costume respectively). It then claims that B (represented by the engraved lines) is also present in the archaeological context. Finally, it infers that A (a "sorcerer") was also present in the archaeological context. Set out like this, the argument's three major weaknesses are clear. First, the association between the two features in the ethnographic source is singular: no evidence is given that "sorcerers" in any other societies dress in plaited fibre. There is therefore no necessary link between the two features once they are abstracted from the Guinea context. Secondly, the postulated horizontal correspondence between the B of the source and the B in the archaeological context is again singular: it is only the converging lines of the archaeological feature that suggest a possible correspondence – although the way in which the engraved lines run in sets is not duplicated by the Guinea "sorcerer's" costume. In any event, we must be clear about the nature of the two items being compared. Neither *is* a costume. The first is a depictive photograph, with its limitations of perspective; the second is a set of engraved lines that may or may not represent something in the "real" world. If, for the sake of the argument, we were to grant that the engraving is depictive, we should still have to allow for a set of Upper Palaeolithic depictive principles possibly very different from photography. Thirdly, given the weakness of this horizontal correspondence, there are scant

Figure 1   Analogical inference from an ethnographic precedent

grounds for inferring the presence of a "sorcerer" in the archaeological context. But even if the engraved lines did represent a disguise there would, because of the weakness of the vertical A–B link in the source, be little reason to infer that it was being worn by a person who had anything in common with a Guinea "sorcerer". Any number of explanations for the engraved lines are equally possible. The problem is that the argument as presented by Breuil is altogether intuitive; it depends upon a deep-seated, but unarticulated, feeling that features of objects exist in sets and go together quite naturally. Indeed, the multiple weaknesses of Breuil's argument recall Gould's (1980, 29) pessimistic citing of the *Fontana Dictionary of Modern Thought*: Analogical reasoning is "peculiarly liable to yield false conclusions from true premises".

Perhaps it is best to think of this use of ethnography as simply the citing of ethnographic precedents. In general terms, consideration of a wide range of ethnographic precedents can help one to avoid too limited and Eurocentric an interpretation; the extraordinary diversity presented by ethnography is a warning against jumping to simple conclusions (Ucko and Rosenfeld 1967, 151). But citing only one potential precedent, as Breuil did, obscures this diversity. More important, citing an ethnographic precedent should not be mistaken for a developed argument leading to a conclusion. As Binford and others have argued, ethnographic precedents should rather be seen as sources for hypotheses. These hypotheses then stand in need of evaluation by procedures quite different from analogical argument (Lewis-Williams 1984a; Lewis-Williams and Loubser 1986, 280–83).

Ethnographic parallels

One way out of the difficulties presented by ethnographic precedents appears to be to seek analogues that have multiple correspondences (more subtle arguments incorporate dissimilarities, but I do not consider them here because they have, as far as I am aware, played no role in Upper Palaeolithic art research). In other words, the more features the ethnographic source of an analogy has in common with the archaeological context, the more likely it is that the archaeological feature needing explanation can be explained in the same way as a similar feature in the source of the analogy. As with Breuil's ethnographic precedent, an intuitive feeling that features "hang together" in sets underlies the inference. By this argument, analogy I in figure 2 is less persuasive than analogy II because it exhibits only three common features, whereas analogy II has six. In each case the archaeological context is seen to be in parallel with the source of the analogy: the more extensive the parallel, the more convincing the inference.

Reinach (1903, 263) adopted this way of supporting analogical inference when he argued that it is more reasonable to look for analogies among hunter-gatherers than among agricultural communities. Taking the Australian Arunta as the source of his analogy, he cited four features that they have in common with the Upper

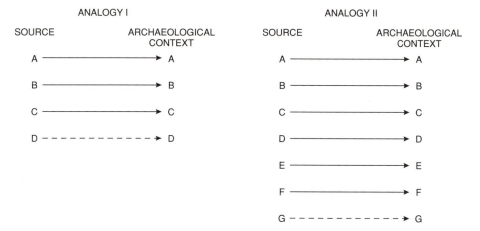

Figure 2 Comparison of analogues by counting common features

Palaeolithic: both societies were hunter-gatherers; both made paintings; both selected for depiction only a few species from their respective environments; access to the Australian painted sites was forbidden to women, children and uninitiated men, and Upper Palaeolithic art is often situated in remote, underground caverns. He considered these parallels sufficient grounds for inferring a fourth: like the Aruntas, the people of the Upper Palaeolithic made paintings to ensure the increase of edible and totemic species.

No matter how much we may rely on this kind of thinking in day-to-day life, counting attributes to establish the degree of similarity between analogues poses problems. As North (1980; 135) argues, the properties of an object are not given and countable: "What is countable are the properties human beings agree to count as properties; and they are far from being absolute or stable enough for an argument to be based on a count of them". All too easily, the features said to be common to the source of an analogy and to the archaeological context may be trival or have no bearing at all on the feature requiring explanation. In Reinach's argument, for instance, there is clearly no *necessary* link between any of the four features he believes the two contexts have in common and the feature he wishes to infer. The four common features cannot therefore be said to imply, singly or collectively, the fifth, the totemic and magical explanations for Upper Palaeolithic art.

In contrast to ethnographic precedents, ethnographic parallels do not demonstrate links on the vertical axis of the ethnographic source; the function of such links is replaced by the sheer weight of the cited parallels. But the piling up of common attributes cannot be said to make one analogy more probable than another (see also Binford and Stone 1988). No amount of unrelated features can make an analogical inference more persuasive.

Relations of relevance

These remarks and the weakness of the relationships between source features presented in figures 1 and 2 lead us to the notion of relevance. As Copi points out (1982, 399), "An argument based on a single relevant analogy connected with a single instance will be more cogent than one that points out a dozen *irrelevant* points of resemblance" (see also Wylie 1988a). Reacting to this kind of criticism of listing what are really irrelevant points of similarity, some writers rightly seek uniformitarian principles, linked aspects of society that can be projected back into the past. They search for behavioural *systems* that produce particular artefactual patterns, that is, persistent sets of behavioural features that are directly *relevant* to material features identical or very similar to those in the archaeological record that need to be explained. The structure of this sort of argument needs to be set out stage by stage.

An argument based on a strong relation of relevance starts by demonstrating the existence of some causal or otherwise determining mechanism that links two features in the source of an analogy (figure 3). In other words, if feature A is present in the source of the analogy, the enabling mechanism or relation of relevance, ensures that B is also present. Then, if we can show that B is present in the archaeological context and if we are confident that the same mechanism existed in the past, we can conclude that A was also present (see Salmon 1982; Wylie 1985; 1988a). The all-important points here are to establish, first, that the archaeological feature B is indeed similar to the B in the source of the analogy, and, second, that the same relation of relevance operated in the past. This is in effect, reducing analogy to a deductive syllogism. The major premiss is that A is inevitably linked by the relation of relevance to B. The minor premiss is that both B and the relation of relevance are present in the archaeological context. The conclusion is that A must also be present. If the premisses are true, the conclusion must follow.

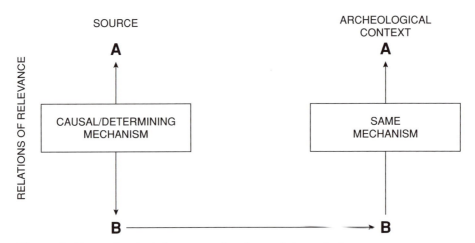

Figure 3   Form of analogical argument based on relations of relevance

The strength of this argument is brought out by a comparison of figure 3 with figures 1 and 2.

Unfortunately, the great diversity of human cultures has diminished many archaeologists' hope of finding any relations of relevance that are not trivial: we cannot be sure that what holds in an ethnographic circumstance also held in the Upper Palaeolithic because similar archaeological remains can be produced by dissimilar activities. Without wishing to pass judgement on the possibility of some day finding cultural relations of relevance that are not trivial, I move on to discuss a specific analogical argument that avoids the problem of cultural diversity and throws considerable light on Upper Palaeolithic art.

Neuropsychology and analogy

In this argument the enabling mechanism is not cultural but rather physiological. Because the nervous system is common to all people, including those who lived in the Upper Palaeolithic, we can assume that the effects of its functioning were the same from at least the Aurignacian to the present and in all parts of the world. More specifically, I highlight the functioning of the nervous system in altered states of consciousness. Neuropsychological research has shown that the *kinds* of hallucination experienced in altered states are cross-culturally uniform (Eichmeier and Höfer 1974; Reichel-Dolmatoff 1969; 1978a; 1978b). This seems to be broadly true whether an altered state is induced by hallucinogens, hyperventilation, sensory deprivation, audio-driving, persistent rhythmic movement and so forth. Although all the senses hallucinate in these various circumstances, we are here concerned principally with visual hallucinations. They are experienced in three stages.

Laboratory experiments have shown that in an initial stage of trance subjects see luminous, pulsating, enlarging, fragmenting and changing geometric forms (Klüver 1942; Siegel 1977; Siegel and Jarvik 1975; Asaad and Shapiro 1986). These are called entoptic phenomena because they are "within the optic system" and are independent of an external source of light (Tyler 1978). The forms include grids, dots, zigzags, nested catenary curves and sets of parallel lines. In a subsequent and deeper stage of trance subjects try to make sense of these forms by construing them as objects known to them (Horowitz 1964, 514; 1975, 177, 178, 181). In religious circumstances subjects construe certain entopic phenomena as important ritual objects (Reichel-Dolmatoff 1978a). In the third and deepest stage of trance the entoptic elements persist, although they tend to be peripheral (Siegel 1977). Now the subject's attention focuses on iconic hallucinations of animals, people, "monsters" and emotionally charged events in which they themselves participate. There are thus two inter-twined elements: geometric entoptic images that derive from the universal human nervous system (neurologically controlled elements) and iconic images that derive from the subject's mind or culture (psychological elements). Both kinds of image are processed or transformed according to neurologically based principles such as fragmentation, combination and rotation. In this way iconic hallu-cinations blend with geometric entoptic images, and various iconic images combine to produce composite animals and therianthropes (forms that are half animal and half human). For a fuller account of this three stage model of altered states of consciousness see Lewis-Williams and Dowson (1988, 202–204).

The usefulness of the model may be gauged by applying it to an art known ethnographically and thus *a priori* to depict hallucinations (fig. 4). The rock paint-ings and engravings of the southern African San (Bushmen) are such an art. Nineteenth- and twentieth-century ethnography has been used to show that San shaman-artists depicted animal symbols of a supernatural power they harnessed to

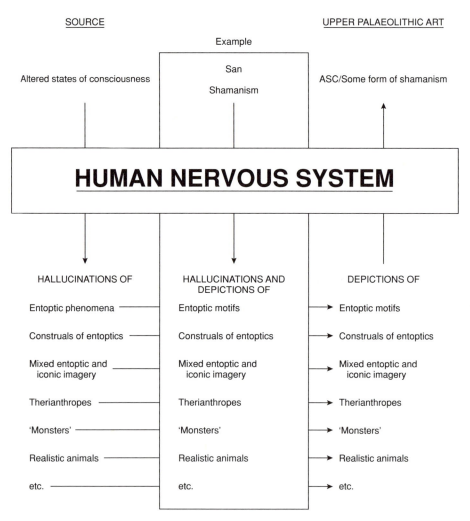

Figure 4   Analogical argument leading from a neuropsychological model of altered states of consciousness (ASC) to Upper Palaeolithic art

enter trance, metaphors of trance experience and hallucinations of the spiritual dimension they believed they entered (Lewis-Williams 1980; 1981; 1982; 1986; Lewis-Williams and Dowson 1989a). Their depictions include zigzags, catenary curves, grids and dots. Because we know independently that the art depicts hallucinations, it is highly likely that these geometric motifs are entoptic in origin (Thackeray *et al.* 1981; Maggs and Sealy 1983; Lewis-Williams 1984b; 1986; Lewis-Williams and Dowson 1989a). San rock art also has construals of certain entoptics (e.g. catenary curves were "seen" as honeycombs; Lewis-Williams 1988; Dowson 1989), as well as the monsters, therianthropes, "realistic" animals and tumultuous events of deep trance (Lewis-Williams 1980; 1982; Lewis-Williams and Dowson 1989a). As figure 4 shows, the human nervous system is the mechanism that induces in the San hallucinations comparable with those experienced by Westerners taking part in laboratory experiments. This is, of course, not to say that the depictions produced by these two groups could be confused or are in any way superficially similar. While the Western subjects hallucinate aeroplanes, motorcars, dogs and other animals familiar to them, San shamans hallucinate antelope, felines, and circumstances, though often bizarre and terrifying, derived ultimately from San life. The similarity exists at a deeper, analytical level that is exposed by the three stage model of altered states of consciousness. Apart from geometric entoptic phenomena which, because of their origin in the nervous system, are very similar, it is only the form, order and structure of the visions that are comparable.

Figure 5, a black and white tracing of a San rock painting, shows how the neuropsychological model makes sense of apparently confused panels of paintings. First painted were the eland and the curved serpent that issues from a step in the rock face. The eland has a grid motif within it and two "tusks"; the serpent has similar tusks and antelope ears. Next, human figures were added. Some of these are in distinctive trancing postures, including a hand raised to the nose, bending forward and the arms extended backwards (for explanations of these postures see Lewis-Williams 1983a; Lewis-Williams and Dowson 1989a). Two of the men have "tusks" like those on the eland and the serpent and are thus conceptually linked to those creatures. Poor preservation makes it hard to determine at what stage the zigzag was added, but it is clear that the dots were painted in two sets. The second set (solid in the copy) was placed so that two dots fell directly on top of dots in the earlier set (stippled in the copy). Although it is not possible to estimate the time that elapsed between each painting episode, the sequence of additions suggests that a series of shamans (or perhaps a single shaman) built up the panel over a period. The apparent confusion that resulted from "sequential composition" is explicable in terms of San beliefs about trance experience and the neuropsychological model. In the Kalahari Desert today San shamans draw one another's attention to hallucinations because they believe that sharing hallucinations is conducive to an especially effective trance dance (Biesele, pers. comm.). The superimposition of one image upon another that can result from this sort of practice is in fact a feature of trance experience. The San notion of sharing and thus building

Figure 5 Tracing of a San rock painting comprising entoptic and iconic hallucinations. Colours: solid: red; close stipple: orange; open stipple: pink; white. Scale in centimetres

up visions seems to lie behind this painting (Lewis-Williams and Dowson 1990; Lewis-Williams 1981).

The way in which the neuropsychological model fits and makes sense of San rock art in general and of an otherwise confused and enigmatic painting like this in particular increases our confidence in its efficacy and encourages us to apply it to arts not known *a priori* to be derived from altered states of consciousness. The Upper Palaeolithic paintings and engravings, both parietal and mobile, are such a case.

This step in the argument, potentially the most controversial, entails assessing the horizontal relationship in figure 4. The structure of the argument itself is probably not in question; it is the more empirical problem of whether the two Bs (fig. 3) of this particular argument can be said to be equivalent or whether the apparent resemblances are simply a matter of chance. First, we must allow reservations similar to those I noted in the case of ethnographic precedents. We are not comparing hallucinations experienced under laboratory conditions with hallucinations experienced in the Upper Palaeolithic. Rather, we are comparing a range of motifs known to be *depictions* of hallucinations experienced by Westerners with the *depictions* of Upper Palaeolithic art. We must therefore allow for a whole range of differentiating cultural factors.

At present there seems to be no way of "proving" the correspondence between the two sets of depictions, but this is, of course, the case with most archaeological correspondences. In the absence of "proof", Dowson and I have stressed the complexity of the "fit" (Lewis-Williams and Dowson 1988). Upper Palaeolithic art includes dots, grids, zigzags, nested catenary curves and other geometric "signs" that fall within the range of entoptic elements determined by laboratory research. Sometimes these motifs are placed on animals, but others, like the grids and fragmented grids at Lascaux, are depicted in isolation. In addition, Upper Palaeolithic art includes a range of depictions equivalent to Stage Three hallucinations: therianthropes, "monsters" and "realistic" animals. Indeed, the neuropsychological model orders and fits Upper Palaeolithic art as well as it does San rock art.

Some critics have tended to assume that the proposed correspondence between hallucinatory images and Upper Palaeolithic art deals only with geometric motifs, and they have pointed out, understandably given their misapprehension, that it is not too difficult to match up a few simple geometric forms. It is therefore important to note that a demonstration of the fit between the kinds of hallucinations determined by neuropsychological research and the depictions of Upper Palaeolithic art does not depend upon the selection of a few look-alike geometric depictions. We are, in fact, dealing with a number of different categories of geometric *and* iconic depictions (fig. 4). The "fit" is by no means simple; it is in fact highly complex, and this increases confidence in the conclusion that it does not result from chance.

The well-known horses at Pech Merle are a useful example of how geometric and iconic images come together (fig. 6). It appears that one horse was drawn and then filled in with dots; then the second horse was drawn and it was filled in with dots (Marshack 1985). Both horses have curiously deformed heads. The dots extend beyond the outlines of the horses and therefore cannot be seen as natural markings on the animals' coats. Other elements include a circle on the first horse's chest, a fish painted along the back of the first horse (only partly shown in the figure), hooked shapes probably made by blowing paint around a bent finger, and stencils of human hands. When allowance is made for cultural differences, it is clear that this panel is, in essence, very similar to the San one in figure 5: both are constructed from Stage One geometric entoptic phenomena and Stage Three iconic hallucinations. Alternatively, the two kinds of motif may have derived from multi-component Stage Three hallucinations.

Following these brief remarks on the fit between the neuropsychological model and Upper Palaeolithic art (for a fuller discussion see Lewis-Williams and Dowson 1988, 205–13), I move on to examine the vertical axis of the archaeological context (fig. 4). The question now is whether the set of geometric and iconic features can more reasonably be ascribed to some source other than altered states. In answering this question, we must remember that the ability of the Upper Palaeolithic people to hallucinate the various types of image is not being inferred from the art. The anatomical modernity of Upper Palaeolithic populations suggests very strongly that they did have that capacity. In other words, the enabling mechanism (the relation of relevance) was present. Indeed, it seems, on the face of it, highly probable that at least some Upper Palaeolithic people experienced hallucinations induced by one or more of the many techniques that range from ingestion of psychotropic drugs to sensory deprivation. The mental imagery of those people would necessarily have included hallucinations very like the range of depictions in their art. The independently established ability to experience this range of hallucinations is thus a further compelling reason for supposing that the graphic imagery of Upper Palaeolithic art derived *at least in part* from the mental imagery of altered states of consciousness.

Figure 6   Simplified copy of rock painting in Pech Merle, France

At this point we must allow that altered states of consciousness can be experienced in a variety of circumstances other than shamanism. For instance, entoptic phenomena can be seen in migraine attacks (Sacks 1970; Richards 1971) and in schizophrenic conditions (Siegel and Jarvik 1975). It has also been shown that some child art displays features similar to entoptic imagery (Kellogg *et al.* 1965). Wylie (1988b) therefore urges that an attempt should be made to develop a measure for showing, first, the origin of Upper Palaeolithic motifs in altered states of consciousness (rather than, say, migraine or child art) and, secondly, the specifically shamanistic circumstances of its generation. It does not seem possible to achieve either of these goals through neuropsychology alone; we have to use a "best fit" argument instead.

In the first instance, there is no need to exclude migraine and schizophrenia. As Sacks (1970) has shown, there is evidence to suggest that migraine visions have played a role in religious experience in Western Christian tradition. Similarly, a variety of mental disorders, including schizophrenia, are accepted as evidence for contact with the spirit world in shamanistic societies (Eliade 1972). Indeed, one may hypothesize pathological conditions ranging from migraine to schizophrenia as well as the induction of altered states of consciousness by hallucinogens, sensory deprivation, rhythmic driving and so forth as contributing to Upper Palaeolithic mental imagery and art. Child art, on the other hand, seems a less likely explanation for any significant portion of the art: the long association during the Upper Palaeolithic of entoptic with often remarkably "realistic" depictions, combinations of entoptic and iconic elements predicted by the neuropsychological model, the occasional combination of different iconic images (therianthropes and "monsters"), the location of much of the art in remote galleries and inaccessible diverticules, as well as evidence for complex Upper Palaeolithic social forms are features better explained by the more extreme varieties of altered consciousness than by infantile perception (Lewis-Williams and Dowson 1988, 236).

Whether these diverse altered states, as experienced by Upper Palaeolithic people, can be said to fall under the rubric of shamanism is the next question. Dowson and I (Lewis-Williams and Dowson 1988) have argued that the harnessing of altered states of consciousness to contact the spirit world, heal, change the weather, divine the future and control animals is the diagnostic element of shamanism; we believe the number of shamans in a group, the role of pathological conditions, the social status of the shaman and other factors are secondary (Bourguinon 1989; Dobkin de Rios and Winkelman 1989). Given the very widespread association of shamanism, so defined, with hunting and gathering societies (e.g. Winkelman 1986) and the strong evidence supplied by our analogical argument for the depiction of hallucinations by Upper Palaeolithic people, we believe that some form of shamanism is a "best-fit" explanation for Upper Palaeolithic art. As a modest first step, we suggest that Upper Palaeolithic religion centred on altered states of consciousness, the seeking of visions in the dark recesses of the caverns (at any rate in the Magdalenian), and some concept of animal power. This is, of course, by no means the first suggestion that shamanism in some form existed in the Upper Palaeolithic (see, among others, Lommel 1967; La Barre 1970; 1972; Eliade 1972; Eichmeier and Höfer 1974; Furst 1976; Halifax 1980, 3, 17; Pfeiffer 1982). We simply try to strengthen the hypothesis by developing an explicit and strong analogical argument based on acceptable relations of relevance.

This is not to say that western European art and belief remained static throughout the Upper Palaeolithic. A more precise assessment of the changing circumstances of the creation of art in different periods, regions and media remains to be essayed. Social and ecological changes would have led to an emphasis on different shaman-istic tasks at different times and in different places, and the social position of shamans would have changed as social conditions changed. It seems highly prob-able that such changes would have been reflected in the subject matter of the depictions, the proportion of mobile to parietal art, whether depictions were indi-vidually or socially produced, the localized or widespread distribution of specific classes of image, the location of parietal images in the entrances or the depths of caves, the proportion of entoptic to iconic imagery, and so forth. Though the analogical argument developed here provides an umbrella explanation, it must not be allowed to obscure the considerable temporal regional diversity nor the multi-faceted nature of shamanism. It should rather be seen as a flexible framework for tackling the diversity and complexity of Upper Palaeolithic art.

Implications

One of the problems that this explanation resolves is the close association of geometric motifs with iconic, sometimes highly realistic, depictions in Upper Palaeolithic art and, moreover, in hunter-gatherer rock art in other parts of the world. The neuropsychological approach shows that, far from being two distinct "systems" of representation or one having evolved out of the other, *both* types of image originate and come together in the functioning of the human nervous system in altered states of consciousness. Indeed, we can go so far as to say that we should expect an art derived from altered states of consciousness to have both types of depiction. On the other hand, we cannot predict exactly which entoptic motifs will be emphasized or what will be the proportion of entoptic elements to iconic depictions. Each society selects a restricted range of elements from the various kinds of hallucination; each art is therefore culturally constituted and not an automatic reaction to the functioning of the nervous system. Similarly, the neuropsy-chological approach tells us about the *origin* of certain kinds of depiction, for example geometric motifs; it cannot, by itself, tell us what those depictions *meant* to the artists and their viewers (Lewis-Williams and Dowson 1988; Dowson 1989). Meaning is always socially constituted. Nevertheless, knowing that at least part or Upper Palaeolithic art derived from altered states of consciousness places us in a more commanding position to address the vexed issues of meaning.

It is also important to note, as figure 4 shows, that this is not an analogical argument from San to Upper Palaeolithic art. Rather, the source of the analogy is a neuropsychological model of altered states of consciousness derived from laboratory research that had nothing to do with rock art (the argument is therefore not circular). It is the strong correlation between the kinds of hallucinations established by neuropsychological research and the depictions of Upper Palaeolithic art, together with the presence of the same relation of relevance, that enables us to postulate some form of shamanism in the Upper Palaeolithic. The source of the analogy is neuropsychological rather than ethnographic.

Because San rock art is not the source of the analogy, it is irrelevant to cite the obvious differences between Upper Palaeolithic and San art. There are, for instance, large numbers of human figures at many – but not all – San rock art sites, but very few in Upper Palaeolithic art. Moreover, there is no point in listing dissimilarities between it and Upper Palaeolithic art any more than there is in listing similarities (cf. figure 2), unless it can be shown that the dissimilar features have, through a relation of relevance, a direct, negative or modifying bearing on the inference of the analogy. Clearly, the proportion of human figures to animals or the proportion of geometric to iconic motifs has no bearing on the origin of an art in altered states of consciousness. Cultural selection is always a potent factor: subjects are not insentiate photocopying machines producing replicas of hallucinations. They are historically situated people who select and modify the products of their nervous system and the symbols of their culture; some particularly sensitive or innovative people produce unique insights and depictions (Dowson 1988; Dowson and Holliday 1989). In the last analysis, social, cultural and personal factors are paramount, and the use of a neuropsychological model cannot be seen as an attempt to reduce certain arts to neurologically determined practices.

On the other hand, if we wish to go further than a general statement about shamanism in the Upper Palaeolithic, it may be possible to use San rock art as well as other arts known to be shamanistic (e.g. Tukano painting; Reichel-Dolmatoff 1969; 1978a) to address specific features of Upper Palaeolithic art. Such arguments would entail setting up a number of analogies each designed to elucidate a specific feature. Because we have moved beyond the kinds of argument represented in figures 1 and 2, we no longer have to seek analogues that are similar in a large number of ways. We need only two features, provided they are linked by a strong relation of relevance. It follows that, in explaining Upper Palaeolithic art, we can draw analogues from a number of sources, even, *pace* Reinach, societies that are not hunter-gatherers (see Wylie 1985 and 1988a on the value of multiple sources). Indeed, because no ethnographically known society is identical, or even in large measure similar, to any Upper Palaeolithic societies, we shall have to appeal to a number of sources, "each of which brings into view different, otherwise unknown, features of the subject" (Wylie 1985, 106). This approach goes some way towards avoiding reducing the unfamiliar to the familiar, always a danger of ethnographically derived explanations (e.g. Ucko and Rosenfeld

1967, 150–58). The congeries of similarities and dissimilarities that multiple analogical arguments will produce will be unlike any known shamanistic society. In the end, the category "shamanism", even as I have loosely defined it, may prove inadequate.

Conclusion

In considering the role of ethnography in Upper Palaeolithic art research it is useful to distinguish three approaches. At the simplest level, the citing of multiple ethnographic precedents can militate against facile Eurocentric and if-I-were-a-horse arguments. Ethnographic precedents do not in themselves constitute an argument, but they may suggest hypotheses that require testing or evaluation by different procedures. Secondly, ethnographic parallels, as I have used the phrase, develop ethnographic precedents into fuller inferential arguments. Whilst some ethnographic parallels are intuitively persuasive, they cannot be said to be based on sound reasoning. Thirdly, arguments incorporating strong relations of relevance offer a more secure foundation for understanding Upper Palaeolithic art. The source of the relation of relevance for the argument adumbrated in this paper is neuropsychological rather than ethnographic, but it may well be possible to devise equally strong arguments from a variety of ethnographic sources to explain specific features of Upper Palaeolithic art. If we deny this third approach or, worse, reject analogy out of hand, we shall never understand Upper Palaeolithic art.

Freud was of course correct when he said, in this paper's epigraph, that "analogies prove nothing". The notion of proof is, in any event, inappropriate in evaluating reconstructions of the past. Positivist researchers may claim that sort of objectivity for their reconstructions, but, when they do so, they are actually saying something about their own social status as arbiters of how the past should be conceived. At best, we can only say that one reconstruction is better than another, though, notwithstanding criteria for discriminating between hypotheses (Lewis-Williams and Loubser 1986), what we mean by "better" is a difficult question, especially when we consider the active life of such reconstructions in the present (e.g. Shanks and Tilley 1987). Even in so apparently remote a field as Upper Palaeolithic art research, the comfort, the feeling of being at home, that Freud believed analogy affords may derive more from cosy compatibility of a reconstruction with present-day ideology than from a sense that it is "right".

Being alive to these considerations of archaeological practice makes us wary of dogmatism, but it need not paralyse our research. We still want to know something about what may well be the greatest of all archaeological enigmas, Upper Palaeolithic art, and we cannot achieve this goal without analogy. Whilst it is true that many analogical arguments are weak and unconvincing, I have tried to show that the kind that is built on strong relations of relevance can lead to compelling conclusions.

References

Asaad, G. and Shapiro, B. (1986). Hallucinations: theoretical and clinical overview. *American Journal of Psychiatry* 143, 1088–97.

Binford, L.R. and Stone, N.M. (1988). Correspondence: Archaeology and theory. *Man* 23, 375–76.

Bourguignon, E. (1989). Trance and Shamanism: what's in a name? *Journal of Psychoactive Drugs* 21, 9–15.

Breuil, H. (1952). *Four Hundred Centuries of Cave Art*. Montignac: Centre d'étude et de Documentation Préhistoriques.

Chalmers, A.F. (1978). *What is this Thing Called Science?* Milton Keynes: Open University Press.

Conkey, M.W. (1987). New approaches in the search for meaning? A review of research in "Palaeolithic art". *Journal of Field Archaeology*, 14, 431–30.

Copi, I.M. (1982). *Introduction to Logic*. London: Macmillan.

Dobkin de Rios, M. and Winkelman, M. (1989). Shamanism and altered states of consciousness: an introduction. *Journal of Psychoactive Drugs* 21, 1–7.

Dowson, T.A. (1988) Revelations of religious reality: the individual in San rock art. *World Archaeology* 20, 116–28.

Dowson, T.A. (1989). Dots and dashes: cracking the entoptic code in Bushman rock paintings. *South African Archaeological Society, Goodwin Series* 6, 84–94.

Dowson, T.A. and Holliday, A.L. (1989). Zigzags and eland: an interpretation of an idiosyncratic combination, *South African Archaeological Bulletin*, 44, 46–48.

Eichmeier, J. and Höfer, O. (1974). *Endogene Bildmuster*. Munich: Urban and Schwarzenberg.

Eliade, M. (1972). *Shamanism: Archaic Techniques of Ecstasy*. New York: Routledge and Kegan Paul.

Furst, P.T. (1976). *Hallucinogens and Culture*. Novato, Calif.: Chandler and Sharp.

Gould, R.A. (1980). *Living Archaeology*. Cambridge: Cambridge University Press.

Halifax, J. (1980). *Shamanic voices*. Harmondsworth: Penguin Books.

Horowitz, M.J. (1964). The imagery of visual hallucinations. *Journal of Nervous and Mental Disease* 138, 513–23.

Horowitz, M.J. (1975). Hallucinations: an information-processing approach. In R.K. Siegel and L.J. West (eds), *Hallucinations: Behaviour, Experience and Theory*, 163–95. New York: Wiley.

Kellogg, R.M., M. Noll and J. Kugler, (1965). Form similarity between phosphenes of adults and pre-school children's scribblings. *Nature* 208: 1129–1130.

Klüver, H. (1942). Mechanisms of hallucinations. In Q. McNemar and M.A. Merrill (eds), *Studies in Personality*, 175–207. New York: McGraw Hill.

La Barre, W. (1970). *The Ghost Dance: Origins of Religion*. Garden City: Doubleday.

La Barre, W. (1972). Hallucinations and the shamanistic origins of religion. In P.T. Furst (ed.), *Flesh of the Gods: The Ritual Use of Hallucinogens*, 261–78. London: Allen and Unwin.

Layton, R. (1987). The use of ethnographic parallels in interpreting Upper Palaeolithic rock art. In L. Holy (ed.), *Comparative Anthropology*, 210–39. Oxford: Blackwell.

Lewis-Williams, J.D. (1980). Ethnography and iconography: aspects of southern San thought and art. *Man*, 15, 467–82.

Lewis-Williams, J.D. (1981). *Believing and Seeing: Symbolic Meanings in Southern San Rock Paintings*. London: Academic Press.

Lewis-Williams, J.D. (1982). The economic and social context of southern San rock art. *Current Anthropology* 23, 429–49.

Lewis-Williams, J.D. (1983a). *The Rock Art of Southern Africa*. Cambridge: Cambridge University Press.

Lewis-Williams, J.D. (1983b). Introductory essay: science and rock art. *South African Archaeological Society, Goodwin Series* 4, 3–13.

Lewis-Williams, J.D. (1984a). The empiricist impasse in southern African rock art studies. *South African Archaeological Bulletin* 39, 58–66.

Lewis-Williams, J.D. (1984b). The rock art workshop: narrative or metaphor? In M. Hall, G. Avery, D.M. Avery, M.L. Wilson and A.J.B. Humphreys (eds), *Frontiers: Southern African Archaeology Today*, 323–27. Oxford: British Archaeological Reports IS 207.

Lewis-Williams, J.D. (1986). Cognitive and optical illusions in San rock art research. *Current Anthropology* 27, 171–78.

Lewis-Williams, J.D. (1988). *Reality and Non-reality in San Rock Art*. Twenty-fifth Raymond Dart Lecture. Johannesburg: University of the Witwatersrand Press and the Institute for the Study of Man in Africa.

Lewis-Williams, J.D. and Dowson, T.A. (1988). The signs of all times: entoptic phenomena in Upper Palaeolithic art. *Current Anthropology* 24, 201–45.

Lewis-Williams, J.D. and Dowson, T.A. (1989a). *Images of Power: Understanding Bushman Rock Art*. Johannesburg: Southern Book Publishers.

Lewis-Williams, J.D. and Dowson, T.A. (1989b). Theory and data: a brief critique of A. Marshack's research methods and position on Upper Palaeolithic shamanism. *Rock Art Research* 6, 38–53.

Lewis-Williams, J.D. and Loubser, J.H.N. (1986). Deceptive appearances: a critique of southern African rock art studies. In F. Wendorf and A.E. Close (eds), *Advances in World Archaeology* 5, 253–89. New York: Academic Press.

Lewis-Williams, J.D. and T.A. Dowson (1990). Through the veil: San rock paintings and the rock face. *South African Archaeological Bulletin* 45, 41–6.

Lommel, A. (1967). *Shamanism: The Beginnings of Art*. New York: McGraw-Hill.

Maggs, T.M. O'C. and Sealy, J. (1983). Elephants in boxes. *South African Archaeological Society, Goodwin Series* 4, 44–48.

Marshack, A. (1985). Theoretical concepts that lead to new analytical methods, modes of enquiry and classes of data. *Rock Art Research* 2, 95–111.

North, J.D. (1980). Science and analogy. In M.D. Grmek, R.S. Cohan and G. Cimino (eds), *On scientific discovery*. pp. 115–140. New York: Reidel.

Pfeiffer, J.E. (1982). *The Creative Explosion: An Enquiry into the Origins of Art and Religion*. New York: Harper and Row.

Reichel-Dolmatoff, G. (1969). El contexto cultural de un alucinogeno aborigen, *Banisteriopsis caapi*. *Revista de la Academia Colombia de Ciencias Exactas, Fisicas y Natureles* 3, 327–45.

Reichel-Dolmatoff, G. (1978a). *Beyond the Milky Way: Hallucinatory Imagery of the Tukano Indians*. Los Angeles: UCLA Latin America Center.

Reichel-Dolmatoff, G. (1978b). Drug induced optical sensations and their relationship to applied art among some Colombian Indians. In M. Greenhalgh and V. Megaw (eds), *Art in Society*, 289–304. London: Duckworth.

Reinach, S. (1903). L'art et la magie: à propos des peintures et des gravures de l'âge du renne. *L'Anthropologie* 14, 257–66.

Richards, W. (1971). The fortification illusions of migraines. *Scientific American* 224, 89–94.

Sacks, O.W. (1970). *Migraine: The Evolution of a Common Disorder*. London: Faber.

Salmon, M.H. (1982). *Philosophy and Archaeology*. New York: Academic Press.

Shanks, M. and Tilley, C. (1987). *Social Theory and Archaeology*. Cambridge: Polity Press.

Siegel, R.K. and Jarvik, M.E. (1975). Drug-induced hallucinations in animals and man. In R.K. Siegel and L.J. West (eds), *Hallucinations: Behaviour, Experience and Theory*, 81–161. New York: Wiley.

Siegel, R.K. (1977). Hallucinations. *Scientific American* 237, 132–40.

Thackeray, A.I., Thackery, J.F., Beaumont, P.B. and Vogel, J.C. (1981). Dated rock engravings from Wonderwerk Cave, South Africa. *Science* 214, 64–67.

Tyler, C.W. (1978). Some new entoptic phenomena. *Vision Research* 18, 1633–39.

Ucko, P.J. and A. Rosenfeld, (1967). *Palaeolithic Cave Art*. London: Weidenfeld and Nicolson.

Winkelman, M. (1986). Trance states: a theoretical model and cross-cultural analysis. *Ethos* 14, 174–203.

Wylie, A. (1982). An analogy by any other name is just as analogical: a commentary on the Gould–Watson dialogue. *Journal of Anthropological Archaeology* 1, 382–401.

Wylie, A. (1985). The reaction against analogy. *Advances in Archaeological Method and Theory* 8, 63–111.

Wylie, A. (1988a). "Simple" analogy and the role of relevance assumptions: implications of archaeological practice. *International Studies in the Philosophy of Science* 2, 134–50.

Wylie, A. (1988b). Comment on J.D. Lewis-Williams and T.A. Dowson "The signs of all times: entoptic phenomena in Upper Palaeolithic Art." *Current Anthropology* 29, 231–32.

PART FOUR

Archaeology and history

INTRODUCTION

Debates about the relationship between archaeology and history have been long-lived in our discipline, and sometimes contentious (see Taylor 1948; Deetz 1988). Typically, they have turned on the question of whether or not archaeology is a generalizing science that reconstructs synchronic events, with the prehistoric past a kind of timeless laboratory useful for cross-cultural studies. The alternative view usually has been one of archaeology as a humanistic field, concerned with describing the particular, and recognizing the importance of historical context if not contingency. Historical contingency – one event only occurs because a previous event has preceded it – is sometimes considered contrary to scientific explanation. Yet other social sciences (such as econometrics) fully acknowledge that the best prediction for future behavior is based precisely on behavior in the past: the best estimate for next year's sales of Wheaties is based on how many Wheaties sell this year. Since prediction is a primary aim of science (retrodiction is the archaeological analog), it is then difficult to deny the importance of history. The past does influence the future, and the question for the archaeologist is whether or not the historical context of the past can be ignored in our reconstruction of it.

The emphasis on the importance of context and the recognition that past conditions were heavily dependent on those immediately preceding them have caused cognitive and post-processual archaeologists to re-examine the relationship of archaeology to history. Two general perspectives may be seen in these reconsiderations. The first derives from R.G. Collingwood (1946), whose influences have been long felt in European archaeology, but less so in America. Collingwood was himself influenced by the turn-of-the-century writings of the Idealist School, the precursor to modern hermeneutics. This hermeneutical perspective is well-revealed by one of his key statements:

> [T]he historian must reenact the past in his own mind. . . . When a man thinks historically, he has before him certain documents

or *relics* of the past. His business is to discover what the past was which has left these relics behind . . . This means discovering the thought . . . expressed [by them]. To discover what this thought was, the historian must think it again himself.
(Collingwood 1946: 282–283; emphasis in original)

As should be immediately clear, calls for an interpretive archaeology based on hermeneutic principles are in keeping with Collingwood's general emphasis on the importance of empathic understandings as opposed to scientific explanations of the past. He can be considered a general influence on post-processual archaeologies at this level.

Another approach to the problem of history has sought inspiration from the French *Annales*, or structural history, school. This originated around the turn of the century but gained prominence in the late 1940s, and is most typically associated with the writing of Fernand Braudel. It appeals to many archaeologists because it at once acknowledges the importance of experienced life (the interest of hermeneutics) and of externally analyzed life (the field of science). Moreover, it explicitly emphasizes the fact that historical processes occur at and within different temporal scales. Climatic change, for example, may be slow and gradual but still influential on human life. Other kinds of change within society, on the other hand, may occur within this longer process of environmental shifts. Yet the recognition of both scales and cycles, and their interplay, is necessary for the full explication of the past.

The two papers in this section expand and explore the value of the *Annales* school approach to archaeological reconstruction. The first, by Christopher Peebles, begins by discussing the archaeological debate between science and history in slightly different terms than has been typical. He frames the distinction as a debate between two modes of cognition: paradigmatic and narrative, respectively. Instead of seeing these as necessarily opposed, he contends that the narrative mode does have a place in paradigmatic (or logico-scientific) thinking. Archaeology necessarily is both an art and a science, one that requires knowledge and understanding. From this view, the *Annales* school provides an appropriate set of conceptual methods for studying the prehistoric past. Yet as Peebles emphasizes in his conclusion, it will not be until archaeology adopts a greater recognition of the importance of the cognitive sciences that this potential will be fully realized. An archaeological concern with history, then, is not solely limited to post-processualists, but also figures among the cognitive archaeologists – a fact that is further emphasized when Flannery's and Marcus's discussion of the importance of ethnohistorical data in archaeological interpretation is recalled.

The second paper is by Charles R. Cobb, who develops a model of long-term change in midcontinental North America prehistory. By taking a view of the *longue durée* ("long duration") – a common *Annales* school concern – he identifies failures in processual explanations that are not evident in the short-term. By considering long-term change in terms of social reproduction, he offers us an improved understanding of the prehistory of this region. And perhaps even more importantly, he shows that an archaeological accommodation of history does not necessarily result in an atheoretical recounting of events. Processual archaeologists were then correct in their rejection of the culture-historical approach of traditional archaeology, but this same critique does not require a rejection of all historical approaches, as many have been led to believe.

■ ■ ■

Further reading

Bintliff 1991
Collingwood 1946

Hodder 1986:77–102, 1987
Taylor 1948

■   ■   ■

References

Bintliff, J. (ed.) (1991) *The Annales School and Archaeology*, London: Leicester University Press.

Collingwood, R.G. (1946) *The Idea of History*, Oxford: Oxford University Press.

Deetz, J.F. (1988) "History and Archeological Theory: Walter Taylor Revisited", *American Antiquity*, 53: 13–22.

Hodder, I. (1986) *Reading the Past: Current approaches to interpretation in archaeology*, Cambridge: Cambridge University Press.

—— (ed.) (1987) *Archaeology as Long-Term History*, Cambridge, Cambridge University Press.

Taylor, W.W. (1948) *A Study of Archaeology*, American Anthropologist, Memoir 69.

Chapter 9

ANNALISTES, HERMENEUTICS AND POSITIVISTS
Squaring circles or dissolving problems

Christopher S. Peebles

By the way of preface, I must emphasize that I seek to dissolve methodological barriers rather than to erect them. Thus, with the exception of so-called "behaviourists", this chapter is not to be taken as an attack on any individual or any school of thought in archaeology. Instead it is an argument for the role of history and of representations in the production of prehistory.

Given that caveat, I would like to discuss prehistory as history – as text and context – and thereby outline the first tentative steps in the formation of an alliance between archaeology, history and the emergent cross-disciplinary movement that has been labelled as cognitive sciences. In taking this path I wish to suggest that both writing about the prehistoric past, and writing about the writings about the prehistoric past, are important tasks for archaeologists. In the former case we ask about the knowledge it took to live one's life in a time and place bereft of written records; in the latter case we ask about the writing of prehistories in the here and now – the knowledge we, as prehistorians, deploy on behalf of this unwritten past. In this quest, I shall argue that prehistory must be in some measure both art and science, in which the latter is embedded in the former. It can be more of one than the other, it can choose to be one rather than the other, but it cannot choose to be neither the one nor the other. That is, prehistory cannot choose a hybrid third way, because to do so leads to an uncritical relativism, solipsism, and perhaps nihilism: a trio to be avoided at all costs.

Prehistory is rapidly becoming an intellectual (and anti-intellectual) battleground. Various individuals, groups, and so-called schools – from hyper-nationalists to post-modernists – compete for the right to assert that theirs is the only legitimate interpretation of the past. Leaving aside the "crazies", who wish to seize the past for various dubious ends (to resurrect Plumb's past, discredited in his *The Death of the Past* (1969), that is dying but, unfortunately, is not completely dead), current battlelines are drawn between two poles, the scientific and the humanistic. On the intellectual side, the clash is between what Jerome Bruner has called the two great modes of cognition, the paradigmatic or logico-scientific and the narrative (Bruner 1986). For Bruner, scientific (empirical) "truth" is the measure of the former, and verisimilitude or "lifelikeness" is the measure of the latter.

Given Bruner's characterization of the two modes of human cognition one might ask: does the narrative mode have a place in the production of scientific history and prehistory? The answer, I believe, is yes. In so far as history and prehistory present temporally ordered descriptions of changes in humankind, society, and culture, then these disciplines are, by definition, involved in the production of narratives. By the same token, it is necessary that these narratives be true to a "real" past: that they be constructed from logico-scientific operations that are both logically and empirically adequate, that the premises entail the conclusions, and that the conclusions are true in the light of the evidence.

Historical narratives, complete with the conceptual bases for inclusion and exclusion of events and other evidence, place the narrator in a privileged position. As Danto has observed: "The historian not only has knowledge they [the participants] lack; it is knowledge they cannot have because the determinate parts of the future are logically concealed" (Danto 1985, p. 350). That is, "the knowledge available to him [the historian] is logically outside the order of events he describes" (Danto 1985, p. 356). Moreover, historical narratives comprise both ahistorical (atemporal and law-like) components as well as elements that are strictly historical. In this task, Danto has observed: "There are limits assigned by historical locations in human affairs that have no counterparts in the natural world" (Danto 1989, p. 274). Consequently:

> To be human is to belong to a stage of history and to be defined in terms of the prevailing representations of that period. And the human sciences must, among other things, arrive at historical explanations of historically indexed representations.
>
> (Danto 1989, p. 273)

In another, far more destructive and profoundly anti-intellectual sense, the current battles among some archaeologists replay those fought by Enlightenment and counter-Enlightenment scholars over the legitimacy of sociology as a discipline with anything important to teach about humankind and society. In the case of nineteenth-century sociology, Wolf Lepenies, in his book *Die Drei Kulturen*, observes:

> In essence . . . the battle lines are drawn as follows: sociology is a discipline, characterized by cold rationality, which seeks to comprehend the structures

and laws of motion of modern industrial society by means of measurement and computation and in doing so only serves to alienate man more effectively from himself and from the world around him; on the opposite side there stands a literature whose intuition can see farther than the analyses of the sociologists and whose ability to address the heart of man is to be preferred to the products of a discipline that misunderstands itself as a natural science of society.

(Lepenies (1985) 1988, p. 13)

As Lepenies points out, when rationality promises too much and cannot deliver, the cult of irrationality prospers. Such was the case among some sociologists and other scholars in late nineteenth and early twentieth-century Europe; such seems to be the case, at least in some quarters, in prehistory today (Shanks and Tilley 1987). Because the "laws" of cultural development have not been forthcoming in history, anthropology, or prehistory, standards of scientific judgement have been abandoned by some in favour of locating archaeology somewhere between the arts and the sciences, but in the grasp of neither the one nor the other (Hodder 1986).

C.P. Snow, who is responsible for the modern contours of the Two Cultures debate (1959, 1964), and of which Hodder is a latter day participant, attempts to find a middle ground in the Third Culture, which Lepenies characterizes as politically expedient but methodologically unstable (Lepenies 1988, ch. 15). Snow envisions the reconciliation of the Two Cultures in a Third, in the historical dimensions of *les sciences humaines*. He observes:

All of them are concerned with how human beings are living or have lived – and concerned not in terms of legend but of fact. I am not implying that they agree with each other, but in their approach to cardinal problems – such as the human effects of the scientific revolution, which is the fighting point of this whole affair – they display, at least, a family resemblance.

(Snow 1964, p. 70)

He is convinced that the third culture will be realized, and he sees its genesis in the communication between the arts and sciences, but he does not endow it with a standard by which we can judge its products – although perhaps some measure of both truth and verisimilitude would suffice.

Jean-Claude Gardin, like Lepenies, argues that the third mode or Third Culture is by definition unstable. It is neither art nor science, and it is measured neither by truth nor by understanding, but by uncertainty. At its worst, it embraces scepticism and various brands of relativism (Gardin 1987). Instead, for Gardin, although archaeological (and historical) constructs – compilations and explanations – may be artful, they are none the less to be judged solely by their logico-semantic structure and their correspondence with the "real" world (Gardin 1980).

The great strength of the *Annales* school, at least as broadly construed, is in its quest to reconcile the paradigmatic (logico-scientific) within the narrative in the study of the past, without either reducing the one to the other or succumbing to unproductive and uncritical relativism and formless scepticism. Coherence, consistency, and lack of contradiction, as well as logical adequacy, are the measures that are used to judge historical concepts and constructs; these constructs, in turn, are assayed against the historical "record" as tests of their validity and opportunities for their falsification. Again, *Annaliste* goals might be said to comprise both knowledge (for which truth claims can be made) and understanding (which, at least in part, includes lifelikeness), which itself may later be cast in paradigmatic, logico-scientific terms.

If the *Annales* school can be described in broad strokes (Stoianovitch 1976), it can be characterized by an absence of dogmatism, a certain non-pathological eclecticism, a general commitment to research directed toward the solution of explicit problems, and longstanding efforts to include the methods and products of the social sciences, especially anthropology and economics, as part of historical methods. Moreover, scholars associated with the *Annales* have sought constantly to broaden the field of historical investigation, bringing in the "people without history" (in the sense meant by Eric Wolf (1982)): the illiterate and the preliterate, the disenfranchised and the distant. These features should have led to an early and easy alliance between the *Annales* brand of history and prehistory. Unfortunately, the *Annales* seem to have made little impact on prehistory, even in France. There have been articles on the archaeology of classical antiquity in their journal, *Annales: Economies, Sociétés, Civilizations*, and one issue (1973, 1) was devoted to archaeology, but otherwise I could not find any articles specifically devoted to topics and problems of prehistory. The three volume synthesis of the *Annales* movement, *Faire de l' Histoire*, edited by Jacques Le Goff and Pierre Nora (1974), contains two articles on archaeology and prehistory. One, by Alain Schnapp (Volume II), "L'archeologie", is a period piece on new approaches in archaeology: mathematics, computers, research methods associated with the new archaeology. The other, by André Leroi-Gourhan (Volume I), "Les voies de l'histoire avant l'écriture", is still vital and instructive.

It is curious that Leroi-Gourhan's article was not among those chosen for translation into English (see Le Goff and Nora 1985). Many of the themes he developed in that chapter have resurfaced lately under the banner of "contextual" or "postprocessual" archaeology. Leroi-Gourhan stressed the point that archaeological sites are not merely to be viewed as calendars for the ordering of isolated finds, but approached as "texts" in which the context of the material remains provides the basis for the construction of contemporary meaning:

> Si l'on considère le document préhistorique non plus comme un calendrier mais comme un texte, l'activité essentielle de la recherche n'est plus dans la réflexion interprétative sur des objects dûment récupérés dans leur ordre stratigraphique, mais dans la lecture du document que constitue la surface dévoilée par la fouille, document éphémère, amalgame de poussìere, de pierres, de débris d'os dont la valeur fondamentale ne réside que dans les rapports mutuels des éléments qui le composent.
>
> (Leroi-Gourhan 1974, p. 140)

He concludes that archaeology has failed to use the scientific apparatus available to it in favour of excavating and reporting sites in the old and underproductive ways (1974, p. 148). In effect, he accuses archaeologists of asking the wrong questions and producing texts that cannot answer the right questions, even if they were asked. He argues that materials gathered in a haphazard manner and from excavations conducted on a vertical face cannot provide the contextual evidence necessary to answer fully questions of technology and economy, let alone those about prehistoric society and beliefs. Leroi-Gourhan stresses that only meticulous, open-area excavations can produce the kind of context (text) necessary to answer questions that go beyond those that can be asked of individual artifacts and assemblages of artifacts.

From the vantage point of North American prehistory, archaeologists have reduced the *Annalistes* to incantations in texts and icons in bibliographies rather than using them as substantive guides to research and exemplars for the writing of prehistories. Thus reconciliation of narrative with science, at least from the *Annales* perspective, has been rendered a sham. Again, from the perspective of North America, prehistory and anthropology, like so many of the other social sciences, have abandoned history as either method or metaphor. In fact, with few exceptions, archaeology has developed a pronounced antipathy to history. American archaeologists have led the search for the nomothetic: the invariant covering laws of human behaviour. In doing so they have eliminated – or at least neutralized – the sentient human and human representation from the prehistoric past.

A search of the *Social Sciences Citation Index* for the years 1982 to 1988 for references in North American journals of archaeology to writings by historians associated with the *Annales* school, especially works by Bloch, Braudel and Le Goff, was generally fruitless. There were few references in the major journals: Mark Leone's citation of Braudel's work in his *American Antiquity* article, "Some opinions about recovering mind" was one of the very few. Even more surprising was the fact that the two Distinguished Lectures of the Society for American Archaeology for 1987, which were given under the general title "History and Archaeological Theory" (Deetz 1988, Young 1988), did not make reference to a single historian associated with the *Annales* school. Instead, exemplars were provided by the works of R.G. Collingwood, E.H. Carr, and Carl Becker. In lesser journals and monographs there have been occasional citations from the *Annales* historians – seemingly for effect rather than for inspiration.

It is important to remove the stigma applied to history by some archaeologists; to eradicate the claim that it and its products are solely ideographic, particularistic, and empathic in structure and content. This assertion is certainly false, and serves only to distance archaeology from historical methods and practice. Bruce Trigger characterizes the roots of this antipathy as based on a false dichotomy:

> that was introduced into American archaeology by Kluckhohn and Steward, and reinforced by the adoption of neo-evolutionism. The latter encouraged prehistoric archaeologists to believe that human behaviour and cultural change

exhibited strong regularities that could be accounted for in terms of evolutionary generalizations, and that doing this constituted scientific explanation. This left history as a humanistic residual, to account for the "unique, exotic, and non-recurrent particulars" of cultural change, all matters that neo-evolutionists judged to be of little, if any, scientific importance.

(Trigger 1989, p. 373)

The patterns among these "particulars", however, turn out to have substantial scientific and historical value. Consequently, it is important to reintroduce the concept and methods of history into prehistory. This suggestion does not imply that science and scientific methods should be eliminated from the intellectual armoury of prehistory. Instead, the scientific and the humanistic should be made to work together, towards knowledge and understanding of humankind and cultural variety. In Bruner's terms, the paradigmatic should be set within the narrative, as long as the result is the production of knowledge and not the kind of understanding gained from fiction. In brief, both scientific truth and verisimilitude are crucial to the construction of history, although the critical judgement appropriate to the former is perhaps more important than the aesthetic considerations of the latter.

Yet at this point, there is a major question: what then does separate history from fiction? Both employ narrative; both exploit verisimilitude. One answer is provided by Paul Ricoeur in his Aquinas Lecture, "The Reality of the Historical Past": "the historian is constrained by what once was. He owes a debt to the past, a debt of gratitude with respect to the dead, which makes him an insolvent debtor". That is, the constructs of the historian (and the prehistorian), be they either hypothetico-deductive constructs or historical narratives – or some combination of both – must be assayed against the remains of a "real" past – remains, which, as Collingwood (1939) pointed out more than fifty years ago, are here with us in the present. In brief, both analytic prowess and rhetorical skill are important in the writing of prehistory. Hayden White's (1973) "trophics of history" are every bit as important as trophic levels in human ecology.

It is perhaps ironic that the "project" of the *Annales* school reads like an indictment of several important aspects of archaeology, both new and old. Ricoeur notes in his Zaharoff Lecture for 1978–9: "Neutral observation, the cult of erudition, empiricism, determinism of the fortuitous, methodological individualism – these form the methodological constellation that the 'Ecole des Annales' set itself the task of dismantling" (Ricoeur 1980, p. 8). They rejected the tyranny of documentary "facts", the primacy of politics, and the straitjacket of nineteenth-century political frontiers. They likewise rejected the prophetic philosophy of history handed down by Hegel and Spengler.

As a consequence of these rejections, the *Annales* historians have provided a potent stock of methods and examples that ought to be of interest to archaeologists. The sense of problem and the breadth of historical vision are their hallmarks and provide considerable overlap with those of archaeology. Both narrative, in the sense of Paul Veyne's (1984) "plots", and scientific arguments, in the sense given in "serial history" by Pierre Chaunu (1968), are important to writing history. For the *Annales* scholars, taken as a group, the line between science and literature does not comprise an either-or choice, but the taking up of a position generally closer to the former than the latter (Chartier 1988, pp. 1–14). Their primary concern is with the questions and problems, answers and solutions embedded in the narrative.

Following Marc Bloch (1953), *Annales* historians have used multiple, shifting scales to measure both time and social phenomenon. The power of these methods is demonstrated by Braudel in his use of the temporal scales that encompass events, conjunctures, and the long duration in the second edition of his book *The Mediterranean and The Mediterranean World in the Age of Philip II* (1972–3) and in his historical "experiments" in the long duration and the geographic, almost timeless expanse of Europe in his *The Identity of France* (Braudel 1988, p. 21). Implicit in these several scales is the varying role played by necessity and contingency as causal factors in stasis and change. The former is far stronger at the level of structure and the long duration; the latter is more strongly associated with the event.

Patricia Galloway is one of the very few North American prehistorians to have incorporated the methods of the *Annales* in her research. In doing so, she has drawn a number of cogent parallels between *Annales* methods in history and those of archaeological research. She notes that ecological and technological analyses in prehistory measure time over the *longue durée*, whereas social and economic approaches look to the *conjoncture* as an appropriate temporal framework. Furthermore, she observes that the facts constructed by *Annales* historians are very much like the facts constructed by prehistorians:

> An *Annales* fact is by and large a tabular fact of some kind, the kind of fact that is gathered in vast quantity in censuses, ledgers, baptismal records, and customs declarations, very much the same kind of fact that archaeologists collect in potsherd counts, records of burial layouts, and distribution of sites over a landscape.

> (Galloway 1990, p. 4)

Galloway's points can be illustrated and amplified with the aid of a brief summary of the current state of research in what is demonstrably a single, late prehistoric (AD 1050–1550) culture (polity) in Alabama, USA. It is an exercise, following Childe (1956), in pre-*history* or *pre*-history, depending on the perspective.

Excavations at the major site, Moundville, began in 1845, were continuous from 1929 to 1941, and have been intermittent from 1948 to the present. Survey and excavation at several other sites of the Moundville phase has been undertaken almost every summer since 1970. The records and collections produced by this research have been conserved, from 1845 to the present, with great care, and are available for use today (see Peebles (1987) and Scarry (1981) for a reasonably complete bibliography on 150 years of research at Moundville).

Moundville, and sites of the Moundville phase, are set in a 500 sq.km portion of the Black Warrior River Valley near Tuscaloosa, Alabama. For purposes of analysis, this portion of the valley can be treated as an "island ecosystem", an oasis of fertile soils and floodplain forests set in the midst of extensive and unproductive pine barrens. For purposes of definition, the Moundville site and phase can be called "Mississipian". The population grew corn (*Zea mays*) and depended on this staple for the majority of their calories, built truncated earthen platform mounds around a plaza, made the right sorts of shell tempered pottery, participated in widespread exchange of manufactured goods and exotic raw materials, had a burial sociology that is consistent with a well-defined hierarchy of social statuses and offices, and through the distribution of "foreign exchange" among specific parts of the settlement and with particular burials give evidence of what has been called a "prestige goods" economy.

The Moundville phase grew (Figure 1) from settlements of hunter-gatherer horticulturists (West Jefferson phase, AD 900–1050). The earliest Moundville phase groups (Moundville I, AD 1050–1200) were fully agricultural, and maintained single temple mounds as foci for regional populations scattered among farmsteads and hamlets. In the later Moundville phases (Moundville II and III, AD 1200–1550) the system grew into a complex system of hamlets, larger villages and single mound centres, in which the site of Moundville was the demographic, economic and symbolic centre. This system began to decline in the later Moundville III period, leaving a series of equidistantly spaced settlements in place of the former hierarchy (Moundville IV, Alabama River phase, AD 1550–1700).

The Moundville site itself (Figure 2) began as a small West Jefferson phase settlement. At some time after AD 1000 a single mound was erected, making Moundville the southernmost of four such regional centres. Four mounds were in place by Moundville II, establishing the bilateral symmetry of the site and raising it from *primus inter pares* to primate among the regional centres. Moundville reached its greatest size during Moundville III, at which point it comprised twenty large mounds which defined a 40 ha plaza; there were, in addition, social spaces devoted to public buildings, workshops, élite residences, and mortuaries. Soon thereafter, in the earliest part of Moundville IV, the site was abandoned.

The extant data from Moundville and from several other sites of the Moundville phase will support the construction of economic and demographic "series", in the sense given this term by the *Annales* (see Peebles 1987 and Steponaitis 1989, for the specifics and for additional citations). Variety in the subsistence economy, the flow of imports and changes in the demographic profile (see also Powell 1988) can be measured with a reasonable degree of accuracy (Figure 3).

This is not the place to redescribe analyses that are already published. In brief, the Moundville subsistence economy becomes less varied over time: the phenotypic diversity in the corn crop declines by one-half, and the variety of animals in the diet, after a brief increase in diversity, declines slightly. The aggregate of imported goods (ceramics and their contents, shell and copper) reach their peak

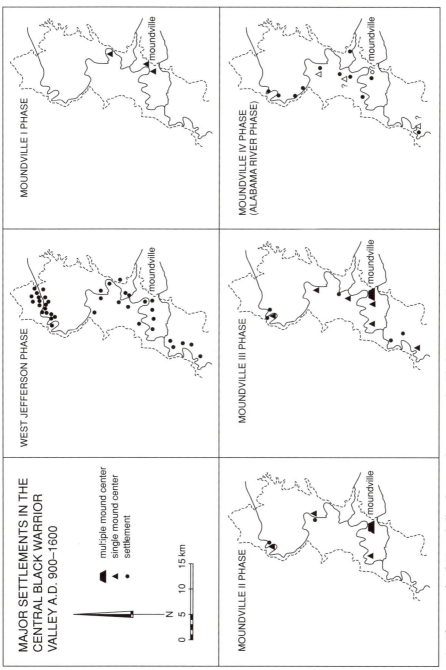

Figure 1 The growth of Moundville phase settlements in the Black Warrior Valley, Alabama from AD 900–1600

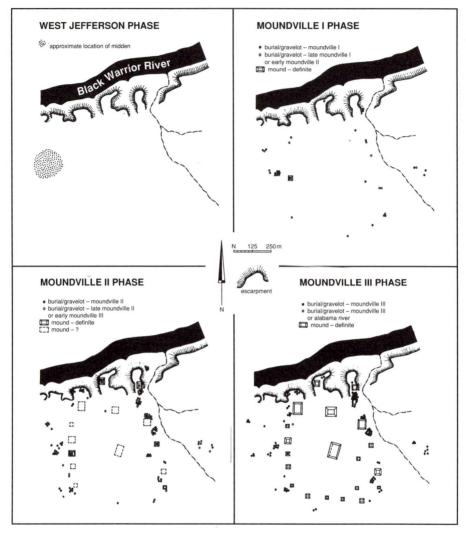

Figure 2 The growth of the Moundville site from agricultural village to major ceremonial center, AD 900–1550

early in the Moundville sequence, at about the time the site begins its major period of growth. Imports decline thereafter and shrink to insignificance late in Moundville III. That is, imports seem to provide "leading economic indicators" of the later collapse of Moundville. If, in fact, Moundville is an example of a "prestige goods economy" then a decline in the volume of essential social currency presages the dissolution of the social hierarchy.

Maximum population size at Moundville was reached in later Moundville II or early Moundville III. Steponaitis has suggested that Moundville served as a necropolis for the whole of the Moundville phase population, and this marked increase

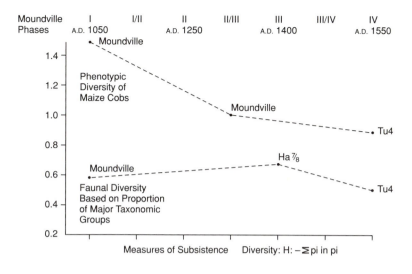

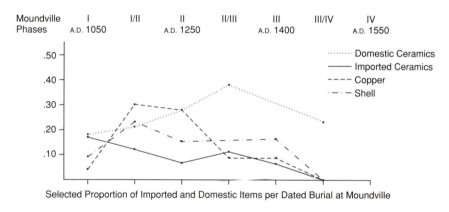

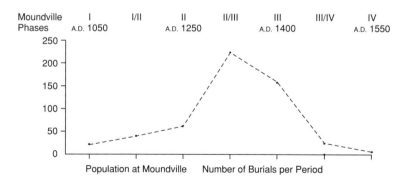

Figure 3 Selected economic, ecologic and demographic measures for Moundville and the Moundville phase, AD 1050–1550

represents the growth of population of the Black Warrior Valley as a whole and not just an increase in the population resident at Moundville. His position is now undergoing critical evaluation. The health of this population, from Moundville I through Moundville III was generally good among both élites and commoners; life expectancy at birth was 28 years and at age 20 was 15 additional years (Powell 1988, p. 184). Thereafter, although the population level in the Black Warrior Valley seems to hold steady for several generations, in the Moundville IV (Alabama River Phase), more than one-half of this population bears signs of malnutrition, and over one-third, many of them adolescents, died before reaching adulthood. With the collapse of valley-wide organization, the population descended into a kind of Hobbesian equality that had profound consequences. As if to pile injury upon injury, the effects of the first European explorers would be felt within a very few generations after the collapse of Moundville.

The example of a prehistory constructed from the Moundville materials may be limited, but it is indicative of a history written using just some of the components of the *Annales* style from an archaeological text.

If space permitted, there would be many more central *Annaliste* themes whose relevance to interpreting the rich Moundville database has been or could be explored: e.g. the interaction of structural constraints and possibilities with contingent events in the production of the historical trajectory of Moundville, or the identification of specific *modes de vie* and *mentalités* within the Mississippian phenomenon and the evaluation of their contribution to the observed cultural dynamics.

There is far more to the *Annales*, moreover, than serial history, problem-directed history, eclectic methods, and *mentalités*. There is, as Samuel Kinser has noted, a profound and deep-seated metaphysic, expressed best in the work of Braudel:

> Braudel's concept of the temporalities making up history is metaphysically anchored, attributable to the very nature of the world. And his three metasigns – Time, Space, Man – stand like sentinels at the edges of Braudel's historical vision; they are the absolutes guaranteeing the rest. . . . The timing that Braudel used is a humanly anchored vision, the product of a historian's reflection about the ideal tempo for human affairs.
>
> (Kinser 1981, p. 99)

It is, again, a human history, in which the unintended consequences of change far outnumber those that were planned and could have been known to the individuals who participated directly. It is only from the vantage points of a past's future that these consequences and their causal structure can be delineated and perhaps explained. Hence the privileged position of the historian and the prehistorian.

It is at this point, with the repeated emphasis on humankind, that the cognitive sciences can be invoked. As Howard Gardner has defined them, in his book *The Mind's New Science*, the cognitive sciences are concerned with "the nature of knowledge, its components, its sources, and its development" (Gardner 1987, p. 6). Thus for Gardner – and for most other cognitive scientists – it is both a natural, biological science and a science of representation and intention – a human and cultural science, if you will. It has interests in brain – and mind – and in knowledge. Moreover, it is a historical science in which each generation builds upon the genetic and representational legacy of preceding generations.

In both history and in anthropology – the past and the present – the touchstone of representation, intention and adaptation is knowledge: the human capacity for knowledge and the content of knowledge itself. It is axiomatic that human cultural abilities have evolved; it likewise is clear that current cognition is dependent on perception and ratiocination – on biological apparatus and mental constructs. What is not (perhaps) so clear is that these capacities and their content have a co-evolutionary history. Mind-brain and culture were, at least in part, the selective environments for each other's evolution. To the extent that the cognitive sciences involve themselves in the study of the production, development and deployment of knowledge, then some of the future of archaeology as paradigmatic science and as narrative is bound up in this study.

In geological time, prehistorians and human paleontologists seek the evolutionary pathways of both mind and brain; in somewhat more recent spans we are interested in archaeological materials and their contexts in the terms laid down four decades ago by V. Gordon Childe: "as concrete expressions and embodiments of human thoughts and ideas – in a world [as embodiments] of knowledge" (Childe 1956, p. 1). Childe is not offering either an idealist's quest or plea for what has derisively been called "paleopsychology". He is arguing for a variant of what Danto has termed "representational materialism". Therein:

> We have the concept of knowledge because we need there to be not simply representations but true ones, and not only true ones but those that are true because of the way the world causes us to have those representations in the first place.
>
> (Danto 1989, p. 272)

In effect, there is both a human ecology and a representational ecology, both of which are important parts of the human career, and both of which are instantiated to varying degrees in the archaeological text.

To the extent that prehistory can include human intention, representations, and knowledge as important aspects of its conceptual framework, it will become a more exciting and relevant discipline. To this end, the only requirements are some form of basic realism (see Lakoff 1987) and a commitment to critical rationality (in the sense meant by Popper and his students). As Stephen Toulmin argues, the metaphysical focus must shift from the certainty of Descartes and Newton to the critical scepticism of Erasmus and Montaigne, from the cosmos to the polis in Cosmopolis (Toulmin 1989). To the extent that prehistory clings to the tenets of behaviourism and positivism, in which logical empiricism sets the goals of invariance and necessity for the scientific study of all human phenomena, it will be relegated to the same musty warehouses that store the last of the Skinner Boxes, abandoned by most psychology departments more than thirty years ago. To the extent that it continues to ignore history, it deprives itself of its anchor in the present. To the extent that it chooses relativism and solipsism and abandons a standard of judgement for its products, it risks becoming totally irrelevant.

References

Bloch, M. 1953 *The Historian's Craft*, Vintage Books, New York.

Braudel, F. 1973 *The Mediterranean and the Mediterranean World in the Age of Philip II*, 2 Vols, trans. by Sian Reynolds, Harper and Row, New York.

—— 1988 *The Identity of France, Volume 1: History and Environment*, trans. by Sian Reynolds, Harper and Row, New York.

Bruner, J. 1986 *Actual Minds and Possible Worlds*, Harvard University Press, Cambridge, Mass.

Chartier, R. 1988 *Cultural History*, Cornell University Press, Ithaca, New York.

Chaunu, P. 1968 *Histoire quantitative, histoire sérielle*, Armand Colin, Paris.

Childe, V.G. 1949 "The sociology of knowledge", *Modern Quarterly* Vol. 4, pp. 302–9.

—— 1956 *Society and Knowledge*, Harper and Brothers, New York.

Collingwood, R.G. 1978 (orig. 1939) *An Autobiography*, Oxford University Press, Oxford.

Danto, A.C. 1985 *Narration and Knowledge*, Columbia University Press, New York.

—— 1989 *Connections to the World*, Harper and Row, New York.

Deetz, J. 1988 "History and archaeological theory: Walter Taylor revisited", *American Antiquity*, Vol. 53, pp. 12–22.

Fink, C. 1989 *Marc Bloch: a life in history*, Cambridge University Press, Cambridge.

Galloway, P. 1990 "*Conjoncture and longue durée*; ethnohistory and anthropology in the Southeast", manuscript in possession of the author.

Gardin, J.-C. 1980 *Archaeological Constructs*, Cambridge University Press, Cambridge.

Gardin, J.C. 1987 Untitled lecture, given in Bloomington, Indiana, 9 October. Transcript in the possession of the author.

Gardner, H. 1987 *The Mind's New Science: A History of the Cognitive Revolution*, Basic Books, New York.

Hodder, I. 1986 *Reading the Past*, Cambridge University Press, Cambridge.

Kinser, S. 1981 "*Annaliste* paradigm? The geohistorical structuralism of Fernand Braudel", *American Historical Review* Vol. 86, pp. 63–105.

Lakoff, G. 1987 *Women, Fire and Dangerous Things*, University of Chicago Press, Chicago.

Leroi-Gourham, A. 1974 "Les voies de l'histoire avant l'écriture", pp. 134–150 in *Faire de l'histoire*, I, Nouveaux problèmes, sous la direction de Jacques le Goff et de Pierre Nova, Gallimard, Paris.

Le Goff, J. and Nora, P. (eds) 1974 *Faire de l'histoire*, 3 Vols, Gallimard, Paris.

—— 1985 *Constructing the Past*, Cambridge University Press, Cambridge.

Lepenies, W. 1985 *Die Drei Kulturen*, Karl Hanser Verlag, Munich.

—— 1988 *Between Literature and Science: The Rise of Sociology* (English translation by Hollingdale, R.J. 1985), Cambridge University Press, Cambridge.

Peebles, C.S. 1986 "Paradise lost, strayed, and stolen: prehistoric social devolution in the Southeast", pp. 24–40 in *The Burden of Being Civilized: An Anthropological Perspective on the Discontents of Civilization*, ed. Miles Richardson and Malcolm C. Webb, Southern Anthropological Society Proceedings, No. 18, University of Georgia Press, Athens.

—— (1987) "The rise and fall of the Mississippian in Western Alabama: the Moundville and Summerville phases, AD 1000 to 1600", *Mississippi Archaeology* Vol. 22, pp. 1–31.

Plumb, J.H. (1969) *The Death of the Past*, Macmillan, London.

Powell, M.L. (1988) *Status and Health in Prehistory*, Smithsonian Institution Press, Washington.

Ricoeur, P. (1980) *The Contributions of French Historiography to the Theory of History*, Clarendon Press, Oxford.

—— (1984) *The Reality of the Historical Past*, Marquette University Press, Milwaukee.

Scarry, C.M. (1981) "The Moundville Archaeological Project", *Southeastern Archaeological Conference, Bulletin* 24, pp. 77–112.

Shanks, M. and Tilley, C. (1987) *Social Theory and Archaeology*, Polity Press, Cambridge.

Snow, C.P. (1959) *The Two Cultures*, Cambridge University Press, Cambridge.

—— (1964) *The Two Cultures and a Second Look*, Cambridge University Press, Cambridge.

Steponaitis, V.P. (1989) "Contrasting Patterns of Mississippian Development", a paper presented at the School of American Research advanced seminar *Chiefdoms: Their Evolutionary Significance*, April 1989.

Stoianovitch, T. (1976) *French Historical Method: The Annales Paradigm.* Cornell University Press, Ithaca, New York.

Toulmin, S. (1989) *Cosmopolis: The Hidden Agenda of Modernity*, The Free Press, New York.

Trigger, B.G. (1989 *A History of Archaeological Thought*, Cambridge University Press, Cambridge.

Veyne, P. (1984) *Writing History*, Wesleyan University Press, Middletown.

White, H. (1973) *Metahistory*, The Johns Hopkins University Press, Baltimore.

Wolf, E.R. (1982) *Europe and the People Without History*, University of California Press, Berkeley.

Young, T.C. (1988) "Since Herodotus, has history been a valid concept?", *American Antiquity* Vol. 53, pp 7–12.

Chapter 10

Cobb

SOCIAL REPRODUCTION AND THE *LONGUE DURÉE* IN THE PREHISTORY OF THE MIDCONTINENTAL UNITED STATES

Charles R. Cobb

In their most recent edition of *A History of American Archaeology*, Willey and Sabloff (1980: 181ff.) argue that one of the signal developments of the new or processual archaeology was the adoption of an explicit evolutionary framework, thereby rejecting the culture-historical formulations guiding earlier archaeological research. That view would meet with little controversy in most quarters today and, with some lag time elapsing between various regions and institutions in North America, it is apparent that by the time of the publication of the 1980 volume the processual program dominated Americanist archaeology. The gains made by the paradigm saw a steady retreat into disfavor of that archaeology oriented toward culture-historical reconstruction, although this form of descriptive research is usually seen as a necessary accompaniment of more "theoretically" based work. Indeed, with various in-depth discussions over the years of the roles of history and historical reconstruction within processual research, and critiques of the limitations of the historical method in archaeology, James Deetz (1988:13) has noted that there is really little more to be added to the subject.

It thus is of no little interest that a resurgence of the historical tradition has occurred in the postprocessual archaeology of the last decade – or at least that branch of the program in Great Britain associated with Ian Hodder and his students (Hodder 1987). From the perspective of the processual school that still dominates on the American side of the Atlantic, the question arises as to whether this particular tradition of British archaeology never rejected historical explanation or has veered into another epistemological tradition that more readily accommodates historical approaches. A third alternative, and one somewhat more unpalatable to the processual program, is that the new archaeology has become a somewhat stultified normal science slow to embrace ongoing theoretical developments in history and other fields, threatening to relegate North American archaeology to a peripheral status in terms of theoretical sophistication (Watson, 1991)

Because of the challenges raised by postprocessual archaeology to some of the basic tenets of processual archaeology, it is of value to reexamine some aspects of the role of historical explanation in archaeology. It thus becomes possible to clarify certain facets of the ongoing debate and to explore possible areas of common ground. It will be argued in this chapter that there is an important place for historically informed models or explanations in archaeology regardless of the epistemological approach utilized. The coevolution of exchange and agricultural systems in the midcontinental United States during the interval of approximately 3000 BC to AD 1400 will serve as a case study demonstrating the value of *social reproduction* as a unit of analysis for addressing historical and general trends over time.

Historical explanation in archaeology

Possibly the major difficulty in evaluating the potential of historical explanation in archaeology is definitional: what constitutes historical explanation for one archaeologist is frequently quite different for another. This problem appears to be commonplace within the processual paradigm, as well as between it and other approaches. For that reason, it is important to examine some of the differences. In broad terms, archaeological treatments of historical explanation can be divided into two categories: (1) history as a concern with the particular and (2) history as an alternative form of explanation to ethnological explanation. Certainly, other ideal divisions of historical explanation and methodology have been made by archaeologists (e.g., Deetz 1988; Taylor 1948); however, I attempt here to address how the discipline (at least in North America) has actually treated historical explanation in practice. Thus, for example, the question as to whether the divide between prehistory and documented history demarcates separate realms of study for archaeologists and historians, respectively, has really represented a minor issue in North American archaeology. We have been happy to subsume under archaeology the study of material culture from any time or place.

The first view of historical explanation given above is one that has traditionally been held by the processual school. From that perspective, historical explanation, as epitomized by the culture-historical school, relies on the reconstruction of time-space systematics. Consequently, research is directed primarily toward developing typological sequences for general regions as a basis for examining change in terms of specific events (e.g., diffusion, warfare). The contraposition to this approach – that archeology should be a generalizing discipline – has served as the great divide between culture-historical and processual programs.

In a major critique of the historical method in archaeology demonstrating the processual views on historical explanation, Binford (1968) examined the Sabloff and Willey study (1967) of the collapse of the Classic Lowland Maya civilization (*ca.* AD 900). Citing evidence for Gulf Coast influence in a number of material realms at the site of Seibal during the ninth century, Sabloff and Willey argued that those remains supported evidence for an invasion from that region that led to the downfall of the Classic Maya. In his criticism, Binford stated that, despite the evidence for Gulf Coast influences, actual evidence for an invasion or warfare had not been demonstrated. The archaeological record was interpreted in terms of sequential, presumably cause-and-effect-related events, without the necessary process of hypothesis testing for rigorously evaluating the presumed relationships between the events. Hence, the "explanation" offered by Sabloff and Willey subscribed to a restricted inductivist philosophy that relied on unfounded inferences. Equally damaging in Binford's view, no attempt was made to incorporate or generate laws of social evolution or function in the model of Maya collapse.

Following the general line of reasoning set forth by Binford, processual archaeology has rejected explanation by antecedent events, if the relationships between the events are not examined in a rigorous manner and do not rely on generalizing explanatory principles. Nevertheless, the basic methodology of historical reconstruction has been welcomed as an important adjunct of processual studies in that control of the specifics of time–space systematics is an important descriptive step – setting the stage, so to speak – for addressing more general explanatory concerns.

A second view of history is that it represents a form of explanation that can be used as an alternative model to the traditional anthropological ties of archaeology. Consequently, archaeology as a method can contribute to either history or ethnological theory (Deetz 1988:20). From the processual perspective, if archaeology is conducted in the service of the former it is not anthropology. From the postprocessual perspective, however, history is a legitimate theoretical discipline that is of equal importance to ethnology as a model for the explanation of long-term change.

It is important to briefly examine some of Hodder's views on historical explanation in archaeology since he has offered the most programmatic statements on the issue from the postprocessual side (see Hodder 1986, 1987). In brief, Hodder has drawn inspiration from two influential historians, Collingwood and Braudel. He proposes that social change must be examined in terms of long-term processes based upon an empathic understanding of past events and that ideational structures are determinant of social processes (Collingwood 1946). Moreover, complete historical description is a necessary avenue for reaching an "inner" understanding of a culture. Underlying the approach is a historically based poststructuralism centering upon the thesis that cultural variability and transformation has as its locus the knowledgeability of specific human actors of their cultural milieu and how they choose to negotiate their role within the ideational system.

For Hodder (1987), Braudel's (1972, 1980) hierarchical and cyclical model of historical process serves as a key heuristic device for understanding the relationship between long-term change and the individual events that lead to the formation of the archaeological record. Braudel (1972:20–21) proposed a three-level cycle of determinance in historical change:

1 Structure: slow-moving recurrent features of change involving geographic, climatic, biological, and productive factors – the *longue durée* of history;
2 Conjuncture: a smaller cycle of rhythmic social history involving economic and social variables that frequently alter structure to reach new points of equilibrium within the longer-lasting structural cycle; and
3 Event: short, rapid oscillations representing specific events or the actions of individuals – history in a more traditional sense.

Whereas Braudel focused on causality as originating on the first tier and viewed the actions and free will of individuals as subordinate to the structural grand currents of geography and ecology, Hodder seems to argue that the structural cycle should be viewed as ideational – and that it is at the third level that action and event become archaeologically visible as individuals manipulate material culture to reproduce the conditions of their existence as mediated by the ideational structure (Hodder 1987:3).

It is evident, then, that the postprocessual approach to historical explanation is not merely an atheoretical recounting of events, the charge typically leveled at the cultural-historical school. And certainly the idea that transformations in material culture are subject to theoretically informed historical models has been advocated by others before (e.g., Glassie 1975:8–12). Despite the possibilities that some historical models may offer for archaeology, however, a justified dissatisfaction with the limitations of past culture-historical studies by processualists has led to an unjustified rejection of any approaches that appear to borrow concepts from historical schools of thought. This stems from the notion that historical explanations are ultimately inductivist and empirical and opposed to the generalizing aims of an archaeology closely wedded to ethnology. Yet even from within the processual camp there have been strong calls to loosen the strong ties to cultural anthropology held in North American archaeology. Gumerman and Phillips (1978), for example, have strongly argued that archaeology would benefit most from the creative borrowing from a number of disciplines and in fact had been leaning that way since the inception of processual archaeology. Rather than viewing archaeology as contributing to (or borrowing from) either history or ethnology, perhaps it is best to retain a sense of pluralism in our borrowing of models to evaluate past behavior. Indeed, Trigger (1988, 1989) has strongly argued that the distinctions between history and anthropology, and between history and science (read evolution), are false cries, and he has been a staunch advocate of historical approaches throughout the heyday of processual archaeology.

Given that historical models may serve an important role in a pluralistic archaeology, one must ask how a processual archaeology is to incorporate notions of the particular or specific events into a discipline that still hopes to make some generalizations about human behavior. This concern is perhaps best addressed by Michael Rowlands, who has noted:

> If specificity is lost altogether, any generalization becomes so general as to be useless, and if too much specificity is retained, then establishing its meaning by relating it to events or cases of a similar class becomes impossible. The problem for many archaeologists is knowing what class of general propositions they might contribute to.
>
> The most consistent answer to this question in recent years has been that archaeology is concerned with processes of change. More specifically, its concern is with the way different types of societies result to changes in their immediate environment and the internal mechanisms that both stimulate and provide the solutions to the internal processes that precede social transformation.
>
> Rowlands 1982:1601

Here Rowlands emphasizes the interplay between specificity and generalization to address issues of change, and it is the renewed emphasis on dealing with change over time that may prove one of the more beneficial critiques of processual archaeology from the postprocessual program. It is ironic for a discipline that, at least within North America, has long proclaimed that its major raison d'être within the larger discipline of anthropology has been its ability to address patterns of long-term change now finds itself under criticism by postprocessualists for neglecting that very approach (Hodder 1987). Processual archaeology has been faulted for its continued heavy reliance upon synchronic cross-cultural generalizations despite years of critiques of systems models, narrow ecological approaches, and other simplified functional explanations (e.g., Kushner 1974; Salmon 1978).

Ecologically based archaeological research does not necessarily lack the conceptual tools to address issues of long-term change, but most studies have chosen not to do so. They typically rely upon the universal type–stage evolutionary sequences developed by Service (1962) and Fried (1967) that ironically incorporate a determinism that is completely at odds with the tenets of evolutionary ecology. As many students of cultural evolution argued before the postprocessual critiques appeared on the scene, cultural evolution, like biological evolution, is opportunistic and nondirectional rather than a process leading inexorably to higher and higher levels of complexity (e.g., Blute 1979:58; Dunnell 1980:48). David Meltzer (1979:654) pointed out 10 years ago that studies in new archaeology that incorporate a more faithful concept of that form of evolution have been largely nonexistent, and this largely holds true today.

More appropriate approaches for addressing the character of social evolution for those who wish to adhere to ecological/evolutionary models seem to include nonlinear or bifurcation models that do not view social systems as static, equilibrium-seeking entities (Adams 1982; Allen 1982; Friedman 1982; Shennan; 1991). Under those approaches, long-term cultural change is conceived of as a discontinuous process, with threshold points of saltation or collapse that are not necessarily predictable and are best understood in terms of historical, particularist parameters. An alternative concept for dealing with long-term change that is in general agreement with that thesis is *social reproduction*, which I will advocate in the following discussion. This unit of analysis provides a potential for bridging patterns of specificity and generality that are pertinent to both historically and ethnologically based approaches to the study of long-term change.

Social reproduction

A major difficulty in broaching problems of long-term change is the delineation of an appropriate unit of analysis; before diachronic description or explanation can take place, there must be a definition of what is to be measured and evaluated with respect to time (Binford 1965:203; Deetz 1988:17; Glassie 1975:8). Of course, a recurring dilemma with that requirement in archaeology is that one frequently finds diachronic "explanation" as the exposition of a series of "static, multiple synchronies" (Deetz 1988:17) rather than a true attempt to deal with process. Thus, we find that our traditional ceramic, lithic, and other artifact typologies that are so efficient for ordering materials chronologically often are inappropriate for other research questions. To these latter ends, we require more processual units of analysis.

Acknowledging that archaeology is a catholic discipline, it is mistaken to assert that only one or a few units of analysis are relevant for examining long-term change from material culture. Instead, the concordance of the goals must be determined by a given research problem. In the case study that concludes this chapter, the concern is with the evolution of exchange systems within a specific region and how that phenomenon was related to dimensions of agricultural intensification and social hierarchy. It is proposed that social reproduction is one concept eminently suited to the explication of these relationships.

To cite Friedman and Rowlands (1978:203), social reproduction represents "a system . . . characterised by a socially determined set of productive relations . . . that distributes the total labour input and output of a population and organises immediate work processes and the exploitation of the environment within limits established by a given level of technological development." The concept of social reproduction is defined largely by both temporal and spatial dimensions and thus is of particular value for archaeological analyses that traditionally excel in those two areas. Because individuals and groups reproduce the conditions of their own existence, history is not merely a passage of events and people but a continual negotiation and transformation of the relations of production and exchange. Consequently, the properties of social reproduction can be defined only with respect to time (Friedman 1975:162; Friedman and Rowlands 1978:204). And while systems of production may have elements that recur through time and space, specific forms of production, exchange, and deploying labor involve specific and historically occurring sets of social relations (O'Laughlin 1975:351; Wolf 1982:75).

At the same time, social systems are not closed; from the most simple bands to modern nation-states, groups engage in external social, economic, and political relationships and alliances at various spatial scales that are imposed upon discrete populations (Bender 1985; Rowlands 1987; Wolf 1982). For that reason the analysis of social reproduction denies the well-worn dichotomy about whether so-called internal or external sources of variation are more important stimuli to the evolution of social systems. Clearly, both are at work in a dynamic interplay. Furthermore, recognition also must be made of the fact that preexisting conditions of technology and demography also represent important constraints upon the course of human action.

The recognition of the overlapping dimensions of variability suggests that Braudel's views of history may still be of some importance for modeling long-term trajectories of social change. However, a concern with social process suggests that it is at the level of conjuncture that the nexus of social reproduction must be addressed. Here in the realm of political and economic action does one find the mediation between the intentions of the individual actor and the larger constraints of ecology, technology, and demography. While individual action may represent a key source of variability in social systems (an argument forwarded by some post-processualists), equally important are the ways in which traits are transmitted to others and why such traits are retained as a feature of the social grouping at large. Conversely, the heavy reliance on such variables as ecology and environment as key instigators of evolutionary processes ignores the importance of social dynamics as begetting social change.

The idea that long-term change in prehistory can be viewed as a series of hierarchical cycles has been the subject of empirical as well as theoretical investigation by several researchers. Jonathan Friedman (1975) has postulated a general cyclical pattern in the reproduction of tribal systems where short-term cycles of political and social variation are affected by a long-term cycle defined by changing patterns of land use and an increasing level of environmental degradation. Similar approaches have been used to tie agricultural intensification in Bronze Age northern Europe to the systematic rise and fall of certain patterns of tribal organization (Kristiansen 1982) and to examine the punctuated nature of political change in Anglo-Saxon England (Hodges 1986).

Cyclical change in the Midwestern United States

This model can be applied with some success to prehistoric developments in the midcontinental United States, a region that clearly demonstrates how long-term trends in ecology and agriculture interact with shorter cycles of social reproduction defined by the emergence and decline of regional exchange networks. The region in question can be broadly defined as that larger area encompassing the Lower Ohio and Central Mississippi valleys (Figure 1). The time period of interest

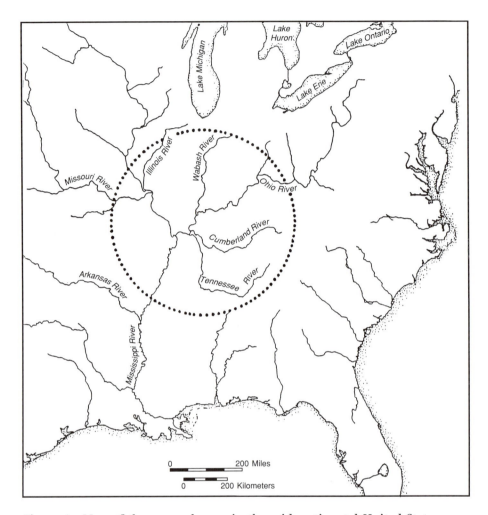

Figure 1   Map of the research area in the midcontinental United States

begins at approximately 3000 BC and ends about AD 1400. During that interval three separate long-distance exchange networks in luxury goods emerged and declined against a backdrop of an overall pattern of subsistence intensification and population increase.

Late Archaic Period

The Late Archaic period (*ca*. 3000–1000 BC) represents the first era in the sequence. At this time certain categories of rare raw materials and finished goods, notably copper from the Great Lakes region, marine shell from the Gulf Coast, and a number of lithic and mineral materials, appear throughout numerous sites in the midcontinental United States (Cook 1976; Goad 1980; Kay 1983; Marquardt and

Watson 1983; Winters 1968). The goods are typically found in mortuary association, but their general distribution in burials suggests a predominantly egalitarian
structure, with signs of ranking and social differentiation at an incipient level (e.g.,
Marquardt and Watson 1983:334, Rothschild 1979).

Although the objects witnessed a fairly extensive distribution, their occurrence
across sites is sporadic. Furthermore, sizeable accumulations of the goods are rare
on specific sites. It thus appears that a limited number of groups participated in
interregional exchange, and there is an absence of the obvious concentrations of
wealth that might indicate the development of strong internal differentiation or
external "core–periphery" relationships.

Within this same time-frame there is the first widespread appearance of cultigens in the Midwest. They include tropical cucurbits and several native species such
as sunflower, sumpweed, and goosefoot. Despite the evidence for a general population increase during the Late Archaic, there is a general consensus that the
subsistence base had a broad spectrum and the role attributed to cultigens was
probably that of a protected garden plant (Marquardt and Watson 1983:335; B.
Smith 1987); they evidently did not serve a critical function in meeting the demands
of a growing population.

Middle Woodland–Hopewell Periods

With some exceptions, the evidence for the participation of midwestern sites in
long-distance trade ceases around 1000 BC. These networks appear again around
200 BC to form the Hopewellian interaction sphere of the Middle Woodland period.
The phenomenon encompassed a large part of the Midwest, with major concentrations of Hopewellian mound sites in southern Ohio and west-central Illinois. In
contrast to Late Archaic exchange, Hopewellian exchange involved a greater diversity and quantity of raw materials and finished goods appearing within many more
sites. They include objects in copper, mica, galena, obsidian, chert, and marine
shell. Regions bordering the Midwest also systematically participated in a far-flung
exchange network that articulated with Hopewellian exchange. Mound sites in the
lower Mississippi Valley, western Georgia, and northern Alabama, for example,
may have contributed raw materials to Hopewell sites and, in turn, may have
received both goods and symbolic or stylistic influences as evidenced on pottery
and other artifacts (e.g., Ford 1963; Jefferies 1979; Jenkins 1979; Smith 1979).

The preferential treatment of some burials, including their accompaniment with
large quantities of nonlocal goods, suggests a more differentiated social system
compared to the Late Archaic period. Yet it is doubtful that those individuals held
the degree of power associated with even simple ranked societies. Their roles may
be better described as positions of negotiation as a consequence of their importance in maintaining external alliances and trade relations (Braun and Plog
1982:517). This notion accords well with the emerging view that Hopewell-related
exchange may have been a fairly unstructured phenomenon (Goad 1978; Seeman

1979). Elites may have enjoyed some differential access to external exchange as a virtue of their status, but factors of primitive transport technology and a fairly weakly differentiated social system limited their control over the external movement of prestige goods.

In contrast to the very minor role held by cultigens in the Archaic diet, in certain areas of the midcontinent during the Hopewellian period certain plants witnessed genetic manipulation, maintenance outside of native habitats, and massive harvesting (Braun and Plog 1982:516). While the same cultigens seen in the Late Archaic period continued to be exploited, several new plants were also added to the subsistence inventory, including knotweed, maygrass, and little barley. This occurs within a context of continued population growth, although numerous wild plant and animal species apparently constituted a major portion of the diet.

Mississippi Period

After a hiatus of several centuries the last great interregional trade systems to appear in the prehistoric midcontinent arose with the advent of the Mississippi period, ca. AD 1000. Continuing the trend seen in Hopewellian times, yet an even greater diversity and abundance of widely traded raw materials and finished goods appear throughout Mississippian sites, both large and small. Most of the raw materials popular in Archaic and Middle Woodland exchange continued to be valued during the Mississippi period, including marine shell, copper, fluorite, galena, and several types of stone. Many of the materials were rendered into a number of recurring symbols, designs, and artifact types referred to as the Southeastern Ceremonial Complex (Brown 1976; Howard 1968; Muller 1966; Waring and Holder 1945). While the common occurrence of the complex across the Southeast and the Midwest has been traditionally viewed as a widespread "cultural" phenomenon, more recently it has been considered in terms of the actual exchange of goods as well as ideas (Brown et al. 1990).

The degree of mortuary elaboration on many Mississippian sites, far exceeding the Archaic and Woodland periods, has led most researchers to concur that social ranking was well developed in many areas. The abundance of exotic sumptuary goods further seems to reflect differential access to external exchange by elites. In addition, the widespread construction of earthworks may indicate more of a control over the deployment of labor than seen during the appearance of earlier interregional exchange networks. Yet it is still unlikely that direct control over interregional exchange was effected by leaders; more likely trade occurred on a down-the-line basis (Muller 1987).

Agricultural systems became fairly intensive during the Mississippi period, seeing a continued heavy use of the cultigens common on Hopewellian sites. Importantly, maize cultivation had now become widespread and in many Mississippian regions constituted the major domesticate and represented a significant portion of the diet. Although no true urban centers developed, large sedentary settlements became commonplace, attesting to a probable significant population increase. There is little question that the potential of maize for intensification was an important factor in surplus production and demographic expansion. The heavy reliance on wild plant and animal foods was a pattern that continued until the Euro-American period, however.

Patterns of cyclical change

What implications do those patterns have for historical and processual perspectives on the prehistory of the midcontinental United States? Three general trends have been documented in studies of cycles of interregional exchange over the long term that are applicable to this example (Parker Pearson 1984): (1) a continual increase in productive capacity through time; (2) a cumulative difference between rich and poor; and (3) an increased quantity and quality of wealth items deposited in ritual contexts as the level of consumption increases in each cycle. The continual increase in productive capacity is evident through the continued expansion of the horticultural economy from the Late Archaic through the Mississippi period. Occurring at different points on this *longue durée* of subsistence intensification, three smaller cycles of interregional exchange emerged and declined, with each successive network incorporating a greater wealth of goods and increasingly marked distinctions of social status (Figure 2).

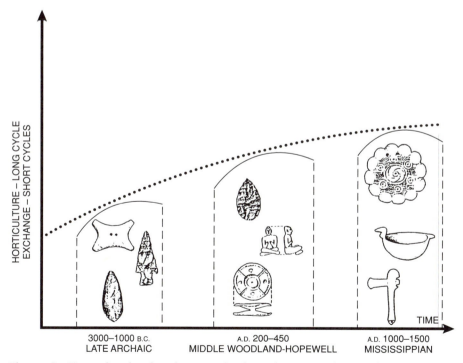

Figure 2   Horticultural and exchange cycles from the Late Archaic to the Mississippian periods

A traditional processual argument would view the coevolution of the intensification of agriculture and development of interregional exchange as related in part to the necessary emergence of elites for their central role in managing the increased information flow associated with higher population densities and complex but risky subsistence systems increasingly dependent upon cultigens (Braun and Plog 1982; Peebles and Kus 1977; Seeman 1979). The interregional circulation of prestige items serves to maintain external alliances that become critical in times of subsistence stress when the exchange of basic goods with established peers in neighboring polities may become critical for overcoming food shortages.

From the perspective of the long term, the argument fails in the midwestern example above because it does not satisfactorily account for why interregional exchange systems would collapse under conditions of increasing agricultural intensification and population growth and then reemerge under the very same conditions.

When viewed as a dynamic system of social reproduction engaged in a prestige goods economy, the emergence and decline of interregional exchange networks can be better understood in terms of elites promoting external exchange primarily for their own benefit and funding their power in part by the increased surplus afforded through intensified production. Nonstratified societies demonstrate a recurrent trend among aspiring elites to intensify subsistence output from immediate and extended families in order to promote status-enhancing feasting and gift-giving (Brookfield and Brown 1963; Mair 1964; Sahlins 1972:135–137). Those activities extend the sphere of production control by elites through a system of debt-obligation inherent in the transactions. This fosters a spiral of ever larger feasts and strategic distribution of prestige goods, providing a means of social control to elites that is not dependent upon a direct control over the means of production.

The widely traded prestige goods frequently are essential within given societies for such important ceremonial or social transactions as conducting important rites of passage, making bride-wealth payments and religious fees, or as markers of prestige (Blanton and Feinman 1984; Ekholm 1978; Friedman 1975; Schneider 1977). Thus, the control over the disbursement of those goods through feasts and bestowals represents a critical link in manipulating labor in a society that finds acquiring those social valuables essential to the reproduction of the social and ideological system. Furthermore, the importance of certain nonlocal goods to localized social transactions promotes a system of interregional alliances between elites and simultaneously discourages the availability of prestige goods locally, further enhancing their value. In contrast to the passive role attributed to exotics as reflectors of status in the processual program, the material goods assume a major active role in the production and reproduction of the social system across space and through time (Hodder 1985:4–5).

Of central importance to the model is the idea that subsistence intensification is not simply viewed as either a dependent or independent variable in culture change – stances frequently adopted in population pressure and agriculture intensification debates. Instead, the intensification of horticulture becomes an important component within a dynamic feedback system of social reproduction. When social systems alter their subsistence strategies – for whatever reason – they introduce new tensions, opportunities, and constraints that potentially alter the conditions of reproduction (Friedman 1975:165), which eventually alter anew the social system. This continues the cycle of change. In this context, it is not denied that increased dependence on horticultural or agricultural economies entails increased subsistence risks brought about by an artificial simplification of the landscape and reduced mobility. However, these problems are in large part an indirect result of competition and social pressures on surplus production.

Where the midwestern data base is perhaps of most interest lies in the question of the decline of the exchange networks. Many of the studies cited above dealing with cyclicity have viewed the collapse of prestige systems founded on agricultural surplus as an outgrowth of growing contradictions between the ability of groups to produce enough surplus for both use and exchange and a widening division between production and consumption where, as consumption increases, production declines from overintensification. Ultimately, these problems lead to social unrest and the threat of environmental degradation, causing social reorganization and the collapse of the interregional alliance systems founded on the exchange of prestige goods (Kristiansen 1982; Parker Pearson 1984).

The patterns described for the midcontinental United States differ in two important ways from this scenario. First, the example in this chapter is a case of relatively pristine development, with no evidence for groups participating in a larger "world system" that involved ties with aggressive complex chiefdoms or stratified societies. Second, this example has its origins in the incipience of horticulture, whereas other studies have tended to deal with fairly well developed agricultural economies. Consequently, there are serious questions as to whether in the Late Archaic, for example, the potential for intensification seen in the minor use of a small number of cultigens was sufficient to afford the surplus production that could engender a prestige economy founded on strongly institutionalized relations of exploitation or whether pressures of competition or exploitation from polities outside the midwest promoted subsistence intensification during the Mississippi period. Finally, with the possible exception of the Mississippi period, it is problematical whether overintensification was a serious problem to subsistence systems in the prehistoric midcontinent.

At the same time, it has been argued that many of the widespread exchange networks were very loosely organized, sporadic, and unstable (Cobb 1989; Goad 1978). The intrinsic fragility of exchange networks in the midcontinent may have been largely due to the lack of institutionalized agricultural systems and the accompanying underdevelopment of the substantial and predictable supply of surplus production, at least until the Mississippi period, necessary to fund expansionist prestige economies of the scale seen in the Old World and Mesoamerica. While this scenario is hypothetical at present, it does suggest that the specific factors underlying cyclicity in the midcontinent may differ from those seen in other cases.

Conclusions

The model for long-term change in the midcontinental United states is in agreement with the processual paradigm in that it implies that there are certain cross-cultural regularities in social behavior that occur diachronically as well as synchronically. Basic elements of the case study accord well with other studies that have examined long-term trends in the evolution of subsistence and exchange systems. This suggests that the occurrence of those trends may be subject to generalizing forms of explanation – although the latter implication has not been followed out in this chapter. Furthermore, such "external" variables as demography and subsistence are seen as an important consideration of addressing change over time. The emphasis of social reproduction is on "social adaptation" rather than ecological adaptation (see Bender 1985: 52), however, or how social action is a primary source of long-term change. Ecological variables on the long cycle are viewed as constraints – negative selection, if you will – on the variability of human behavior, not as sources of variability.

Certain aspects of the nature of the cyclicity of the exchange networks also seem to be understandable only in terms of their historic context. For example, the potential of the short cycles of exchange to reverse back to their point of origin becomes irreversible as a function of their tangent along the historical trajectory of the long cycle (see Friedman 1975: 187). Consequently, each new cycle of exchange represents a new order understandable only in terms of prior conditions peculiar to this trajectory. Further, the exact points on the long cycle where exchange systems emerge and collapse are determined by social pressures on production – not environmental ones – that appear to culminate in threshold effects whose timing does not seem predictable.

In short, social reproduction incorporates the notion that addressing antecedent and particularist conditions is an important objective for understanding long-term trajectories. Yet generalizations from social theory are also seen as a valuable source of explanatory potential. Obviously, however, the concept will not be a panacea for all researchers concerned with addressing patterns of sociocultural evolution. Major divisions between and among processual and postprocessual camps over such issues as materialist versus idealist approaches, and the possibility of building true theories of social evolution, are likely to be continuing sources of contention over what should be appropriate units of analysis in the study of long-term change.

■   ■   ■

References

Adams, Richard N. (1982) *Paradoxical Harvest*. Cambridge University Press, Cambridge.

Allen, P.M. (1982) The Genesis of Structure in Social Systems: The Paradigm of Self Organization. In *Theory and Explanation in Archaeology: The Southampton Conference*, edited by Colin Renfrew, Michael J. Rowlands, and Barbara A. Segraves, pp. 347–374. Cambridge University Press, Cambridge.

Bender, Barbara (1985) Emergent Tribal Formations in the American Midcontinent. *American Antiquity* 50:52–62.

Binford, Lewis R. (1965) Archaeological Systematics and the Study of Culture Process. *American Antiquity* 31:203–210.

—— (1968) Some Comments on Historical Versus Processual Archaeology. *Southwestern Journal of Anthropology* 24:267–275.

Blanton, Richard, and Gary Feinman (1984) The Mesoamerican World System. *American Anthropologist* 86:673–682.

Blute, Marion (1979) Sociocultural Evolutionism: An Untried Theory. *Behavioral Science* 24:46–59.

Braudel, Fernand (1972) *The Mediterranean and the Mediterranean World in the Age of Phillip II*. Vol. I. Translated by Sian Reynolds. Harper Colophon, New York. Originally published 1949.

—— (1980) *On History*. University of Chicago Press, Chicago.

Braun, David P. and Stephen Plog (1982) Evolution of "Tribal" Social Networks: Theory and Prehistoric North American Evidence. *American Antiquity* 47:504–525.

Brookfield, H.C. and Paula Brown (1963) *Struggle for Land: Agriculture and Group Territories Among the Chimbu of the New Guinea Highlands*. Oxford University Press, Melbourne.

Brown, James A. (1976) The Southern Cult Reconsidered. *Midcontinental Journal of Archaeology* 2:115–135.

Brown, James A., Richard A., Kerber, and Howard D. Winters (1990) Trade and the Evolution of Exchange Relations at the Beginning of the Mississippian Period. In *Mississippian Emergence: The Evolution of Ranked Agricultural Societies in Eastern North America*, edited by Bruce D. Smith. Smithsonian Institution Press, Washington, D.C.

Cobb, Charles R. (1989) An Appraisal of the Role of Mill Creek Chert Hoes in Mississippian Exchange Systems. *Southeastern Archaeology* 8:79–92.

Collingwood, Robin G. (1946) *The Idea of History*. Oxford University Press, Oxford.

Cook, Thomas (1976) *Koster, An Artifact Analysis of Two Archaic Phases in West Central Illinois*. Prehistoric Records No. 1; Koster Research Reports No. 3. Northwestern University Archaeological Program, Evanston, Illinois.

Deetz, James (1988) History and Archaeological Theory: Walter Taylor Revisited. *American Antiquity* 53:13–22.

Dunnell, Robert C. (1980) Evolutionary Theory and Archaeology. In *Advances in Archaeological Method and Theory*, vol. 3, edited by Michael B. Schiffer, pp. 35–99. Academic Press, New York.

Ekholm, Kajsa (1978) External Exchange and the Transformation of Central African Systems. In *The Evolution of Social Systems*, edited by Jonathan Friedman and Michael J. Rowlands, pp. 115–136. Duckworth, London.

Ford, James A. (1963) *Hopewell Culture Burial Mounds Near Helena, Arkansas*. Anthropological Papers of the American Museum of Natural History 50(1). New York.

Fried, Morton H. (1967) *The Evolution of Political Society*. Random House, New York.

Friedman, Jonathan (1975) Tribes, States, and Transformations. In *Marxist Analyses and Social Anthropology*, edited by Maurice Bloch, pp. 161–202. Tavistock, New York.

—— (1982) Catastrophe and Continuity in Social Evolution. In *Theory and Explanation in Archaeology: The Southampton Conference*, edited by Colin Renfew, Michael J. Rowlands, and Barbara A. Segraves, pp. 201–276. Cambridge University Press, Cambridge.

Friedman, Jonathan, and Michael J. Rowlands (1978) Notes Towards an Epigenetic Model of the Evolution of "Civilisation." In *The Evolution of Social Systems*, edited by Jonathan Friedman and Michael J. Rowlands, pp. 201–276. Duckworth, London.

Glassie, Henry (1975) *Folk Housing in Middle Virginia: A Structural Analysis of Historic Artifacts*. University of Tennessee Press, Knoxville.

Goad, Sharon I. (1978) A Reconsideration of the Hopewellian Interaction Sphere in Prehistory. *Early Georgia* 6:4–11.

—— (1980) Patterns of Late Archaic Exchange. *Tennessee Anthropologist* 5:1–16.

Gumerman, George J. and David A. Phillips, Jr. (1978) Archaeology Beyond Anthropology. *American Antiquity* 43:184–191.

Hodder, Ian (1985) Post-Processual Archaeology. In *Advances in Archaeological Method and Theory*, vol. 8, edited by Michael B. Schiffer, pp. 1–26. Academic Press, New York.

—— (1986) *Reading the Past: Current Approaches to Interpretation in Archaeology*. Cambridge University Press, Cambridge.

—— (1987) The Contribution of the Long Term. In *Archaeology as Long-Term History*, edited by Ian Hodder, pp. 1–8. Cambridge University Press, Cambridge.

Hodges, Richard (1986) Peer Polity Interaction and Socio-Political Change in Anglo-Saxon England. In *Peer Polity Interaction and Socio-Political Change*, edited by Colin Renfrew and John F. Cherry, pp. 69–78. Cambridge University Press, Cambridge.

Howard, James H. (1968) *The Southeastern Ceremonial Complex and Its Interpretation*. Memoir 6. Missouri Archaeological Society, Columbia.

Jefferies, Richard W. (1979) The Tunacunnhee Site: Hopewell in Northwest Georgia. In *Hopewell Archeology: The Chillicothe Conference*, edited by D.S. Brose and N. Greber, pp. 162–170. Kent State University Press, Kent, Ohio.

Jenkins, Ned J. (1979) Miller Hopewell of the Tombigbee Drainage. In *Hopewell Archeology: The Chillicothe Conference*, edited by D.S. Brose and N. Greber, pp. 171–180. Kent State University Press, Kent, Ohio.

Kay, Marvin (1983) Archaic Period Research in the Western Ozark Highland, Missouri. In *Archaic Hunters and Gatherers in the American Midwest*, edited by James L. Phillips and James A. Brown, pp. 41–70. Academic Press, New York.

Kristiansen, Kristian (1982) The Formation of Tribal Systems in Later European Prehistory: Northern Europe, 4000–500 B.C. In *Theory and Explanation in Archaeology*, edited by Colin Renfrew, Michael J. Rowlands, and Barbara A. Segraves, pp. 241–280. Cambridge University Press, Cambridge.

Kushner, Gilbert (1974) A Consideration of Some Processual Designs for Archaeology as Anthropology. *American Antiquity* 35:125–132.

Mair, Lucy (1964) *Primitive Government*. Penguin Books, Baltimore.

Marquardt, William H. and Patty Jo Watson (1983) The Shell Mound Archaic of Western Kentucky. In *Archaic Hunters and Gatherers in the American Midwest*, edited by James L. Phillips and James A. Brown, pp. 323–339. Academic Press, New York.

Meltzer, David J. (1979) Paradigms and the Nature of Change in American Archaeology. *American Antiquity* 44:644–657.

Muller, Jon (1966) Archaeological Analysis of Art Styles. *Tennessee Archaeologist* 22:25–39.

—— (1987) Salt, Chert, and Shell: Mississippian Exchange and Economy. In *Specialization, Exchange, and Complex Societies*, edited by Elizabeth M. Brumfiel and Timothy K. Earle, pp. 10–21. Cambridge University Press, Cambridge.

O'Laughlin, Bridget (1975) Marxist Approaches in Anthropology. *Annual Review of Anthropology* 4: 341–370.

Parker Pearson, Michael (1984) Economic and Cyclical Change: Cyclical Growth in the Pre-State Societies of Jutland. In *Ideology, Power, and Prehistory*, edited by Daniel Miller and Christopher Tilley, pp. 69–92. Cambridge University Press, Cambridge.

Peebles, Christopher S. and Susan A. Kus (1977) Some Archaeological Correlates of Ranked Societies. *American Antiquity* 42: 421–448.

Rothschild, Nan A. (1979) Mortuary Behavior and Social Organization at Indian Knoll and Dickson Mounds. *American Antiquity* 44: 658–675.

Rowlands, Michael J. (1982) Processual Archaeology as Historical Social Science. In *Theory and Explanation in Archaeology*, edited by Colin Renfrew, Michael J. Rowlands and Barbara A. Seagraves, pp. 155–174. Academic Press, New York.

—— (1987) Centre and Periphery: A Review of a Concept. In *Centre and Periphery in the Ancient World*, edited by Michael J. Rowlands, Mogens Larsen and Kristian Kristiansen, pp. 1–11. Cambridge University Press, Cambridge.

Sabloff, Jeremy A., and Gordon R. Willey (1967) The Collapse of Maya Civilization in the Southern Lowlands: A Consideration of History and Process. *Southwestern Journal of Anthropology* 23: 311–336.

Sahlins, Marshall D. (1972) *Stone Age Economics*. Aldine, Chicago.

Salmon, Merilee H. (1978) What Can Systems Theory Do for Archaeology? *American Antiquity* 43: 174–183.

Schneider, Jane (1977) Was There a Pre-Capitalist World System? *Peasant Studies* 6(1): 20–29.

Seeman, Mark F. (1979) The Hopewell Interaction Sphere: The Evidence for Interregional Trade and Structural Complexity. *Indiana Historical Society, Prehistory Research Series* 5(2). Indianapolis.

Service, Elman R. (1962) *Primitive Social Organization*. Random House, New York.

Shennan, S.J. (1991) "Tradition, Rationality, and Cultural Transmission", in R. Preucel (ed.) *Processual and Postprocessual Archaeologies: Multiple Ways of Knowing the Past*, Center for Archaeological Investigations, Southern Illinois University of Carbondale, Occasional Paper No. 10.

Smith, Betty A. (1979) The Hopewell Connection in Southwest Georgia. In *Hopewell Archaeology: The Chillicothe Conference*, edited by D.S. Brose and N. Greber, pp 181–187. Kent State University Press, Kent, Ohio.

Smith, Bruce D. (1987) The Independent Domestication of Indigenous Seed-Bearing Plants in Eastern North America. In *Emergent Horticultural Economies of the Eastern Woodlands*, edited by Willian F. Keegan, pp. 3–47. Occasional Paper No. 7. Center for Archaeological Investigations, Southern Illinois University at Carbondale.

Taylor, Walter W. (1948) *A Study of Archaeology*. American Anthropological Association Memoir No. 69. Menasha, Wisconsin.

Trigger, Bruce (1988) History and Contemporary American Archaeology: A Critical Analysis. In *Archaeological Thought in America*, edited by C.C. Lamberg-Karlovsky and Philip L. Kohl, pp. 19–34. Cambridge University Press, Cambridge.

—— (1989) *A History of Archaeological Thought*. Cambridge University Press, Cambridge.

Waring, Antonio J., Jr., and Preston Holder (1945) A Prehistoric Ceremonial Complex in the Southeastern United States. *American Anthropologist* 47: 1–34.

Watson, P.J. (1991) "A Parochial Primer: The New Dissonance As Seen from the Midcontinental United States, In R. Preucel (ed.) *Processual and Postprocessual Archaeologies: Multiple Ways of Knowing the Past*, Center for Archaeological Investigations, Southern Illinois University of Carbondale, Occasional Paper No. 10.

Willey, Gordon R., and Jeremy A. Sabloff (1980) *A History of American Archaeology*. 2nd ed. W.H. Freeman, San Francisco.

Winters, Howard D. (1968) Value Systems and Trade Cycles of the Late Archaic in the Midwest. In *New Perspectives in Archaeology*, edited by Sally R. Binford and Lewis R. Binford, pp. 175–221. Aldine, Chicago.

Wolf, Eric R. (1982) *Europe and the People Without History*. University of California Press, Berkeley.

PART FIVE

Gendering the past

INTRODUCTION

The last few decades have been marked by a number of changes in western societies. Not the least of these have involved shifts in the place, perception and status of women, and a rethinking of traditional gender roles. Archaeology has not been immune to these changes, either in the structure of the discipline, or in the way that we view the past. While gender parity in employment may still be a long way off, there is little question that women now are more common participants in a discipline that was, traditionally, dominated by males. Likewise, significant steps have been taken towards changing our view of prehistory from an androcentric, or male-dominated, one, with women as invisible or barely visible participants, to one where both sexes (and, perhaps, multiple genders) played their parts.

The importance of this change is no better seen than in hunter-gatherer archaeology. The traditional western view of hunter-gatherers was enshrined in a "Man the Hunter" ideology (Collier 1988), a fact signalled by an edited volume of that same name which aimed to summarize the status of hunter-gatherers worldwide (see Lee and DeVore 1968). Yet one ironic outcome of this volume was a recognition that, among many hunter-gatherers, it was woman-the-gatherer rather than man-the-hunter that provided the majority of the diet. Our own traditional division of labor, with men going out to work and "bringing home the bacon" while women stayed at home to tend the kids, provided a perfectly false model of the relative contributions of the sexes for many of the non-western, small-scale societies that archaeologists study (Falk 1997).

Sex – male, female – is of course a biological division, most visible in the primary and secondary sexual characteristics of the human body. Gender – masculine, feminine – concerns the culturally ascribed values placed on sex categories, often used to provide a conceptual organization of the world. Sex and gender don't necessarily overlap in a given culture, and their meaning can vary between different cultures. The result is a spider-web of potential relationships that give the lie to simplistic analogies between our own cultural traditions and those in the prehistoric past.

A good example of the interplay between sex and gender, how these differ, and the difficulties they present for the archaeologist is found in the ethnographic record in the area where I work, the Great Basin. The Numic inhabitants of this region conceptually organized the world in terms of a structural opposition shared by many cultures – masculine: feminine (Whitley forthcoming). The world was created when a masculine principle, the sky, united with a feminine principle, the earth. One result of this conceptualization was the belief that high elevations on the landscape, like mountain peaks, were masculine places. This was linguistically-encoded in a place-name-ending that is usually glossed as "mountain peak", but that literally translates as "penis erected". Low places on the landscape, including caves and springs (often near the base of mountain ranges) were, by the same logic, feminine places. (The name for one spring, for example, translates literally as "vulva-water"). Both high and low places were considered sacred. Like sacred places for most Native American groups, they were believed to be portals into the supernatural world (Walker 1991).

Yet I emphasize that these were masculine and feminine, not male and female, places. The reason for this becomes evident when their use is considered. Sacred places that are (relatively speaking) low on the landscape, and therefore feminine, were used by male shamans for vision quests, after which they created petroglyphs to record their visionary experiences. (Following the same symbolic inversion, high peaks were sometimes associated with female spirits, but these weren't used for vision questing). There were two reasons for the male shaman's use of feminine places. At one (ideological) level, male shamans appropriated feminine places and thus power, thereby serving to support a gender bias that existed in society (see Whitley, this volume). At another (symbolic) level, male shamans used feminine places for their vision quests because vision questing involved an entry into the supernatural world. The supernatural, however, was the perfect inverse of the natural world. Because of this inversion, male shamans, seeking masculine supernatural power, entered the sacred at feminine locations. Here, in other words, we see an example of how gender was used to conceptualize and categorize the world, but we also see that the use of gendered locations did not follow the biological division of the sexes in any simple way. Yet while this is complicated enough, this Numic case cannot even be generalized to surrounding cultures. In nearby western Arizona, for example, the landscape was symbolically conceptualized in terms of three gender divisions, rather than two: masculine, feminine, and transvestite (Whitley forthcoming).

Once the ethnographic complexity of the use of sex and gender categories is recognized, the fallacy of our "common sense" use of these categories in archaeology becomes apparent. One of these is the common attribution of female figurines as necessarily equating with "fertility" or "mother-goddess cults", as Russell (1993) has shown. Sex and gender, then, are fundamental categories that cultures use to conceptualize their world, and to organize relationships between peoples within it (Conkey and Spector 1984). But we cannot assume that our categories for sex and gender held for prehistoric peoples. Instead, these need to be explicitly brought into our archaeological analyses, if we aim for any sophisticated understanding of prehistoric cultures.

Probably no archaeological problem has greater implications for sex and gender than subsistence change, precisely because it involves one of the most universal societal organizing divisions: the sexual division of labor. Patty Jo Watson and Mary Kennedy raise this point in the first paper in this section, a reconsideration of the origins of agriculture in the eastern woodlands of North America. Over the last few decades considerable data have been accumulated about the different plants involved in this process. But, as these archaeologists note, little consideration has been made of the people that were also part of this equation: previous studies were largely unpeopled, and gender-neutral. In an effort to rectify this botano-centric view of agricultural origins, they look to a gendered view of the beginnings of farming, as well as the genetic improvements in maize that occurred once it was domesticated. Using ethnohistorical and cross-cultural data as part of their argument, they infer that women were most likely responsible for the origins of agriculture in this region. This challenges a traditional view that innovation and change were typically instigated by people highly ranked in the social system – specifically, male political and religious leaders.

Gender is of course *at least* a two-part conceptual division. This implies that a gendered archaeology is not exclusively an archaeology of women, as Bernard Knapp reminds us in the second paper in this section. Feminist scholarship has been important to western science, in general, because it has shown that our traditional views of society represented a kind of androcentric universalism, which is hardly an objective point of view of present or past. Yet in engendering archaeology, Knapp rightly contends, it is important that the androcentric traditional view not be replaced by a modern gynaecentric one. Males too were gendered, sometimes in various different ways, as the ethnographic western Arizona case (above) implies. This recognition is as much a part of a properly gendered archaeology as the perspective provided by the feminist point of view.

■ ■ ■

Further reading

Conkey and Spector 1984
Gero and Conkey 1991
Hays-Gilpin and Whitley 1998
Wylie 1991

■ ■ ■

References

Collier, J.F. (1988) *Marriage and Inequality in Classless Societies*, Stanford: Stanford University.
Conkey, M.W. and Spector, J. (1984) "Archaeology and the Study of Gender", *Advances in Archaeological Method and Theory* 7:1–38, New York: Academic.
Falk, D. (1997) "Brain Evolution in Females: An Answer to Mr Lovejoy", in L.D. Hagar (ed.) *Women in Human Evolution*, London: Routledge.
Gero, J.M. and Conkey, M.W. (eds) (1991) *Engendering Archaeology: Women and Prehistory*, Oxford: Blackwell.
Hays-Gilpin, K. and Whitley, D.S. (eds) (1998) *Reader in Gender Archaeology*, London: Routledge.
Lee, R.B. and DeVore, I. (eds) (1968) *Man the Hunter*, Chicago: Aldine.
Russell, P. (1993) "The Paleolithic Mother-Goddess: Fact or Fiction?", in H. du Cross and L. Smith (eds) *Women and Archeology: A Feminist Critique*, Occasional Papers in Prehistory 23, Department of Prehistory, Research School of Pacific Studies, Canberra: Australian National University.
Walker, Jr., D. (1991) "Protection of American Indian Sacred Geography", in C. Vecsey (ed.) *Handbook of American Indian Religious Freedom*, New York: Crossroad.
Whitley, D.S. (forthcoming) "Finding Rain in the Desert: Rock Art, Gender and Landscape in Far Western North America", in C. Chippindale and P.S.C. Taçon (eds) *The Archaeology of Rock Art*, Cambridge: Cambridge University Press.

Chapter 11

THE DEVELOPMENT OF HORTICULTURE IN THE EASTERN WOODLANDS OF NORTH AMERICA
Women's Role

Patty Jo Watson and Mary C. Kennedy

Introduction

We begin with the words of some famous anthropologists:

> The sound anthropological position is that certain sex-linked behaviors are biologically based, although subject to cultural modifications within limits.
>
> (Hoebel 1958: 391)

> A limited number of sex-associated characteristics also appear to be transmitted at the genetic level, such as an apparent tendency shared with many other animals for dominance and passivity in the male and female, respectively.
>
> (Keesing 1966: 75)

> The community recognizes that women must be accompanied by their babies wherever they go; hence they cannot hunt or fish as efficiently as the unencumbered males. Males are therefore free to be mobile and active while females have been accorded, by nature, a prior responsibility or obligation to rear additional members of the community in the only way this can be done. Hence the community assigns work involving more mobility to men and work involving less mobility to women.
>
> (Jacob and Stern 1952: 145–6)

> Man, with his superior physical strength, can better undertake the more strenuous physical tasks, such as lumbering, mining, quarrying, land clearance, and housebuilding. Not handicapped, as is woman, by the physiological burdens of

pregnancy and nursing, he can range farther afield to hunt, to fish, to herd, and to trade. Woman is at no disadvantage, however, in lighter tasks which can be performed in or near the home, e.g., the gathering of vegetable products, the fetching of water, the preparation of food, and the manufacture of clothing and utensils. All known human societies have developed specialization and cooperation between the sexes roughly along this biologically determined line of cleavage.

(Murdock 1949: 7)

Up to about nine thousand years ago all human populations lived by hunting and most of them also by fishing, supplemented by the picking of berries, fruits and nuts, and the digging of roots and tubers. Perhaps the first division of labor between the sexes was that the male became the hunter and the female the food-gatherer.

(Montagu 1969: 134)

Even in those societies where there are no professional or semi-professional artisans, all ordinary manufactures are delegated either to men or to women. Moreover, this sex division of labor is much the same wherever it occurs. Such universal patterns derive from universally present facts, such as the greater size and strength of the male, and his greater activity based on the differing roles of the two sexes in connection with the production and care of children. These factors unquestionably led to the earliest differentiation in food gathering activities. This must have begun at an extremely remote period. The males became the main providers of animal foods, since they were able to run down their prey and engage it in combat. The females being hampered throughout most of their adult lives by the presence either of infants *in utero* or in arms, were unable to engage in such active pursuits, but were able to collect vegetable foods and shell fish. . . . Thus to this day in the American family dinner the meat is placed in front of the father to be served and the vegetables in front of the mother. This is a folk memory of the days when the father collected the meat with his spear and the mother the vegetables with her digging stick.

(Linton 1955: 70–1)

Thus, the sexual division of labor is neatly laid out, and simply and cogently explained. Men are strong, dominant protectors who hunt animals; women are weaker, passive, hampered by their reproductive responsibilities, and hence, consigned to plant gathering. Not only is that the case for every ethnographically observed society, but it is carried back to "extremely remote" periods. This received view could be schematized as:

men>hunt>animals>active
women>gather>plants>passive

All the introductory texts from which these excerpts were taken were written before the women's movement and the reorganization of contemporary American life that made women working outside the domestic sphere an inescapable reality.

Introductory texts are much more cautious these days. Conspicuously absent is the explicit male/active, female/passive dichotomy (e.g. Harris 1987: 127; Oswalt 1986: 104–5; Peoples and Bailey 1988: 254–60). Current texts acknowledge that in every known society there is a sexual division of labor; that men do hunting and women gathering seems almost always to be the case, but that beyond this there is tremendous variation in which labors a particular society assigns to a particular sex. The received view today is that in foraging societies:

> men>hunt>animals
> women>gather>plants

For purposes of argument we accept this premise and attempt to formalize this very division of labor for a particular time, region, and cultural historical process: the origin and early development of plant cultivation and domestication in the Eastern Woodlands of North America. We draw upon three lines of evidence: archaeological data, ethnohistoric data, and general schemes of human social organization derived from ethnography.

Data sources and arguments of relevance

Archaeological and archaeobotanical data

The time period relevant to the origin and early development of horticulture in the Eastern Woodlands is approximately 7000–2000 BP. Primary evidence for plant use during these five millennia comes from a variety of archaeological contexts, but only two basic categories: charred and uncharred plant remains. Charred plant remains are usually recovered by flotation-water separation systems; uncharred plants are recovered from dry caves and rockshelters; both categories are then analysed by paleoethnobotanists (Hastorf and Popper 1988; Pearsall 1989).

The evidence to date suggests three different episodes of domestication in the Eastern US (Smith 1987a; Watson 1989; Yarnell 1986). The first began about 7000 BP when a gourd-like cucurbit (*Cucurbita* sp.; perhaps *C. pepo*, perhaps *C. texana*, or even *C. foetidissima*) and bottle gourd (*Lagenaria siceraria*) begin to appear in archaeological deposits in the Eastern US. The second is from 3500 BP onward when domesticated forms of the weedy plants sumpweed, chenopod, and sunflower begin to appear. The third is the development of varieties of maize specific to the requirements of the Eastern US, a process that took place between 2000 and 1000 BP.

We are in the pioneer phase of knowledge expansion about prehistoric plant use. One characteristic of this pioneer phase is a scramble by interested scholars to synthesize the new data as they become accessible, not only in annotated inventories of the primary evidence (Yarnell 1977, 1983, 1986, forthcoming), but also in comparative discussions of regional developments (Asch and Asch 1985; Chapman and Shea 1981; Watson 1985, 1988, 1989), and in more general theoretical formulations (*e.g.* Chomko and Crawford 1978; Crites 1987; Lathrap 1987; Smith 1987a, 1987b). It seems desirable to launch an inquiry at yet another level: that of the women and men involved in the events and processes. While a great deal is being written about the evidence, it is, for the most part, gender-neutral writing; when actors are mentioned they are "people," or "humans," or "individuals". These accounts tend to be discussions of the archaeological evidence, the plant remains, rather than the people who manipulated the plants. We depart from that pattern here.

The ethnohistoric record

Although the archaeological record of plant use has only recently been sought, information about plant use by living peoples in the Eastern Woodlands has been available since the time of European entry in the sixteenth century. Thus, one source of data is historical or ethnohistorical such as that provided by Dye (1980), Hudson (1976), Le Page du Pratz (n.d.), Parker (1968), Swanton (1948), Will and Hyde (1917), Willoughby (1906), Wilson (1917), and Yarnell (1964). For example, in an often-quoted passage, Le Page du Pratz (n.d.: 156–7) describes the planting of *choupichoul* (Smith 1987c), an Eastern Woodlands cultigen being grown in Louisiana by the Natchez at the time of European entry into the Southeast: "I have seen the Natchez, and other indians, sow a sort of grain, which they called Choupichoul, on these dry sand-banks. This sand received no manner of culture; and the *women and children* covered the grain any how with their feet, without taking any great pains about it" (emphasis added). Throughout the ethnohistoric and ethnographic literature of the Eastern US are similar examples of women planting, reaping, collecting, and processing plants.

License to use the ethnographic and ethnohistorical information for archaeological inference would presumably be granted because it fulfills the criteria for the use of ethnographic analogy (the most comprehensive recent discussion is Wylie 1985, but see also Ascher 1961; Salmon 1982: 57–83; Watson, LeBlanc, and Redman 1971: 49–51, 1984: 259–63). That is, the information in question comes from the same or a very similar physical environment, and from people who are closely related physically and culturally. Therefore, the ethnographic/ethnohistoric information carries a certain degree of prior probability, of plausibility or likelihood, with respect to the archaeological materials. That does not mean, however, that it is to be accepted uncritically.

Social organization

There is another necessary source, and that is the more abstract and theoretical literature in anthropology about the organization and functioning of human groups at various levels of technological complexity. For present purposes we are content to evoke Fried (1967), Friedl (1975), Murdock and Provost (1973), Sahlins (1963, 1968), Service (1962, 1971), Steward (1948), and White (1959) and refer to them in general as the authority for some basic assumptions:

1   In small-scale, non food-producing, egalitarian societies, subsistence activities are divided on the basis of age and sex.
2   For biological reasons relating to gestation and lactation, adult women are primarily responsible for nourishing and socializing infants and small children, although various others can assist in these tasks.
3   For biological reasons relating to greater physical strength and hormone levels, adult men are charged with the primary responsibility for safeguarding the social units in which children are born and reared, and – in general – with tasks that require sudden bursts of energy, such as running after game.
4   Because of these biological constraints on men and women, groups tend to divide labor between the sexes so that women are responsible for activities that do not interfere with childcare and that can be performed near the habitation – cooking and "domestic activities" as well as the collecting of stationary resources such as plants and firewood. Men are responsible for exploiting mobile resources, primarily the hunting of game, as well as for defense, and a variety of other such tasks.

Using these assumptions about the sexual division of labor, as well as evidence from the archaeological record and the ethnohistoric/ethnographic record, we depart from the usual gender-neutral perspective to discuss one of the most recent and most comprehensive theoretical treatments we know for the development of horticulture in the Eastern Woodlands: Bruce Smith's (1987a) paper, "The Independent Domestication of Indigenous Seed-Bearing Plants in Eastern North America."

The domestication of plants

Women and coevolution in the Eastern Woodlands: weedy plant domestication

Smith's interpretive formulation may be rendered schematically as follows: at about 8000 BP, the beginning of the Middle Archaic period, human populations in the Eastern Woodlands are thought to have been small, few, and dispersed rather widely across the landscape. Their subsistence systems – hunting-gathering-foraging with some emphasis on deer and several kinds of nuts, especially hickory and acorn – were further characterized by residential mobility, probably cycling through similar or the same series of locales, season after season, year after year. Occupation sites were small, although summer camps on river terraces or levees were probably considerably larger than winter residential units in the uplands.

Geological studies indicate significant changes in Mid-Holocene (8000–5000 BP) fluvial systems throughout the East, partly as a result of a long drying trend, the Hypsithermal. Rivers stabilized and aggraded so that previously ephemeral or rare features such as meanders and oxbow lakes, bars and shoals, sloughs and backwater lagoons became much more common and long-lasting than in the previous post-Pleistocene millennia. As a result of these changes, human subsistence-settlement patterns also changed. When slackwater habitats, shoals, etc. took shape as relatively permanent features, then the abundant flora (edible bulbs, rhizomes, shoots, seeds) and fauna (many different kinds of fish, amphibians, mollusks, and waterfowl) characterizing them became readily accessible on a predictable, seasonal, long-term basis. Human settlements – in the form of base camps occupied from late spring to summer and on through fall, and oriented to these resource points – increased in size and were permanently occupied for at least four to five months each year for hundreds of years. This process resulted in the first recognizable anthropogenic locales in the archaeological record of the Eastern US; i.e. these sites represent the first long-lasting impact on this physical environment produced by human activity. Archaic shell mounds and midden mounds are then the scene where the rest of the story unfolds: these "domestilocalities", as Smith calls them, are the crux of his formulation.

The mounds and middens are significant and long-lived disturbed areas, highly congenial to the weedy species ancestral to the earliest cultivated and domesticated food plants. Smith discusses a series of four important factors in the coevolutionary interplay between human and plant populations at the domestilocalities; sunlight, fertile soil, continually disturbed soil, and continual introduction of seeds. He also stresses that some of the selective pressures operating on the weedy plants colonizing such locales are congruent with the best interests of humans who harvest them for food, most significantly big seeds and thin seed coats.

Intense competition among pioneer species in these rich openings favors seeds that sprout quickly and grow quickly. These traits translate botanically into seeds with reduced dormancy (a thin seed coat is one good means of effecting reduced dormancy) and large endosperm (food reserves to sustain rapid, early spring growth), the two morphological characteristics enabling identification of the earliest domesticates: sumpweed and sunflower (bigger seeds than in wild populations) and *Chenopodium berlandieri* ssp. *jonesianum* (seeds with thinner seed coats than in wild *C. berlandieri*).

Finally, Smith outlines the main stages or steps in the general coevolutionary trajectory between *ca.* 6500 and 3500 BP numerous places in the Eastern Woodlands.

At about 6500 BP. In the first stage, domestilocalities are inhabited by humans and by a series of weedy, colonizing, or pioneering plant species for several months during each growing season. Natural selective pressures operate on the plants in the directions just noted to produce big seeds and thin seed coats.

In the second stage, humans tolerate the useful edible species, but ignore, or even occasionally remove the useless or harmful species.

In stage three, humans actively encourage the useful species (which have gradually become even more useful), and while systematically harvesting them also systematically remove competing non-useful plants. Thus, the incidental gardens of stage 2 become true managed gardens, the proceeds of which are stored to augment the winter and early spring diet.

In stage four, humans deliberately plant seeds of the useful species each year, carefully tending and caring for the resulting crops.

At about 3500 BP. In stage five, plants emerge that are clearly recognizable morphologically as domesticates.

The entire process is quite low-key, and there is no drastic alteration in the diet as a result of it, but there is an increase in dependable plant resources.

If we populate Smith's evolutionary stages with gendered human beings chosen to accord with the four operating assumptions for the division of labor already noted, and with the ethnographic record for the Eastern Woodlands, then we must conclude that the adult women are the chief protagonists in the horticultural drama of the domestilocalities. Although the entire human group contributes to the sunlight and soil fertility factors, it is the women who are primarily responsible for soil disturbance and continual introduction of seeds. Smith lists as examples of disturbance: the construction of houses, windbreaks, storage and refuse pits, drying racks, earth ovens, hearths. Most of these probably represent women's work as do the majority of other examples he mentions: primary and secondary disposal of plant and animal debris, and a "wide range of everyday processing and manufacturing activities."

As to the continual introduction of seeds, Smith notes harvesting plants for processing and consumption at the domestilocality. Seed loss during processing, storage, and consumption (plus defecation subsequent to consumption) continually introduce seeds to the fertile soil of the domestilocality. Once again – although everyone joins in consumption and defecation – it is the women who are responsible for processing, and for food preparation and storage.

Have we not then definitively identified woman the gatherer, harvester, and primary disturber of domestilocalities in the prehistoric Eastern Woodlands as woman the cultivator and domesticator? Yes, we have. But anyone persuaded by Smith's or similar coevolutionary constructions would doubtless respond "So what?" Our conclusion, with which they would probably readily agree, is at best anti-climactic because the co-evolutionary formulation downplays stress, drive, intention, or innovation of any sort on the part of the people involved, in this case the women. The coevolutionary formulation highlights gradualness; the built-in mechanisms adduced carry plants and people smoothly and imperceptibly from hunting-gathering-foraging to systematic harvesting to at least part-time food production with little or no effort on anyone's part. The plants virtually domesticate themselves.

> While a number of the initial and ongoing selective pressures acting on these plants within such disturbed habitats were clearly related to human activities,

these activities were unintentional and "automatic" rather than the result of predetermined and deliberate human action toward the plant species in question.

. . . It is this simple step of planting harvested seeds, even on a very small scale, that if sustained over the long-term marks both the beginning of cultivation, and the onset of automatic selection within affected domestilocality plant populations for interrelated adaptation syndromes associated with domestication.

. . . This continuing evolutionary process did not require any deliberate selection efforts on the part of Middle Holocene inhabitants of domestilocalities in the Eastern Woodlands. All that was needed was a sustained opportunistic exploitation and minimal encouragement of what were still rather unimportant plant food sources.

(Smith 1987a; 32, 33, 34)

This is in keeping not only with the current scheme for division of labor

women>gather>plants,

but also with the earlier (Keesing, Linton, *et al.*) scheme

women>gather>plants>passive.

Are we to be left with such a muted and down-beat ending to the Neolithic Revolution in the Eastern Woodlands?

Shaman the cultivator: gourd domestication

The domestication of the native cultigens described by Smith was apparently preceded by introduction of another type of domesticate, *Cucurbita* gourd and bottle gourd, in various parts of the Eastern US beginning about 7000 years ago. In an article entitled, "The Origins of Plant Domestication in the Eastern United States: Promoting the Individual in Archaeological Theory," Guy Prentice (1986) constructs a scenario for that earlier transformation.

Prentice first details the evidence for the tropical squash, *Cucurbita pepo*, in archaeological deposits dating from 7000–3500 BP, some of the earliest evidence for domesticated plants in Eastern North America. Investigators agree that *Cucurbita pepo* fruits would have been used primarily as containers, or perhaps as rattles, rather than food (Prentice 1986: 104). He then argues (ibid.: 106) that the species was probably introduced through some form of trade with the tropical areas in which it grows naturally. The sites at which the earliest evidence for *Cucurbita pepo* is found are those of Archaic period, hunting and gathering, band-level societies. He notes that authoritarian controls in such societies would have been weak, and that shamans and headmen were probably exercising the strongest control within these groups (ibid.: 107). Prentice presents information from studies indicating that change is not an automatic process in human societies, that certain conditions must be met before an innovation is accepted (ibid.: 108–11). An innovation will take hold if it is introduced by an individual of high status, a specialist, an ambitious person who is in contact with outsiders and who is oriented toward commerce rather than subsistence:

> By postulating a ritual use for cucurbits during the Archaic period, one is led to conclude that it would be the shaman who would be most likely to adopt cucurbit agriculture. He would be the one most interested in new religious paraphernalia. He would have the greatest knowledge of plants. He would have been in communication with other shamans and probably exchanging plants and plant lore. If gourds were introduced as magical rattles and ritualistic containers for serving stimulants and medicines, he would have gained a very impressive "medicine" in the eyes of his patients. In fact, the gourd itself may have provided the medicine.
>
> (Prentice 1986: 113)

Here is an instance in which at least one archaeologist is not arguing for

women>gather>plants.

Why not? Perhaps because this is a discussion of innovation, and

women>gather>plants>passive

– although it might lead to dinner – would not lead to *innovation*. Rather, this is a scenario for

man>trade>ceremony>active>innovation>cultivation>domestication.

Perhaps it really was like that (see Decker 1988 and Smith 1987a for alternative views on the development of *Cucurbita* cultivation in eastern North America), but we are leary of explanations that remove women from the one realm that is traditionally granted them, as soon as innovation or invention enters the picture.

Women and maize agriculture in the Eastern Woodlands: the creation of northern flint

Maize was the most important domesticate among the horticultural societies of North America at the time of European contact. Although there was enormous variety among the indigenous subsistence economies in the Eastern and Western United States, wherever crops were grown maize was central, often being literally deified (e.g. Cushing 1974; Hudson 1976; Munson 1973; Stevenson 1904; Swanton 1948). Yet, as the latest evidence makes clear (Chapman and Crites 1987; Conard *et al.* 1984; Doebly, Goodman, and Stuber 1986; Ford 1987; Yarnell 1986), maize is a rather late entrant into the Eastern Woodlands, probably introduced from the Southwest, and appearing about 1800 BP. The development of horticulture in the Southwest seems to have been very different from that in the East (Minnis 1985, in prep.; Wills 1988), and maize is much earlier there, apparently present by *ca.* 4000 BP.

There is great unclarity in the literature about the exact definitions and time-space distributions of contemporary maize varieties, but there is some consensus that the earliest kinds known in the East (and grown together with sunflower, sump-weed, chenopod, maygrass, knotweed, etc.) are of a type with 10 to 12 rows of kernels, and called Chapalote, Tropical Flint, North American Pop, and/or Midwestern 12-row. These varieties were developed from the earliest Maize, which was originally created from wild populations occurring in Mesoamerica, Central America, or South America (or all three), but exactly where and how has been hotly debated for some 20 years (e.g. Galinat 1985b; Lathrap 1987).

Our concern here, however, is with the transition in the more northerly Eastern Woodlands from the early, higher row-number maize to a lower row-number variety variously known as Maiz de Ocho, Northern Flint, or Eastern 8-row maize, which appeared in the Northeast around AD 800–900, became quite standardized, and was the dominant agricultural crop of this region from approximately AD 1000 to historic times (Wagner 1983, 1987). There are at least three alternatives as to how this happened: (1) Eastern 8-row was created in the Eastern Woodlands from the Earlier Midwestern 12-row varieties; or (2) it, like the older form itself, was developed somewhere south of the Border and later diffused to the Eastern US; or (3) both (1) and (2) are too simple, and the origin of Northern Flint/Eastern 8-row involved more complicated combinations of both southerly (the Tropical Flint or Chapalote type) and northerly (the Northern Flint/Eastern 8-row type) maize varieties originating in several parts of northern, central, and southern America. Lathrap (1987) provides a comprehensive presentation of the second alternative (see also Upham *et al.* 1987), and Bruce Smith favors the third (Smith in prep.). Although there is now a very solid corpus of information on Fort Ancient maize (Wagner 1983, 1987), primary evidence about Middle Mississippian maize is only beginning to be available (Blake 1986; Fritz 1986; Scarry 1986), so it is not yet possible to assess definitively the relative merits of these three suggestions.

At the moment one can suggest, without contravening the scanty available evidence and in fact remaining congruent with it, that the original form of Northern Flint (Eastern 8-row) was developed from a Chapalote (Midwestern 12-row, Tropical Flint) type of maize at one or several places in the northerly portions of Eastern North America. The earliest date now known for Northern Flint is *ca* AD 800–900 from one site in western Pennsylvania and two near the north shore of Lake Erie (Blake 1986; Blake and Cutler 1983; Stothers 1976). Northern Flint is present by AD 1000 in the cultural context called Fort Ancient located in the Ohio River drainage of southern Ohio and Indiana, northern Kentucky, and northern West Virginia (Wagner 1983, 1987). On the present evidence, robust forms of Northern Flint appear later or not at all as one moves west and south from Fort Ancient territory (Blake 1986; Fritz 1986; Johannessen 1984; Scarry 1986). Thus, we believe we are justified in accepting, at least for purposes of our argument here, that the Northern Flint variety of maize was developed indigenously in northeastern North America from an older, Chapalote form that came into the east 1800 or 1900 years ago.

We assume that the first Chapalote or Chapolote-like forms of this tropical cultigen to enter northern latitudes in the Eastern US were not well suited to that physical environment, even if the plant diffused northward gradually from Mesoamerica. Day-length, annual temperature and moisture cycles, growing-season length, and substrate characteristics probably all differed significantly from those of the locales where Chapalote was initially grown. Hence, the Middle Woodland groups who planted and hoped to harvest this novel crop in the most northerly North American regions may have had more failures and near failures than successes. Lower row numbers on maize cobs are thought to be a botanical reflection of poor growing conditions such as short growing seasons, drought, or even unchecked competition from weeds (Blake and Cutler 1983: 83–4). Thus, it is possible that adverse climate was compounded by neglect in the development of Northern Flint.

We think it more likely, however, that cultivators in the northeasterly portions of North America actively encouraged, against environmental odds, the new starchy food source. Accepting the AD 800–900 dates from the Lake Erie and western Pennsylvania sites as the first establishing of Northern Flint, and noting the rapidity with which Northern Flint agriculture spread throughout the central Ohio River drainage (Fort Ancient) area immediately thereafter, we conclude that deliberate nurturing of maize in an inhospitable environment is a more plausible interpretation than is neglect in the development of this hardy variety.

Two points are implied from the above discussion: (1) maize acceptance and cultivation north of the Border was purposeful and deliberate; and (2) it was surely the women sunflower-sumpweed-chenopod gardeners in Middle and Late Woodland communities who worked (with varying success and interest) to acclimatize this imported species, by planting it deeper or shallower, earlier or later, in hills or furrows, and who crossed varieties to obtain or suppress specific traits. From *ca.* AD 1100–1200 to the time of European contact in the sixteenth century, Northern Flint was the main cultivated food of the hamlets, villages, towns, and chiefdoms that arose in the Ohio River Valley and the vast region north to the Great Lakes. To the west and south, in the Mississippi River and its tributary drainages, Northern Flint was also sometimes grown but in combination with other varieties having higher row-numbers (Blake 1986; Fritz 1986; Johannessen 1984; Scarry 1986; Smith in prep.) Thus Northern Flint, together with pumpkins, squashes, sunflowers, and a long list of other cultigens, planted, tended, harvested, and processed by the women agriculturalists (Hudson 1976; Parker 1968; Swanton 1948; Will and Hyde 1917; Willoughby 1906; Wilson 1917), supported many thousands of people each year for hundreds of years. The accomplishments of these women cultivators is even more impressive when one realizes that their creation, Northern Flint, is the basis (together with Southern Dent, a maize variety that entered the southeastern

United States somewhat later) for all the modern varieties of hybrid "Corn Belt Dent" maize grown around the world today (Doebley *et al.* 1986; Galinat 1985a).

Conclusions

We close with a few further thoughts about the first women gardeners in the Late Archaic domestilocalities. Their contribution of domesticated sumpweed, sunflower, and chenopod (and possibly maygrass as well) to the diet and the archaeological record of initial Late Holocene human populations in the Eastern Woodlands may not have been so automatic a process with so insignificant a result as the coevolutionary formulation makes it out to be.

In the first place, the natural history, natural habitat and distribution, ecology, and genetic structure of most of the Late Archaic/Early Woodland cultigens and domesticates are not well understood. On closer inspection, it may turn out to be the case that some if not all the species initially domesticated would have required special, self-conscious, and deliberate treatment to convert them to garden crops, and to cause the very significant and progressive changes in seed size that at least two of them (sumpweed and sunflower) exhibit. Sunflower and maygrass were apparently being grown outside their natural ranges by 3000–2500 BP, and this must have been done purposefully.

Secondly, the best and most comprehensive dietary evidence for the early horticultural period comes from the long series of human paleofecal and flotation derived remains in Salts Cave and Mammoth Cave, west central Kentucky. The fecal evidence dates to 2800–2500 BP and is quite clear and consistent. Over 60 per cent of the plant foods consumed were seeds of indigenous domesticates and cultigens: sunflower, sumpweed, and chenopod (Gardner 1987; Marquardt 1974; Stewart 1974; Watson and Yarnell 1986; Yarnell 1969, 1974, 1977, 1983, 1986, forthcoming). If maygrass, whose status is uncertain but which is here beyond its natural range, is added, then the total proportion of indigenous cultigens rises to well over two-thirds. This single and well-established datum for a period relatively early in the history of the indigenous domesticates might be taken to cast some doubt on the generalization that the addition of the domesticate species had only a slight dietary impact. The doubt is strengthened by corroborating evidence from Newt Kash (Jones 1936; Smith and Cowan 1987), Cloudsplitter (Cowan 1985), and Cold Oak (Gremillion 1988; Ison 1986; Ison and Gremillion 1989) shelters in eastern Kentucky (see also Smith 1987b).

A third matter to think about is the fact that – quite apart from all other considerations – the women plant collectors and gardeners of 3500–2500 BP were the first to devise and use techniques of tilling, harvesting, and processing the new domesticates. These same techniques must have been in use throughout the later periods, and were then applied to the production and processing of maize as well as the older cultigens. As Bruce Smith (1987a) points out, more than 60 years ago

Ralph Linton described significant differences in the tools and techniques used for maize production and processing in Eastern North America vs. those of the Southwest and Mexico, and suggested that in the East maize "was adopted into a preexisting cultural pattern which had grown up around some other food or foods" (Linton 1924: 349).

The fourth and last point is somewhat more tenuous, but we think it is important to consider the implications of one issue unanimously demonstrated by all the relevant ethnographic and ethnohistorical literature: the extensive and intensive botanical and zoological knowledge possessed by people in hunting-gathering-foraging societies. Botanical knowledge is (and would have been in prehistory) greatest among the women who gather, collect, harvest, and process plant resources. Such knowledge goes far beyond foodstuffs to include plants and plant-parts useful for dyes and for cordage and textile manufacture, as well as a vast array of medicinal leaves, bark, roots, stems, and berries. The ethnographically-documented women who exploited these various plant resources knew exactly where and when to find the right plant for a specific purpose. Surely their prehistoric predecessors controlled a similar body of empirical information about their botanical environments, and were equally skilled at using it for their own purposes. Viewed against such a background, the image of unintentional and automatic plant domestication by Late Archaic women pales considerably.

We think that archaeologists operate under at least two different schemes for explaining gender and labor in prehistoric foraging groups. The first is based upon the assumption that women are seriously encumbered and disadvantaged by their reproductive responsibilities and that men are unencumbered by theirs. In this scheme, these physical limitations are combined or conflated with certain personality traits that are thought by some to apply universally to the sexes. This is the scheme of Linton, Montagu, Hoebel, Keesing, etc.; in it women cannot be responsible for culture change because they are not men and therefore they are not active:

men>hunt>animals>active
women>gather>plants>passive

The second scheme is based upon a universal sexual division of labor for hunter-gatherers derived from available ethnographic evidence, but does not suppose that any innate psychological characteristics or activity levels separate males and females:

men>hunt>animals
women>gather>plants

We do not know who domesticated plants in the prehistoric Eastern Woodlands, but faced with a choice between an explanation that relies on scheme number one and one that relies upon scheme number two, we prefer the alternative we have presented: based on available ethnographic evidence for the Eastern United States in particular and the sexual division of labor in general, women domesticated plants. We would like to think that they domesticated them on purpose because they were bored, or curious, or saw some economic advantage in it, that they acted consciously with the full powers of human intellect and that their actions were a significant contribution to culture change, to innovation, and to cultural elaboration. We prefer this explanation because it makes explicit a formulation that anyone who has ever studied anthropology has to some degree absorbed, i.e. that food plants in foraging societies are women's business. Neither Prentice nor Smith argues that women did *not* domesticate plants in prehistoric North America, yet Prentice does argue that a particular group of men were responsible for this major innovation and Smith argues that the innovation was not consciously achieved. It may be the case that shamans were responsible for the introduction of horticulture. It may be that the invention of horticulture was largely unintentional, or passive. But until there is convincing evidence for either of these hypotheses, we prefer to pursue a third alternative: prehistoric women were fully capable not only of conscious action, but also of innovation.

References

Asch, David L. and Nancy B. Asch (1985). "Prehistoric Plant Cultivation in West-Central Illinois." In *Prehistoric Food Production in North America*, Richard Ford, ed. Ann Arbor: University of Michigan Museum of Anthropology, Anthropological Papers No. 75, 149–204.

Ascher, Robert (1961). "Analogy in Archaeological Interpretation." *South-western Journal of Anthropology* 17: 317–25.

Blake, Leonard (1986). "Corn and Other Plants from Prehistory into History in the Eastern United States." In *The Prehistoric Period in the Mid-South; 1500–1700. Proceedings of the 1983 Mid-South Archaeological Conference*, D. Dye and R. Bristler, eds. Mississipi Department of Archives and History, Archaeological Report 18, 3–13.

Blake, Leonard and Hugh C. Cutler (1983). "Plant Remains from the Gnagey Site (36SO55)." Appendix II, in R. George, "The Gnagey Site and the Monongahela Occupation of the Somerset Plateau." *Pennsylvania Archaeologist* 53: 83–8.

Chapman, Jefferson and Gary Crites (1987). "Evidence for Early Maize (*Zea mays*) from the Icehouse Bottom Site, Tennessee." *American Antiquity* 52: 352–4.

Chapman, Jefferson and Andrea Brewer Shea (1981). "The Archaeological Record: Early Archaic to Contact in the Lower Little Tenneessee River Valley." *Tennessee Anthropologist* 6: 64–84.

Chomko, Stephen A. and Gary W. Crawford (1978). "Plant Husbandry in Prehistoric Eastern North America: New Evidence for its Development." *American Antiquity* 43: 405–8.

Conard, N., D. Asch, N. Asch, D. Elmore, H. Gove, M. Rubin, J. Brown, M. Wiant, K. Farnsworth, and T. Cook (1984). "Accelerator Radiocarbon Dating of Evidence of Prehistoric Horticulture in Illinois." *Nature* 308: 443–6.

Cowan, C. Wesley (1985). "From Foraging to Incipient Food-Production: Subsistence Change and Continuity on the Cumberland Plateau of Eastern Kentucky." Unpublished Ph.D. dissertation, University of Michigan.

Crites, Gary (1987). "Human–Plant Mutualism and Niche Expression in the Paleoethnobotanical Record: A Middle Woodland Example." *American Antiquity* 52: 725–40.

Cushing, Frank H. (1974). *Zuni Breadstuff*. New York: Museum of the American Indian Hey Foundation, Indian Notes and Monographs 8 (reprint edn).

Decker, Deena (1988). "Origin(s), Evolution, and Systematics of *Cucurbita pepo* (Cucurbitaceae)." *Economic Botany* 42: 4–15.

Doebley, J., M. Goodman, and C. Stuber (1986). "Exceptional Genetic Divergence of Northern Flint Corn." *American Journal of Botany* 73: 64–9.

Dye, David (1980). "Primary Forest Efficiency in the Western Middle Tennessee Valley." Ph.D. dissertation, Department of Anthropology, Washington University, St. Louis.

Ford, Richard I. (1987). "Dating Early Maize in the Eastern United States." Paper read at the 10th Annual Conference of the Society of Ethnobiology, Gainesville, FL.

Fried, Morton H. (1967). *The Evolution of Political Society*. New York: Random House.

Friedl, Ernestine (1975). *Women and Men: an Anthropologist's View*. New York: Holt, Rinehart, and Winston. Reprinted 1984 by Waveland Press, Prospect Heights, IL.

Friedman, J. and M.J. Rowlands, eds (1977). *The Evolution of Social Systems*. London: Duckworth.

Fritz, Gayle (1986). "Prehistoric Ozark Agriculture: the University of Arkansas Rockshelter Collections." Ph.D. dissertation, Department of Anthroplogy, University of North Carolina, Chapel Hill.

Galinat, Walton C. (1985a). "Domestication and Diffusion of Maize." In *Prehistoric Food Production in North America*, Richard Ford, ed. Ann Arbor: University of Michigan Museum of Anthroplogy, Anthropological Papers No. 75, 245–78.

—— (1985b). "The Missing Links between Teosinte and Maize: A Review." *Maydica* 30: 137–60.

Gardner, Paul S. (1987). "New Evidence Concerning the Chronology and Paleoethnobotany of Salts Cave, Kentucky." *American Antiquity* 52: 358–67.

Gremillion, Kristin J. (1988). "Preliminary Report on Terminal Archaic and Early Woodland Plant Remains from the Cold Oak Shelter, Lee County, Kentucky." Report submitted to Cecil R. Ison, USDA Forest Service Station, Stanton Ranger District, Stanton, Kentucky.

Harris, Marvin (1987). *Cultural Anthropology*, 2nd edn. New York: Harper & Row.

Hastorf, Christine and Virginia Popper, eds (1988). *Current Paleoethnobotany: Analytical Methods and Cultural Interpretations of Archaeological Plant Remains*. Chicago: University of Chicago Press.

Hoebel, E. Adamson (1958). *Man in the Primitive World: An Introduction to Anthropology*. New York: McGraw-Hill.

Hudson, Charles (1976). *The Southeastern Indans*. Knoxville: University of Tennessee Press.

Ison, Cecil R. (1986). "Recent Excavations at the Cold Oak Shelter, Daniel Boone National Forest, Kentucky." Paper presented at the Kentucky Heritage Council Annual Conference, Louisville.

Ison, Cecil R. and Kristin J. Gremillion (1989). "Terminal Archaic and Early Woodland Plant Utilization Along the Cumberland Plateau." Paper presented at the Society for American Archaeology Annual Meeting.

Jacobs, Melville and Bernhard Stern (1952). *General Anthropology*. New York: College Outline Series, Barnes and Noble. Reprinted 1964.

Johannessen, Sissel (1984). "Paleoethnobotany." In *American Bottom Archaeology*, C. Bareis and J. Porter, eds. Urbana and Chicago: University of Chicago Press, 197–214.

Jones, Volney (1936). "The Vegetal Remains of Newt Kash Hollow Shelter." In *Rock Shelters in Menifee County, Kentucky*, William Webb and W. Funkhouser, eds. Lexington: University of Kentucky, Reports in Archaeology and Anthropology 3.

Keesing, Felix M. (1966). *Cultural Anthropology: The Science of Custom*. New York: Holt, Rinehart, and Winston.

Lathrap, Donald W. (1987). "The Introduction of Maize in Prehistoric Eastern North America: The View from Amazonia and the Santa Elena Peninsula." In *Emergent Horticultural Economies of the Eastern Woodlands*, William Keegan, ed. Carbondale: Center for Archaeological Investigations, Southern Illinois University, Occasional Paper No. 7, 345–71.

Le Page du Pratz, Antoine Simon (n.d.). *The History of Louisiana*. Pelican Press, Inc.

Linton, Ralph (1924). "The Significance of Certain Traits in North American Maize Culture." *American Anthropologist* 26: 345–9.

—— (1955). *The Tree of Culture*. New York: Alfred A. Knopf.

Marquardt, William H. (1974). "A Statistical Analysis of Constituents in Paleofecal Specimens from Mammoth Cave." In *Archaeology of the Mammoth Cave Area*, Patty Jo Watson, ed. New York: Academic Press, 193–202.

Minnis, Paul (1985). "Domesticating Plants and People in the Greater American Southwest." In *Prehistoric Food Production in North America*, Richard Ford, ed. Ann Arbor: Museum of Anthropology, University of Michigan, Anthropological Papers No. 75, 309–40.

—— (in prep.). "Earliest Plant Cultivation in Desert North America." In *Agricultural Origins in World Perspective*, Patty Jo Watson and C.W. Cowan, eds. MS chapter. For submission to Smithsonian Institution Press.

Montagu, Ashley (1969). *Man, His First Two Million Years: A Brief Introduction to Anthropology*, New York: Columbia University Press.

Munson, Patrick J. (1973). "The Origins and Antiquity of Maize-Beans-Squash Agriculture in Eastern North America: Some Linguistic Implications." In *Variation in Anthropology; Essays in Honor of John C. McGregor*, D. Lathrap and J. Douglas, eds. Urbana: Illinois Archaeological Survey, 107–35.

Murdock, George P. (1949). *Social Structure*. New York: The Free Press.

Murdock, George P. and Caterina Provost (1973). "Factors in the Division of Labor by Sex: A Cross-cultural Analysis." *Ethnology* 12: 203–25.

Oswalt, Wendell H. (1986). *Life Cycles and Lifeways: An Introduction to Cultural Anthropology*, Palo Alto, CA: Mayfield Publishing.

Parker, Arthur C. (1968). "Iroquois Uses of Maize and Other Plant Foods." In *Parker on the Iroquois*, W. Fenton, ed. Syracuse: Syracuse University Press, 1–119.

Pearsall, Deborah (1989). *Paleoethnobotany: Reconstructing Interrelationships Between Humans and Plants from the Archaeological Record*. San Diego, CA: Academic Press.

Peoples, James and Garrick Bailey (1988). *Humanity: An Introduction to Cultural Anthropology*. St. Paul, MN: West Publishing.

Prentice, Guy (1986). "Origins of Plant Domestication in the Eastern United States: Promoting the Individual in Archaeological Theory." *Southeastern Archaeology* 5: 103–19.

Sahlins, Marshall (1963). "Poor Man, Rich Man, Big-Man, Chief: Political Types in Melanesia and Polynesia." *Comparative Studies in Society and History* 5: 285–303.

—— (1968). *Tribesmen*. Englewood Cliffs, NJ: Prentice-Hall.

Salmon, Merrilee (1982). *Philosophy and Archaeology*. New York: Academic Press.

Scarry, C. Margaret (1986). "Change in Plant Procurement and Production During the Emergence of the Moundville Chiefdom." Ph.D. dissertation, Department of Anthropology, University of Michigan, Ann Arbor.

Service, Elman (1962). *Primitive Social Organization*. New York: Random House.

—— (1971). *Primitive Social Organization*, 2nd edn. New York: Random House.

Smith, Bruce D. (1987a). "The Independent Domestication of the Indigenous Seed-Bearing Plants in Eastern North America." In *Emergent Horticultural Economies of the Eastern Woodlands*, William Keegan, ed. Carbondale: Center for Archaeological Investigations, Southern Illinois University, Occasional Paper No. 7, 3–47.

—— (1987b). "Hopewellian Farmers of Eastern North America." Paper presented at the 11th International Congress of Prehistoric and Protohistoric Science, Mainz, West Germany.

—— (1987c). "In Search of Choupichoul, the Mystical Grain of the Natchez." Keynote Address, 10th Annual Conference of the Society of Ethnobiology, Gainesville, Florida.

—— (in prep.). "Prehistoric Plant Husbandry in North America." In *Origins of Agriculture in World Perspective*, Patty Jo Watson and C.W. Cowan, eds. MS chapter. For submission to Smithsonian Institution Press.

Smith, Bruce D. and C. Wesley Cowan (1987). "The Age of Domesticated *Chenopodium* in Prehistoric North America: New Accelerator Dates from Eastern Kentucky." *American Antiquity* 52: 355–7.

Stevenson, Matilda G. (1904). *The Zuni Indians*. Washington: Annual Report of the Bureau of American Ethnology 1901–1902, vol. 23.

Steward, Julian (1948). *Patterns of Cultural Change*. Urbana: University of Illinois Press.

Stewart, Robert B. (1974). "Identification and Quantification of Components in Salts Cave Paleofeces, 1970–1972." In *Archaeology of the Mammoth Cave Area*, Patty Jo Watson, ed. New York: Academic Press, 41–8.

Stothers, David M. (1976). "The Princess Point Complex: A Regional Representative of the Early Late Woodland Horizon in the Great Lake Area." In *The Late Prehistory of the Lake Erie Drainage Basin*, David Brose, ed. Cleveland: Cleveland Museum of Natural History, 137–61.

Swanton, John R. (1948). *The Indians of the Southeastern United States*. Washington: Bureau of American Ethnology Bulletin 137. Reprinted 1979 by Smithsonian Institution Press.

Upham, S., R.S. MacNeish, W.C. Galinat, and C.M. Stevenson (1987). "Evidence Concerning the Origin of Maiz de Ocho." *American Anthropologist* 89: 410–19.

Wagner, Gail E. (1983). "Fort Ancient Subsistence: The Botanical Record." *West Virginia Archaeologist* 35: 27–39.

—— (1987). "Uses of Plants by Fort Ancient Indians." Ph.D. dissertation, Department of Anthropology, Washington University, St. Louis.

Watson, Patty Jo (1985). "The Impact of Early Horticulture in the Upland Drainages of the Midwest and Midsouth." In *Prehistoric Food Production in North America*. Richard Ford, ed. Ann Arbor: University of Michigan Museum of Anthropology, Anthropological Papers No. 75, 73–98.

—— (1988). "Prehisroric Gardening and Agriculture in the Midwest and Midsouth." In *Interpretation of Culture Change in the Eastern Woodlands During the Late Woodland Period*, R. Yerkes, ed. Colombus: Ohio State University, Department of Anthropology, Occasional Papers in Anthropology No. 3, 38–66.

—— (1989). "Early Plant Cultivation in the Eastern Woodlands of North America." In *Foraging and Farming: the Evolution of Plant Exploitation*, D. Harris and G. Hillman, eds. London: Allen and Hyman, 555–70.

Watson, Patty Jo and Richard A. Yarnell (1986). "Lost John's Last Meal." *Missouri Archaeologist* 47: 241–55.

Watson Patty Jo, Steven A. LeBlanc, and Charles L. Redman (1971). *Explanation in Archaeology: An Explicitly Scientific Approach* New York: Columbia University Press.

—— (1984). *Archaeological Explanation: The Scientific Method in Archaeology*. New York: Columbia University Press.

White, Leslie (1959). *The Evolution of Culture*, New York: McGraw-Hill.

Will, George F. and George E. Hyde (1917). *Corn Among the Indians of the Upper Missouri*. Lincoln: University of Nebraska Press.

Willoughby, Charles C. (1906). Houses and Gardens of the New England Indians. *American Anthropologist* 8: 115–32.

Wills, W.H. (1988). *Early Prehistoric Agriculture in the American Southwest*. Sante Fe, NM: School of American Research Press.

Wilson, Gilbert L. (1917). *Agriculture of the Hidatsa Indians, an Indian Interpretation*. University of Minnesota Studies in the Social Sciences 9. Reprints in Anthropology 5 (May 1977), J&L Reprint Co. Lincoln, NB.

Wylie, Alison (1985). "The Reaction Against Analogy." In *Advances in Archaeological Method and Theory*, vol. 8, Michael Schiffer, ed. Orlando, FL: Academic Press, 63–111.

Yarnell, Richard A. (1964). *Aboriginal Relationships Between Culture and Plant Life in the Upper Great Lakes Region*. Ann Arbor: University of Michigan, Museum of Anthropology, Anthropological Papers No. 23.

—— (1969). Contents of Human Paleofeces. In *The Prehistory of Salts Cave, Kentucky*, Patty Jo Watson, ed. Springfield: Illinois State Museum. Reports of Investigations No. 16, 41–54.

—— (1974). "Plant Food and Cultivation of the Salt Cavers." In *Archaeology of the Mammoth Cave Area*, Patty Jo Watson, ed. New York: Academic Press, 113–22.

—— (1977). "Native Plan Husbandry North of Mexico." In *Origins of Agriculture*, C. Reed, ed. The Hague: Mouton 861–75.

—— (1983). "Prehistory of Plant Foods and Husbandry in North America." Paper presented at the Annual Meeting of the Society for American Archaeology, Pittsburgh.

—— (1986). "A Survey of Prehistoric Crop Plants in Eastern North America." The *Missouri Archaeologist* 47: 47–59.

—— (forthcoming). "Sunflower, Sumpweed, Small Grains, and Crops of Lesser Status." In *Handbook of North American Indians*, W. Sturtevant, ed. Washington, DC: Smithsonian Institution Press.

Chapter 12

BOYS WILL BE BOYS
Masculinist Approaches to a Gendered Archaeology

A. Bernard Knapp

The study of gender in archaeology has made significant strides since the ground-breaking article of Conkey and Spector in 1984 (Zarmati 1994). Male archaeologists, however, continue to show reluctance in adopting gender as a key concept in archaeological theory. This seems all the more curious since "masculinist" writers have been treating gender-related concepts in an intelligent and informed manner for at least the past decade (e.g., Connell 1987, 1995; Seidler 1989; Stoltenberg 1989). Since many feminists equate "masculinist" with male dominance, my use of the term "masculinist" may be disquieting. I would like to suggest here an alternative meaning for those who associate the term "masculinist" exclusively with a reactionary, gender-biased, androcentric position. In this paper, "masculinist" is used exclusively as a gender-based concept widely adopted by psychologists, social scientists, historians and literary critics to define or categorise both a contemporary social movement and an academic position, each of which attempts to formulate the masculine subject. Furthermore, I argue that masculinity, or better, masculinities, must become a focus of gender-based social or cultural enquiry, not least because the social sciences have for so long presented men as gender-neutral and thus as universal, but also because – in my opinion – there is no point in replacing an androcentric account of the world with a gynaecentric one. An exclusionary, feminist worldview is no less likely than any other to obliterate the significance of gender, or to portray gender asymmetry as a consequence of other, somehow more "essential" forces.

Archaeologists of whatever gender need to rethink their traditional research priorities and writing styles, as well as the objects and subjects of their study. Feminist theory has proved to be a fulcrum for the study of gender in archaeology because it has paid closer attention to gender as an analytical category than any other body of theory. I proceed in this paper by looking briefly at the background of feminist scholarship, after which masculinist reactions to feminism are defined: in many ways, masculinist approaches may be regarded as heavily reliant on feminist scholarship. One important contribution of masculinist research has been to insist upon the existence of divergent, multiple masculinities rather than the binary oppositions that once characterised most gender-based research. In drawing upon a cross-section of new studies on masculinities, I want to emphasise that an engendered archaeology must involve both women and men. The study of sexual, social and gender issues should not become the exclusive domain of either women or men; the goal is an archaeology informed by feminism, one that looks critically at theories of human action and uses archaeological data to challenge existing structures of knowledge.

Feminist and masculinist

The women's liberation movement emerged forcefully during the 1960s when it began to make noticeable inroads into a complacent, strongly male-dominated American society. Before long, the corporate world and Madison Avenue had co-opted the movement for purely economic ends: "You've come a long way, baby" (advertisement for Virginia Slims cigarettes) was a typical example. The co-optation, however, was purely economic, since the women's liberation movement was far too controversial socially and politically. Alongside the student and civil rights movements in the USA, and the New Left movement in Britain, a new kind of women's scholarship emerged (e.g., Strathern 1972; Weiner 1976), while a flood of political commentary and soul-searching associated with the movement led to a very different way of looking at the world (e.g., Rosaldo and Lamphere 1974).

The male reaction to feminism that emerged over the succeeding two decades took two main directions, while gay scholarship evolved in other directions:

1   *reactionary masculinities*: the "weekend warriors", "wild men" who engaged with their "Zeus energy" and communed with nature, legend, myth and other "real men";
2   *motivated masculinities*: "feminist" writers who took on board the radical implications and ideology associated with feminism in their writing on masculinity.

The authors engaged in reactionary masculinities tend to be psychologists or else to write with a psychological orientation; those engaged in motivated masculinities tend to be sociologists, and to write with a strong political commitment. Robert Bly's *Iron John* (1990) is the most notorious of the biosocial, almost mythological, writings where biological sex is seen as the fundamental difference between genders. The most compelling of the motivated masculinity studies is perhaps John

Stoltenberg's *Refusing to be a Man* (1989), where the political becomes intensely personal, and where all gender-based research stems from radical feminism.

But how has "masculinist" theory contributed to the study of gender, and how might it contribute to a gendered archaeology? Can men study gender and masculinity using feminist insights but avoiding an androcentric perspective? Masculinist approaches are usually regarded with extreme scepticism, not least because feminists are concerned that masculinist writers will simply co-opt all of the advances made since the 1970s (Canaan and Giffen 1990; Hammer 1990). Of course, such concerns are entirely justified in response to reactionary writers, but otherwise they may prove to be counter-productive to a holistic study of gender that incorporates females, males and any of several other possible realities (Cornwall and Lindisfarne 1994: 29–34).

A feminist political position logically regards "men" or "male" as an oppositional category (Threadgold and Cranny-Francis 1990). Yet some of the critiques of "radical" or "cultural" feminism which appeared in the American literature of the 1980s (e.g., Jaggar 1983; Ringelheim 1985) articulated well the general objections to a "remedial" feminism that simply inverted the gender categories it meant to challenge (Alison Wylie, personal communication). Along with the classical self-critique by Rosaldo (1980), these writings represent a burgeoning feminist literature and practice which questioned an essentialist myopia and certain, narrowly focused, approaches in feminist political theory and enquiry.

Assertions about gender differences are bound closely to specific political positions, but gender does not conform to any fixed identity nor does it preordain any inevitable type of human action (Lorber 1994: 80–96). On the contrary, gender identity is tenuously constituted in time and through space, and gender differences are built and maintained through discourses pertaining to agency, identity and causation (Strathern 1988: 5; Butler 1990: 140). For some, gender is regarded as nothing more than a performance, one way that human agents negotiate their social reality (Morris 1995). Some feminists, moreover, believe that gender should be eliminated as an organising principle in post-industrial and post-colonial society (Lorber 1986: 568; Coltrane 1994: 43). Still others argue that there is no distinction between sex and gender, and that it is no longer acceptable to advocate biological sex as the basis from which the cultural construction of gender proceeds (e.g., Laqueur 1990; Butler 1993: 1; detailed arguments in Knapp and Meskell 1997).

The ideologies that privilege both men and women have been termed "hegemonic masculinities" (Carrigan *et al.* 1985), which themselves necessitate an "essentialist", male/female binary system. Binary approaches have always formed an integral part of Western metaphysics, and contain an inbred, judgmental bias which privileges one over the other (Bruner 1994: 98; Conway-Long 1994: 77). Postmodernist theory largely ignores such biological, dualistic typologies and views gender as a spectrum, rather than a dichotomy. Postmodernist studies, however, have yet to reconcile satisfactorily the binary typology of human beings with the culturally-fashioned spectrum of gender (di Leonardo 1991; Wylie 1991). No matter how central this biological dualism may be to human culture, gender does not simply follow on directly from sex.

The movement of human beings between the diverse social aspects of their lives, and the pluralistic elements on which these movements depend, help to conceptualise gender (Strathern 1988). This somewhat radical notion of "personhood" makes it possible to think about difference beyond binary opposites. The category of "woman," or "feminist," is no more monolithic than that of "man," or "masculinist." Masculinity, then, like femininity, is a relational construct: understanding gender in relational terms is important because hegemonic masculinities function best when they assert their power over some "other" group or individual. Power relations between different men also involve struggles to define hegemony, and so serve to construct different masculinities. It should be apparent that no single factor constitutes masculinity: it is not only divergent and often competing, but above all continuously changing.

Analysing the nature of difference has always been central to anthropology: one way to validate both difference and similarity, and at the same time to highlight both human agency and structural pattern, is to delineate the motivations, conditions and settings through which gender becomes salient in everyday life (Coltrane 1994: 57; Lorber 1994: 172–193). There is a constant, active process in which gender is created and re-created, in response to specific tasks, roles and changing power relations. Gender is never static, but instead interacts with the structures that surround it and the agents that act it out (Kaufmann 1994: 147). The systematic study of these "gender strategies" (Hochschild 1989) helps in understanding their origin and the way that they are constructed and used within various cultural, economic, institutional and spatial contexts.

Gendering archaeology

In what follows, my aim is simply to outline briefly what I regard as the most problematic as well as the most promising aspects of a gendered archaeology. The feminist critique of academic research traditions has proceeded in stages, from exposing androcentrism, to "remedial" research, and finally to reconceptualisation. Archaeologists, in turn, have engaged with gender in at least two distinctive ways (Conkey and Tringham 1995):

1   the "add women and stir" approach (cf. Conkey and Spector 1984), where gender issues are tacked on to existing, usually androcentric, paradigms.

2   the "gender attribution" approach, which is essentially static and fails to engage any of the rich theoretical resources on gender (Conkey and Tringham 1995; Dobres 1995).

The fundamental critiques of essentialism that have appeared during the last decade (e.g., Spelman 1988; Fuss 1989) have been pivotal in the shift from an "add women and stir" approach to programmes of feminist research that accept the challenge in taking gender seriously as a category of analysis (Alison Wylie, personal communication). Within anthropology, recent feminist thought has focused on analysing gender differences in relation to class, age, culture, ethnicity and identity (e.g., Moore 1988, 1995; di Leonardo 1991; Conkey and Tringham 1995). More recent work on the anthropology of sex and gender revolves in large part around the concept of the body as an essential site for theorising about society and the self (e.g., Shilling 1993; Grosz 1994; Morris 1995). Within archaeology, gender increasingly is accepted as a key organising principle of all human beings through time and space (Conkey and Spector 1984); accordingly it should be recognisable in the material remnants of past human groups and individuals (Roberts 1993: 18; Beck and Balme 1994: 39–40).

Roberts (1993: 18–19) distinguishes what she terms a "gendered archaeology", which rejects the binary oppositions and biological determinism implicit in earlier gender-based research and in structuralist or post-structuralist approaches in archaeology (Conkey and Gero 1991: 8; Gilchrist 1991: 488). Despite these ideals and desiderata, there remain certain problems in making gender a central concern of archaeology. Although Conkey and Gero (1991: 11) have emphasised that a gendered archaeology is not dependent on the actual visibility of various gender categories in the archaeological record, certain questions seem inescapable: for example, if we regard material data as a record, how does the evidence indicate different kinds of gender-based activity? Alternatively, if we regard the material record as text, and agree that certain codes may signify gender in particular socio-cultural contexts, how are such texts to be read (Barrett 1988: 12)? Even where the use of cross-cultural data derived from an ethnoarchaeological or ethnohistoric approach allow us to link certain materials, tools or trinkets to gender-specific activities, is it justifiable to retrodict present or recent cultural expressions of gender into the remote past?

Archaeologists should not attempt to understand gender simply in terms of female or male activities, or their residues. At a minimum, this paper suggests that the categories female and male, or feminine and masculine, have been destabilised substantially, and that multiple genders must be acknowledged. Gender, moreover, is based not just in material or economic conditions, but also in the structuring of ideology (Dommasnes 1990: 29). If gender serves to constitute social relations, then it may be constructed as a relationship, while gender categories may be reproduced as a relationship in which women, men or others control specific cultural–resource sets (Rosaldo 1980). A gendered archaeology therefore accepts that gender is based on culturally perceived and inscribed similarities and differences between and among diverse human individuals (Gilchrist: 1991: 497).

Feminist and masculinist theory alike are critical for studying gender in archaeology, not least because they promulgate a pluralistic approach or multiple interpretations while rejecting "runaway relativisms" (Conkey and Tringham 1995) Ambiguity is inherent in the archaeological record, and alternative interpretations are inevitable. Moreover, the recognition of difference and ambiguity encourages dialogues between data and theory, past and present, writer and reader, text and context. Feminist theory not only offers insight into the way gender affects and is affected by social being and social practice, it also challenges contemporary "scientistic" reconstructions of the past that proclaim "truth" or exclusive knowledge (Conkey and Tringham 1995).

Conclusion

"Malestream" archaeologists still regard gender as an intractable field of discourse. Indeed, the study of gender and the issues raised by feminist theory present real challenges to archaeology, which must be confronted if ever we wish to incorporate gender as a dynamic, historical process, or to produce better understandings of the past. Feminist theory can help archaeologists to balance objectivism against extreme relativism, and to realise a more encompassing archaeology that acknowledges contexts, contingencies and ambiguities. Based as it is in categories and typologies, archaeology can only benefit from placing gender at the analytical centre of the categories and typologies we construct. Engaging gender in this manner should also help archaeologists to comprehend the social construction of particular human roles and relationships, and to foreground the individual as an active social agent.

If it is true that the study of the human past thus far has involved largely an appraisal of patriarchy (Kokkinidou and Nikolaidou 1993: 163), the significance of feminist theory and gender in archaeology will only be realised when androcentric attitudes are demolished and bridges built to integrate gender fully within the wider discipline (Gilchrist 1991: 500).

Fotiadis (1994: 546) points out that authors must pass an "epistemological tribunal" even to discuss an "engendered" archaeology or to critique "malestream" practices, and of course to ensure that the work represents "legitimate disciplinary pursuits". If, as seems evident (e.g., Hodder 1991: 10), a backlash against theoretical archaeology asserts itself in the wake of the processual/postprocessual debate, an archaeology informed by feminist theory may discover that the archaeological establishment has become even less receptive to their ideas.

Finally, it is necessary to consider the wisdom of arguing that a total commitment to feminist archaeology must result in a new archaeology, where both the praxis and theory of the discipline must be radically transformed (Dommasnes 1990: 28; Conkey and Tringham 1995). In terms of social change, this presents a real dilemma: while such a transformation must remain a feminist goal, and although gender cannot be separated from other archaeological concerns and marginalised as a "speciality" within the discipline (Conkey and Gero 1991: 17), I reiterate that it will do no good simply to replace an androcentric archaeology with a gynaecentric one.

I have argued in this study that gender forms an important theoretical aspect of work by "masculinist" writers, and that careful attention to this work can help archaeologists to engage the study of multiple, engendered pasts. The critical point is that a gendered archaeology must involve both women and men in order to make gender a more dynamic, multifaceted concept within archaeological interpretation. Any serious debate on gender within a social archaeology must engage both feminist and masculinist perspectives, reconceptualise the categories within which we construct the past, and define new and alternative modes of archaeological discourse and interpretation.

■ ■ ■

References

Bacus, E., Barker, A.W., Bonevich, J.D., Dunavan, S.L., Fitzhugh, J.B., Gold, D.L., Goldman-Finn, N.S., Griffin, W. and Mudar, K.M. (1993) *A Gendered Past: A Critical Bibliography of Gender in Archaeology*. Ann Arbor: University of Michigan. University Museum of Anthropology, Technical Report 25.

Barrett, J.C. (1988) "Fields of discourse: reconstituting a social archaeology". *Critique of Anthropology*, 7(3):5–16.

Beck, W. and Balme, J. (1994) "Gender in aboriginal archaeology: recent research". *Australian Archaeology*, 39:39–46.

Bly, R. (1990). *Iron John: A Book About Men*. Rockport, Mass.: Addison-Wesley Publishing.

Bruner, E.M. (1994). "Abraham Lincoln as authentic reproduction: a critique of postmodernism". *American Anthropologist*, 96:97–415.

Butler, J. (1990) *Gender Trouble: Feminism and the Subversion of Identity*. London and New York: Routledge.

Butler, J. (1993) *Bodies that Matter: On the Discursive Limits of Sex*. London and New York: Routledge.

Canaan, J.E. and Giffen, C. (1990) "The new men's studies: part of the problem or part of the solution?" In J. Hearn and D.H.J. Morgan (eds) *Men, Masculinities and Social Theory*, London: Unwin Hyman, pp. 206–214.

Carrigan, T., Connell, R.W. and Lee, J. (1985) "Towards a new sociology of masculinity". *Theory and Society* 14:551–603.

Coltrane, S. (1994) "Theorizing masculinities in contemporary social science". In H. Brod and M. Kaufmann (eds) *Theorizing Masculinities*, London: Sage, pp. 39–60. Research on Men and Masculinities 5.

Conkey, M.W. and Spector, J.D. 1984 "Archaeology and the study of gender". In M.B. Schiffer (ed.) *Advances in Archaeological Method and Theory* 7:1–38. New York: Academic Press.

Conkey, M.W. and Gero, J.W. 1991 "Tensions, pluralities, and engendering archaeology: an introduction to women in prehistory". In J.W. Gero and M.W. Conkey (eds) *Engendering Archaeology: Women and Prehistory*, Oxford: Basil Blackwell, pp. 3–30.

Conkey, M.W. and Tringham, R.E. 1995 "Archaeology and the goddess: exploring the contours of feminist archaeology". In A. Steward and D. Stanton (eds) *Feminisms in the Academy: Rethinking the Disciplines*. Ann Arbor: University of Michigan Press.

Connell, R.W. 1987 *Gender and Power: Society, the Person, and Sexual Politics.* Oxford: Polity Press.

—— 1995 *Masculinities.* London: Polity Press.

Conway-Long, D. 1994 "Ethnographies and masculinities". In H. Brod and M. Kaufmann (eds) *Theorizing Masculinities*, London: Sage, pp. 61–81. Research on Men and Masculinities 5.

Cornwall, A. and Lindisfarne, N. 1994 "Dislocating masculinity: gender, power and anthropology". In A. Cornwall and N. Lindisfarne (eds) *Dislocating Masculinities: Comparative Ethnographies*, London and New York: Routledge, pp. 1–10.

Di. Leonardo, M. (ed.) 1991 *Gender at the Crossroads of Knowledge: Feminist Anthropology in the Postmodern Era.* Berkeley: University of California Press.

Dobres, M.-A. 1995 "Beyond gender attribution: some methodological issue for engendering the past". In J. Balme and W. Beck (eds) *Gendered Archaeology: Proceedings of the Second Australian Women in Archaeology Conference*, pp. 51–66. Canberra: ANH, Research School of Pacific and Asian Studies, Australian National University. Research Papers in Archaeology and Natural History 26.

Dommasnes, L.H. (1990) "Feminist archaeology: critique or theory building?" In F. Baker and J. Thomas (eds) *Writing the Past in the Present*, Lampeter: Saint David's University College, pp. 24–31.

Fotiadis, M. (1994) "What is archaeology's 'mitigated objectivism' mitigated by? Comments on Wylie". *American Antiquity* 59:45–555.

Fuss, D. (1989) *Essentially Speaking: Feminism, Nature and Difference.* New York and London: Routledge.

Gero, J.M., and Conkey, M.W. (eds) 1991 *Engendering Archaeology: Women and Prehistory.* Oxford: Basil Blackwell.

Gilchrist, R. (1991) "Women's archaeology? Political feminism, gender theory, and historical revision". *Antiquity* 65/248:495–501.

Grosz, E. (1994) *Volatile Bodies.* St Leonards (Sydney): Allen and Unwin.

Hammer, J. (1990) "Men, power and the exploitation of women". In J. Hearn and D.H.J. Morgan (eds) *Men, Masculinities and Social Theory*, London: Unwin Hyman, pp. 21–42.

Hochschild, A. (1989) *The Second Shift.* Berkeley: University of California Press.

Hodder, I.A. (1991) "Interpretive archaeology and its role". *American Antiquity* 56:7–18.

Jaggar, A.M. (1983) *Feminist Politics and Human Nature.* Totowa, NJ: Rowman and Allanheld.

Kaufmann, M. (1994) "Men, feminism, and men's contradictory experiences of power". In H. Brod and M. Kaufmann (eds) *Theorizing Masculinities*, London: Sage, pp. 142–163. Research on Men and Masculinities 5.

Knapp, A.B. (1996) "Archaeology without gravity: postmodernism and the past". *Journal of Archaeological Method and Theory* 3: 127–158.

Knapp, A.B. and Meskell, L.M. (1997) "Bodies of evidence on prehistoric Cyprus". *Cambridge Archaeological Journal* 7: 183–204.

Kokkinidou, D. and Nikolaidou, M. (1993) *I Arheoloyia ke i Kinoniki Taftotita tu Filu: Prosengisis stin Eyeaki Proistoria.* Thessaloniki: Vanias Editions. (in Greek, English summary)

Laqueur, T. (1990) *Making Sex: Body and Gender from the Greeks to Freud.* Cambridge, Mass.: Harvard University Press:

Lorber, J. (1986) "Dismantling Noah's ark". *Sex Roles* 14:567–580.

Lorber, J. (1994) *Paradoxes of Gender.* New Haven and London: Yale University Press.

Moore, H.L. (1988) *Feminism and Anthropology*. Cambridge: Polity Press.

Moore, H.L. (1995) (ed.) *The Future of Anthropological Thought*. London and New York: Routledge.

Morris, R.C. (1995) "ALL MADE UP: Performance Theory and the New Anthropology of Sex and Gender". *Annual Review of Anthropology* 24:567–592.

Ringelheim, J. (1985) "Women and the holocaust: a reconsideration of research". *Signs* 10:741–761.

Roberts, C. (1993) "A critical approach to gender as a category of analysis in archaeology". In H. du Cros and L. Smith (eds) *Women in Archaeology: A Feminist Critique*, Canberra: Dept of Prehistory, Research School of Pacific Studies, Australian National University. pp. 16–21. Occasional Papers in Prehistory 23.

Rosaldo, M.Z. (1980) "The use and abuse of anthropology: reflections on feminism and cross-cultural understanding". *Signs* 5:389–417.

Rosaldo, M.Z. and Lamphere, L. (eds) (1974) *Women, Culture and Society*. Stanford: Stanford University Press.

Seidler, V.J. (1989) *Rediscovering Masculinity*. London and New York: Routledge.

Shilling, C. (1993) *The Body and Social Theory*. London: Sage.

Spelman, E.V. (1988) *Inessential Woman: Problems of Exclusion in Feminist Thought*. Boston: Beacon Press.

Stoltenberg, J. (1989) *Refusing To Be a Man: Essays on Sex and Justice*. Boulder, Oxford: Westview Press.

Strathern, M. (1972) *Women in Between: Female Roles in a Male World, Mount Hagen, New Guinea*. London: Seminar Press.

Strathern, M. (1988) *The Gender of the Gift: Problems with Women and Problems with Society in Melanesia*. Berkeley: University of California Press.

Threadgold, T. and Cranny-Francis, A. (eds) (1990) *Feminine, Masculine and Representation*. London: Allen and Unwin.

Weiner, A. (1976) *Women of Value, Men of Renown*. Austin: University of Texas Press.

Wylie, A. (1991) "Feminist critiques and archaeological challenges". In D. Walde and N.D. Willows (eds) *The Archaeology of Gender*, Calgary: Archaeological Association of the University of Calgary, pp. 17–23.

Zarmati, L. (1994) "Review of Bacus *et al.* 1993", in *American Journal of Archaeology* 98:773–774.

PART SIX

Ideology and social theory

INTRODUCTION

A key concern of processual archaeology has been social process: the manners in which societies operate, whether this involves (diachronic) change over time, or (synchronic) interactions between or within societies at a given moment. Many cognitive and post-processual archaeologists share this interest, although they take a slightly different view of it than processualists, for two reasons. First, they view more aspects of material culture as directly tied to social processes than is implied by process-ualism. This is because they maintain a wider perspective on the meanings of things than found in the processualist technocentric view of material culture. Second, they largely reject the structural-functionalist model of society common to processualism, and seek alternative models for social processes. These circumstances are best expressed with reference to two related issues: ideology and social theory.

As Flannery and Marcus (this volume) have pointed out, ideology concerns political beliefs, yet it is not a political system, *per se*. This important distinction is best understood in terms of our own govern-ment and society. The American form of participatory democracy incorporates a well-structured political *system* (federal, state and local governments; executive, legislative, and judiciary branches; etc.), but this is not our democratic *ideology*. Our ideology, instead, is one that has been encoded in the Declaration of Independence and our Bill of Rights: that we are all born equal; that we all have equal opportunity in our society; and that our form of government yields a just and equi-table society for all. Do American reality and ideology match perfectly? Without moralizing the issue, suffice it to say that many people would argue no. (Of course, these same people differ on whether this is good or bad and, if bad, how deleterious it may be). For example, until the election of John F. Kennedy in 1960, no Catholic had ever been pres-ident of the country, even though 23 per cent of Americans are Catholic, and Catholicism is our single largest religion. (Kennedy's religion was, in fact, an issue in the 1960 campaign, and we have not had a Catholic president since). Similarly, we have yet to see a female president although, again, 51 per cent of our population is female. If American society were truly democratic and equitable, per our ideology, we could expect that the largest proportion of our presidents would be Catholic, and about half would be women.

Yet this is not the way the statistics play out. Our presidential history has been androcentric and WASP dominated. Something has happened (and continues to happen) that has prevented what should have occurred (based on the "law of averages") from developing. The cause of this circumstance is in part due to our ideology. Inculcated in all of us almost from birth, it tells us that we are all equal even when, sometimes, maybe we are not. Ideology is then a system of knowledge, values and beliefs. Its purpose is to legitimize the social and political *status quo*. It does this by making this *status quo* appear to be the normal and therefore unchangeable nature of things. We are led to believe that we have a perfectly just society when, at even the most obvious level (such as the sex and religious backgrounds of our presidents), it is clear that this is not quite so. Again, how serious we view this matter is another issue, but the empirical evidence in our own case is straightforward.

How is ideology broadcast and promoted within a society? One key criticism of processual archaeology has precisely been that it has served as part of our society's dominant ideology (see Tilley, this volume). Processual archaeology denies that ideology matters, partly because its behaviorism denies the importance of cognitive phenomena. It insists that the structural-functionalist model of society, an inductively-derived analogy based on Protestant Euro-America, is appropriate for past societies. Both of these positions serve to support the belief that our existing society is, in fact, the natural order of things – because it has existed in all societies, throughout the prehistoric past. Yet as should be clear, this simply is not so.

Archaeology of course is not the only, or even a primary, way that an ideology may be promoted. In prehistoric societies it is obvious that archaeology played no part. In traditional, smaller-scale prehistoric societies ideologies were instead broadcast and reinforced in other ways: through rituals, myths and oral traditions, common practices and repeated behaviors and, especially, material culture. Though ideology may be primarily understood as a political concern, ideologies are often expressed in religious beliefs and practices, because of the inseparability of religion and politics in most societies. Similarly, ideologies support the social *status quo*, and so social structure, including gender systems, are also reflected in them.

This is why a concern with ideology figures so prominently in many cognitive and post-processual studies. Ideology is one of the key kinds of meanings that are encoded in the things we study: artifacts and monuments. Archaeologists have then identified ideological meanings in wide aspects of the archaeological record, ranging from architecture (e.g., Freidel and Schele 1988), to rock art (e.g., Lewis-Williams 1982), to ceramics (e.g., Pauketat and Emerson 1991), even to foodstuffs (e.g., Hastorf and Johannessen 1993). Far from epiphenomenal, the cognitive system we call ideology influenced many aspects of societies.

Closely related is the question of social theory, in more general terms. An acknowledgement of the importance of ideology in the functioning of a society implies something important. This is that societies are not necessarily well-integrated systems, with all parts working in harmony. Most cognitive and post-processual archaeologists recognize instead that conflicts of different sorts exist within all societies. In larger-scale societies, such as states, these differences may be class-based. In smaller-scale societies, such as bands, they may instead consist of special interest groups, such as genders, or age- or status-groups. But in all societies some degree of conflict is assumed to exist. It is precisely the role of ideology to smooth this conflict out. And it is exactly the archaeologist's job, in attempting to reconstruct the past, to determine how a prehistoric sociopolitical system operated, and how this operation is expressed in material cultural remains, rather than to assume it was like our own, and that the primary meaning of artifacts lies in their technological functions. This requires an explicit concern with social theory, the model of how a society is assumed to operate.

These points are developed in different ways in the two papers in this section. The first, which is my own contribution, addresses a straightforward empirical problem: why did a culture that subsisted primarily on seeds and nuts create tens of thousands of petroglyphs portraying game animals and weapons? I argue that the reason for this lies in the ideological function of the petroglyphs. But to understand this, it is necessary first to determine how the society responsible for this art itself operated. Much like our own culture, the Numic of the Great Basin also maintained a "Man the Hunter" ideology. This was necessary to support the androcentric bias of Numic society because, in fact, males were dependent on women for the majority of their foodstuffs. Moreover, this ideological emphasis developed in this region along with a subsistence change: a transition from generalized foraging, which involved more large game and thereby more direct male participation, to one emphasizing the women's contributions. Petroglyphs of animals and weapons may portray things related to hunting, but they were about men and women, and the socioeconomic and political relationships between them.

Randy McGuire and Dean Saitta look more directly at social theory in the second chapter in this section. Their concern is a major problem in Southwestern prehistory, and one that has led to one of the more contentious recent debates in this region. This is whether Late Prehispanic western Pueblo social organization was egalitarian or hierarchical. This polarized view can be attributed to processualist social theory, which necessarily defines societies in terms of such oppositional constructs. But, using a dialectical methodology (see also Marquardt 1992), they argue instead that Pueblo societies were both egalitarian *and* hierarchical – hence, the inability of archaeologists to decide between the two functionalist alternatives. McGuire and Saitta do not propose a formal social model of traditional societies, intended to replace structural-functionalism. They demonstrate instead a method for developing a model of the operation of a small-scale society. This, importantly, is based on the lived experiences of the people involved, rather than some implicit analogy with our own form of society.

■   ■   ■

Further reading

Demarest and Conrad 1992
Freidel and Schele 1988
Hastorf and Johannessen 1993
Lewis-Williams 1982
Marquardt 1992
Pauketat and Emerson 1991

■   ■   ■

References

Demarest, A.A. and Conrad, G.W. (eds) (1992) *Ideology and Pre-Columbian Civilizations*, Santa Fe: School of Research.
Freidel, D. and Schele, L. (1988) "Kingship in the Late Preclassic Maya Lowlands: The Instruments and Places of Ritual Power", *American Anthropologist* 90: 547–67.

Hastorf, C.A. and Johannessen. S. (1993) "Pre-Hispanic Political Change and the Role of Maize in the Central Andes of Peru", *American Anthropologist* 95: 115–38.

Lewis-Williams, J.D. (1982) "The Economic and Social Contexts of Southern San Rock Art", *Current Anthropology* 23: 429–49.

Marquardt, W.H. (1992) "Dialectical Archaeology", *Archaeological Method and Theory*, 4: 101–40. Tucson: University of Arizona.

Pauketat, T.R. and Emerson, T.E. (1991) "The Ideology of Authority and the Power of the Pot", *American Anthropologist* 93: 919–41.

Chapter 13

BY THE HUNTER, FOR THE GATHERER
Art, Social Relations and Subsistence Change in the Prehistoric Great Basin

David S. Whitley

Since the writings of Roland Barthes (1967), certain literary critics and now some archaeologists have embraced the notion that cultural products may be read, in the sense that they fulfill communicative functions parallel to language, and in that they may be semantically structured in manners similar to texts (e.g., Hodder 1986; Tilley 1990). There are obvious epistemological and ontological commitments attached to this textual approach to archaeological analysis (cf. Taylor 1971), taken literally. It can also be perceived more generally as an analytical metaphor, however, for surely our archaeological record is neither a text in the denotative sense, nor must an interpretation of this record proceed only in a way that is fully equivalent to reading. But that "reading art" may be taken literally or metaphorically is more than merely anecdotal. Just as there are two different meanings of this phrase, so too does a similar tension exist between literal and metaphoric interpretations of prehistoric art and symbolic systems. Indeed, as Lewis-Williams and Loubser (1986) have demonstrated, understanding prehistoric art requires acknowledgement of its fundamentally metaphoric intent.

In considering metaphoric readings of art, my concern is the Late Prehistoric (post-AD 500) archaeological record of the Coso Range, located in the southwestern Great Basin of North America (Fig. 1). This region was occupied to Euro-American contact (*c.* 1860) by hunter-gatherers speaking Numic languages, and is notable because it contains one of the largest concentrations of rock engravings in the hemisphere. It is also advantaged because directly relevant "salvage ethnography", collected early in the century, provides a useful adjunct to archaeological data. In this study I

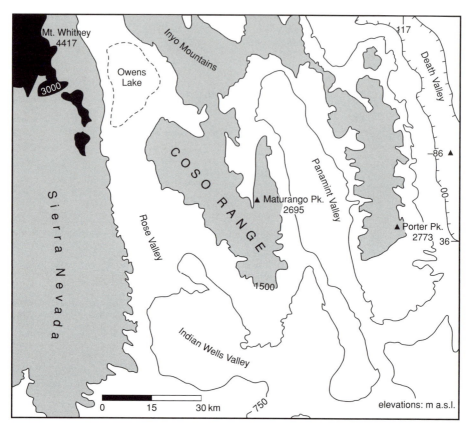

Figure 1 Location of the Coso Range, a portion of the western Great Basin, lying in eastern California, North America

combine analyses of archaeological and ethnographic data to build an interpretation of the traditional Numic culture of the Coso region, and to explain why people who principally ate seeds and nuts made art that emphasized mountain sheep and bows and arrows. I begin with the archaeological record, as traditionally described, before turning to an analysis of aspects of the ethnography. Then, in conjoining these two lines of inquiry, I examine the implications for art, social relations and gender amongst these putatively egalitarian hunter-gatherers, and show how the metaphor "killing a mountain sheep" played a central symbolic role in changing prehistoric subsistence practices.

Settlement and subsistence in the Coso Range

The archaeological record of the Coso Range region has been studied in a relatively thorough manner through a series of large-scale settlement surveys and test and intensive site excavations. Abstracting from a previous synthesis (Whitley 1992a; Whitley *et al*. 1988), the Late Prehistoric settlement and subsistence pattern for the Cosos can be summarized as follows.

Late Prehistoric Coso settlement, to *c*. AD 1200, represents a continuation of a pattern first established during the Late Archaic at *c*. 1500 BC, itself reflecting a local manifestation of a major, far western North American-wide expansion in human population and settlement (W and S Consultants 1991). In the Cosos this was expressed, first, by the establishment of three large seasonally occupied, aggregation-phase villages. These are found at permanent water sources, on the western (wetter) side of the range, at elevations of approximately 1,200m. Second, this was matched by the first intensive use of upland environments (to above 1,830m), where a series of smaller, multi-functional sites was established. These include "residential bases", representing dispersal-phase camps, as well as special activity areas, used for plant collecting and processing, hunting, quarrying and lithic production around a major obsidian source, and ritual activity in the form of rock engraving.

Subsistence to *c*. AD 1200 was based on a generalized hunting-gathering strategy. At aggregation-phase villages, occupied during the winter, faunal assemblages are dominated by black-tailed hares (*Lepus californicas*) and other small game. There is also a small but probably significant proportion of large game in the assemblages (mountain sheep, *Ovis canadensis*, and mule deer, *Odocoileus hemionus*), with surface finds of projectile points in upland environments confirming the importance of mobile, big-game hunting strategies. Paleoethnobotanical remains suggest the seasonal exploitation of piñon nut (*Pinus monophylla*) sources, and of small, local catchments of seeds (Gumerman 1985). This contrasts with the paleoethnobotanical evidence from the residential bases, where seed exploitation, involving a wide diversity of species, is indicated. That is, settlement and subsistence data suggest the use of a wide-range of lowland to upland environments, the exploitation of essentially all available resources, and seasonal variability in plant gathering and use.

After *c*. AD 1200, during the Numic temporal phase, a shift in subsistence and settlement occurred in the Coso region. Aggregation-phase village occupation diminished, with one of the three villages abandoned, while the remaining two were used with reduced intensity. Exploitation of upland areas also changed: with the exception of one class of Numic phase sites (see below), upland occupation was limited to residential bases, typically represented by small middens near springs. Special activity sites such as hunting locales and quarries are all but absent during this phase.

Although low Numic archaeological visibility makes the interpretation of subsistence difficult, the tool assemblages from the aggregation-phase villages suggest a shift from the earlier temporal phases: at one of the Coso villages, Lanning (1963) reported that 52 per cent of the plant processing implements was derived from the Numic occupation levels, while projectile points from these same levels contributed only 7 per cent to the site total. This dramatic reduction in the use of projectile points during Numic times has been confirmed by recent, extensive re-excavations at this site (Yohe 1992). That is, Numic phase evidence suggests an increasing importance in plant foods at the expense of hunting and game, and a more logistically organized, less mobile use of the upland zones relative to the previous phase. A similar pattern has been noted in other portions of the western Great Basin. Noting that the Numic phase was marked by the migration of Numic-speaking peoples out of eastern California, Bettinger and Baumhoff (1982, 1983; Young and Bettinger 1992) have suggested that this migration was effected by the widespread adoption of a higher cost, lower mobility subsistence strategy. This emphasized the exploitation of small seeds, and provided a competitive advantage over the greater reliance on big game by earlier peoples, as well as allowing the Numic to achieve higher population densities than their competitors.

Coso engravings and literal readings

As implied above, there is one variation on the pattern of diminished use of special-ized activity areas during Numic times: rock art sites. These are very common in the Cosos, with rock engravings present virtually wherever non-vesicular basalt outcrops are found. Grant (1968: 120–1) estimated that there are more than 14,000 individual engravings in the Cosos; subsequent field checks suggest that this may be an underestimation by as much as two-thirds. Regardless of exact total, however, his counts of motif types provide a fair estimate of the themes and subject matter of the art. Most common by class are engravings of mountain sheep (51 per cent); followed by various "geometric" patterns (29 per cent); male anthropomorphs (13 per cent); canids/felines (1.6 per cent); "medicine bags" (1.3 per cent); and snakes (1 per cent). Thematically, "killed/hunted sheep" represent 0.7 per cent of the total and 1.5 per cent of the sheep alone. Depictions of weapons, "hunting scenes" and anthropomorphs with weapons comprise 1.9 per cent of the corpus.

This emphasis on putative game, weaponry, hunt scenes, and anthropomorphs resulted in a widely accepted, literal reading of the art: sympathetic hunting magic (e.g., Heizer and Baumhoff 1959; 1962; Grant 1968; Wellman 1979). Aside from the general logical, methodological and empirical problems inherent in this hypoth-esis (cf. Lewis-Williams 1982), it was problematic in the specific case because it contradicted existing ethnographic information that categorically denies the exis-tence of Numic mountain sheep hunting magic. This contradiction was "resolved" by Heizer and Baumhoff (1962: 226–30) who, in an inferential circumlocution, argued away the existence of directly relevant ethnography on the rock engravings: if the ethnography did not support their inductive interpretation, they argued, then the art must be older than ethnographic Numic culture. Their conclusion was then straightforward: all of the art was necessarily prehistoric rather than potentially historical/ethnographic in age. Bettinger and Baumhoff (1982) extended this infer-ence by contending that the hunting magic ritual was solely attributable to Late Prehistoric "Pre-Numic", hunting-oriented peoples and that, with the appearance of the Numic peoples and their intensive seed exploitation strategy at AD 1200, the manufacture of this "hunting art" terminated.

This literal reading of the engravings began to unravel empirically once real attention was paid to dating. The Coso rock engraving corpus has been dated in three ways. Direct, numerical and calibrated ages on a limited number of engravings have been obtained using cation-ratio and AMS^{14}C varnish dating (Whitley and Dorn 1987; 1988; Dorn et al. 1992). This indicates production beginning in the Late Pleistocene and continuing through the Numic phase, and provides no support for previously suggested, intuitively defined stylistic chronologies (e.g., Heizer and Baumhoff 1962; Grant 1968).

Thematic evidence also yields important temporal information, in two ways. First, anthropomorph engravings include a number of "hunter" motifs, portrayed with weapons. According to Grant's (1968: 120–1) tabulations, 96 per cent of the hunter engravings carry a bow and arrow, which was only introduced into the region after AD 500 (cf. Yohe 1992), whereas 4 per cent hold the earlier atlatl. This indicates that a significant proportion, if not large majority, of the art dates to the last 1,500 years. Second, that the production of this art continued into the Numic phase, contrary to previous speculations, is also demonstrated by certain historical motifs. Although not common, a handful of Coso horse and rider engravings clearly indicate creation of the art after Euro-American contact at c. AD 1860 (Whitley 1982). This is confirmed by the large amount of ethnographic data now known to exist on this art (see below).

An examination of the degree of re-varnishing on certain motif types also allows some indication of relative age. Dorn (1982: 15) has noted that although the relative darkness of a rock varnished surface is more contingent upon the manganese to iron ratio than age once a surface has a complete varnish coating, a general assessment of relative age can be obtained by visual examinations of motifs prior to complete re-varnishing. A systematic visual examination and comparison of 352 sheep engravings (5.2 per cent of this motif class, using Grant's (1968) totals) from the three major Coso sites (Lower Renegade, Big Petroglyph and Sheep Canyons) indicates that fully 81 per cent had little or no evidence of re-varnishing; 18 per cent were moderately re-varnished; and 1 per cent completely re-varnished. An equivalent examination was made of 392 anthropomorphs (21 per cent of the Coso total) from the same sites, including "patterned body", "solid body" and "hunter" types. Little or no re-varnishing was visible on 56 per cent of the anthropomorphs; 35 per cent were moderately re-varnished; and 8 per cent completely re-varnished. All of the "hunter" anthropomorphs with bow and arrow, which must be less than 1,500 years old in the region, had little or no re-varnishing.

Since varnish formation can begin within approximately 100 years in eastern California (Whitley and Dorn 1987), the engravings that exhibit little or no re-varnishing can be interpreted as less than roughly 1,000 to 1,500 years old. That is, the majority of these classes of engravings appear to be relatively recent in age. The obvious inference is that the Numic phase experienced not simply continued rock art manufacture, but in fact an accelerated production specifically of anthropomorph, mountain sheep and "hunter" motifs, that far exceeded the number of engravings made during earlier periods. That is, the seed-eating Numic produced a massive corpus of art that, taken literally at least, emphasized hunting, an activity of reduced importance to them.

Art and vision quests

Understanding this apparent paradox, "hunting art" produced by a seed gathering culture, is aided by a consideration of aspects of Numic ethnography. The first of these concerns the art, per se. I summarize here a series of detailed descriptions of the ethnographic evidence for Numic rock art production (Whitley 1992b; 1992c).

Numic rock art was produced by shamans and shaman-initiates following the altered states of consciousness (ASC) experiences of their vision quests. These were considered perilous and usually began with a supernatural test of worthiness and inner strength. They were conducted at locales believed to concentrate *poha*, or supernatural power. The distribution of engraving sites, then, corresponds to the perceived distribution of *poha* across the landscape, which was correlated with high peaks, rocks and caves, and permanent water sources. Notably, the Coso Range was thought the point at which humans were created during mythic time, and thus was particularly potent. Shamans undertook vision quests and entered the supernatural world at these locales to acquire *poha*, usually manifest in the spirit helpers, shamanistic songs and ritual paraphernalia they received during their ASCs. Because of his intimate, personal connection with *poha*, a shaman was a *pohagunt*, "man of power", while rock art sites were *pohakanhi*, "house of power". Some sites yielded specialized kinds of shamanic power; from other sites, any of a variety of kinds of *poha*, including generalized curing power, could be obtained.

The ethnography is also explicit concerning what is depicted in the art: the spirits (including spirit helpers) and visual hallucinations experienced during the ASC, as well as the shaman himself transformed into a supernatural being. In that we have a number of descriptions of culturally-conditioned visions, it is possible to abstract the common ASC imagery experienced by shamans and compare it to the art. It includes: male anthropomorphic figures; animal spirit helpers; weapons; power objects (e.g., feathers, crooked staffs); fighting/battle scenes; hunt scenes; footprints/tracks; and geometrical forms (entoptic patterns; cf. Lewis-Williams and Dowson 1988). As should be expected, this ASC imagery correlates very closely with the motif types and themes found in Numic rock art.

Because certain spirit helpers/trance experiences conferred specific kinds of *poha*, it is then possible to relate particular engravings to specialized types of shamanic power. "Rattlesnake shamans", who cured snake bites, saw rattlesnakes (*Crotalus* spp.) during their vision quests and, correspondingly, made snake engravings. The historical class of "bullet-proof shamans", derived from earlier "arrow shamans", had two kinds of power: the ability to cure wounds from, and invulnerability to, arrows/bullets. They saw images of weapons, and scenes of battles and fighting during their ASCs. Another specialty, "horse cure shamans", was important historically as horses became important means of transportation. Horses were their spirit helpers. Perhaps the most important of the shamanic specialties, however, was weather control. Rain shamans could summon the wind, thunder and lightening, and thus bring rain. The ethnography demonstrates, in a number of different ways, the strong association between the rain shaman and the mountain sheep, not incidentally the dominant rock engraving type in the Coso Range.

First, much of the rain shaman's ritual paraphernalia was derived from mountain sheep products. His characteristic ceremonial object, for example, was the bull-roarer. As noted by Kelly,

> wooden bull-roarers were toys, but those of mountain sheep horns were for rainmaking (1936: 137), while "a mountain sheep singer [i.e., shaman] always dreamed of rain, a bull-roarer and a quail tufted cap of mountain-sheep hide" (ibid: 142), indicating that the bull-roarer and quail tufted sheep-hide cap were ritual objects "obtained" during his vision quest (Figure 2). Similarly, he hung a thong of mountain sheep hide wrapped with eagle down from

Figure 2 Coso patterned body anthropomorphic engraving, depicted wearing a headdress made with the curved topknot feathers of the California quail (*Callipepla californica*). As noted by Kelly (1932: 202), a cap with quail topknots was one of the characteristic features of the ritual dress of the weather shaman. Note also that the figure is depicted with bird claw feet (height of figure, 1.5m)

his belt or staff "to strengthen his power and aide his spirit helper"

(Kelly 1939: 160)

and demonstrated his power by throwing pieces of dried sheep fat or meat onto coals, magically transforming them into fresh kill (ibid: 164).

Second, the mountain sheep, along with the natural phenomena of rain, thunder, lightening and ripe fruit, served as the rain shamans' specialized spirit helpers (Kelly 1936: 138–9, 142; 1939: 159, 165; Steward 1941: 262; Laird 1976). But the mountain sheep vision of a rain shaman was not simply a dream of a sheep as a beneficent spirit helper, with whom the shaman maintained a symbiotic supernatural relationship. Instead, "It is said that rain falls when a mountain sheep is killed. Because of this some mountain sheep dreamers thought they were rain doctors" (Kelly 1936: 139). That is, "a dream of killing a mountain sheep gives power" (Steward 1941:259). "Killing a mountain sheep", then, was a metaphor for the acquisition and application of a particular kind of shamanistic power, weather control.

The large proportion of Coso mountain sheep engravings, including killed sheep and "hunters" shooting sheep (Fig. 3), thus, should not be interpreted in a literal sense, as the remains of a prehistoric hunting magic cult that disappeared prior to

Figure 3   "Killed mountain sheep" and "hunter and mountain sheep" engravings. Like most such motifs in the Coso Range, these engravings exhibit essentially no re-varnishing, suggesting that they are less than roughly 1,000 years old. Although interpreted typically as signifying hunting magic, "killing a mountain sheep" was a Numic metaphor for the practice of rain shamanism (maximum size of "killed mountain sheep", 1.1m; height of "hunter", 29cm)

the historical period, and that (conveniently enough) cannot be documented ethno-graphically. The majority of the Coso motifs, as the ethnography demonstrates, were graphic expressions of the visions of rain shamans that, themselves, were metaphors for the rain shaman's supernatural control over weather. Importantly, Numic ethnography provides independent support for this metaphoric interpreta-tion. As noted above, certain Numic vision quest/rock art sites were cited as endowing specialized *poha*; the Coso region was widely acknowledged as the center of weather control shamanism. Not only did surrounding groups seek out shamans from the Coso region for rain-making ceremonies, but the last living Numic rain shaman travelled specifically to the Cosos to make rain (Zigmond 1977: 89). Thus, while there is no reason to assume that only weather control power could be obtained in the Cosos, it is none the less apparent that this was a major emphasis of the vision questing and resulting production of rock engravings in the region.

Gender and power

Although the interpretation of Coso engravings as resulting largely from rain shamanism provides us with one reading of the art, more insight is gained by exam-ining their social context, as Lewis-Williams (1982) has demonstrated in a parallel example for the southern San. In the Numic case this is obtained by, once again, looking to the ethnographic record. But in that much of this was collected under the guise of Julian Steward's (e.g., 1955) cultural ecology, the importance of art, symbolism and ritual are diminished. Using the existing ethnography to define the social context of the art necessarily, therefore, requires a re-analysis of it; specifi-cally, of Numic social relations, and how the engravings articulated with them.

The Numic are often viewed as the archetypal egalitarian society (e.g., Steward 1936: 561–2). Summarizing from a detailed analysis presented elsewhere (Whitley 1992a; in press) however, asymmetrical social relations were established by the institution of marriage, creating a system of gender inequality in Numic society. Additionally, *poha* served to further distinguish and inequitably differentiate two categories of males, shamans and non-shamans. After showing how these two struc-tures of inequality manifest in Numic social relations, we can turn to how the art articulated with social structure.

Male versus female

Although Numic society was demonstrably kin-based, non-stratified, and lacked leaders with rights to give orders to others, it is evident that kinship, through the institution of marriage, established a system of inequality that favored males over females, and married men over bachelors. This is apparent, following Collier's (1988) model of marriage and inequality in classless societies, when it is recognized that inequalities are expressed not only in the rights held by individuals, but equally by the differing obligations they maintain. For the Numic these were most dramatically expressed by the sexual division of labor and the subsistence obligations these entailed; through differing access to means of production; in forms of circulation within the family, as opposed to outside the family; and in social discourse.

Numic men were solely responsible for big-game hunting. Women were the suppliers of gathered plant foods and small (captured) game, such as rabbits and rodents. Little or no specialization in craft was practised, so that each individual made his own tools and implements. Meat obtained by a male was communally shared, guaranteeing that all inhabitants of a camp would have access to some large game. Gathered plant foods and the other subsistence products of the woman, in contrast, were reserved for her immediate family, were not considered a commodity (Park 1938: 68), and therefore were not traded.

The implications of this sexual division of labor and pattern of circulation are extreme. Women's subsistence activities were the primary contributors to diet and, except in winter, had to be conducted daily. Male hunting was less important, uncertain in its returns, and could be undertaken less frequently, if at all. Women, in other words, did not need husbands, because the division of large game in a camp guaranteed them some portion of this meat; they were economically independent. Marriage, however, tied them to a relatively strict plant-gathering regimen, as well as burdening them with primary responsibilities for child care, and the hauling of water and firewood. For the male, in contrast, a wife was necessary to obtain a steady supply of dietary staples; the only alternative was to accrue obligations to other married males (usually by entering into a polyandrous marriage, and temporarily sharing a wife). Marriage was thus necessary for a man to be independent of other men and, given that hunting was optional, it did not burden him with any obligations he did not already hold. Marriage, then, resulted in an asymmetrical division of obligations that released men from duties, as well as potential obligations to other men, while tying women to them.

Moreover, although women were not necessarily considered inferior to men, the prescribed Numic means for acquiring and maintaining respect, prestige and ultimately authority essentially excluded them from it. Prestige, for example, was measured by the number of wives a person could obtain and hold, and discourse emphasized masculine traits and accomplishments, to the complete exclusion of feminine activities and undertakings, as hallmarks of success. Since success was exclusively defined in masculine terms, causality was necessarily linked to male activities and attributes, and feminine skills like gathering and child-rearing were devalued. And shamanistic power, believed the key to all success and authority, was inimical to menstrual blood, thereby effectively excluding women from prestige. Given that the concept of femininity was then unelaborated among the Numic (cf. Collier 1988: x), it is apparent that women were the objects of prestige, not the subjects of it.

As implied above, marriage also established an asymmetrical relationship between groups of men: husbands and bachelors. Since prestige was in part measured by the number of wives a man maintained, and because marriages were brittle and often short-lived, conflicts over women were a major source of Numic social disruption. Bachelors were, by definition, men looking for women; due to the fact that divorce threatened a man's independence from other men, bachelors were then seen by husbands as competitors over women. This had one important outcome. Although the Numic lacked leaders with the power to dominate and order all others, it is nonetheless true that authority, the ability to influence, convince and/or coerce fellow men towards a desired action, existed and was prized. This was obtained by senior men who had gained prestige and demonstrated their trustworthiness to their cohorts. Trust resulted in part when it was recognized that another male was not in competition for one's women. Until bachelors married, in other words, they were considered the consummately untrustworthy members of Numic society. Marriage, then, in structuring men's relationships with other men, enabled men to become political actors and, in a reversal of Numic conceptions of causality, allowed them to accrue prestige.

Shamans versus non-Shamans

Marriage structured one kind of relationship between men, but access to supernatural power created an additional asymmetrical relationship, pertaining specifically to the incipient forms of political leadership present among the Numic. Although the Numic are often conceived as egalitarian and as representing the base-line stage in human sociopolitical evolution, it is nonetheless true that authority and leadership were invested in particular individuals. Typically this was limited to the village or band level, although leadership for occasional district-wide communal activities (e.g., ceremonial fandangos, raiding parties) was exercised when needed. The most common leader, though, was the village or band headman. He was a "man of influence who 'told his people what to do and where to hunt' – who entertained visitors at camp, interviewed thiefs [sic] and directed [the] return of stolen property" (Kelly 1932: 182). His authority also covered hunts, dances, war and ceremonies; he kept himself informed about seasonally-available plant resources, and was responsible for organizing group gathering forays (Steward 1938: 240–7).

The headman ruled at the will of the people, in the sense that allegiance was by residential preference: the dissatisfied could simply change their village and ally themselves with a new headman if unhappy with their existing conditions. There were limits, then, to the authority of the headman, and his power was constrained by the fact that he ruled by achieving consensus rather than by exercising dictatorial prerogatives. Still, the headman served as the organizational nexus for Numic society, in terms of both ceremonial and subsistence activities, and represented the pinnacle of prestige within the male population. Thus, although the headman did not accumulate wealth over and above his fellow villagers, this was not due to some inflexibly egalitarian social structure, but because stockpiling material wealth was maladaptive for these nomadic peoples (Park 1938: 68).

The critical point of this is that headmen were, almost invariably, shamans (Park 1938: 67, 103; Steward 1938: 82, 88, 159; Harris 1940: 59, 77; Whiting 1950: 22; Laird 1976: 28). It is important then to note that shamanism was largely hereditary (Lowie 1924: 294; Kelly 1932: 191, 1939: 161; Driver 1937: 141; Park 1938: 22; Harris 1940: 70; Steward 1943: 282; Whiting 1950: 31; Malouf 1974: 81; Laird 1976: 19, 35); as was village headmanship (Kelly 1932: 183; Steward 1938: 82). Thus, although the Numic may represent the most egalitarian society known to anthropology, it is none the less true that a certain degree of incipient hereditary social differentiation existed among them.

Not all shamans, however, were headmen; any individual theoretically could receive a spontaneous shamanistic "calling". Like the headmen, though, their *poha* gave them a considerable amount of prestige and influence. According to Park, shamans, whether headmen or not, were "very influential in every aspect of the political and social life" (1938: 103). In fact, Numic cultural logic specified that it was exactly the possession of supernatural power that allowed success, whether measured in health and long life, status, hunting skills, or the acquisition of numerous wives: *poha* enabled a man to become an "outstanding member" of society and, by the same logic, success was taken as a *de facto* demonstration of shamanistic power. Thus, as Kelly (1936: 134) noted, people "are always jealous of an older man and think he must be a doctor [i.e., shaman]. They cannot understand how he has lived so long . . .".

Although marriage served to structure the relationship between husbands and bachelors, individuals' perceived relationships to supernatural power served as a deeper foundation for these relationships. It was only through the acquisition of shamanistic power that men could truly become political actors, and gain prestige and status in Numic society. In turn, this advantaged them in a number of ways: women desired such men as preferred marriage partners (Whiting 1950: 100), and the population at large respected them, largely out of fear of their potentially malevolent *poha* (Park 1938: 69). And in that shamanistic power was partly inherited, but in any case limited to a small segment of the population (estimated at about 2 per cent by Harris 1940: 102 and Whiting 1950: 28), it is apparent that a very restricted, incipient "elite" group, comprised of shamans/headmen, existed within the ostensibly egalitarian Numic society.

Art, ideology and social relations

As stated at the outset, my goal has been to explain the apparent paradox by which principally seed and nut eating peoples made art emphasizing mountain sheep, bows and arrows, "hunters" and male anthropomorphic figures; and to explain in a larger sense the workings of Numic society. My perspective is informed, however, by a cognitive, not behaviorist, theory of culture (cf. Whitley 1992a: 60). Thus, I seek explanation in cognitive cultural systems, rather than simply in adaptive behavioral responses. The articulation between culture and society then results because of the inherently ideological, albeit conservative, nature of culture (cf. Keesing 1987: 161). That is, culture can be defined as a cognitive system of beliefs and world-view. Recognizing that, even in classless societies, culture in part serves an ideological purpose by masking the real nature of social relations and thereby supports the status quo, it is then apparent that the articulation of art and social relations occurs within a larger cultural system of ideological symbols. How the Coso rock engravings relate to Late Prehistoric and especially Numic subsistence patterns, as well as Numic social relations, can then be reconstructed as follows.

The Late Prehistoric but Pre-Numic (pre-AD 1200) occupation of the Coso region involved a generalized, mobile hunting and gathering strategy. With the transition to a less mobile, seed-oriented gathering economy at c. AD 1200, it must be inferred that the then-existing social relations were, at least, threatened: the increasing emphasis on foods supplied by women and diminished importance of game hunted by men had the potential to change gender relations. In particular, this change made women effectively independent economically. And since male independence (from other males) was predicated on marriage and the resulting control of a woman's gathered foodstuffs, this increased men's dependence on women and marriage.

While there could have been a series of solutions to avert the potential social disruption that might have resulted by this changing subsistence pattern, the archae-ological evidence suggests that a response in the Cosos involved a dramatic increase in the production of rock engravings. As noted previously, a majority of certain key classes of engravings appear to have been made in roughly the last 1,000 years. These are the mountain sheep, anthropomorph, weapons and "hunter" motifs; i.e., those engravings that are literally read as pertaining to a sympathetic hunting magic cult. But as we know from the ethnography, no such cult existing among the Numic. Instead, as the ethnography also demonstrates, these motifs were metaphors for the shaman and his relationship with the supernatural world, while the mountain sheep – the dominant engraving in the region – specifically was associated with the rain shaman. That is, the changing subsistence system in the western Great Basin appears to have precipitated a dramatic increase in weather control shamanism.

The adaptive logic for this is straightforward. Rain shamans called the wind to bring rain clouds. In turn, following Numic cultural logic, this served an impor-tant purpose: to enable plants to grow during periods of drought (Harris 1940: 60; Zigmond 1977:88). As Kelly noted: "When the ground was parched and food plants were withering, the [rain] shaman sang night and day, accompanied at times by the people. He dreamed and told the rain, 'We need moisture so that the seeds will grow'" (1939:159). And, of course, when the rain shaman dreamed to bring the rain, he dreamed of killing a mountain sheep, as recorded in the rock engrav-ings of the Coso Range.

The response to the threat to established gender relations precipitated by the change in subsistence, then, was to emphasize male – specifically, the male shaman's

– control over women's plant gathering activities. In a region of extreme aridity, it was the rain shaman who brought the rain and, by controlling nature, caused the seed plants to grow.

It is also apparent, however, that all of the symbols of the shaman are masculine. Completely absent in the Coso engravings are representations of women's crafts and utensils (e.g., basketry) or, for that matter, their product: the plants they gathered and that served as the staples of diet. Male shamans controlled women's plant gathering, then, not because they controlled plants and the ritual symbols of women. Instead, it was because of their relationship with an important part of the world of men, the supernatural, from which they obtained *poha*, as symbolized metaphorically by hunting mountain sheep; and due to their control of the symbols of men – hunted game and weaponry. Women's plant gathering, in other words, was only possible when the importance of male hunting was valorized and ritualized. The shaman thus demonstrated his importance to women's subsistence activities by metaphorically killing a mountain sheep and by recording this supernatural act in rock art, as well as emphasized the continuing importance of male hunting, in general, by the selective use of these literal masculine symbols.

In this sense, parallels with Lewis-Williams's (1982) analysis of the social context of southern San rock art are immediately apparent. Not only did the Numic shaman control nature through his rain rituals, and thereby directly aid the material reproduction of society, but he also fostered the stability of Numic social relations. In this case it was by maintaining the established gender asymmetry, by re-affirming the dominance of males even in the face of the changing importance of the sexes's differing contributions to diet.

But as I have emphasized earlier, Numic social relations did not solely consist of an asymmetrical relationship between the sexes. Also present, and equally requiring explanation, was an asymmetry between groups of males: those with and those without *poha*. This is particularly important because, given the correlation between political and shamanistic power, in the origin of this distinction lies the origin of the incipient political organization of the Numic.

My contention is that changing subsistence practices, and thus the potential for changing social relations between the genders, precipitated an alteration in the relationships between males. The asymmetrical relationship between men and women was maintained, even in the face of changing contributions to diet, by an acceleration in shamanistic activities, as recorded in the art. But this was not without cost for the males as a whole. By allowing the emergence of shamans as part-time ritual specialists, responsible for maintaining the position of men in relation to women, the males effectively laid the stage for the emergence of asymmetrical relationships between men. This favored those with *poha* – the shamans – over those without, as measured by prestige, respect, authority and, in some sense (given their enhanced desirability to women), increased access to females. Moreover, given their ownership of esoteric knowledge, shamans were advantaged at a fundamental level: their access to the supernatural enabled them not only to cure (and cause) disease, and thereby exercise some social control through fear, but more generally enabled them to manipulate the workings of the universe to their own benefit. And, of course, since political authority was homologuous with shamanistic power, and because both were at least in part inherited, the emergence of incipient political organization was the immediate result.

Although speculative, there is archaeological support for this reconstruction. Given that village/band headmen were responsible for scheduling and directing subsistence activities, it follows that the appearance of these political functionaries should correlate with observable changes in subsistence organization; specifically, with an increase in the logistical organization of hunting and gathering. As noted earlier, and in addition to the obvious increase in rock art ritual during Numic times, the transition from Pre-Numic generalized foraging to Numic seed-oriented subsistence involved a dramatic reduction in the number of small, specialized activity sites, in favor of upland residential bases. Apparently, the transition to the Numic subsistence pattern involved just the kinds of logistical changes the emergence of incipient political organization would be expected to have precipitated.

Finally, if the *status quo* domination of men over women required ideological support, it follows that the emerging asymmetry of shaman-cum-headman over other males also necessitated ideological bolstering. This was provided in two ways. In part it resulted from the shaman's use of exclusively masculine symbols. By emphasizing metaphors such as killing mountain sheep to make rain, the shaman underscored the relationship of the supernatural to male activities, as well as the importance of men to social relations and subsistence in general, thereby mediating the disparity in authority, prestige and respect between him and other males. Further, cultural perceptions held that all success and authority resulted from *poha*. Since the receipt of this power was believed somehow to be predicated on the independent agency of the supernatural world in its own right, then the distinction between males was, in a sense, cosmically ordained: power was believed to "select" its recipient, while belief in the inherently dangerous nature of the vision quest apparently stymied most males from seeking power without a previous "calling". Thus, ethnographic informants consistently stated that anyone could be a shaman or a headman, even when ethnographic genealogies systematically demonstrate that shamanism and political authority ran, patrilineally, in family lines.

Conclusion

One general point needs be emphasized in concluding this reading of the rock engravings of the Coso Range, particularly in light of Julian Steward's (1938:46) oft-cited contention that Numic culture was principally "gastric" in character. This is that subsistence change is not simply a mechanical or even evolutionary alteration in diet, as much of our recent archaeological literature might suggest. A subsistence system is, after all, a conceptual entity, only indirectly expressed in the archaeological record, that is based on cultural perceptions of food preference, sexual divisions of labor, decisions about scheduling, selections between competing resources, social organization, and so on (cf. Lévi-Strauss 1969; Hastorf and Johannessen 1993). It is actualized neither solely by hunger, then, nor only through competition with other members of an ecosystem, but by negotiated commitments from various groups in society. To divorce these cognitive aspects from the analysis of subsistence, thus, can only result in something very different: a study of the physical act of eating – bodily movement and digestion.

Moreover, subsistence change can require larger cognitive adjustments, exactly because it can result in changing social relations between groups in a society. Just such a change is evident in the Coso engravings, with the transition from a generalized foraging to more specialized seed-oriented subsistence, and the potential disruption in social relations that this could have engendered. To study subsistence change, then, is to commit to the study of prehistoric cognition, something many materialist archaeologists have been reluctant to admit. But as I hope I have demonstrated here, understanding subsistence change requires an understanding of prehistoric culture, a cognitive system of beliefs and worldview, and the study of art and symbolism more generally are a necessary adjunct in such an endeavor.

■ ■ ■

References

Barthes, R. 1967. *Elements of Semiology* (trans. A. Lavers and C. Smith). London: Jonathan Cape.

Bettinger, R.L. and Baumhoff, M.A. 1982. The Numic spread: Great Basin cultures in competition. *American Antiquity*, 47: 485–503.

Bettinger, R.L. and Baumhoff, M.A. 1983. Return rates and intensity of resource use in Numic and Prenumic adaptive strategies. *American Antiquity*, 48: 830–4.

Collier, J.F. (1988). *Marriage and Inequality In Classless Societies*. Stanford University Press.

Dorn, R.I. (1982). Observations on the use of "desert varnish" in the age-determination of surfaces. *Society for California Archaeology Newsletter*, 1(1): 15–18.

Dorn, R.I., Clarkson, P.B., Nobbs, M.F., Loendorf, L.L. and Whitley, D.S. (1992). New approach to the radiocarbon dating of rock varnish, with examples from drylands. *Annals of the Association of American Geographers*, 82: 136–51.

Driver, H. (1937). Cultural element distributions: VI, southern Sierra Nevada. *Anthropological Records* 1(2): 53–154.

Grant, C. (1968). *Rock Drawings of the Coso Range, Inyo County, California*. China Lake: Maturango Museum.

Gumerman IV, G. (1985). An optimal foraging approach to subsistence: the Coso Junction ranch site. Master of Arts thesis, Department of Anthropology, University of California, Los Angeles.

Harris, J.S. (1940). The White Knife Shoshoni of Nevada. In *Acculturation in Seven American Indian Tribes* (ed. R. Linton). New York: D. Appleton-Century, pp. 39–116.

Hastorf, C.A. and Johannessen, S. (1993). Pre-Hispanic political change and the role of maize in the central Andes of Peru. *American Anthropologist*, 95: 115–38.

Heizer, R. and Baumhoff, M.A. (1959). Great Basin petroglyphs and game trails. *Science*, 129: 904–5.

Heizer, R. and Baumhoff, M.A. (1962). *Prehistoric Rock Art of Nevada and Eastern California*, University of California Press.

Hodder, I. (1986). *Reading the Past: Current approaches to interpretation in archaeology*. Cambridge: Cambridge University Press.

Keesing, R.M. (1987). Anthropology as interpretive quest. *Current Anthropology*, 28: 161–76.

Kelly, I.T. (1932). Ethnography of the Surprise Valley Paiutes. *University of California Publications in American Archaeology and Ethnology*, 31(3): 67–210.

Kelly, I.T. (1936). Chemehuevi Shamanism. In *Essays in Anthropology, Presented to A.L. Kroeber In Celebration of His Sixtieth Birthday* (no editor). University of California Press, pp. 129–42.

Kelly, I.T. (1939). Southern Paiutes Shamanism. *Anthropological Records*, 2(4): 151–67.

Laird, C. (1976). *The Chemehuevis*. Banning: Malki Museum.

Lanning, E.P. (1963). Archaeology of the Rose Spring site, Iny-372. *University of California Publications in American Archaeology and Ethnology*, 49(3): 237–336.

Lévi-Strauss, C. (1969). *The Raw and the Cooked*. New York: Harper & Row.

Lewis-Williams, J.D. (1982). The economic and social context of southern San rock art. *Current Anthropology*, 23: 429–49.

Lewis-Williams, J.D. and Dowson, T.A. (1988). The signs of all times: entoptic phenomena in Upper Paleolithic art. *Current Anthropology*, 29: 201–45.

Lewis-Williams, J.D. and Loubser, J.N.H. (1986). Deceptive appearances: a critique of southern African rock art studies. *Advances in World Archaeology*, 5: 253–89.

Lowie, R.H. (1924). Notes on Shoshonean ethnography. *Anthropological Papers, American Museum of Natural History*, 20: 185–314.

Malouf, C. (1974). The Gosiute Indians. In *Shoshone Indians* (no editor). New York: Garland Publishers, pp. 25–172.

Park, W.Z. (1938). *Shamanism in Western North America: A Study in Cultural Relationships*. Northwestern University Studies in the Social Sciences, No. 2.

Steward, J.H. (1936). Shoshoni polyandry. *American Anthropologist*, 38: 561–4.

Steward, J.H. (1938). Basin-plateau aboriginal sociopolitical groups. *Bureau of American Ethnology*, Bulletin 120.

Steward, J.H. (1941). Culture elements distributions: XIII, Nevada Shoshoni. *Anthropological Records*, 4(2): 209–359.

Steward, J.H. (1943). Culture element distributions: XXIII, Northern and Gosiute Shoshoni. *Anthropological Records*, 8(3): 263–392.

Steward, J.H. (1955). *Theory of Culture Change: the methodology of multilinear evolution*. University of Illinois Press.

Taylor, C. (1971). Interpretation and the science of man. *Review of Metaphysics*, 25: 3–51.

Tilley, C. (ed.). (1990). *Reading Material Culture: Structuralism, Hermeneutics and Post-Structuralism*. Oxford: Basil Blackwell.

W and S Consultants (1991). Phase II archaeological test excavations at CA-VEN-478, -1038, -1042/H, -1043, -1044, -1045 and -1046, TPM 4687, Ventura County, California. Unpublished manuscript on file, Institute of Archaeology, University of California, Los Angeles.

Wellman, K. (1979). *A Survey of North American Indian Rock Art*. Graz, Austria: Akademische Druck u. Verlagstanstalt.

Whiting, B.B. (1950). *Paiute Sorcery*. Viking Fund Publications in Anthropology, 15.

Whitley, D.S. (1982). Notes on the Coso petroglyphs, the etiological mythology of the western Shoshone, and the interpretation of rock art. *Journal of California and Great Basin Anthropology*, 4: 210–22.

Whitley, D.S. (1992a). Prehistory and post-positivist science: a prolegomenon to cognitive archaeology: In *Archaeological Method and Theory* Vol. 4, (ed. M.B. Schiffer). University of Arizona Press, pp. 57–100.

Whitley, D.S. (1992b). Shamanism and rock art in far western North America. *Cambridge Archaeological Journal*, 2: 89–113.

Whitley, D.S. (1992c). The vision quest in the Great Basin. Paper presented at the twenty-third biennial Great Basin Anthropological Conference, Boise.

Whitley, D.S. In press. Etiology and ideology in the Great Basin: or, Coyote's first date. In *Numic Myth and Ritual* (ed. L.D. Myers).

Whitley, D.S. and Dorn, R.I. (1987). Rock art chronology in eastern California. *World Archaeology*, 19: 150–64.

Whitley, D.S. and Dorn, R.I. (1988). Cation-ratio dating of petroglyphs using PIXE. *Nuclear Instruments and Methods in Physics Research*, B35: 410–14.

Whitley, D.S. Gumerman, G., IV, Simon, J.M. and Rose, E. (1988). The Late Prehistoric period in the Coso Range and environs. *Pacific Coast Archaeological Society Quarterly*, 24(1): 2–10.

Yohe, R.M. (1992). A re-evaluation of western Great Basin cultural chronology and evidence for the timing of the introduction of the bow and arrow to eastern California based on new excavations at the Rose Spring Site (CA-INY-372). Doctoral dissertation, Department of Anthropology, University of California, Riverside.

Young, D.A. and Bettinger, R.L. (1992). The Numic spread: a computer simulation. *American Antiquity*, 57:85–99.

Zigmond, M. (1977). The supernatural world of the Kawaiisu. In *Flowers of the Wind: Papers on the Myth and Symbolism in California and the Southwest* (ed. T.A. Blackburn). Socorro, NM: Ballena, pp. 59–95.

Chapter 14

ALTHOUGH THEY HAVE PETTY CAPTAINS, THEY OBEY THEM BADLY
The Dialectics of Prehispanic Western Pueblo Social Organization

Randell H. McGuire and Dean J. Saitta

Southwestern archaeologists have been unable to decide whether fourteenth-century pueblos were democratic societies that existed many centuries before the signing of the Declaration of Independence (Wormington 1947:19) or hereditary oligarchies in which a small number of individuals dominated leadership positions over generations (Upham 1982:199). In the 1980s this controversy manifested itself in the Chavez Pass–Grasshopper debate (Upham 1982; Upham and Plog 1986; Upham *et al.* 1989; cf. Graves 1987). The debate remains unresolved despite major methodological advancements and the steady accumulation of new data on subsistence, settlement, and exchange behavior. While the debate has subsided somewhat in recent years, given both sides' failure to present a compelling case (Cordell and Gumerman 1989:13; Kohler 1993:269), the question, remains: why do southwestern archaeologists have so much difficulty characterizing Prehispanic pueblo social organization? Why have they been unable to resolve the issue even with new methods and abundant new data?

We suggest that the issue of late Prehispanic pueblo social organization remains unresolved because archaeologists have been asking the wrong question. Most have framed the question of late Prehispanic social organization in the Southwest in dichotomous either–or terms: i.e., was a given organizational entity simple or complex, egalitarian or stratified, acephalous or authoritarian (McGuire 1990; Plog 1995)? Questions about causality have been similarly framed. They ask whether change was environmentally or politically induced (e.g., Lightfoot 1984), with investigators' preferences usually tied to their position on complexity. This kind of oppositional thinking originates in a processual view of social organization and causality. It has persisted through methodological refinements, and the collection of new data. It has also survived theoretical reevaluations of the concept of complexity and even widespread advocacy of continuous, as opposed to typological, approaches to variation (Sebastian 1991; Upham *et al.* 1989).

What impresses us most about modern and past pueblo societies is not that they are/were egalitarian or stratified, but that they embodied *both* consensual hierarchical social relations (see also Plog 1995). Oppositional thinking does not accommodate the paradoxical reality of pueblo life or the empirical realities of the archaeological record. This means that a radical change in perspective is required, one that breaks with oppositional thought. For us, the best hope for new insights lies in framing different questions about the past, and adopting a different framework of inquiry. This alternative framework is grounded in a dialectical epistemology, and reflects an interest in the *lived experience* of past peoples, i.e., their actions within fields of social relations *and* cultural meanings, and their roles as conscious creators and negotiators of culture. We do not ask if the Southwest was egalitarian or stratified – thereby forcing Prehispanic cases into conventional categories – but rather we ask what was the dialectical relationship between egalitarianism and stratification? Or, put differently, how did consensual and hierarchical social relations structure pueblo society, and how did the tensions and contradictions in these relations propel cultural change?

Such questions can only be asked and answered in the context of specific historical experiences. After a brief comparison of the processual approach with a dialectical alternative, we will examine the Chavez Pass–Grasshopper debate to illustrate what our approach delivers in a concrete archaeological setting. We offer an alternative model open to the possibility that late Prehispanic western pueblo society may have varied in ways that conventional analytical categories cannot capture.

Oppositional thinking and processual archaeology

Processual archaeology embraces a logical positivist epistemology and a systemic view of culture. Positivists emphasize the acquisition of general and "objective" knowledge and the ability to predict future events based on this knowledge. The processualist metaphysic is explicitly nomothetic rather than particularistic in orientation. It ultimately seeks to generate laws of human behavior good for all times and places. Processualists study pueblo prehistory to learn about that past, but also to fulfill more general goals such as making contributions to methodology and evolutionary anthropology (Cordell and Plog 1979: 424; McGuire 1983).

The processualist emphasis on generality and predictability springs from a systemic and atomistic view of culture. Processualists imagine that culture consists of subsystems functionally integrated into a larger whole. This view emphasizes stability as the normal state of social systems. In most cases the system functions as a means of human adaptation to the physical environment. Given that cultural subsystems are functionally related and geared to produce stability, the cause for change must be found in independent variables that lie outside the system. Many processualists believe that changes in the technological subsystem determine change in other aspects of the cultural system. Therefore, processualists tend to find causality in the material relations of the economy and the environment. For example, Cordell and Plog's (1979:410) reading of the whole of puebloan prehistory is predicated on the assumption that "human societies are continually involved in experimentation with different strategies for coping with the changing environment."

Processual archaeology, and its attending values, performed a useful service for southwestern archaeology (Redman 1991). The new archaeology advocated explicit methods, directed us to variation as the proper focus of study, specified questions of social relevance, and undermined simple appeals to authority as the basis for inference justification. Cordell and Plog's (1979) seminal paper opened up the study of the puebloan past to diverse organizational strategies that may not be reflected in the ethnographic record. Processual archaeology's stress on material relations led to impressive gains in our understanding of Prehispanic pueblo environments and economies that we continue to build on.

Many archaeologists have concluded, however, that the philosophy of processual archaeology has made limited contributions to understanding cultural change. Numerous detailed critiques of processual archaeology exist in the literature, both from within (Cowgill 1993; Renfrew 1982:8) and without (Hodder 1982; McGuire 1992; Shanks and Tilley 1987). Two specific points drawn from these critiques inform our rethinking of late Prehispanic pueblo social organization: (1) processual archaeology has failed to attain its nomethetic ambitions and (2) processual archaeology's objectivist ideals preclude the expansion of archaeological inquiry into several important realms, such as social power and ideology. In other words, the processual paradigm has not delivered law-like knowledge or general theories of culture change, and restricts our understanding of the full spectrum of human organizational possibilities.

We feel that the limits of processualism lie in the inherent ambiguity and complexity of all societies. The advocates of processual archaeology underestimate these features, and oppositional thinking cannot capture them. For many critics, the New Archaeology's failure to arrive at general laws of cultural change suggests that there is more shaping society than the broad adaptive, systemic, and evolutionary "macro forces" championed by processual archaeology (Binford 1986: 469). Specifically, "internal" ethnographic variables or "structuring principles" seem to make a difference (Wylie 1989). These variables include power, ideology, and gender, characteristics that make up the everyday lived experience of people (Gailey 1987; Kus 1989; Roseberry 1989; Silverblatt 1987; Wolf 1982). Change in structuring principles can occur on a temporal scale visible to the participants in a culture; that is, people are aware of them and act upon this knowledge (Paynter and McGuire 1991). Thus, human lived experience, and specific historical context, are indispensable in considering cultural process and change.

All of this suggests that study of ethnographic detail or "micro forces" is just as important as study of those systemic "macro forces" invisible to the participants in a society. By failing to address internal dynamics we miss the variation created by real trajectories of social change, as well as the lived experience that is to be found in the particulars of an empirical case. The task should not be to privilege one or another kind of inquiry as providing *the* truth about past societies (as is wont to happen on both sides of the "processual–postprocessual" debate), but to recognize that sensitivity to both kinds of organizational forces can lead to richer, more nuanced understandings of the past (Tringham 1991:99–103).

Dialectics

A dialectical approach to knowledge and society reveals the rich tapestry of the human past. The dialectic is both a worldview and a method of inquiry (Ollman 1976; Saitta 1989; Sayer 1987). As a way of thinking it differs radically from atomistic and systemic modes of thought (Gramsci 1971:435). Dialectics is underpinned by different ideals while at the same time retaining – albeit in a slightly different form – the generalizing and predictive aspirations of processual archaeology.

Epistemology

Like logical positivism, dialectics accepts that we can gain empirical knowledge of, and learn from, the world of experience. Dialectics differs, however, in recognizing that our specification of causality is fully dependent on particular sets of theoretical assumptions, conceptions of culture and society, and values. Knowledge is *constructed* about, rather than discovered in facts. Wylie puts it well: a "rich theoretical judgement" (1989:100) is required to make sense of empirical facts and gain an understanding of underlying relations and processes.

We do not endorse the radical subjectivism of the sort condemned by Watson (1991). A dialectical epistemology accepts that there are empirical and logical criteria for evaluating knowledge-claims (Saitta 1989; Wylie 1989). It also endorses generalization and prediction as admirable aspirations, albeit in particular senses. Specific cases can suggest what prior conditions, actions, and consequences we should examine to understand change in other broadly similar cases.

Our bottom line is that dialectics does not force a choice between objectivism and subjectivism, or science and humanism, or particulars and generalities. In other words it does not force a choice between an archaeology that is "either explanatory, empirical and capable of obtaining objective truth or intuitive and particularistic and a matter of personal interpretation" (Rowlands 1984:112). The debate over subjectivity and objectivity is a false one that serves only to obscure the dialectic between reality and consciousness, past and present, facts and values (Kohl 1985; Patterson 1989; Rowlands 1984).

Social theory

A dialectical approach eschews ideal types in favor of social forms as constituted in history and out of the everyday lived experience of their participants. It views the social world not in terms of compartmentalized subsystems, but as a complex web of internal relations. Every real social form is a field of interconnected relations. A dialectical approach acknowledges that human *individuals* are embedded in these relations; indeed, relations have no existence independent of people. Individuals are recognized as conscious, intentional creators of culture rather than passive carriers of culture (Paynter 1989). People interact with social structures (e.g., arrangements for allocating resources, dividing labor, exercising authority, and so on), and they are differentially positioned with respect to these structures.

The dialectic embraces that which is paradoxical to oppositional thinking. In oppositional terms a society must be either egalitarian or stratified, or possibly in transition between the two. Dialectical thinking allows, however, that in some historical instances equality may necessitate the existence of certain forms of political stratification. That is, there are certain situations where forms of political hierarchy based on strongly regularized, even hereditary access to decision-making positions are crucial to maintaining communalism.

Such seeming paradoxes exist because social oppositions do not exist independently of each other, but rather form a unity whereby the existence of one necessarily entails the existence of the other. For example, the existence of a slave requires the existence of a master. The underlying relationship of slavery defines both the slave and the master. As should be obvious, the slave and the master experience this relationship differently, and because of the inherent inequality of it, find themselves in conflict. Social relations create parts in uneasy tension (if not outright conflict) so that the whole manifests tensions and conflict as much as harmony and integration. The tensions and conflicts that drive social change always have their origins in relationships between people in concrete environmental and historical settings. Instability is endemic to social forms (Paynter 1989).

Herein lies a notion of causality and change different from that in processual archaeology. We cannot identify some relationships as determinants and others as effects. We can, however, point to the role that one entity or subset of relations has in altering one or more of the other relations with which it is enmeshed (Ollman 1976:17). In doing so we are singling out an influence as being worth analyzing in a particular case, not saying that it was causal in the same way that causality is understood within processual archaeology.

Dialectics thus recognizes a complex social landscape that cannot be fully appreciated through oppositional thinking. Dialectics challenges us to define the operative forms or expressions of social differentiation (generational, gender, or class-based) in concrete instances; to take stock of individual and group interests vis-à-vis patterns of inclusion and exclusion; and to clarify the instabilities and conflicts (over material conditions and cultural meanings) that they can produce. Change in social forms in turn springs from the myriad possibilities for conflict inherent in the nature of social relations. Every social form has within it the seeds of its own transformation. These seeds will not totally destroy the old form, but rather will change it into something that is both new and old. In this mix of new and old are *other* potential tensions that will, in the end, transform the new social form. Thus, history is a critical element in a dialectical account of change. Incorporating history means that explanation is "contingent," sensitive to the complex interweaving of environmental conditions, human interests and choices, interregional contacts, regional spheres of interaction, and particular local dynamics. In the next section, we use these theoretical concepts to develop a more specific model of a pueblo social landscape.

The pueblos as complex communal societies

The key opposition in understanding pueblo social organization hinges on a distinction between the pueblos as egalitarian societies and as stratified societies. The traditional position argues for egalitarian pueblos lacking in formal hierarchies beyond age and sex, and organized by cross-cutting ties (sodalities) immanent in social structure (Eggan 1950; Reid 1985; Vivian 1990; Whittlesey 1978). The recent "revisionist" position sees the pueblos as hierarchical polities that may manifest significant inequalities of wealth and power (Brandt 1994; Smith 1983; Upham 1982; Whiteley 1988; Wilcox 1981).

The revisionists argue that these inequalities derive from differential control of esoteric knowledge and ceremonial objects. This differential access to wealth and power is further understood to follow clan lines. The revisionist literature notes the differential participation of particular clan leaders (from core lineage segments) in a variety of regulative processes, including the allocation of land and permits relating to the use of land and water, the scheduling of ceremonial activity, the appointment of ceremonial and secular officials, the utilization of communal surpluses, and general planning for the future (Reyman 1987; Upham 1982; Whiteley 1988). Primary producers support elites via work parties that prepare, plant, and harvest elite land, maintain their houses, and periodically prepare their food. Upham (1982) and Brandt (1994) see this support of elites as reflecting institutionalized inequality if not coercive, exploitative relations. Finally, revisionist scholarship underscores how positions of leadership are hereditarily transmitted within clans. In short, for these revisionist authors access to ritual knowledge and power translates into control over the very economic foundations of society.

As Brandt (1994) points out, however, the pueblo ethnographic literature "is neither deep nor thick." Information was collected over a period of more than 100 years, from different intellectual perspectives and with different interests in mind. Thus, at present one can find empirical support in pueblo ethnography for either model of pueblo social organization.

Our review of this literature – and our suspicion that empirical patterns in pueblo prehistory defy explanation with either model – suggests the need for alternative formulations. We seek to open a third space for theory development, and from this space we propose that the Prehispanic pueblos, while not egalitarian, were not stratified either; in fact, they were simultaneously *both*. We capture this situation with a model of the pueblos as complex *communal* societies.

A communal society exists when constituent social groups hold the means of production – the land, game, plants, fish, tools, technical knowledge, and other resources needed to sustain life – in common, and where surplus appropriation is *collective* in form; i.e, where the extractors of surplus labor are simultaneously the producers (Amariglio 1984; Diamond 1974; Handsman 1991; Leacock 1972; Lee 1990; Saitta and Keene 1990). It would be a mistake, however, to assume that because production is communal, wealth and power differentials between interest groups – the indicators of "complexity" in revisionist literature – do not exist. The communal ownership of property and the collective appropriation of social labor do not necessarily imply that each communal group will have the same or equal amounts of property, that people within these groups will have equal access to resources, or that some groups will not be in a position to make demands on the labor of other groups (Bender 1989: 84–87; Brumfiel 1989:128–132; Handsman 1991:342). Inequalities can exist within and between social groupings (Brumfiel 1989:128–132). Reproduction and ideology can become the means by which some members within a group dominate others, or by which one social group gains dominance over another. Cultural knowledge can be unevenly distributed and have important political and economic effects depending on environmental, and historical circumstances.

Communalism can take a variety of forms that cannot be captured by the simplistic opposition of egaliterian vs. stratified society. It is possible to have hierarchy and even institutionalized social ranking *without* the erosion of collective appropriation or differential effects on the biological well-being of members of the society. That is, we can imagine situations or contexts where political hierarchy exists without the sort of wealth and power monopolies that generate class divisions. Indeed, political hierarchy in some circumstances may even be crucial to the maintenance of egaliterian collectives, depending on how those hierarchies articulate with other aspects of communal social life.

Saitta (1994) develops this idea for "tribal" groupings generally, and the pueblos specifically. He sees historic pueblo hierarchies as responsive to, rather than exploitative of, the commune. Pueblo leaders were "subsumed" to the commune and did not form a distinct class exploiting the labor of kinfolk and neighbors. The pueblo elite's subsumption to the commune implies a paradoxical position within the communal social order. Subsumed elites are limited by kin and civil obligations, and they struggle with each other over access to communally extracted and allocated surpluses. While a "communal ethos" or "ideology of community" (Handsman 1991:343) in this case tempers the use of power and softens its impact on the daily life of people, power relationships and social struggles among elites and between subsumed elites and primary producers provide an internal dynamic of daily life and social change.

In short, we are mistaken to assume that communal hierarchies and inequalities will always have the same form, or exist in the same spaces where we find them in our own lives. Prehispanic societies may have been quite variable with respect to the nature and sources of social conflict, and we miss an opportunity to explore this variation when we make conventional assumptions about hierarchy and its structural position in society. Identifying the sources of social power and its relationship to wealth and labor flows is a real challenge to building a theory of communal forms. Evidence for the pueblos as complex communal societies may be found in the same gamut of ethnographic and ethnohistoric sources used to sustain egalitarian and stratified models of puebloan social life.

Whiteley (1988), in his reexamination of classic puebloan ethnographies, challenges the assumptions of clan corporateness and equality in economic, jural, and ritual affairs that underwrite the egalitarian model. He shows that clans have differential access to ceremonies and duties in the social order. Further, he demonstrates that inequality existed within clans and between family/lineage segments, and that some family/lineage segments had differential access to land and ceremonial knowledge. Whiteley's reexamination suggests that the economic, social, and ceremonial relations structuring Puebloan society (specifically, those determining landholding and inheritance patterns, and participation in ritual) were far more variable and flexible than either pole of the existing opposition allows. These relations were also more open to modification and negotiation by agents than either an egalitarian or a stratified model permits.

Ownership of pueblo land is clearly a complex and ambiguous relation that is subject to negotiation. Whiteley underscores a point made by Titiev (1944) that *no* producers are left landless at Hopi regardless of how land distribution is regulated (Whiteley 1988). This suggests the existence of a fundamentally communal mechanism for guaranteeing producer access to, and control over, the means of production. However, Jorgenson (1980:239) notes that in some cases dominant clans could confiscate farmland. These observations suggest that the defining condition of pueblo communalism was not equivalent access, but rather *guaranteed* access to resources. This guarantee embodied ambiguities and contradictions that could, in extreme conditions, render it null and void.

Jerrold Levy (1992) explicitly confronts these contradictions in his analysis of the 1906 split at Orayvi. He demonstrates a contradiction in Hopi society between an ideology of cooperation and integration, and a stratified system of land control. He describes two ranks for clans in Hopi society, the *pavansinom* clans, who control the major ceremonies and the best agricultural land, and the *sukavungsinom*, who control neither ceremonies nor good agricultural land. The superior economic position of the *pavansinom* clans did not, however, translate into obvious economic benefit for these clans. Levy argues that this was because the Hopi society was organized to manipulate scarcity and not abundance.

Among the turn-of-the-century Hopi the manipulation of scarcity created a social contradiction. Although cooperation was necessary for the economy and society to work, resources could not be distributed evenly because in times of extreme scarcity starvation and destruction of the social order would result from such egalitarian distributions. The resolution of this contradiction led to a social organization that was neither egalitarian nor stratified (Levy 1992). Powerful clans controlled both the best agricultural lands and the ceremonial cycle of the villages, while poor clans held inferior lands and had only minor roles in the ceremonial cycle. In good times, social relations and ideology stressed egalitarianism, cooperation, and peaceful relations among all members of the community — relations that urged all to work for the common good. When insufficient rains fell or the frost came too early, the economically powerful and ceremonially more important clans had food and stayed in the village, while lack of food forced poorer clans out to hunt and gather, or to depend upon the charity of the Navajo or other pueblos.

The revisionist claim that elites coerced labor from others in the society seems problematic. Titiev (1944:65) noted that individuals in work parties organized for a leader's benefit at Hopi contributed their labor voluntarily, without prodding or fear of reprisals. He also remarked on a general lack of mechanisms to compel labor performance in other activities such as cleaning springs or sponsoring dances (Titiev 1944:63). Ellis (1981:414, 423) expands on this point by noting the frequent participation of caciques in such activities. In light of these observations, it seems reasonable to hypothesize puebloan elites as subsumed to the communal order. That is, the personal consumption of labor by political leaders represents communally allocated shares of surplus labor (given as compensation for the performance of those regulative processes described by revisionists), the size and timed distribution of which is controlled by the commune. Exemption of individuals from certain labors and their realization of material support through labor performed elsewhere in a wider social division of labor does not necessarily imply a relationship of domination or exploitation.

Still other information indicates the existence of a complex subsumed communal hierarchy organized along the lines imagined here. Parsons (1933:77) reports an informant's observation that there was not one but "many bosses" at Zuni, a comment that suggests a complex set of checks on power wielding. Whiteley (1988) buttresses this inference with his observation that, at least at Hopi, society (sodality) chiefs had a considerably more important role in political life than traditional pueblo ethnographies allow. He argues that society chiefs were not subservient assistants to village chiefs, but rather were independent participants within a group of decision makers — village chiefs were only "first among equals." Bolton (1908) makes a further point about the communal limits on political power in his reporting of Oñate's observation on the pueblos: "In their government they are free, for although they have petty captains, they obey them badly and in very few things" (see also Titiev 1944:65). Goldman (1937) noted that individuals did not seek the ceremonial offices carrying greatest responsibility (and that consequently should bestow greatest opportunity for economic control), but rather that they were filled only with great difficulty because they involved the holder in unwelcome and heavy obligations (see also Ellis 1981: 426).

We should note that Brandt (1994) sees this reluctance to hold office as a product of an ideology fostered by elites so as to limit interest in leadership and thereby preserve differential access to resources. We doubt Brandt's conclusion. It ascribes to primary producers an ignorance of inequality and oppression that seems hard to square with observations made by other ethnographers about the reality of pueblo political and economic life.

While we have only cited shreds of evidence here, these observations suggest the plausibility of alternative models of puebloan social structure and dynamics, models that cannot be neatly described as egalitarian or stratified. A model of puebloan society as communal in the sense advocated here allows for the great variability in patterns of authority, property relations, and forms of labor mobilization and circulation noted by ethnographers from Kroeber (1917) through Whiteley (1988), and that we take as an implicit message of Jorgenson (1980). We believe, based on Fried's (1975) comments on tribalization in contact situations and the well-documented patterns of twentieth-century change in pueblo society (Whiteley 1988), that this variability was even greater before the Spanish Entrada. We suspect that early Spanish and later United States regimes stabilized what had been much more dynamic political and economic patterns.

Thus, the longstanding debate about the nature of pueblo social organization results from a false opposition. The pueblos are neither egalitarian nor stratified, but rather they are both (Plog 1995). While our model acknowledges political power differentials and even deep social hierarchies, this power is far from the coercive kind that stratification theory invokes. We believe that the revisionist literature overstates the effects of hierarchy and holds to a particularly narrow view of power in pueblo society.

A dialectical perspective on the pueblos "decenters" this political aspect, showing it to be complexly shaped by the other, nonpolitical relations of the commune. We suggest that each household/individual in puebloan society was/is faced with a set of distinct and potentially conflicting kin and non-kin (civil) interests and allegiances that are conditioned by their differential participation in the communal labor process and communal political and socio-ceremonial processes. This strikes us as an alternative and potentially profitable way to begin exploring and *specifying* the tensions and tendencies toward factionalism in pueblo groups that ethnographers and archaeologists have noted (Eggan 1950; Kintigh 1985).

The archaeological and ethnohistoric evidence for specialized political, economic, and ritual activity in puebloan society provides the substantive foundation for proceeding in this direction (Ellis 1981; Ferguson 1981; Ford 1972; Snow 1981). Such specialization raises the possibility of conceivably intense conflict and struggle occurring both within, and across, kin groupings. Individuals filling subsumed communal leadership positions and charged with regulating the many aspects of communal social life stand to be especially conflicted by these struggles. That is, they stand to be torn by different kin and sodality obligations. To proceed under this model we need to determine the extent to which the subsumed leadership structure of puebloan society is internally differentiated; how communal economic, political, and religious functionaries receive support; to what extent subsumed leaders participate in the performance of everyday labor; how subsumed leaders are squeezed by competing demands for communal surplus production; and where structural points of tension and conflict lie in this ensemble of interacting processes. We do not expect these dynamics to be the same for all polities across the puebloan Southwest; rather, they will vary in time and space so that any analysis must be historically contextualized.

It is clear that traditional ethnographies can provide only limited creative guidance for building such models. The ethnographic literature is problematic because it represents only a brief moment in the long history of pueblo peoples. This moment comes after 300 years of interaction between puebloan society and Europeans. While expanding the search for ethnographic parallels would help – for example, adopting the less provincial ethnographic perspective suggested by Cordell and Gumerman (1989) – that strategy is compromised by the same fact. At best, the ethnographic literature can be useful as a source of clues to meaningful relationships existing between different aspects of social life. Imaginative work drawing on the "subject side" of the interpretive equation – i.e., the archaeological record – is also required. Reflexive use of both ethnographic and archaeological sources can allow development of "hunches" about the possibilities for variation in the past and the contradictory forces conditioning Prehispanic development (Sacks 1979:106–107).

The Grasshopper Pueblo–Chavez Pass debate

Perhaps the hottest recent debate in southwestern archaeology has been the decade-long controversy about the nature of Prehispanic social organization at Grasshopper Pueblo and Chavez Pass. Like most notable scholarly debates, it embodies theoretical, substantive, institutional, and personal quarrels. It gained prominence in the field because of the eminence of the individuals and institutions involved, and because it highlights the fundamental opposition in scholarly views about pueblo social organization. The debate exemplifies a fissure that divides most of the archaeologists in the Southwest. On one side of the divide stand those archaeologists who see a Prehispanic Southwest populated by egalitarian communities. On the other side are scholars who envision a landscape dotted with hierarchically organized stratified polities.

Grasshopper Pueblo and Chavez Pass

Grasshopper Pueblo and Chavez Pass are two late Prehispanic pueblos located in the mountainous zone of central Arizona. Pueblo people established both communities at the end of the thirteenth century, and occupied each until the late fourteenth or early fifteenth centuries. They built their pueblos in broadly similar environments at locations about 100 km apart.

Grasshopper Pueblo includes approximately 500 rooms divided into 13 room blocks. These room blocks include three enclosed plazas, one of which the inhabitants converted into a great kiva. The pueblo grew through a process of aggregation as populations abandoned smaller communities in the area and moved into Grasshopper Pueblo. Reid and Whittlesey (1990:195) argue that a major motivating factor for this aggregation was defense. Researchers initially attributed the abandonment of the pueblo to the failure of the burgeoning community to develop the requisite social complexity for managing changes in societal scale (Graves *et al.* 1982). While not disagreeing with this interpretation, Reid (1989:89) links abandonment of the community to declining rainfall at the end of the fourteenth century.

Researchers at Grasshopper Pueblo have consistently interpreted the social organization of the site as egalitarian. They have categorically rejected the idea that a social hierarchy with an established elite was present at any time in the pueblo's history. Reid has invariably argued that social complexity at Grasshopper did not exceed that which Eggan (1950) and Jorgenson (1980) describe in their egalitarian interpretations of western pueblo social organization. Reid (1989:88) states, "The implication is that Grasshopper social organization is an example of a Prehispanic sequential hierarchy with community decision-making vested in sodalities."

The Chavez Pass ruin, which archaeologists also refer to by its Hopi name, *Nuvakwewtaqa*, is a large pueblo of around 1,000 rooms. The ruin includes several enclosed plazas, a great kiva, and a possible ball court. Extensive agricultural features cover the countryside surrounding the pueblo. These features include terraces, linear grid systems, agricultural check dams, and field houses. Researchers at the Arizona State University (ASU) located many smaller settlements in the general region of Nuvakwewtaqa. They interpreted these as evidence of a Prehispanic site hierarchy with an administrative center, Nuvakwewtaqa, encircled by smaller hamlets (Upham 1982). They made production estimates for the agricultural features, and population estimates for the settlements. Based on these estimates they concluded that the catchment area of the pueblo could not have supported the population that was present (Upham and Plog 1986). In their interpretation the pueblo was home to a managerial elite. This elite controlled access to a variety of strategic resources, and managed a large sedentary population that exceeded the carrying capacity of the area. This elite also interacted with the elites of other similarly organized polities that filled the late Prehispanic landscape of the Southwest.

A critical evaluation of the debate

The Grasshopper Pueblo–Chavez Pass debate has shed some light on southwestern prehistory, produced quite a bit of heat, and lots of smoke. Despite considerable data collection, methodological critique, and theoretical disputation, however, we seem no closer today to resolving the egalitarian versus stratified debate than we were over a decade ago. Both sides have identified three substantive issues as key in the debate: agricultural intensification, mortuary behavior, and regional exchange. Each side has engaged these issues with different methods and theoretical assumptions.

The first thing to recognize in the debate is that real differences do exist between the two pueblos. Grasshopper Pueblo is only about half the size of Nuvakwewtaqa. The two sites participated in different trade spheres, as indicated by polychrome pottery. Jeddito Yellow wares predominate at Nuvakwewtaqa, and White Mountain redwares and Salado redwares at Grasshopper. Researchers have not found extensive agricultural features like those at Nuvakwewtaqa around Grasshopper. Upham and Plog (1986:229) claim that the catchment area of Grasshopper would have been able to support the population of the community, while the catchment area at Nuvakwewtaqa would not have been adequate for the local population. We would agree, however, with the principals in the debate that these differences are not great enough to account for the very different interpretations of social organization for the two communities.

Upham (1982) based his initial arguments for hierarchy at Nuvakwewtaqa on an inference of dramatic intensification of agriculture in the area. He interpreted the appearance, growth, and spread of agricultural features as evidence of this intensification. Researchers at Grasshopper Pueblo also inferred increases in agricultural productivity around Grasshopper, but stopped short of calling it intensification.

The hottest exchanges in the debate have concerned the interpretation of mortuary behavior at the two pueblos. The distribution of grave goods at the two sites is very similar, but the distributions have been interpreted very differently.

The mortuary sample from Nuvakwewtaqa is not very large or complete. Archaeologists excavated over 100 individuals, but pothunters had intensively looted the cemetery so that the researchers viewed their conclusions from the sample as provisional. They found a differential distribution of grave goods in the burials and inferred three tiers of graves with goods, and a fourth tier without goods.

At Grasshopper there is little or no evidence of pothunting and the sample of burials is bigger and more complete: over 400 individuals. These burials exhibit a differential distribution of goods very similar to the distribution at Nuvakwewtaqa, Whittlesey (1978), however, interprets this distribution as evidence of differential membership in sodalities or societies. Based on an assumption that individuals were buried in their sodality ceremonial costumes, Whittlesey identified six sodalities and labeled them according to the distinctive attributes of the costumes: (1) a female ring society, (2) a coed shell bracelet society, (3) a male conus tinkler society, (4) a male bone hair pin society, and (5) a male arrow society. One male burial, number 140, stood out both because of the quantity of grave goods, more than 190, and their variety. This burial had emblems of the arrow, bone hairpin, and shell bracelet societies. Whittlesey (1978) interpreted this individual as a community leader and head of the arrow society.

One of the most striking things about both the Grasshopper and Nuvakwewtaqa collections is the large quantity of trade items, especially polychrome pottery, at each site. At Nuvakwewtaqa only four of the 80 pottery types found were locally produced. Other trade items included obsidian, turquoise, and copper bells. These items occur at Nuvakwewtaqa, but not in the surrounding smaller sites. The ASU researchers hypothesized that these goods were used in a "banking" strategy controlled by a managerial elite. They also used these goods to infer the existence of specialized production at the pueblo. Grasshopper exhibits the same kinds of objects, with the addition of macaws. Here researchers interpreted exchange as a buffering mechanism against hard times. They suggested that such exchange occurred in a down-the-line fashion with Grasshopper households linked to other settlements via trading partnerships.

The disparity in these interpretations, and the critiques by each side of the other, reflect substantive, methodological, and theoretical differences. Neither the Grasshopper Pueblo field school, nor the Chavez Pass project, have adequately published the data necessary to evaluate their positions. These disparities also obscure the shared assumptions underlying each position, further impeding resolution of the debate.

The Chavez Pass substantive critique of the Grasshopper position has tended to focus on errors in statistical analyses and the use of ethnographic analogy. Chavez Pass researchers have repeatedly questioned the representativeness of the Grasshopper burial sample, and pointed to specific mistakes in statistical analyses (Cordell et al. 1987; Plog 1985). They have also questioned the use of ethnographic analogy in the interpretation of social organization at Grasshopper. Upham and Plog (1986: 237) note that the historic pueblos had undergone severe contact-induced changes, and that pueblo ethnography is biased by an "Apollonian" view of pueblo culture conceivably inconsistent with the reality of pre-contact situations.

Proponents of the Grasshopper critique are very empirical. They note that the quantity and quality of the Grasshopper data are superior to Chavez Pass and, therefore, the Grasshopper interpretations are more likely to be correct. They question the interpretative conclusions at Chavez Pass because they believe that the archaeologists there did not adequately control archaeological formation processes. They question the inference of a hierarchical settlement pattern at Chavez Pass and argue instead that the smaller communities were earlier.

The Chavez Pass researchers tend to view material culture as a direct reflection of culture and social organization. Thus, when confronted with a positively skewed distribution of grave goods, they conclude that a hierarchical social organization existed. They critique the Grasshopper researchers for failing to accept such direct interpretation. For example, Plog (1985: 162) comments on Whittlesey's (1978) analysis of Grasshopper burials: "A given table will show, for example, that only 13 per cent of the burials between 20 and 30 years of age contain high status grave goods. In a hierarchical system would one expect otherwise?"

University of Arizona archaeologists tend to reject the idea that artifact distributions will be a direct reflection of social organization. They are careful in interpreting skewed distributions because such distributions could be the product of intervening formation processes, rather than direct reflections of Prehispanic social reality (Reid and Whittlesey 1990). Accordingly, they interpret the differential distribution of whole vessels on room floors at Grasshopper to indicate variation in patterns of room abandonment as opposed to differences in wealth or status. The skewed distribution of goods in burials that Plog notes becomes evidence for membership in sodalities.

The interpretations of Chavez Pass are based on an explicitly developed evolutionary social theory, but the social theory of the Grasshopper research is largely implicit. This makes examination of the Grasshopper social theory difficult, but clear differences from the Chavez Pass position are apparent. Cordell *et al.* (1987) criticize the University of Arizona archaeologists for making the object of study behavior, rather than culture. They then point to substantive errors that they believe result from this focus. Reid *et al.* (1989: 803) reply that Cordell *et al.*'s approach does not allow "the archaeologist to understand how various sources of systemic variability (e.g., functional, occupational, and cultural variability) as well as formation processes influenced the production of archaeological variability."

Developing an alternative view

The standoff in the Grasshopper–Chavez Pass debate is not resolvable through the collection of new data, or through new interpretations of existing data. The standoff results from the oppositional thinking that informs the debate. This thinking derives from a shared functionalist view of culture, a shared notion of power, and a common use of analogy in the analyses.

The social theory that shapes both positions is pervasively functionalist. In the case of Grasshopper it is a structural-functionalist view derived from Eggan's (1950) and Jorgenson's (1980) analyses of western pueblo society. Structural-functionalism answers the question of why societies do not fly apart by showing how social parts function to maintain the social whole. Functionalism underpins the Chavez Pass researcher's invocation of a managerial elite. This functionalism is derived largely from information theory. It assumes that once a certain number of nodes or levels of organization exist, some centralized control must also develop to maintain the smooth functioning of the system.

Neither variety of functionalism provides an internal motor for cultural change. Because in each theory the different parts of society function to maintain the whole, change must originate outside while a subsumed elite remain in the community and maintain the social and ideological continuity necessary for the survival of the pueblo. When times are good again, the sojourners may be welcomed back into the communal whole.

Neither the environment nor the technological level of society in any way determines that these contradictions, or this social form, will exist. There are other ways for human populations to survive in this environment. The ethnographic and archaeological record of the Southwest gives us many examples of these other ways, even when domestic livestock are removed from the picture.

One such successful adaptation is to spread the population thinly over the land-scape. Such populations may mix agriculture with hunting and gathering, with such diversity compensating for the uncertainty of the environment. Various combinations of exchange, exogamy, and fictive kinship may link small groups. When times are really hard each small group is on its own. This dispersed adaptation was predominant in certain periods of prehistory, such as Pueblo I, and was an available option in all others. In all periods of southwestern prehistory there were areas, often immense areas, suitable for agriculture that lacked appreciable (that is, archaeologically visible) populations. In the historic period, low-ranked Hopi groups would go out and live with the Navajo when agricultural production was inadequate; when they alienated themselves from other Hopi; or when epidemic disease hit (Parsons 1936). When times got better these groups might return to the Hopi, or stay among the Navajo. (The Navajo have a Hopi clan comprised of the descendants of these people; see Young and Morgan 1980.) In the absence of the Navajo, dispersed groups could have taken up hunting and gathering with low intensity agriculture either on their own or with an existing low intensity population (Upham 1988).

Another successful adaptation is to aggregate into larger communities. As structural functionalist scholars of western pueblo society recognize (Eggan 1950; Jorgenson 1980), the bonds of pueblo society are very difficult to maintain. Clans and lineages are small enough that the vagaries of reproduction do not guarantee that each group will have the right number of offspring in the necessary sex ratio to reproduce itself each generation. This internal dynamic constantly reworks the social fabric. Aggregation allows linked clans to reside together and facilitates the transfer of individuals between groups to maintain important clans and lineages. Aggregation also leads to safety in numbers when conflicts erupt between different villages.

Social relations also involve power and the contradictions of equality and hierarchy. Higher ranked clans have the best farmland, but they may lack sufficient labor to work all of that land and to reproduce the clan (Levy 1992). Therefore, they may have to draw on lower ranked clans for labor. Matrilineal inheritance means that the corporate land base will not be diluted by marriage down in clan rankings, but such marriages do establish reciprocal relations of sharing and labor with lower ranked husbands. Matrilineal inheritance, however, also meant that these husbands could be discarded without weakening the clan membership. Sodalities and societies also crosscut kin groups to further reinforce communal relations. But, the leaders of these groups were usually from high-ranked clans, and these leaders controlled the esoteric knowledge necessary for the sodalities and societies to survive. Thus, sodalities and societies linked everyone in the pueblo, but only a small leadership group was essential to maintaining the organization in hard times.

Two different functionalist perspectives have been used to interpret western pueblo religion. In a structural functionalist model, religious organizations such as the katsina cult functioned to bind together the diverse social groups of the community (Adams 1991). In an adaptive functionalist, or cultural ecological, model, such organizations provide stability by redistributing agricultural products among social groups. In contrast Plog and Solometo (1993) have highlighted the connections between the katsina religion and warfare. They suggest that the communal aspects of the religion were products of population declines that resulted from European conquest of the Southwest. We would accept that religious practices functioned in social and adaptive ways, but we would argue that religion was a locus of struggle where the contradictions between hierarchy and communalism in pueblo society were realized. Religion carried meaning and embodied power relations.

Western pueblo religion is ascetic and esoteric. Religious activities maintain and enhance the people's harmony with the world. Without such activities this harmony would be broken, and the world destroyed or transformed. Thus, western pueblo people have a special role because it is only through their acts that the cycle of nature will be maintained. Their identity as a people is a product of this role. These acts require adherence to strict rules of conduct, and the making of offerings or sacrifices to the supernatural. Individuals who break these rules can be severely disciplined or even killed. The ceremonial calendar includes many rituals, each of which must be performed to make the religion whole. Some of these rituals must be private, while others must involve the entire community. The rituals are to benefit all people, plant, animal, and spirit life, yet the knowledge of individual rituals is the property of specific clans and is carried by special individuals in those clans. The religion can work only through the communalism of the whole, yet its parts are restricted to a few.

A number of inequities are embedded in this communal ceremonial cycle. Not all rituals, or even parts of rituals, are of equal importance or centrality. There is a ranking of clans historically based on the sequence of clan arrival in their communities. Older clans control more important rituals and knowledge, and some clans make only minor contributions to the cycle. The Hopi distinguish between highly ranked *pavansinom* clans and lower ranked *sukavungsinom* clans (Levy 1992:30–32). At Zuni, a poor person is *tewuko?liya*, without religion (Tedlock 1979:501). Even within clans, ritual information is not uniformly shared because only clan leaders have full access to the most esoteric knowledge of rituals. These clan rankings establish a hereditary ranking of social groups based on the control of ceremonial knowledge in western pueblo society.

What archaeologists refer to as aggregation and agricultural intensification are more than just adaptive strategies, they are also the essence of self in western pueblo life. To be Hopi or Zuni is to stand in good relation to the supernatural. To do this the individual must farm, participate in communal rituals, make ritual offerings and sacrifices, have a good heart, and cooperate with his and her fellows. To do so is to be special, to have the responsibility and honor of ensuring the harmony of nature. The coming together and breaking apart of late Prehispanic populations was, therefore, not just a functional response to changes in the environment, but meaningful human action undertaken by social groups with different and sometimes contradictory interests in an environmental context.

Our reading of late Prehispanic western pueblo social organization suggests a process of social change much different from that stipulated by processualist models. The evolutionary assumptions of processualist models suggest that pueblo society was either egalitarian, or locked in an evolutionary trajectory of intensification and deepening social hierarchy. Archaeologists have tended to assume that population growth, aggregation, environmental changes favouring corn farming, and the intensification of agriculture would lead to increased complexity and social stratification in society. Recognizing the paradoxical relationship between equality and hierarchy and its roots in the material, social, and ideological conditions of life suggests that the ebb and flow of aggregation and dispersal in the archaeological record does not relate to environmental change in a simple additive way.

We would argue for a much more dynamic, variable, and historically contingent process of cultural change. In the initial stages of aggregation founding clans would benefit materially, socially, and ideologically by attracting others. They would maintain their primary status, but give new arrivals good land and an important position in the ritual calendar. A growing settlement would attract newcomers by its promise of social and material stability and the allure of rich and meaningful ceremonial life. Material, social, and ritual thresholds exist in this process. The good land will be taken up, the list of ranked clans will grow large, and the sacred dates of the calendar will become crowded. As these thresholds are approached, established clans have less to gain from newcomers, and newcomers would be given less and less to join the community, or not allowed to join at all. The lived experience of the community would start out communal and become reconfigured as the thresholds approach, possibly resulting in greater political hierarchy. This political hierarchy would be an ambiguous one, however, enmeshed in a paradoxical relationship with the other social relations of the commune.

In this process, increasing population, environmental change, aggregation, and agricultural intensification affect the interplay of communality and hierarchy in different ways. Initially, population growth and aggregation would favor communalism until thresholds were approximated; then they would favor hierarchy as more and more people divided up the material, social, and ritual resources of the community. At this point any decline in population, such as the massive declines of the historic period, would strengthen communalism. Contrary to processualist assumptions, any factor that increased production (e.g., environmental change, agricultural intensification) would support communalism, while drought or agricultural failure would expose the full force of hierarchy. With plenty there is more to share and strengthen the position of high-ranked clans through communal ideals, and with want high-ranked clans justify the expulsion of others for the survival of the whole.

Any such change would be socially negotiated. Social groups' fortunes and position in ranked hierarchies could rise and fall through the vagaries of reproduction, the manipulation of histories, and jostling for ceremonial position. Clans would have the options of fissioning to form new communities, or possibly joining other communities at different stages of the development cycle, albeit at some social and ritual cost. Finally, there would always be the option of spreading out and living a different life. Such a life, however, would entail a different relationship to the supernatural and require a new definition of self.

All of this would be played out on the dynamic environmental stage of the region. Long-term trends would differentially affect communities depending on their position in the developmental cycle, and would expand or contract the size of the stage. They would not, however, determine the process.

The coming of the Spanish after 1540 would have altered but not qualitatively changed this dynamic. The massive population decline that resulted from disease and warfare would have favored communality in social relations and disrupted clan rankings. The expansion of horse-mounted nomads – the Comanche, Ute, Navajo, and Apache – would have made community shifts and colonization of new areas more difficult. This and the European threat of violence would have displaced some populations and encouraged aggregation in large villages. Finally, the development of closed corporate communities would have been a response to European attempts to control pueblo life directly.

In the end our interpretation of late Prehispanic pueblo social organization may not be more correct than either the Grasshopper or Chavez Pass interpretations. What is important about our scenario is that it moves us away from oppositions to asking questions about social variation and dynamics. We hope that it will be more productive for archaeologists to ask how the tension between equality and hierarchy played itself out over time, rather than to argue about which conceptual box western pueblo social organization best fits into. Archaeologists need to examine specific instances of change with a framework that acknowledges a complex interaction of material, social, and ideological processes. The results of these efforts will not be predictive models of prehistory or grand schemes of human evolution but instead be a history of pueblo lived experience over the ages.

Conclusion

We have outlined an alternative approach to understanding variation in Southwest prehistory, one situated within a critique of prevailing positivist and evolutionist ways of thinking. A dialectical approach radically changes traditional assumptions about the organization of society. We have used this approach to make sense of late Prehispanic pueblo society. It should be clear that we understand the communal formations of this time period to be moments in the historical development of pueblo society, not exemplars of conventional evolutionary stages.

We recognize that this exercise is incomplete. The aim here has been to frame issues, problems, and directions for further work. The task as we see it is to use archaeological and ethnographic materials together to imagine alternative organizational possibilities for late Prehispanic pueblo societies. The task also involves inquiring into the diversity of social relations and experiences that structure pueblo society, and how material culture is used within those relations and experiences. Archaeologists may never resolve the debate over pueblo social organization, but with a dialectical approach we can at least move away from the traditional oppositions that preclude other, and perhaps richer, understandings of puebloan history.

References

Adams, E.C. (1991) *The Origin and Development of the Pueblo Katsina Cult*. University of Arizona Press, Tucson.

Amariglio, J. (1984) *Forms of the Commune and Primitive Communal Class Processes*. Association for Economic and Social Analysis Paper 19. Department of Economics, University of Massachusetts, Amherst.

Bender, B. (1989) The Roots of Inequality. In *Domination and Resistance*, edited by D. Miller, M. Rowlands, and C. Tilley, pp. 83–95, Unwin and Hyman, London.

Binford, L.R. (1986) In Pursuit of the Future. In *American Archaeology: Archaeology Past and Future*, edited by D. Meltzer, D. Fowler, and J. Sabloff, pp. 459–479. Smithsonian Institution Press, Washington D.C.

Bolton, H. (1908) *Spanish Explorations in the Southwest, 1542–1706*. Barnes and Noble, New York.

Brandt, E. (1994) Egalitarianism, Hierarchy, and Centralization in the Pueblos. In *The Ancient Southwestern Community*, edited by W. Wills and R. Leonard, pp. 9–23. University of New Mexico, Albuquerque.

Brumfiel, E.M. (1989) Factional Competition in Complex Society. In *Domination and Resistance*, edited by D. Miller, M. Rowlands, and C. Tilley, pp. 127–139. Unwin and Hyman, London.

Cordell, L.S. (1984) *Prehistory of the Southwest*. Academic Press, New York.

—— 1985 Status Differentiation and Social Complexity in the Prehistoric Southwest: A Discussion. In *Status, Structure, and Stratification*, edited by M. Thompson, M. Garcia, and F. Kense, pp. 191–195. Archaeological Association of the University of Calgary, Calgary.

Cordell, L.S., and G.J. Gumerman (editors) (1989) *Dynamics of Southwestern Prehistory*. Smithsonian Institution Press, Washington, D.C.

Cordell, L.S., and F. Plog (1979) Escaping the Confines of Normative Thought: A Reevaluation of Puebloan Prehistory. *American Antiquity* 44: 405–429.

Cordell, L.S., S. Upham, and S.L. Brock (1987) Obscuring Cultural Patterns in the Archaeological Record: A Discussion from Southwestern Archaeology. *American Antiquity* 52:565–577.

Cowgill, G. (1993) Distinguished Lecture in Archaeology: Beyond Criticizing the New Archaeology. *American Anthropologist* 93: 551–573.

Crown, P.L., and W.J. Judge (editors) (1991) *Chaco and Hohokam: Prehistoric Regional Systems in the American Southwest*. SAR Press, Santa Fe, New Mexico.

Crumley, C.L., and W. Marquart (1987) *Regional Dynamics: Burgundian Landscapes in Historical Perspective*. Academic Press, Orlando, Florida.

Diamond, S. (1974) *In Search of the Primitive: A Critique of Civilization*. Transaction Books, New Brunswick, New Jersey.

Eggan, F. (1950) *Social Organization of the Western Pueblo*. University of Chicago Press, Chicago.

Ellis, F.H. (1981) Comments on Four Papers Pertaining to the Protohistoric Southwest. In *The Protohistoric Period in the North American Southwest, AD 1450–1700*, edited by D. Wilcox and W. Masse, pp. 410–433. Anthropological Papers No. 24. Arizona State University, Tempe.

Ferguson, T.J. (1981) The Emergence of Modern Zuni Culture and Society: A Summary of Zuni Tribal History 1450–1700. In *The Protohistoric Period in the North American Southwest, AD 1450–1700*, edited by D. Wilcox and W. Masse, pp. 336–353. Anthropological Research Papers No. 24. Arizona State University, Tempe.

Ford, R.I. (1972) An Ecological Perspective on the Eastern Pueblos. In *New Perspectives on the Pueblos*. edited by A. Ortiz, 1–17. University of New Mexico Press, Albuquerque.

Fried, M. (1975) *The Notion of Tribe*. Cummings, Menlo Park.

Gailey C.W. (1987) Culture Wars: Resistance to State Formation. In *Power Relations and State Formation*, edited by T.C. Patterson and C.W. Gailey, pp. 35–56. American Anthropological Association, Washington D.C.

Gibson, D.B., and M. Geselowitz (1988) The Evolution of Complex Society in Late Prehistoric Europe: Toward a Paradigm. In *Tribe and Polity in Late Prehistoric Europe*, edited by D.B. Gibson and M. Geselowitz, pp. 3–37. Plenum, New York.

Goldman, I. (1937) The Zuni Indians of New Mexico. In *Cooperation and Competition Among Primitive Peoples*, edited by M. Mead, pp. 313–353. McGraw Hill, New York.

Gramsci, A. (1971) *Selections from the Prison Notebooks*. International Publishers, New York.

Graves, M. (1987) Rending Reality in Archaeological Analysis: A Reply to Upham and Plog. *Journal of Field Archaeology* 14:243–249.

Graves, M., S.J. Holbrook, and W.L. Longacre (1982) Aggregation and Abandonment at Grasshopper Pueblo: Evolutionary Trends in the Later Prehistory of East-Central Arizona. In *Multidisciplinary Research at Grasshopper Pueblo*, edited by W.A. Longacre, S.J. Holbrook, and M.W. Graves, pp. 110–122. Anthropological Papers No. 40. University of Arizona, Tucson.

Handsman, R.G. (1991) Whose Art Was Found at Lepenski Vir? Gender Relations and Power in Archaeology. In *Engendering Archaeology*, edited by J. Gero and M. Conkey, pp. 329–365. Basil Blackwell, Oxford.

Hodder, I. (1982) *Symbols in Action*. Cambridge University Press, Cambridge.

Jorgenson, J. (1980) *Western Indians*. W.H. Freeman, San Francisco.

Kintigh, K. (1985) *Settlement, Subsistence and Society in Late Zuni Prehistory*. Anthropological Papers No. 44. University of Arizona, Tucson.

Kohl, P.L. (1985) Symbolic, Cognitive Archaeology: A New Loss of Innocence. *Dialectical Anthropology* 9:105–117

Kohler, T.A. (1993) News from the Northern American Southwest: Prehistory on the Edge of Chaos. *Journal of Archeological Research* 1(4):267–321.

Kroeber, A. (1917) *Zuni Kin and Clan*. Anthropological Papers No. 18:39–205. American Museum of Natural History, New York.

Kus, S. (1989) Sensuous Human Activity and the State: Towards an Archaeology of Bread and Circuses. In *Domination and Resistance*, edited by D. Miller, C. Tilley, and M. Rowlands, pp. 140–154. Unwin and Hyman, London.

Leacock, E.B. (1972) Introduction. In *Origins of the Family, Private Property and the State*, by F. Engels, pp. 7–68. New World Paperbacks, New York.

—— (1983) Interpreting the Origins of Gender Inequality: Conceptual and Historical Problems. *Dialectical Anthropology* 7(4):263–285.

Lee, R.B. (1990) Primitive Communism and the Origin of Social Inequality. In *The Evolution of Political Systems: Socio-Politics in Small Scale Sedentary Societies*, edited by S. Upham, pp. 225–246. Cambridge University Press, Cambridge.

Levy, J.E. (1992) *Orayvi Revisited: Social Stratification in an "Egalitarian" Society*. SAR Press, Santa Fe, New Mexico.

Lightfoot, K. (1984) *Prehistoric Political Dynamics: A Case Study from the American Southwest*. Northern Illinois University Press, Dekalb.

Longacre, W., and J.J. Reid (1974) The University of Arizona Archaeological Field School at Grasshopper: Eleven Years of Multidisciplinary Research and Teaching. *Kiva* 40:3–38.

McGuire, R.H. (1983) Breaking Down Cultural Complexity: Inequality and Heterogeneity. *Advances in Archaeological Method and Theory* 6:91–142.

—— (1990) Introduction: Elites and Regional Systems. In *Perspectives on Southwestern Prehistory*, edited by P.E. Minnis and C.L. Redman, pp. 167–172. Westview Press, Boulder, Colorado.

—— (1992) *A Marxist Archaeology*. Academic Press, Orlando, Florida.

Miller, D., M. Rowlands, and C. Tilley (1989) Introduction. In *Domination and Resistance*, edited by D. Miller, M. Rowlands, and C. Tilley, pp. 1–26. Unwin Hyman, London.

Ollman, B. (1976) *Alienation*. 2nd ed. Cambridge University Press, Cambridge.

Parsons, E.C. (1933) *Hopi and Zuni Ceremonialism*. Memoirs of the American Anthropological Association No. 39. American Anthropological Association, Menasha, Wisconsin.

Parsons, E.C. (editor) (1936) *Hopi Journals of Alexander M. Stephen*. Contributions to Anthropology No. 23. Columbia University, New York.

Patterson, T.C. (1989) History and the Post-Processual Archaeologies. *Man* 24(3):555–566.

Paynter, R. (1989) The Archaeology of Inequality. *Annual Review of Anthropology*. 18:369–399.

Paynter, R., and R.H. McGuire (1991) The Archaeology of Inequality: An Introduction. In *The Archaeology of Inequality*, edited by R.H. McGuire and R. Paynter, pp. 1–11. Basil Blackwell, Oxford.

Plog, F. (1985) Status and Death at Grasshopper: The Homogenization of Reality. In *Status, Structure, and Stratification*, edited by M. Thompson, M.T. Garcia, and F.J. Kense, pp. 175–180. Archaeological Association of the University of Calgary, Calgary, Alberta.

Plog, S. (1995) Equality and Hierarchy: Holistic Approaches to Understanding Social Dynamics in the Pueblo Southwest. In *The Foundations of Social Inequality*, edited by T.D. Price and G.M. Feinman, pp. 189–206. Plenum, New York.

Plog, S., and J. Solometo (1993) Alternative Pathways in the Evolution of Western Pueblo Ritual. Paper presented at the Chacmool Conference, Calgary, Alberta.

Redman, C. (1991) Distinguished Lecture in Archaeology: In Defense of the Seventies. *American Anthropologist* 93:295–307.

Reid, J.J. (1985) Measuring Social Complexity in the American Southwest. In *Status, Structure, and Stratification*, edited by M. Thompson, M.T. Garcia, and F.J. Kense, pp. 167–174. Archaeological Association of the University of Calgary, Calgary, Alberta.

—— (1989) A Grasshopper Perspective on the Mogollon of the Arizona Mountains. In *Dynamics of Southwestern Prehistory*, edited by L.S. Cordell and G.J. Gumerman, pp. 57–87. Smithsonian Institution Press, Washington D.C.

Reid, J.J., M.B. Schiffer, S.M. Whittlesey, M.J. Hinkes, A.P. Sullivan III, C.E. Downum, W.A. Longacre, and H.D. Tuggle (1989) Perception and Interpretation in Contemporary Southwestern Archaeology: Comments on Cordell, Upham, and Brock. *American Antiquity* 54:802–814.

Reid, J.J., and S.M. Whittlesey (1990) The Complicated and the Complex: Observations on the Archaeological Record of Large Pueblos. In *Perspectives on Southwestern Prehistory*, edited by P.E. Minnis and C.L. Redman, pp. 184–195. Westview Press, Boulder, Colorado.

Renfrew, C. (1982) Explanation Revisited. In *Theory and Explanation in Archaeology*, edited by C. Renfrew, M.J. Rowlands, and B.A. Segraves, pp. 5–24. Academic Press, New York.

Reyman, J. (1987) Priests, Power and Politics: Some Implications of Socioceremonial Control. In *Astronomy and Ceremony in the Prehistoric Southwest*, edited by J. Carlson and W.J. Judge, pp. 121–148. Maxwell Museum of Anthropology Papers No. 2. University of New Mexico, Albuquerque.

Roseberry, W. (1989) *Anthropologies and Histories*. Rutgers University Press, New Brunswick, New Jersey.

Rowlands, M. (1984) Objectivity and Subjectivity in Archaeology. In *Marxist Perspectives in Archaeology*, edited by M. Spriggs, pp. 108–114. Cambridge University Press, Cambridge.

Sacks, K. (1979) *Sisters and Wives: The Past and Future of Sexual Equality*. University of Illinois Press, Urbana.

Saitta, D. (1989) Dialectics, Critical Inquiry, and Archaeology. In *Critical Traditions in Contemporary Archaeology*, edited by A. Wylie and V. Pinsky, pp. 38–43. Cambridge University Press, Cambridge.

—— (1994) Class and Community in the Prehistoric Southwest. In *The Ancient Southwestern Community: Models and Methods for the Study of Prehistoric Social Organization*, edited by W. Wills and R. Leonard. University of New Mexico Press, Albuquerque.

Saitta, D.J., and A.S. Keene (1990) Politics and Surplus Flow in Prehistoric Communal Societies. In *The Evolution of Political Systems: Socio-Politics in Small Scale Sedentary Societies*, edited by S. Upham, pp. 203–224. Cambridge University Press, Cambridge.

Sayer, D. (1987) *The Violence of Abstraction: The Analytical Foundations of Historical Materialism*. Basil Blackwell, Oxford.

Shanks, M., and C. Tilley (1987) *Reconstructing Archaeology*. Cambridge University Press, Cambridge.

Sebastian, L. (1991) Sociopolitical Complexity and the Chaco System. In *Chaco and Hohokam: Prehistoric Regional Systems in the American Southwest*, edited by P. Crown and W.J. Judge, pp. 109–134. School of American Research, Santa Fe, New Mexico.

Silverblatt, I. (1987) *Moon, Sun, and Witches: Gender Ideologies and Class in Inca and Colonial Peru*. Princeton University Press, Princeton, New Jersey.

Smith, M.E. (1983) Pueblo Councils: An Example of Stratified Egalitarianism. In *The Development of Political Organization in Native North America*, edited by E. Tooker and M. Fried, pp. 32–44. American Ethnological Society, Washington D.C.

Snow, D. (1981) Proto-historic Rio Grande Economics: A Review of Trends. In *The Protohistoric Period in the North American Southwest, AD. 1450–1700*, edited by D. Wilcox and W. Masse, pp. 354–377. Anthropological Research Papers No. 24. Arizona State University, Tempe.

Stuart, D.E., and R.P. Gauthier (1981) *Prehistoric New Mexico: Background for Survey*. State Historic Preservation Bureau, Santa Fe, New Mexico.

Tedlock, D. (1979) Zuni Religion and World View. *Handbook of North American Indians 9, Southwest*, edited by A. Ortiz, pp. 499–508. Smithsonian Institution Press, Washington, D.C.

Titiev, M. (1944) *Old Oraibi: A Study of the Hopi Indians of Third Mesa*. Papers of the Peabody Museum of American Archaeology and Ethnology Vol. 22(1). Harvard University, Cambridge, Massachusetts.

Trigger, B. (1990) Maintaining Economic Equality in Opposition to Complexity: An Iroquoian Case Study. In *The Evolution of Political Systems: Socio-Politics in Small Scale Sedentary Societies*, edited by S. Upham, pp. 119–145. Cambridge University Press, Cambridge.

Tringham, R.E. (1991) Households with Faces: The Challenge of Gender in Prehistoric Architectural Remains. In *Engendering Archaeology*, edited by J. Gero and M. Conkey, pp. 93–131. Basil Blackwell, Oxford.

Upham, S. (1982) *Politics and Power*. Academic Press, New York.

—— (1988) Archaeological Visability and the Underclass of Southwestern Prehistory. *American Antiquity* 53:245–261.

Upham, S., K.G. Lightfoot, and R.A. Jewett (editors) (1989) *The Sociopolitical Structure of Prehistoric Southwestern Societies*, Westview Press, Boulder, Colorado.

Upham, S., and F. Plog (1986) The Interpretation of Prehistoric Political Complexity in the Central and Northern Southwest: Towards a Mending of Models. *Journal of Field Archaeology* 13:223–231.

Vivian, R.G. (1990) *The Chacoan Prehistory of the San Juan Basin*. Academic Press, Orlando, Florida.

Watson, R. (1991) Ozymandias, King of Kings: Postprocessual Radical Archaeology as Critique. *American Antiquity* 55:673–689.

Whiteley, P. (1988) *Deliberate Acts*. University of Arizona Press, Tucson.

Whittlesey, S.M. (1978) *Status and Death at Grasshopper Pueblo: Experiments Towards an Archaeological Theory of Correlates*. Unpublished Ph.D. dissertation, University of Arizona, Tucson.

Whittlesey, S.M., and R. Ciolek-Torrello (1992) A Revolt Against Rampart Elites: Towards an Alternative Paradigm. In *Proceedings of the Second Salado Conference*, edited by R.C. Lange and S. Germick, pp. 312–324. Arizona Archaeological Society, Phoenix.

Wilcox, D.R. (1981) Changing Perspectives on the Protohistoric Pueblos, A.D. 1450–1700. In *The Protohistoric Period in the North American Southwest, AD. 1450–1700*, edited by D.R. Wilcox and R.B. Masse, pp. 378–409. Anthropological Research Paper No. 24. Arizona State University, Tempe.

Wolf, E.R. (1982) *Europe and the People Without History*. University of California Press, Berkeley.

Wormington, H.M. (1947) *Prehistoric Indians of the Southwest*, Denver Museum of Natural History, Denver.

Wylie, A. (1989) Matters of Fact and Matters of Interest. In *Archaeological Approaches to Cultural Identity*, edited by S. Shennan, pp. 94–109. Unwin Hyman, London.

Young, R.W., and W. Morgan (1980) *The Navajo Language: A Grammar and Colloquial Dictionary*. University of New Mexico Press, Albuquerque.

PART SEVEN

Archaeology and social responsibility

INTRODUCTION

What is the social responsibility of the archaeologist, if any? Does it end with our ethical requirement to serve as managers of the archaeological record? Or are we, as archaeologists, instead implicated in larger social concerns? Is there, or should there be, a politics of archaeology? And where might one's archaeological commitments to science, anthropological interests in traditional societies, and the differing views of Native Americans intersect? These and related issues have been increasingly important to archaeology in the last decade. Moreover, they have shaped the nature of archaeology in profound ways, and promise to continue influencing it into the future.

The political and social implications of archaeology, of course, have been an issue of great concern among many cognitive and post-processual archaeologists. They have contended that archaeological practise is, on at least some level, a political act. This is partly because we project our own ideological beliefs about the past on to our interpretations of it, and partly because, by promoting our interpretations, we serve to reinforce these beliefs in society as a whole.

Many processual archaeologists have reacted quite strongly to these assertions, preferring to see science as value-neutral. Their view is that, if archaeologists create an ideologically-biased interpretation of the past based on current beliefs, then there can be no real purpose to doing archaeology. What is the point of archaeology, if all we create is a reflection of our implicit biases about prehistory? Yet as Mark Leone (1991) has perceptively noted, it is precisely because of its social and political implications that archaeology can be important. These implications are what can make it relevant and, in fact, more relevant than is implied by some vague and abstract notions about the general value of accumulating scientific knowledge, as processualism assumes. The point of archaeology (especially critical archaeology, as he practices it) is not so much to reconstruct an objective past, then, but to help us achieve a more objective, less value-laden present.

Leone also has noted that, even while processualists insist that archaeology is apolitical, its political implications are reverberating ever more strongly through the discipline. The outfall from the US Native American Graves Protection and Repatriation Act (NAGPRA) of 1990 shows this very clearly. This demonstrates precisely that many of the political and social contentions of cognitive and postprocessual archaeologists are correct, yet few processualists seem to make this connection between theory and the empirical reality within which they now conduct their work. NAGPRA is instead seen by many archaeologists as a narrow problem between archaeologists and Native Americans, either because we "don't get along", or because Native Americans are using archaeology to "get even" for a history of abuse and domination. Few seem to realize that neither Native Americans nor archaeologists passed NAGPRA. Yet its implications are extreme because, against a background of archaeological protests, it represents society at large speaking, and telling us that what we have been doing is no longer very relevant. Leone's predictions have come true in less than half a decade.

The two papers that conclude this volume illustrate and explore some of these points. The first is by Christopher Tilley, who has been one of the more prominent voices in the post-processual debate. His paper addresses the larger issues of the social and political relevance of archaeology. He emphasizes that it is non-critical archaeology, archaeology that fails to reflect on its own social and political biases, that is the most ideological, exactly because it fails to acknowledge its own internal problems and political commitments. Tilley also suggests a program of action intended to move archaeology away from its traditional ideological posture toward one that is both more self-aware, and that can help transform society in positive ways.

One component of this proposed program is a transformation of museums along with public archaeological interpretation in more general terms, a topic that has also concerned Leone (e.g., Handsman and Leone 1989). Museums are of course one of our primary means for communicating our interpretations of the past to the public, and their importance cannot be underestimated. But consider the general organizational structure of many American museum systems. Native American prehistory and ethnology are commonly found in natural history museums, along with dinosaurs, gemstones and stuffed zoological specimens. The archaeology of classical and western civilizations, on the other hand, is more commonly displayed in art museums, alongside Rembrandts and Van Goghs. The message of this organizational structure (which admittedly we have inherited from the nineteenth century) is that Native Americans are part of nature, not culture. They are not really humans, like us Euro-Americans. Granted, few if any of us would explicitly support such a view today. But does this excuse us from having implicitly perpetuated it, almost into the twenty-first century? Where is our professional and social responsibility in such circumstances? This is why critical archaeology, aimed at revealing and correcting biases such as these, is so important, as Tilley contends.

The Native American issue is directly addressed by Gary White Deer, a Choctaw and Keeper of the Treasures, in the last paper in the volume. White Deer lays out, in a clear fashion, some of the problems that Native Americans have with our western scientific empiricism, perhaps helping us to understand why NAGPRA has come about, and why it has been necessary. His suggested solution to the problems between Native Americans and archaeologists is informed by his Native American sensibility, yet it is so obvious in its practicality and humanness that it is almost shaming. Ultimately, what he asks for is simply respect and balance. He (and other Native Americans) are perfectly willing to accommodate scientific archaeology. But White Deer asks for a scientific archaeology that also accommodates Native American concerns. Central among these is a consideration of the sacred.

The reasonableness of this request cannot be assailed. The problem with it, from the perspective of many American archaeologists, is that sacredness is to archaeology like oil is to water. Many archaeologists would contend that sacredness cannot be the solution, precisely because it is the problem. What we want to study cannot be studied, because it is sacred. But the problem between Native Americans and archaeologists, as White Deer implies but archaeologists often don't understand, is not that certain kinds of remains are sacred. It has resulted because we refuse to admit that they are, and to act accordingly.

The point of this is not just Native American–archaeologist relations – critically important though these are. The point of this also concerns cognitive and post-processual archaeologies, because one subtext of White Deer's paper serves to tie this Native American concern directly to the matter of archaeological method and theory. This is the question that White Deer's article implicitly raises. Why is the study of stone tool or ceramic technology more important than the study of religious beliefs and practices? What tells us more about a people: what they ate, or what they believed? Which is more important in charting socio-cultural evolution: changes in tool technology, or advances in knowledge?

The reason for the failure to acknowledge the sacredness of certain Native American remains lies at least partly in the behaviorism of processual archaeology. This denies that beliefs, religious practices and, in essence, knowledge, is important or studiable. Because these are cognitive phenomena, they are epiphenomenal and therefore analytically irrelevant. Archaeologists then cannot accommodate the contention that certain Native American remains are sacred, because their scientific worldview denies that sacredness has any meaning. Meanwhile, Native American beliefs, through NAGPRA, strip away processual archaeology's museum collections. Try telling museum curators, after completing their NAGPRA inventories and de-accessioning their collections, that Native American beliefs are epiphenomenal, and can be categorically dismissed.

This problem can also be presented more personally. How do you, as an archaeologist, wish to be remembered: by your intellectual accomplishments (which are, like beliefs, mental constructs), or the tools that you once used to dig holes in the ground? Which should be preserved for posterity, your trowels and brushes and mattocks? Or your monographs and journal articles? Processual archaeology would, implicitly, tell you the first. Cognitive and post-processual archaeologies, in contrast, would argue for the second. These approaches contend that ritual and belief, like our own intellectual contributions, are important. They have also shown, in theory and practice, that these are perfectly studiable by prehistoric archaeologists (e.g., Renfrew 1994). And they demonstrate, at least in my own experience with rock art research, that archaeologists can study the sacred, often with the enthusiastic participation of Native Americans.

Ultimately, White Deer asks us to find a balance between spirit and matter. This, in essence, is also the message of cognitive and post-processual archaeologies.

■ ■ ■

Further reading

Handsman and Leone 1989
Leone 1991
Renfrew 1994
Swidler *et al.* 1997
Trigger 1980

■ ■ ■

References

Handsman, R.G. and Leone, M.P. (1989) "Living History and Critical Archaeology in the Reconstruction of the Past", in V. Pinsky and A. Wylie (eds) *Critical Traditions in Contemporary Archaeology*, Cambridge: Cambridge University Press.

Leone, M.P. (1991) "Materialist Theory and the Formation of Questions in Archaeology", in R. Preucel (ed.) *Processual and Postprocessual Archaeologies: Multiple Ways of Knowing the Past*, Center for Archaeological Investigations, Southern Illinois University at Carbondale, Occasional Paper No. 10.

Renfrew, C. (1994) "The Archaeology of Religion", in C. Renfrew and E.B.W. Zubrow (eds) *The Ancient Mind: Elements of Cognitive Archaeology*, Cambridge: Cambridge University Press.

Swidler, N., Dongoske, K.E., Anyon R. and Downer, A.S. (eds) (1997) *Native Americans and Archaeologists: Stepping Stones to Common Ground*, Walnut Creek: AltaMira.

Trigger, B. (1980) "Archaeology and the Image of the American Indian", *American Antiquity*, 45: 662–76.

Chapter 15

ARCHAEOLOGY AS SOCIO-POLITICAL ACTION IN THE PRESENT

Christopher Tilley

Introduction

To say that we live in an unfair world is a commonplace understatement of the contemporary problem. A few indices may be of use to remind us, in our rather small and parochial discipline of archaeology, of the realities.

In the United States average calorie intake is estimated to be 3,537 kilocalories per person per day. In Africa the comparable figure is 2,303 kilocalories with about one-fifth of the continent's population, approximately 100 million people, either starving or undernourished. An average of 1,000 kilograms of grain products per person per year is consumed in America. The largest part of this (93 per cent) goes to feed animals for meat production. To produce 1 kilogram of beef about 10 kilograms of grain is required. The meat, once produced, is subsequently used to promote, in part, "The McDonalds Way of Living", the products of Colonel Sanders and the like. Five huge multinational companies – Cargills, Continental Grain, Cook Industries, Bunge Corporation and the Louis Dreyfeus Corporation – control, together and through their subsidiaries, about 80 per cent of the entire world grain-market (wheat, rice, maize, etc.) from the seeds sown in the ground to the food arriving on our tables. Market division is such that there is little effective competition. Grain produced in underdeveloped countries utilising cheap labour and land is sold to the rich industrialised world rather than used for feeding the local population. Between 1960 and 1970 the world's gross national product (GNP) is estimated to have grown by 1,000 billion dollars (i.e. $1,000 million million). Of this increase, 80 per cent went to the industrialised West, 5 per cent to the underdeveloped nations.

Every year 100,000 square kilometres of tropical rain forest, an area roughly two and a half times the size of Denmark, is felled and exported in one form or another to industrialised nations at a capital value of 120 billion dollars. Exploitation quadrupled between 1950 and 1960, and is still increasing. Should people in under-developed countries use as much paper as is used in the industrialised world for such things as packaging, all the forests would be cut down more quickly than they could grow up. Similarly, should the world's population adopt an American-style meat diet, it would only be possible to feed 1.7 billion of the estimated 5 billion people on earth.

Multinational companies are now so huge in terms of sheer capital and degree of horizontal or vertical market integration that it is virtually impossible to effectively control their activities on a nation state basis. The two largest, Exxon (Esso) and General Motors, have an annual capital turnover that exceeds the GNP of all but ten of the world's nations. A doubling of consumption in the industrialised world leads to roughly six times the amount of pressure on dwindling world resources than would a doubling of the population in the underdeveloped countries. "We" provide "them" with contraceptive pills, but where are our consumption pills?

Since the beginning of the twentieth century, a hundred million people have died in connection with 160 smaller and 16 larger wars. During thirty-five years since the end of World War II there have only been between twenty-six and thirty days without a war somewhere on the planet. Today it is estimated that over 54,000 nuclear weapons exist in the world. Their combined destructive potential is equiv-alent to over one million of the two bombs that were dropped on Hiroshima and Nagasaki. The world's military expenditure comes to about one million dollars every minute. Every day 20,000 people die because of lack of clean water. In total, 1.7 billion people on the earth lack clean water. The use of money spent on arma-ments for a one-week period would eliminate this problem. Meanwhile the profits to be made from sales of weapons are enormous.

Labour, in capitalist production, has been reduced to an unfeeling, empty, mundane and repetitive process. Capitalism has created a uniquely alienated and estranged world in which, as Giddens describes it,

> The gearing of daily life into comprehended tradition is replaced by the empty routines of everyday life. On the other hand, the whole of humanity now lies in the shadow of possible destruction. This unique conjunction of the banal and the apocalyptic, this is the world that capitalism has fashioned.
>
> (1981, p. 252)

Living in Western society of the 1980s is to be involved with and, in part, responsible for prevailing social conditions. The statements above, which present as bluntly as possible information drawn from a recent publication (Carlson *et al.* 1983), are intended to challenge and promote reflection: where does archaeology stand in relation to all this? Where are its values? What is its purpose? In which direction should the discipline develop? Is archaeology relevant or irrelevant to the world? Is doing archaeology like playing the fiddle while Rome burns? In short, why archaeology?

The argument that follows is conducted in two stages. First, it is suggested that archaeology, as presently practised by many, sustains rather than challenges the contemporary social order. Second, an alternative is outlined: an archaeology conceived as a form of social and political action in the present with emancipatory potential.

Contemporary archaeology and contemporary politics

Development of the new archaeology

During the past twenty years archaeology has been besotted with methodological procedures presumed essential in the quest for supposedly objective knowledge. The scientistic "new archaeology" of the 1960s and 1970s was born and rapidly gained ascendancy in Britain and the United States, the oldest and the most powerful of capitalist states. This conjunction would seem to be no mere historical accident, but rather an integral part of the prevailing social and political climate. Prior to the advent of the new archaeology the discipline was seen as essentially historical rather than scientific in character (e.g., Clark 1939; Piggott 1959). Clarke (1968, p. 12) felt it necessary to rail against any continued writing of counterfeit history books. In the last two decades, a majority of archaeologists have donned the white coat of the scientist and distanced themselves from history. Why is this the case? It would seem closely tied to acceptance of the myth of science's supremacy as the ultimate mode of human understanding, and that of the scientist as hero, as producer of certain knowledge, as one who dispels illusions, and as one who is blessed with an incisive sacred rationality. Indeed, the use of the terms "science" and "objectivity" in the literature are almost magically self-legitimating where questions about the worth of particular research are concerned. Given the ever-increasing dominance and celebration of science and technology in contemporary society, to be cast in this image, as producing (or purporting to produce) objective knowledge, was to gain intellectual respectability and power. Archaeologists abandoned the concept of their discipline as a humanistic delving into the past of direct relevance to modern society, and reconceived it as a science that could have definite rewards. An instrumental justification for the discipline thus arose.

This concept of archaeology as an instrument in the present, as having something to say and contribute to the world, suffered a curious inversion; it amounted to suppressing speech altogether. One of the polemical claims associated with the advocacy of "hard science" was that the ability to both formulate and test laws of cultural process, given the unique time-depth of the archaeological record, could put archaeology in a position to contribute actively to the wider social sciences (Watson et al. 1971, p. 162). Fritz and Plog expressed it darkly: "We suspect that unless archaeologists find ways of making their research increasingly relevant to the modern world, the modern world will find itself increasingly capable of getting along without archaeologists" (1970, p. 412). Consequently, archaeologists no longer dealt with the archaeological record as such; it became a "natural laboratory" (Plog 1974, p. 35). Binford, for example, demanded "instruments that permit and facilitate unambiguous meaningful observation" (1983, p. 415). This scientism is viewed as having definite monetary advantages for the discipline. Grant proposals framed as objective and scientific are more likely to be successful (Plog 1982, p. 30), while American rescue archaeology has metamorphosed into "cultural resource management", and an entire literature devoted to it is associated with federal government legislation.

By opposing science to history, archaeologists believed themselves to be increasingly respectable academically, and socially relevant. This, in turn, proved to have certain financial advantages. Archaeology was no longer the handmaiden of history with a humanistic emphasis, but a science involved in the technical control of the past, cemented together by means of methodological guidelines concocted in the image of the natural and physical sciences.

However, this concern for contemporary relevance was not construed in political terms. The proponents of relevance never really addressed the question, "To whom is this work to be relevant and why?"; it was simply assumed that the work would be relevant if properly scientific (see Wobst 1989). In fact, the commitment to (useful) involvement in scientific activity entailed a deliberately apolitical stance; it required that politics be kept out of archaeology in order not to distort the interpretation of the data. This produced a concept of the past that was by no means neutral. It was much more an exact mirror-image of the capitalist present than that ever achieved in the berated traditional archaeology which, despite its many failings, always incorporated awareness of the essential *difference* between past and present.

Strident advocacy of the view that archaeology should be conducted as science, specifically, a natural rather than a social science, has obscured the fact that people, and not inanimate machines, write and create the past. Archaeology is a process, a system of social relationships in the present within which the production of meanings takes place. An essential part of the process of investigating the past is that the data are constantly re-articulated in relation to each other. The selfsame materials are repeatedly placed in different analytical contexts and associations and put to different uses; new meanings are discovered as the relationships between them are reshuffled. In order adequately to come to grips with this process of the production of meanings, we must constantly re-evaluate the *Lebenswelt* that is presupposed by any and all forms of archaeological theory and practice.

As archaeology is a relationship between past and present mediated by individuals, groups and institutions, it has, inescapably, some contemporary relevance. Inevitably it becomes political and ideological in character. The knowledge it produces does not in any sense consist of a body of detached subject matter to be transmitted and learnt. It is, and always will be, a form of individual and cultural experience which is continually being shaped and modified.

Archaeology with a "radical" message

The context-relativity and relevance of archaeology is clearly seen in some recent work of Clark, one of the most respected of the more traditional archaeologists. He has made a remarkable series of assertions, of an overtly political nature, concerning the relationship between past and present (Clark 1979, 1983). He suggests that archaeology poses "questions more radical than those commonly asked by political science or sociology because they are framed in an ampler perspective" (1979, p. 5). In what does this radicalism consist? The message Clark derives from a study of archaeology is as follows: firstly that egalitarian and illiterate peasant societies produce "dull and boring" culture; and secondly, "the finest artefacts made by man, the most superb and diverse embodiments of his humanity were produced in hierarchical societies" (*ibid.*, p. 12). Thus, for Clark, archaeological research documents the attainment of "humanity" through the gradual emergence of hierarchy, where it is presumed that the diversity expressed through cultural products is a differential measure of the degree of humanity attained. He views contemporary industrial society with exasperation: "the archaeologist finds himself confronted in his daily life by an increasingly rapid reversion toward the intraspecies homogeniety of a prehuman situation" (*ibid.*, p. 13). This, he holds, is a process of cultural impoverishment. The greatest threat to the contemporary quality of life derives, moreover, from the "proponents of self-styled progressive philosophies" (*ibid.*, p. 14). We are told that the rich are now taxed so heavily that they can no longer indulge in the kind of conspicuous consumption that promotes the maintenance of high culture. He maintains that "[We must] hold fast to the values defined by our history. . . . If our common aim is to enhance our lives, our guiding light must surely be quality rather than quantity, hierarchy rather than equality, and diversity rather than homogeneity" (*ibid.*, p. 19). To whom is the "our" in this passage supposed to refer? Is it an élite that Clark wishes to protect? Clark's entire argument turns on the presumption that a clearcut definition can be given of what constitutes "high" culture and worthwhile cultural products. Inasmuch as no such rigid distinction can be systematically drawn between "high" and "low" culture, the argument is ultimately incoherent. In addition, it is not at all clear that hierarchy, wealth, or status necessarily foster culture; Clark's argument embraces an enormous over-simplification. What cultural status would he give, for example, to palaeolithic cave art? Is this crude and nasty compared with an Etruscan bronze? Is the work of Jackson Pollock inferior to that of Rubens?

Considered in its own individual and historical setting, Clark's argument is self-evidently part of an aristocratic tradition which is inspired by some aspects of Plato's philosophy (namely the differentiation of children of "bronze" from children of "gold"), and finds expression in the British public school system and certain sectors of élitist universities such as Cambridge. It bears a remarkable similarity to the work of T. S. Eliot (1948) who also identified the most worthwhile aspects of culture with the existence of a small governing leisured class. Its central élitist tenet is that diffusion of the precious quality of *culture* among the masses can only lead to a dilution of quality and diversity. Clark attempts to legitimate this message by appeal to the past; its "radical" content is that contemporary capitalism apparently is not sufficiently hierarchical or exploitative to foster cultural diversity and high attainment.

Commodifying the past

The political implications of Clark's view of the past are clear and unabashed. He spells them out for us. The new archaeology is no less political. The difference is that its politics are less obvious and generally concealed under its self-professed veil of a science of the past.

American archaeology, rather than opposing the values of the capitalist system, appears more and more to be embedding itself in them. This is seen especially in the literature of cultural resource management and in a recent book effectively summarising the central issues involved, *Ethics and Values in Archaeology* (Green 1984). The range of values and ethical issues considered in this book is disappointingly narrow; it is largely concerned with the relationship of archaeology as discipline and profession to business and government. The past is regarded as a non-renewable resource which requires management by a body of specialists, while the proposed science of managing this resource is understood to be best realised by means of problem-oriented research designs. The central problem of such management is that of evaluating the significance of the past: "Is this site worth preserving or excavating rather than another site?" (Dunnell 1984). The consequence of this is that the past is treated as a commodity. Like any other commodity, sites become abstract equivalents for one another; each has a price-tag and, when the demands of business efficiency raise questions about who can do the requisite work for the least money the past may be tagged with competing prices. The commodification of the archaeological record thus turns archaeologists into entrepreneurs who treat the past as an abstract system of exchangeable equivalents which can be marketed for sale in various ways.

In this process of commodification archaeologists possess the necessary cultural capital (i.e., knowledge) to establish a hegemonic claim on the past and exclude other non-professional interest groups (see Gero 1989). The professional élite decides, on the basis of *its* knowledge claims and interests, what is important in the past and then recovers or preserves it. After subsequent interpretation the public is told that this is its past. This sets up and perpetuates a total disjunction between the professionals who produce the past and the public who are firmly placed in the role of passive consumers and in the end are alienated from it. Their reaction to this sense of alienation may sometimes take the form of unauthorised excavation or pot hunting which, in turn, elicits from the professional archaeological community various attempts to punish the offenders, namely, those who have attempted to discover their own past and have dared to transgress the divide (see Hodder 1984, p. 29).

Asserting professionalism, establishing codes of ethics, talking about responsibilities, promoting science, and so on, do nothing to lessen public alienation from the past. In fact, they only exacerbate the situation. The primary concern of the discipline, at present, is with its own interests. The justifications typically given for its practice ring a little hollow; they divert attention inward towards the discipline. Archaeology is done because it entertains, educates, or stimulates "us", it allows "us" to understand the achievements of humanity or the symbolic unity of the earth's population in terms of its common roots. The past is "ours" and "we" need it. Why archaeology, and why do we need it? Because it is natural; "we" all need a past. Because "we" can learn from the past; the past has aesthetic value, it is a social duty to preserve the past. Why? Because we know and we are telling you. Who exactly are the "we" of "our" past? Those who speak and write are, of course, professional archaeologists, the self-appointed guardians of the past. These professionals know the true worth of the past which, they usually claim, is intrinsic. If the public do not accept that the past produced for them is important then they must be educated. In fact, the very question of justification is the product of a guilty conscience. All archaeologists are implicated in this cycle of mystification and self-legitimation whatever kind of work they do. Most, if not all, know it.

Concepts and the past as functionally conservative

Much of present-day archaeological practice is clearly ideological. It is not a normatively neutral discourse on the past, but rather has definite socio-political consequences for the present. It is ideological not because it propagates false consciousness or entails a political bias which might be corrected through a process of neutralisation or removal of distortion, but because it is a form of social practice which helps, in however minor a way, to sustain, justify and legitimate the values of a capitalist society. This is a product of the work being *non-critical* in conception, which results, in turn, in a rationalisation of present social and economic processes, and of the values associated with them, in terms of the past.

Perhaps it is not very fruitful to ask whether the concepts employed by archaeologists, such as rationality, adaptation, role, function or system, are true or false descriptions of past social action. They may be illuminating or even in part applicable. It is more pertinent to inquire: why these concepts rather than others? What kind of archaeology or view of the past do these concepts produce? It might be profitable to distinguish between those types of theories and concepts that are productive of change and critical of the existing social order, and those which aid and abet the preservation of the contemporary social order. Many of the theories utilised in the new archaeology are *status quo* theories of the social.

A prime example is systems theory with its emphasis on persistence and stability. Equilibrium, smooth functioning, and the interconnection of sub-systems are always stressed in these theories while social conflict and contradiction are either underplayed or ignored. Clarke (1968, pp. 48–52) defines seven different equilibrium states which are, in essence, different states of system stability. Stability is taken to be the norm and systems are presumed to change only in order to remain stable: they are characterised as searching out and converging on desirable states, a process which Clarke terms "goal-seeking" or homeostasis (*ibid.*, p. 52). He observes that "the ideal is for man to act without dislocation because [this] . . . communicates a set of contradictory values – capable of causing confusion, loss of cohesion and ultimately social anarchy" (*ibid.*, p. 97). Renfrew, likewise, states that the "conservative nature of culture cannot be too strongly stressed. In terms of our model it is the *natural* tendency of culture to persist unchanged. . . . It is change, any change, which demands explanation" (1972, p. 487). Hill claims that it merely "begs the question" of why internal tensions arise to suggest that they might promote change (1977, p. 76). Flannery (1972) talks of internal "pathologies" in the system promoting change, implying that quite extreme failure of internal functioning is required to overturn the norm of stability. Systems theory is a model imposed on archaeological data. It is not altered by that data. The past, of course, is found to be conservative. It is assumed that stability simply occurs rather than being made to happen by definite forms of social intervention. It is easy to make the connection between a conservative theory and conservative politics, but that is inadequate and does not take us far enough. Systems theory lends support to any social order. It is founded on an uncritical set of concepts. It tends to legitimate and naturalise that which exists; it does not promote the will for change. Any pre-existing state, apparently, is a state for the good. "Goodness" becomes equated with social stability, "pathologies" with social unrest.

Language and evolution – passing judgement

Political values are embodied in the very language in which we write and have had a profound influence on cultural evolutionary theories. The choice of descriptive terms is value-laden. For example, archaeologists frequently use the term "civilisation" as a description of certain sets of remains encountered in the archaeological record. According to *The Oxford English Dictionary*, the verb "to civilise" means to improve to a better state. Whether what we might be prepared to label a civilisation actually does constitute a better state is a question of social and political values which are built into the linguistic term "civilisation". In cultural evolutionary theories (e.g., Flannery 1972; Sanders and Webster 1978; Service 1975) societies are treated in a way which equates them with football teams. The archaeologist lays down the ground rules for the game – differential adaptive success. The teams, conveniently labelled "bands", "tribes", "chiefdoms", and "states", are then placed in the adaptive arena. The higher divisions subsequently may be called civilisations, but if they are not deemed suitably adaptive, they are relegated to the lower status of chiefdoms or tribes. Far from being a normatively neutral process, this is a direct politicisation of time in which the archaeologist passes judgement, leaving the accused no opportunity for defence. The archaeological subject is either found guilty of adaptive failure at one time or another (hence the decline of civilisation occurs), or is commended for achieving increasing complexity and increasingly sophisticated control of the environment (hence the rise of civilisation). No concept of social evolution, whatever terminology it might be wrapped in, can be divorced from the political and social idea of progress. In the literature of the new archaeology, the term progress is exorcised in virtually all accounts, but it persists, nonetheless, as an abstract measure, a yardstick, for differentiating between societies. This measure is adaptation which often serves in a tautologically triple role as cause, consequence, and outcome of change. The implicit but ideologically resonant conclusion that this yields for us in the present is either a legitimation of our own society or the promise of an even better future.

Biologising the social

Another area of archaeology in which political and social values can be seen to operate is in the work of the Cambridge palaeoeconomic school. We are exhorted to "formulate models with specifically archaeological objectives and data in mind" (Higgs and Jarman 1975, p. 1). As there are probably as many archaeological objectives as there are archaeologists to formulate them, this proposal appears rather loose. In practice, palaeoeconomists have allowed their perceptions of what constitutes hard archaeological data to shape their objectives. They attempt to relate population, resources, and technology over the long term. This "long-term" perspective legitimates a fairly mechanistic analysis in which social phenomena are either written-off as "short-term trivia" (*ibid.*, p. 2) or presumed, more mildly, to be "largely reflections of economic activity" (Jarman *et al.* 1982, p. 4). The object of research is the formulation of natural laws governing the population/environment/technology triplet. Populations are always viewed as pressing against resource ceilings. Paleoeconomists admit that this is a purely theoretical argument (*ibid.*, p. 9); population pressure is presumed to select between more and less viable populations inasmuch as only those with the stronger economic base survive inevitable resource conflict. They also recognise that their work has political implications:

> A lesson which can be drawn from the study of prehistory is that wars, starvation, exploitation and conservation are not simply moral, ethical or political issues. There is an important, indeed a primary biological component to these phenomena, without recognition of which no really effective consideration of them can be made.

> (*ibid.*, p. 12)

They add, by extension of this, that "the possible demonstration that there are laws which govern human behaviour in the long term ought to have an effect on the way in which we view our behaviour today" (*ibid.*).

Palaeoeconomists cannot, in fact, lay claim to actually having discovered any laws, consequently, the "lesson" of prehistory is no lesson at all. It has been theoretically constituted prior to the study of the archaeological record. Such statements about the relevance of the past to the present have alarming implications. They may indeed be valuable to certain political interests inasmuch as they can be readily used to further and legitimate virtually any existing form of immoral action. They are especially effective in this given their claim to support rigorous objective science. On this account it would seem that the Gulag and the concentration camps of Nazi Germany can be represented as inevitable because of a "primary biological component". Are the Vietnam war or the possibly impending nuclear holocaust also inevitable? Fortunately, we all know that future destruction of the earth can be avoided by political and social reconstruction. These implications of the palaeoecological lesson should not be taken seriously and the authors probably did not intend them. The point is that they illustrate just what a lack of self-critical awareness, sheltering under the guise of positivist science, can come to: the inadvertent support of a very objectionable politics.

Much the same kind of point can be made concerning the recent importation of Darwinian evolutionary theory by Dunnell (1978, 1980b) and Wenke (1981) in order to "explain" the archaeological record. Sahlins (1976) has discussed at length the theoretical and political implications of socio-biology and has subjected it to a lengthy and devastating critique. These arguments will not be repeated here. The essential threat of such a perspective, especially as displayed in Wilson's most widely read but least satisfactory discussions (1975, 1978), comes from the argument that human actions are determined by a combination of genes and environment. Concomitantly, it follows from this that the only political action that could change the world or social life would be eugenic. However, it is by means of the concepts of this very theory of evolutionary biology that we can demonstrate convincingly that any attempt to apply such a theory to the study of human social organisation is untenable or at least so deeply difficult that the value of the application is completely undermined. Social relationships are not in any primary sense biological relationships and may not be explained, except in the most reductionist scenario, by appeal to the physical attributes of human beings.

The same conclusions apply to attempts to biologise the study of material culture. Dunnell and Wenke argue for a primacy of function over style and suggest that style is a reservoir of variability which may in the end acquire selective value (Dunnell 1978, p. 199; Wenke 1981, p. 114). In reply, two questions may be posed: where does the style of pot shape end and function begin? In what circumstances would a pottery vessel decorated with curvilinear lines have a selective value over one with scalene triangles? These questions are not trivial, or extreme, or suitably chosen, since similar questions can be raised in relation to the entire gamut of human culture, material and non-material. If it is to work at all, such application of a perspective like Darwinian evolutionary theory must reduce the almost limitless variety of human actions and material production to self-sameness. In so doing it destroys what it purports to explain. These comments can be extended to a great deal of what constitutes present-day archaeological practice.

Rationalising the economic

In much of the literature of the new archaeology, there is an emphasis on various forms of manipulation and control of the archaeological record (e.g., by means of computer simulation studies) in which human subjects are reduced to the status of passive objects shuffled around from one adaptive state to the next. The overriding concern has always been to produce a neat fit between theory and data irrespective of the tacit politics involved in making this fit.

This manipulation, control, and rationalisation of present social practices in terms of the past can be seen most nakedly in game theory and decision-making models of socio-economic relation (e.g., Christenson 1980; Earle 1980; Jochim 1976; Keene 1979, 1981). One representative example makes this clear:

> There is no universal tendency toward profit maximization in the unrestricted sense. However, maximization when referring to efficiency can be considered a restrictive kind of profit maximization where output (consumption) is fixed. This kind of maximization is quite relevant to an understanding of early human subsistence behaviour.
>
> (Christenson 1980, p. 33)

Is it relevant? Maximisation and optimisation are key terms in all this work; the theory is built around the assumption that a central tenet of the value system of contemporary capitalist western economics – the imperative to realise maximum profit for minimum risk and cost – can be projected onto the past without difficulty. Such values, no doubt, would be readily endorsed by those playing the stock exchanges of London, New York, Tokyo or Stockholm. Executives in the Chase Manhattan Bank would feel very much at home with such a view. Such accounts assume that maximising and optimising strategies have been features of social life from the dawn of prehistory. They suggest, moreover, that contemporary economic practices are the only possible ones, and in the absence of a self-conscious critical approach, have the ideological effect of naturalising them. All that has happened between the palaeolithic past and the present is that profit maximisation has become more extensive and efficient.

Such models treat rationality not as a relative concept but as an absolute. In effect, it becomes a value in itself by means of which any other form of action or system of values is judged and deemed irrational. The *technical rationality* of efficiency and cost-minimisation is designated, on *a priori* grounds, as definitive of what rationality *is*; humans are deemed rational in just this one sense, and other supposedly "non-rational" values not directly relevant to economic maximisation are reduced to independent (but, arguably, far more important) variables. These models and other frameworks employed in the new archaeology are not just simply interpretations of the archaeological record but are statements of a tacit and implicit ideology; they affirm that features such as profit maximisation are not just valued by some in particular historical circumstances, but are essential to the human condition and to human survival.

Discussion

Such examples of the projection of the social processes and values of the capitalist West into the past are not the exception but, rather, the rule (see Shanks and Tilley 1987a). Space will not be taken up here with unnecessary duplication of arguments for this point. In reducing the past to a mere stuttering repetition of the present we rob it of its emancipatory force, which must be its difference or otherness. It is only through maintaining a radical discontinuity between past and present that the past may be brought powerfully to the fore in the process of changing the latter.

Differing conceptions of the past are given shape in accordance with definite interests, values, and presuppositions which form part of the contemporary social milieu. Past facts, constituted by the archaeologist, cannot be separated from present values. This is to say that our social and political values determine or influence what becomes constituted as the factual, and this factual basis for interpretation cannot be divorced from prior value-judgements. What counts as knowledge is a social production from which there is no possible escape into a past reality of untainted facts. There is no need to drag politics into archaeology. It has been there from the beginning. All archaeological theories have been inextricably bound up with political beliefs and ideological values. No body of knowledge can avoid this. Any attempt to reduce archaeology to the science of the artefact would entail silence. This is the central contradiction embodied in *Analytical Archaeology* (Clarke 1968), a contradiction between "pure" archaeology as archaeology as archaeology, and actually being able to say something about material culture; the latter inevitably entails going far beyond the tangible and into the realms of social, economic, and political theory. An apolitical archaeology is a dangerous academic myth. The problem is not that archaeology is a political discourse, but that its politics largely take place on a tacit or unconscious level. Kossina's work is now generally condemned for its overt racist implications in relation to German nationalism (Daniel 1962, p. 123), but what is so objectionable in his work is not that it is political, but, rather, the type of politics professed. Many would say that Kossinna gravely distorts the archaeological record to insert a political reading, but this supposes that some real opposition and distinction can be set up between "distorted" and "nondistorted" work. All interpretations are in a fundamental sense distorted; the attempt to hide or minimise the intrusion of values can never be very successful. All that can happen is that they may be rendered less obvious and, therefore, potentially more insidious.

The positivist conception of value-free knowledge of the past is both impossible to realise and psychologically disturbing. Such a view, in effect, sets up a notion of the subject-observer – the interpreter of the past – as renegade and treacherous. The archaeologist is told to deny self in order to independently establish the facts. This is impossible because the self must inevitably provide mediation for the object, the facts which have no meaning, significance, or importance other than that which can be ascribed to them. A lack of value-neutrality should be regarded not as a weakness but as a strength; it provides us with a more realistic and critical basis for doing research. Binford and Sabloff (1982) agree that knowledge of the past is completely dependent on meanings given to it by the archaeologist, but this does not lead them to a further understanding that all archaeology is political archaeology. They would probably reject this as compromising the scientific objectivity to which they wish to adhere. While they mention meanings they do not discuss values.

One cannot connect facts and meanings without taking the step of linking facts and values. Much of the archaeology produced in the Anglophone world by and large has tended to strengthen the present power system in the West rather than challenge it. Clarke (1973), in his paper, "Archaeology: the loss of innocence", proclaimed the new archaeology as a raising of disciplinary self-consciousness vis-à-vis traditional research. According to Clarke, it put archaeologists in a position to "control the direction and destiny" of the discipline. In certain respects, however, the new archaeology represents innocence *par excellence*. Far from encouraging self-determination, it enjoined archaeologists to allow their direction to be controlled by a vision of a deductive empirical and concrete science which would somehow miraculously guarantee the validity of the statements made about the past on a non-social basis. Scientism in archaeology was, and is, the programming, production and advocacy of a body of knowledge which can bypass and remain untroubled by debates about social and political factors. The pertinence of such debates inevitably induces in students of other social sciences an awareness of the shortcomings of dominant forms of thought and of their inextricable connection with patterns of social control. Attempts to maintain neutrality are spurious whether they be attempts to discover laws or atemporal, aspatial statements of culture process, or to produce high-level generalisations of use to all, irrespective of divergent social and political values. The onus must be placed on those who adopt such an approach to show exactly how it is value-free. In fact, value-freedom is always an implicit assumption.

Archaeological work, I have argued, is firmly bound up with social processes and values in the capitalist West. These specific values, in part, are political in nature. The past is politicised in the process of interpretation whether archaeologists like it or not. All too often the vision of the past produced is a capitalist vision, in which present-day values such as maximisation are simply transposed to the past, with an unfortunate naturalising effect in the present. What has been said here should not be taken as a form of personal or disciplinary character assassination. Indeed, assumptions similar to those criticised above can be found in my own work (Tilley 1979). It is not suggested that theories and their development can be reduced simply to the effects of the operation of social and political values but that these values form components is of our theorising which cannot be separated one from another. The central problem of the politics of archaeology described here is that the politics is not generally recognised. It needs to be made clear. It is essential to be critically self-conscious in research and to make research itself critically relevant to the present. The alternative to a past of supposedly neutral and intrinsic worth is an actively instrumental archaeology.

Elements of a programme for action

Abandoning the myth of value-freedom

What has been largely overlooked in the archaeological literature is that discourse on the past is produced socially by men and women located in specifiable historical and political circumstances. In his XIth thesis on Feuerbach, Marx wrote that the "philosophers have only *interpreted* the world, in various ways; the point is to *change* it" (1970, p. 123). In similar vein we might say that archaeologists have so far only interpreted the past; they should undertake to change it in service of the present. This will require attention to and work on those determinants which condition various conceptions of the past, with the aim of changing the uses to which the past is put. In other words, archaeology should not primarily be concerned with the past for its own sake and as a means of escape from the socio-political reality of the present, but with using the past as a basis for strategic intervention in the present. Here we can introduce a parable:

> The story is told of an automaton constructed in such a way that it could play a winning game of chess, answering each move of an opponent with a countermove. A puppet in Turkish attire and with a hookah in its mouth sat before a chessboard placed on a large table. A system of mirrors created the illusion that this table was transparent from all sides. Actually, a little hunchback who was an expert chess player sat inside and guided the puppet's hand by means of strings.
>
> (Benjamin 1973, p. 255)

The "puppet" of objective, value-free, apolitical knowledge is a strong candidate as a philosophical counterpart to the device described in Benjamin's aphorism; it functions to create the illusion of certainty which must always win. Its critics are usually dismissed as ideologically motivated extremists. However, this strategy ultimately betrays its own credentials as a social and political myth the purpose of which is to preserve, rather than to challenge, existing bases of power in society. The quasi-religious commandment of positivist/empiricist discourse, "Thou shalt not commit a value judgement", must be abandoned. The pursuit of value-freedom is extremely dangerous as *the very attempt to eradicate values precludes any possibility of taking an open and critical stance towards society and is supportive of the existing order*. The notion of value-free research commits those who wish to adopt it to a rejection of any critique of society. In practice it results in political conservatism (see Marcuse 1955).

Establishing conceptual frameworks

Work on problems in philosophical and sociological theory must be a primary concern in any rejuvenated archaeology. These problems are not alien to archaeological concerns. They are central problems of archaeology because, apart from its concern with the artefact, archaeology is utterly non-distinctive as a form of knowledge.

Merely borrowing theories from elsewhere and "applying" them to archaeological data does not result in a critical perspective but rather in the reverse. Some more traditional archaeologists might attempt to adhere to the principle that while the work of others is infected with theories which might very well have political implications, their own work is a straightforward attempt to come to terms with how the past really was. However, the power of ideology is probably no more clearly marked than in the claim that interpretations are essentially innocent. The presentation of work as the obvious stuff of common sense raises the following problem: commonsense is never called upon to demonstrate its own consistency and validity. The "obvious" and the "natural" are by no means given to consciousness at birth but are created in a determinate set of socio-historical relations. In reality, common sense betrays its inadequacy via its contradictions and silences, providing an entirely unsatisfactory foundation for archaeology. Empiricist common sense as recently glorified by Flannery (1982) in his aversion to theory and declaration of the "need" to get back to the "real business of archaeology" (namely, to the construction of solid culture history without worry about the niceties of theory), provides no miraculous cure, no guarantee of objectivity. It is a dangerous retreat from the requirements of critical thought.

Developing a critical approach to tests

A post-processual archaeology constituted as socio-political action and cultural critique will be centrally concerned to lay bare the assumptions involved in non-critical archaeological theory and practice. Such texts must not be left unchallenged. Such an archaeology will provide a critique of prevailing contemporary conditions and a critique of the theoretical models articulated with these conditions. Archaeological texts are not to be conceived as documents that merely reflect existing reality like a mirror. They play a role in helping to shape that reality and may shore up particular sets of norms and values. Archaeological texts are all themselves contemporary artefacts and we may very well learn far more from them about the present than about the past. Because much archaeological work can be viewed as a textual self-interpretation of capitalist society, any attempt to criticise those texts and offer an alternative account of the past must criticise and intervene in the social milieu from which they arise.

By virtue of their location in contemporary society, archaeologists work and write in a field of power relations and political struggle. The statements and interpretations made by archaeologists are thus interventions in contemporary society. The past is always worked over, analysed and re-analysed. Its resuscitated existence in the present is always overlain by a series of different interpretations: the uses to which it is put for scholarly and public consumption. Theory must be seen, therefore, as a form of practice. In a properly dialectical conception of archaeology there can be no radical split between theory and practice for just these reasons. The crude division of subject and object, with its parallel referents "subjective" and "objective", must be abandoned (see Rowlands 1984).

The critical process of considering archaeological texts on the model of Marx's critique of political economy would involve three distinct steps:

1   A demonstration of the inadequacy of the theories criticised that proceeds on the basis of the assumptions or presuppositions employed; that is to say, an internal critique;
2   A sorting out of the origin of these inadequacies and the development of a critique of them; this inevitably reconstructive process will take as its starting-point both its own assumptions and the point of view of an alternative conceptual structure;
3   A demonstration of the manner in which the theory criticised is embedded in a particular set of social relations and reproduces them in its conceptual networking.

(see Suchting 1983)

This is a critical process of reading and interpreting texts, an analysis of the ways in which archaeological uses of language are mediated by factors which cannot be simply reduced to factual predication or direct authorial assertions about the nature of archaeological "reality". No radical opposition can be held to exist between what is inside or part of, and what is outside archaeological texts. These texts can be viewed as part of a process of interaction between language and the social world in which they are situated. The precise nature of the relationship between the content of individual archaeological texts and the social matrix in which they are situated needs investigation. This means that we must rethink the relation between author and text. The text is something other, something that has a mode of existence apart from the author. The meaning of a text cannot be held to be solely what the author intended. The author has no necessary, proprietary relationship to the text, nor has the text necessarily any unitary meaning (Barthes 1977; Foucault 1981). The question is, then, what relationship holds between the author's intentions, in so far as these can be plausibly reconstructed, and what the text may be argued to do or disclose. We need to investigate the sedimented layers of meaning given the past and the ideology they disclose, showing how these are situated in the text in terms other than instantiation or simple reflection.

Archaeological texts present views about the past which may ultimately contribute to a public awareness and understanding of the culture in which we live. It is vital to adopt a critical approach to the writing, reading and analysis of these texts since the manner in which the subject matter is presented, the data selected, and the analyses performed all provide messages with meanings relevant to the present.

Knowledge as practical and strategically relevant

The capitalist West is in a perpetual state of social crisis. This crisis consists not in the periodic economic recessions which can always be interpreted rather glibly by certain Marxists as signifying the final demise of capitalism, but rather in the very resilience of capitalism, the fact that things just carry on, that structures of social domination and inequality existing on a global and national scale continue to be reproduced and the political process is never effectively challenged. A bourgeois social order always champions the freedom of the individual. What this means in practice is that some make fat profits while others starve; some live off the backs and labours of others. Benjamin reminds us that "there is no cultural document that is not at the same time a record of barbarism" (1979, p. 359). Archaeology is such a cultural document, such a product of barbarism. Professional archaeologists are only able to perform their work as a result of the labours of others who are deprived of the chance to live off and through culture. This is why archaeology must be made practically relevant to the present and must not remain merely an arcane discourse on the past. In the conclusion of *The Idea of Prehistory*, Daniel states that the justification for archaeology is pleasure (1962, p. 169). It is hard to accept such a hedonistic thesis, especially given that most archaeological literature is anything but pleasurable to read. However, the principle underlying Daniel's remark would seem to be that the past is to be constituted for the idiosyncratic pleasure of an archaeological scholarly élite, at everyone else's expense.

The production of an alternative to the account of the past espoused by much contemporary archaeology is an indispensable project; that which is valuable needs to be taken and the rest left on one side. The past is not in any sense immobile or fixed or written indelibly. Rather, it is something to be strategically reconstructed in relation to contemporary social and historical conditions, to be actively reinterpreted and reinscribed within the present social order. The empirical phenomena on which we work must be dismantled, rediscovered and rearticulated – drawn into a fresh constellation of conceptual relations and structures that cut through the timeworn categories of conventional theory. The empirical data base is of vital importance. This concern to be empirical, to consider the data in all its fullness and contextual associations, should not be confused with empiricism; it does not grant the data any primacy in terms of conceptual structure. Theory and data need to be put on an equal and dialectical footing such that neither is considered "soft" nor "hard". Theories do not compromise data, and data is not "hard" in relation to theory; together they make up a productive and potentially expansive dialectical unity. This entails that we move beyond the sterile and pseudo-scientific methodologies of imposing external and absolute measures for determining truth or falsity by granting primacy to the observational data base. Not to do so would be irrational, since by virtue of our theoretical networks we necessarily decide what is to count as emperical data and in what its empirical attributes consist; there can be no imposed, external testing procedure. To suggest that there can be involves circular reasoning, since there can be no independent test of theory against that which has itself been theoretically constituted. The meaning and significance of the data is not obvious, it is not "given" to us in any real sense as subject observers. We inevitably make it what it is according to a particular conceptual framework. The move recommended here is not from science to the creation of fairy tales about the past, but from a pseudo-science to a dialectically conceived science. Such a science is not radically different from other modes of human understanding. It comprehends and embraces the creative human element in the construction of knowledge and recognises that, for knowledge to be useful, it must be practical and have implications for practice and reconstruction in the present (i.e., for those contemporary social conditions mentioned at the beginning of this essay). Statistics, mathematical modelling and the use of computers are important, not as ends but as descriptive means. The task of such work will be not merely to transmit an understanding of the past, but to engage the reader to challenge, to pinpoint inadequacies, and to stimulate him or her to reflect on the current political and social situation. Such knowledge of the past will always be frail, always liable to substitution and change; it cannot and should not be conceived as rigid and immobile. Such knowledge is *strategic*.

Transforming museums and relations with the public

So far the discussion has been concerned almost entirely with archaeology as political practice within an academic environment. Few members of the general public read academic texts such as this, however. Probably even fewer visit archaeological excavations than read the intermittent and academically self-styled popularisations. The museum remains the major institutional connection between archaeology as a discipline and profession and the wider society.

Museums ostensibly have educative value in presenting the past to the public; here one can visit the past, but it is a past which is not at all relevant to most interest-groups in society. In their present structure, museums serve by and large to distance and disenfranchise people from their past. They have an ever-present tendency to commodify and objectify the artefact. The past becomes a succession of pre-interpreted, securely named or labelled objects, astheticised by means of the museum display. Picturesque and pleasant, or icy in its solemnity, the museum is unavoidably part of the commodity system and systematically divorces people from the past rather than linking them to it:

> It is tourists who are the main modern pilgrims, carrying guide books as devotional texts. Moving from one architectural feature of the church to the next, or, in museums, passing from glass case to glass case or from painting to painting . . . they may scarcely look at the exhibit or monument: their essential function is to read the guide books, the explanatory cards or commemorative plaques, or listen to hired cassettes. What matters is *what they are told* they are seeing . . . what finally matters may be a souvenir postcard, perhaps even the admission ticket, kept for years afterwards with other mementoes of passing visions of how life might have been.
>
> (Horne 1984, p. 10, emphasis added)

Behind the obligatory exaltation of the austere severity of the museum and the "mediation" it encourages, there are sometimes glimpses of the true nature

of the visit – an always somewhat laborious task which the devotees set themselves and duly perform with methodical determination. The museum left
me with an impression of silence. Emptiness, too, but perhaps because of
the silence. That helps you concentrate on the works, helps them sink into
you. I wasn't bowled over by it, it's very tedious. Looking at everything
systematically is tiring. It was self-imposed discipline. It's constraining and
you get indigestion. I think I got through it quickly because I wanted to be
able to tell myself I'd done that museum. It was very monotonous, one picture
after another. They ought to put something different in between the paintings to break it up a bit.

(Engineer in Bourdieu 1984, p. 273)

Rather than establishing any real link with the past for the visitor, the museum
very effectively serves to establish the modernity of the viewing public. The "real"
past belongs to the specialist, the curator. The museum might be viewed as a power
structure in which the past is given only to be taken away. The past is not the past
of the public, but belongs to a small clique who water it down, disseminate it,
asceticise it, select it, control it, and present it. The public become passive
consumers and the reduction of the public to consumers establishes their power-
lessness in relation to the past; this is reflected in the boredom experienced by
many, if not most, museum visitors. To be bored means one cannot enter the past,
open it out, get it going. The past remains aloof, controlled, mediated, and all that
is permitted is a passive response and acquiescence. A number of effective critiques
of the role of museums in contemporary society are beginning to appear in the
literature (Horne 1984; Leone 1981a, 1981b, 1984b; Wallace 1981) but further
work of this nature is required. Its aim, as in all critical work, is not to destroy
but to open out possibilities for change and intervention. A major research project
now in progress under Leone's direction, "Archaeology and the public", has great
potential for such opening up of new avenues and fresh directions (and see
Handsman and Leone, 1989)

The analogy between contemporary museums and capitalist processes of production is striking, although it is obscured in everyday life. Commodities are sold in
shops and are thus divorced from the place and process of their fabrication; adver-
tisements never depict the conveyor belt and the social relations of the factory floor.
Museums, likewise, tend to suppress the theoretical labour involved in constructing
the past and the indeterminances in, and contradictions between, the various theoretical frameworks utilised. The past is not seen as a construct, a social production,
but as a self-evident body of facts. Just as commodities appear to have a value in
themselves rather than by virtue of being a product of labour, so too the past appears
to have an eternal value or meaning in itself divorced from creative thought.

The transformation of museums must play an important role in archaeology
that is practised as a form of social and political action. Museums should, but do
not, provide the public with the intellectual means to assess, criticise, define and

redefine the past. In a society which is truly open to different opinions and beliefs, the museum should be deconstructed and restructured to enable people to create their own pasts. The goal will be to make the visitor no longer a passive consumer but an active producer of the past. In a political role, museums should bring an awareness that people *do* make their own history and can change it by their actions in the present. The museum display should not promote acquiescence but *shock* people into reflection on their past and their current situation.

We should try to build into museum displays alternative accounts of the phenomena, diverse explanations, and a variety of perspectives on, and rival theoretical interpretations of, the factual data so as to encourage a critical and creative outlook. Deconstructing the conventional manner of production of the past in this way would make the museum a cultural experience to be shaped and modified at will. In essence museums should provide people with the materials they need to make the past they want and would value. Political content could be introduced into conventional displays to show how the past may be manipulated and misrepresented for present purposes. The "objective third-person narrative" of the ordinary display might be supplemented with exaggeration, irony, humour, or absurdity as a means of stripping away the supposedly self-evident meaning of the artefact. Community use of artefacts should be promoted and the institutionally hallowed space of the museum broken down (see Shanks and Tilley 1987b).

Revealing the social and historical contextuality of rationality

Individuals, interest groups, and societies all have different views of the past and this is potentially productive for social reconstruction. Archaeology should be sensitive to these different views. Hodder notes that:

> There are signs that groups other than white, . . . middle class intellectuals want to write their own pasts. Other social groups in England, women in England and America, ethnic minorities and archaeologists in less-developed countries are beginning to make claims to their own archaeology. . . . If these different but coherent viewpoints can be discussed openly, then the past will play a rôle in unearthing and objectifying alternative viewpoints and social dispositions, contributing to social change.
>
> (Hodder 1984, pp. 30–31)

This is a point of the utmost importance. There is and can be no monolithic *past*. Rather, there are multiple and competing pasts constructed in accordance with ethnic, cultural and sexual social and political values (see Gero 1989). The assertion of a crude scientism fragments concerns and is not at all productive. Hall (1984) and Ucko (1983) discuss the very real social divide between the archaeology of the white investigator and that which the indigenous populations wish to create and sustain in Zimbabwe and Australia. Similarly, a feminist archaeology is likely to involve very different concerns than those taken at present and will create a different version of the past (Conkey and Spector 1984). The conflicts of interest between American Indian groups and archaeologists are well known (e.g., Meighan 1984). This conflict has its roots not only in the issue of whether or not archaeologists have the right to uncover Indian remains but also in the images created of the people who lived in the past (Trigger 1980). Knowledge of the past may or may not have truth value. It certainly can have politically effective power as a technological discourse operating partly to reproduce the relationship between the dominant and the dominated. A pluralistic dialectic between different groups interested in the past reveals different contexts for the development of differing rationalities or modes of understanding. It allows us to recognise otherness and, more than anything else, it underlines the irretrievably social character of archaeological theory and practice – why the past is created in one manner rather than another.

Understanding material culture in relation to power and ideology

One redeeming and potentially important feature of archaeology is that it studies material culture and is the major discipline to do so in a systematic and serious manner. Given that we live in a world of material objects, a self-critical archaeology should be especially concerned to examine the ways in which material culture is and can be used to legitimate power strategies and ideological practices both in the past and the present. Such an archaeology will consider the ways in which material culture, as material discourse, sign system, and signifying practice, is related to the maintenance or transformation of systems of power. To unmask this role of material culture in specific social and historical contexts is to make a political statement and, potentially, to develop a critique of the social order (for preliminary attempts see Faris 1983, and contributions in Miller and Tilley 1984).

The major challenge confronting archaeologists has always been to confer meaning and significance in terms of the social on a world of otherwise meaningless objects. Material culture is a human production and, as such, it is charged with meaning and is structured in relation to social processes. People order their activities in the world and simultaneously effect an ordering of the representation of those activities as a symbolic scheme, apart from which their activities cannot be understood. Meanings are not simply the reflection of the extant material conditions of existence and of the social relations necessary for social reproduction, they are constitutive of this existence and these relations, and are therefore essential for any archaeological unravelling of past and present. We can, in fact, posit that all social life consists of the constitution and transformation of the frames of meaning through which agents orient and reorient their conduct in relation to others and the natural environment. Material culture is an integral part of social life and may play an active role in constituting and transforming frames of meaning. It is embodied in social relations and social practices and plays an important role in facilitating interventions in the natural and social world. Any determinate social formation is characterised by distinctive temporally, spatially, and socially situated practices in which material culture patterning is interlinked. Material culture can only be realistically interpreted once it is contextually situated. To begin to understand the nature of this patterning requires a process of double contextualisation. First, explanations must be related to the totality of practices of a particular social formation. To make cross-cultural generalisations and pretend one can gain significant insight is like taking a series of British, French, and Swedish coins, grinding down the edges, erasing the heads, figures, and valuations, and then suggesting that they are all in some very basic way comparable. Second, that which is analysed must be interpreted within the framework of particular social strategies in the social formation under consideration. Material culture, as a sign system, may serve to channel and structure power in social strategies primarily as a producer and organiser of consensus. It makes that which is contingent appear natural. In many instances social actors may not realise that they are using a sign system or a series of embedded codes. In this case the sign system may, rather, tend to use them. Concomitantly, consensus may seem not only natural but actually spontaneous. Hence, contrasts and relationships can be exploited as part of a semiotic code in the structuring, restructuring, and reproduction of specific sets of social practices and relations. There is a pressing need for an adequate understanding of the manner in which material culture operates in relation to social strategies if emancipation in the present is to be realised. Archaeological work in this area is only just beginning to be done but it is here that it has a major contribution to make.

There can be no *a priori* guidelines for a critical archaeology determining what is or is not appropriate to study. Both Greek red figure ware and modern beer cans are equally important; it does not matter what particular kind of data are used or whether they are past or present-day materials. What is vital is that our studies have critical, transformative intent which enables us to view past, present, and the connection between the two in a new light. A deconstruction of conventional archaeology will build on a critique of the notion that it is only appropriate for the archaeologist to bury his or her head in the distant past (Gould and Schiffer 1981). The goal of modern material culture studies will not be just to aid in an understanding of the past or to help to relate past to present, but also to effect a critical understanding of the present using contemporary material.

Conclusions

This discussion has moved a long way from the political and social issues mentioned at the beginning of the chapter. Is it, then, just another piece of academic self-justification which in the end fails to relate archaeology to the world? Yes and no. Yes, because archaeology can have no dramatic reconstructive effect on contemporary capitalism, war, or the problem of global inequality. Only a radical change in all areas of society could accomplish that. No, because it does not follow from this that archaeologists are entirely impotent. Archaeology forms one small but nevertheless significant part of contemporary culture. Changing the nature of archaeology will filter through and have an effect on other areas, especially through interaction between professional archaeologists and the public. Because prehistoric social actors are dead and gone it is only too easy to treat them as mere objects, subject to the whims of an imposed technocratic reason, or to suggest that they were involved in maximising strategies or were inherently conservative. None of these ideas is altered by the archaeological data; the data can always be interpreted in this manner whatever "tests" might be attempted. Such interpretation of the past *does* have an effect on the present. In the absence of a critical approach it can suggest that the capitalist present is in some basic way natural rather than culturally created in a particular set of historical and social conditions.

The transformation of the capitalist social order which many might like to see cannot be achieved only through normal political processes. The events of Paris in 1968 demonstrated this quite clearly. Essentially, and in most cases, societies are not just held together by brute force or coercion. These are relatively weak and extreme forms of power. There is a much more subtle and pervasive form of power: the power of ideology that infects and invades all areas of social life, including academic environments. The challenge to and critique of ideology cannot just involve criticism of the political establishment but must extend to all areas of society and social life, to the entire social, political, moral and intellectual culture of today. Archaeology is a part of that culture and provides a source and medium for critique.

The seven proposals advanced above are little more than preliminary suggestions. This does not in any sense mean that they are the only arguments and proposals to be made, or that they are entirely correct. They are both personal and social, social because no work is produced in a vacuum; there is no sanctity of pure personal thought. All thought is social although individuals may stamp it with their names. Just as the theories criticised in the first section of this essay cannot be reduced to the effects of social and political values and have a conceptual worth or inferiority independent of these values, so the arguments made here may have some importance irrespective of the values embedded in them. Nevertheless, there is no "pure" statement that can be radically separated from these values. The values explain, at least in part, why these particular positions were adopted rather than others, why certain concepts were employed rather than others, and finally why this paper is being written rather than another. It has been suggested that no text is to be interpreted in any simple sense, for example, purely in terms of the intentions attributed to it by the author either at the time of writing or afterwards. A text lives beyond the person who constructed it. Naturally, this caveat applies to this text. Critical work is essential, and it is not simply destructive and pessimistic. It keeps archaeologists on their toes, and, more fundamentally, it ensures that archaeology will be a critical discipline, critical of itself and critical of the world. A non-critical archaeology tends to be an ideological archaeology because it is not aware of its embedment in the social. The critics of the critic are left to their work.

References

Barthes, R. (1977) "The death of the author", in R. Barthes *Image – Music – Text*, Hill and Wang, New York, pp. 142–8

Benjamin, W. (1973) *Illuminations*, Fontana, London

—— (1979) *One Way Street*, New Left Books, London

Binford, L.R. (1983) *Working at Archaeology*, Academic Press, New York

Binford, L.R. and Sabloff, J.A. (1982) "Paradigms, systematics and archaeology", *Journal of Anthropological Research*, 38: 137–53

Bordieu, P. (1984) *Distinction: A Social Critique of the Judgement of Taste*, Routledge and Kegan Paul, London

Carlson, B-G., Wall, H. and Sandegård, E. (1983) *Varlden i Forskolan*, 2 vols., Tjanstemannens Bildningsverksamhet, Stockholm

Christenson, A. (1980) "Change in the human niche in response to population growth", in T. Earle and A. Christenson (eds.) *Modelling Change in Prehistoric Subsistence Economies*, Academic Press, London, pp. 31–72

Clark, J.G.D. (1939) *Archaeology and Society*, Methuen, London

—— (1979) "Archaeology and human diversity", *Annual Review of Anthropology* 8: 1–20

—— (1983) *The Identity of Man*, Methuen, London

Clarke, D.L. (1968) *Analytical Archaeology*, Methuen, London

—— (1973) "Archaeology: the loss of innocence", *Antiquity* 47: 6–18

Conkey, M. and Spector, J. (1984) "Archaeology and the study of gender", in M.B. Schiffer (ed.) *Advances in Archaeological Method and Theory*, vol. 7, Academic Press, London, pp. 1–38

Daniel, G. (1962) *The Idea of Prehistory*, Watts and Co., London

Dunnell, R.C. (1978) "Style and function: a fundamental dichotomy", *American Antiquity* 43 (2): 192–202

—— (1980) "Evolutionary theory and archaeology", in M.B. Schiffer (ed.) *Advances in Archaeological Method and Theory*, vol. 3, Academic Press, London, pp. 35–99

—— (1984) "The ethics of archaeological significance decisions", in E. Green (ed.) *Ethics and Values in Archaeology*, The Free Press, New York, pp. 62–74

Earle, T. (1980) "A model of subsistence change", in T. Earle and A. Christenson (eds.) *Modelling Change in Prehistoric Subsistence Economies*, Academic Press, London, pp. 1–29

Eliot, T.S. (1948) *Notes Toward a Definition of Culture*, Faber and Faber, London

Faris, J. (1983) "From form to content in the structural study of aesthetic systems", in D. Washburn (ed.) *Structure and Cognition in Art*, Cambridge University Press, Cambridge, pp. 90–112

Flannery, K.V. (1972) "The cultural evolution of civilizations", *Annual Review of Ecology and Systematics* 3: 399–426

—— (1982) "The golden Marshalltown: a parable for the archaeology of the 1980s", *American Anthropologist* 84: 265–78

Foucault, M. (1977)

—— (1981) "The order of discourse", in R. Young (ed.) *Untying the Text*, Routledge and Kegan Paul, London, pp. 48–78

Fritz, J.M. and Plog, F. (1970) "The nature of archaeological explanation", *American Antiquity* 35: 405–12

Gero, J.M. (1989) "Producing prehistory, controlling the past: the case of New England beehives". In V. Pinsky and A. Wylie (eds) *Critical Traditions in Contemporary Archaeology: Essays in the Philosophy, History and Socio-politics of Archaeology*, Cambridge: Cambridge University Press, pp. 96–103.

Giddens, A. (1981) *A Contemporary Critique of Historical Materialism*, Macmillan, London

Gould, R.A. and Schiffer, M. (eds.) (1981) *Modern Material Culture: The Archaeology of Us*, Academic Press, London

Green, E. (ed.) (1984) *Ethics and Values in Archaeology*, The Free Press, New York

Hall, M. (1984) "The burden of tribalism: the social context of Southern African Iron Age studies", *American Antiquity* 49: 455–67

Handsman R.G. and M.P. Leone (1989) "Living history and critical archaeology in the reconstruction of the past," In V. Pinsky and A. Wylie (eds) *Critical Traditions in Contemporary Archaeology: Essays in the Philosophy, History and Socio-politics of Archaeology*, Cambridge: Cambridge University Press, pp. 117–135.

Higgs, E. and Jarman, M. (1975) "Palaeocconomy", in E. Higgs (ed.) *Palaeoeconomy*, Cambridge University Press, Cambridge pp. 1–7

Hill, J.N. (1977) "Systems theory and the explanation of culture change", in J. Hill (ed.) *The Explanation of Prehistoric Change*, University of New Mexico Press, Albuquerque, pp. 59–103

Hodder, I. (1984) "Archaeology in 1984", *Antiquity* 58: 25–32

Horne, D. (1984) *The Great Museum: The Re-Presentation of History*, Pluto Press, London

Jarman, M., Bailey, G.N. and Jarman, H.N. (eds) (1982) *Early European Agriculture*, Cambridge University Press, Cambridge

Jochim, M.A. (1976) *Hunter-Gatherer Subsistence and Settlement: A Predictive Model*, Academic Press, London

Keene, A. (1979) "Economic optimization models and the study of hunter-gatherer subsistence-settlement systems", in C. Renfrew and K. Cooke (eds) *Transformations: Mathematical Approaches to Culture Change*, Academic Press, London, pp. 369–404

—— (1981) *Prehistoric Foraging in a Temperate Forest: A Linear Programming Model*, Academic Press, London

Leone, M.P. (1981a) "Archaeology's relationship to the present and the past", in R. Gould and M.B. Schiffer (eds) *Modern Material Culture: The Archaeology of US*, Academic Press, London, pp. 5–14

—— (1981b) "The relationship between artifacts and the public in outdoor history museums", *Annals of the New York Academy of Sciences* 376: 301–14

—— (1984) "Interpreting ideology in historical archaeology: The William Paca Garden in Annapolis, Maryland", in D. Miller and C. Tilley (eds) *Ideology, Power and Prehistory*, Cambridge University Press, Cambridge, pp. 25–35

Marcuse, H. (1955) *Reason and Revolution*, Routledge and Kegan Paul, London

Marx, K. (1970) "Theses on Feuerbach", in K. Marx and F. Engels *The German Ideology* (ed. C. Arthur), Lawrence and Wishart, London, pp. 121–3

Meighan, C. (1984) "Archaeology: science or sacrilege", in E. Green (ed.) *Ethics and Values in Archaeology*, The Free Press, New York, 208–23

Miller, D. and Tilley, C. (eds) (1984) *Ideology, Power and Prehistory*, Cambridge University Press, Cambridge

Piggott, S. (1959) *Approach to Archaeology*, A. and C. Black, London

Plog, F. (1974) *The Study of Prehistoric Change*, Academic Press, New York

—— (1982) "Is a little philosophy (science?) a dangerous thing?", in C. Renfrew, M.J. Rowlands and B.A. Segraves (eds) *Theory and Explanation in Archaeology: the Southampton Conference*, Academic Press, New York, pp. 25–33

Renfrew, C. (1972) *The Emergence of Civilisation: The Cyclades and the Aegean in the Third Millenium BC*, Methuen, London

Rowlands, M. (1984) "Objectivity and subjectivity in archaeology", in M. Spriggs (ed.) *Marxist Perspectives in Archaeology*, Cambridge University Press, Cambridge, pp. 108–13

Sahlins, M. (1976) *The Use and Abuse of Sociobiology*, Tavistock, London

Sanders, W. and Webster, D. (1978) "Unilinealism, multilinealism and the evolution of complex societies", in C. Redman, M.J. Berman, E.V. Curtin, W.T. Langhorne Jr, N.M. Versaggi and J.C. Wanser (eds) *Social Archaeology: Beyond Subsistence and Dating*, Academic Press, London, pp. 249–302

Service, E.R. (1975) *Origins of the State and Civilization*, Norton, New York

Shanks, M. and Tilley, C. (1987a) "Facts and values in archaeology", in M. Shanks and C. Tilley, *Re-constructing Archaeology: Theory and Practice*, Cambridge University Press, Cambridge, pp. 46–67

—— (1987b) "Presenting the past: towards a redemptive aesthetic for the museum", in M. Shanks and C. Tilley *Re-constructing Archaeology: Theory and Practice*, Cambridge University Press, Cambridge, pp. 68–99

Suchting, W. (1983) "Knowledge and practice: towards a Marxist critique of traditional epistemology", *Science and Society* 47: 2–36

Tilley, C. (1979) *Post-glacial Communities in the Cambridge Region: Some Theoretical Approaches to Settlement and Subsistence*, British Archaeological Reports, no. 66, Oxford

Trigger, B. (1980a) "Archaeology and the image of the American Indian", *American Antiquity* 45: 662–76

Ucko, P.J. (1983) "Australian academic archaeology: aboriginal transformation of its aims and practices", *Australian Archaeology* 16: 11–26

Wallace, M. (1981) "Visiting the past: history museums in the United States", *Radical History Review* 25: 63–96

Watson, P.J., LeBlanc, S.A. and Redman, C.L. (1971) *Explanation in Archaeology: An Explicitly Scientific Approach*, Columbia University Press, New York

Wenke, R. (1981) "Explaining the evolution of cultural complexity: a review", in M.B. Schiffer (ed.) *Advances in Archaeological Theory and Method*, vol. 4, Academic Press, London, pp. 79–127

Wilson, E. (1975) *Sociobiology: A New Synthesis*, Harvard University Press, Cambridge, Massachusetts

—— (1978) *On Human Nature*, Harvard University Press, Cambridge, Massachusetts

Wobst, H.M. (1989) "Commentary: a socio-politics of socio-politics in archaeology". In V. Pinsky and A. Wylie (eds) *Critical Traditions in Contemporary Archaeology: Essays in the Philosophy, History and Socio-politics of Archaeology*, Cambridge: Cambridge University Press, pp. 136–140.

Chapter 16

RETURN OF THE SACRED
Spirituality and the Scientific Imperative

Gary White Deer

White Deer

> *The communication of the dead*
> *is tongued with fire*
> *beyond the language of the living.*

These words grace a tombstone, somewhere near Dylan Thomas's grave, in Westminster Abbey, London. In that gray place, the paving blocks are, quite literally, tombs. Somewhere between when you pay admission and when your eyes adjust to that dim light, it occurs to you that you are in the middle of an immense burial ground.

Everywhere there are bodies. Graves line the floor, impossible to avoid, endless chiseled names and descriptions, stepping stones to walk upon. Bodies are buried in the walls. Bodies molder between the relics and altar pieces, and under sculpted mausolea on which Byzantine images of their diminutive occupants stare with fixed expressions past endlessly curious lines of tourists.

Over the centuries, this venerable sanctuary has produced a solitary ideal, distilled to a strict taboo, posted – in bold letters: NO PHOTOGRAPHY PLEASE.

The temptation here is to suggest that if science is indeed a religion, then Westminster Abbey could easily qualify as archaeology's Mother Church simply by lifting its ban on photography. Especially apparent to Native American sensibilities, however, is that within this sepulcher of western theology dwells a profound absence of the sacred.

It is this singular absence of the sacred that constitutes the gulf between empiricism and Native American spirituality. If we as particular groups are molded in part by the space between ourselves, then the separation between spirit and science must be a definitive chasm.

Into this void new federal laws have thrown two groups that have, in living form, been for the most part mutually exclusive: archaeologists and Native Americans. There seems to be some tension here. To archaeologists, the idea of consulting with potential specimens must seem annoying. For Native Americans, it's yet another version of this country's oldest and deadliest game: Cowboys and Indians.

Right at this moment it's obvious where both groups are; we're contemplating the void between ourselves, looking for a common ground. At this moment, the space between ourselves is neither sacred nor scientific, neither spirit nor matter. Welcome to the Twilight Zone.

Within this great space there is growing communication. Memos, faxes, formal letters, phone calls, and official visits between tribes and institutions now litter the chasm. Early on, tribal governments received a blizzard of summaries, then inventories, all required by the new federal mandate, from prestigious institutions and agencies that for years had avoided any interaction with Native Americans as living people. Depending on how well various tribal nations understand the new federal mandate, or how seriously its agenda is taken, those required manifests are now either the basis for ongoing consultations or they remain in cardboard containers, somewhere.

In regard to ongoing consultation, tribes, agencies, and institutions are constructing a trail mostly of letters, memos, and faxes. We should always be careful when using such paper trails, lest we make for ourselves and others the worst kind of common ground: an enormous landfill that will be made almost entirely of official communications. Our next task obviously will be to begin the process of crafting a true common ground, one that will in practice bridge the spaces between all concerned parties.

How do we begin to craft a true common ground across the chasm that separates archaeology and tribal nations? I suggest that we start by celebrating the obvious; it's our void, yours and mine. It's a unique tribal/archaeology space – a place we have entered, to be sure, by federal mandate, but ours anyway. Let us reflect on, and appreciate, what we have. Let's celebrate our great space, our common space in order to consider what kind of mutually inclusive landscape we wish to create.

At this moment, we are the ethos of the space between spirituality and the Scientific Imperative. It is for us to realize what sort of notions we may bring into our space, and what we may have to leave behind.

The scientific imperative

At University College, London, there is on display the body of Jeremy Bentham, the utilitarian philosopher. Bentham willed his body to the university medical department, and after he died they did the predictable thing any utilitarian could reasonably expect – they promptly stuffed and mounted him. There exists a notion that empiricism has an overriding mandate to do such things, called the Scientific Imperative. It's a notion with which Indian Country has long been familiar.

The Scientific Imperative presumes an unqualified right to suspend social ethics and cultural taboos in the name of a greater social good: objective discovery.

In the name of objective discovery, empiricism distinguishes for us between animal torture and scientific enquiry, corpse mutilation and medical examination, grave robbery and archaeology. Unfortunately, this notion also amounts to an ethical blank check for visits to Indian Country, a blank check that has purchased, among many other things, thousands of Native American grave goods and remains, many of which, like Jeremy Bentham, have been displayed for public consumption.

Public consumption of Indian remains is a long-standing practice that is just now being abandoned by most reputable venues. Not too long ago the University of Memphis sponsored a tour of Chukalissa, a Mississippian site, which featured the viewing of human remains. I can recall a display of skeletal remains at Woolaroc Museum in Oklahoma. The museum also had on exhibit a collection of shrunken heads. For Native America, such public viewings of the dead are only slightly more objectionable than the mass warehousing of hundreds of thousands of Indian skeletons now on shelves and in boxes across the country.

Now that some of those blank checks are bouncing, and remains and objects are starting to be returned, it is clear that the Scientific Imperative no longer has the currency it once did. It is a notion that we may bring to our mutually inclusive landscape only if we are prepared to recognize its limited applications.

The buried treasure syndrome

Many corollaries to the Scientific Imperative exist as reflex cultural notions. One, we might call the Buried Treasure Syndrome. The other is its close companion, Collecting.

The idea that anything old, or otherwise unique and in the ground, is buried treasure is a notion reinforced by American pioneer-styled property rights. There is a loose consideration about such objects; most often they are regarded as part of the public domain and are therefore up for grabs. Of course, certain federal laws prohibit some of this loose regard. Still, the finders-keepers notion of buried objects as being, in effect, "pay dirt" seems to be a cultural reflex that archaeology has enshrined as a basic tenet.

Collecting also apparently requires a certain kind of cultural instinct. Collecting has been explained to me several different ways by archaeologists and others as a simple desire to possess a unique physical object, one that no one else may have. This instinct to possess the unique and unusual accounts for a range of phenomena, including Elvis memorabilia, butterfly collections, antique shops, art museums, and the ongoing reluctance of some archaeologists regarding repatriation and the subsequent reburial of artifacts.

Recently, an Alabama archaeologist citing the Scientific Imperative proposed that a state collection of Native American remains should not be repatriated since they might one day be used for cancer research. Her proposal raises questions as to what other ethnic collections of remains various agencies and institutions may possess. Are there hundreds of thousands of Irish American, Asian American, Jewish American, or any other American remains now on perpetual tap, ready to be studied for, say, cancer research? Of course not. Only collections of Native American remains are warehoused on a scale of grand proportions.

Collecting within certain ethical limits is fine. Collecting Indian remains and grave objects as buried treasure, however, is no longer acceptable. It is a notion that does not deserve a place within our common ground.

Advocacy

In my community a young boy was buried with his Game Boy tapes. His grave was quickly looted, and the tapes were stolen. Some months previous to this event, tribal members had reburied Woodland period remains that a top soiling operation had unearthed. At the reburial site just beyond a tree line, pot hunters waited, hopeful that we were reburying artifacts as well. The top soiling activity occurred on private property and had been the subject of much regional debate and objection. It was only abated, however, when it was discovered that a soil overburden constituted a wetland fill, a clear violation of the Clean Water Act.

A few issues are apparent in these narratives. How much time elapses before science considers it proper to dig up a burial? What about the destruction of graves by industrial development? What about grave looting, now a major growth industry in America? How viable is the notion of cultural affiliation? What about state and federal laws that protect the environment but ignore human rights?

Archaeologists have always been ideologues, since they are followers of the empiricist notion of linear social progression. As a profession, archaeology needs to realize that the federal mandate has widened the proper scope of their concerns. Social issues are no longer abstract ideas. The entry of tribal governments into the general field of historic preservation has politicized those issues for archaeology. Archaeology and Native America need to maintain an ongoing dialogue, to identify basic common interests, and then to agree on strategies to achieve common goals.

Proactive advocacy, both on a political and professional level, is a notion that now is inevitable. We only need to agree on what form it should take within our mutually inclusive landscape.

Tribal sovereignty

Tribal sovereignty is a notion that predates the contact period. To Native Americans it is a birthright; to European Americans it is a codified concept that stems from two other notions rooted in English Law, the Right of Discovery, and Eminent Domain.

If the Right of Discovery legitimized (for Europeans) land claims in the name of a foreign power, then Eminent Domain legitimized (again, for Europeans) the right of original inhabitants to live on the land being claimed. In order to settle discovered lands, therefore, and assume full title, the foreign power in question was first required to treat or deal with the original occupants, offering (ideally, at least) just compensation.

This mitigating process was codified into a series of treaties between the United States and the original inhabitants of this continent. These original inhabitants were federally recognized in treaty language as sovereign nations. The Native American Graves Protection and Repatriation Act clearly reaffirms the notion of tribal sovereignty by naming federally recognized tribal governments as sole respondents for culturally affiliated, and unidentified objects and human remains.

Historically, the exercise of tribal sovereignty has ebbed and flowed depending on the political, military, and economic strength of Native America. For our purposes, it is important to note that the reason the Scientific Imperative is in question in Indian Country is because of the continuous reaffirmation of tribal sovereignty by the federal government. The notion of tribal sovereignty is one that we must recognize as part of our common ground.

Spirituality

To Native America, the world is composed of both spirit and matter. This, of course, is not a unique concept, as the world is full of variations on this common theme. What is important for our consideration is that to Native America, burials are sacrosanct, certain geographies are counted as holy places, and the earth itself is a living entity.

Certain objects, too, are considered as being imbued with spiritual presence and power. These objects of cultural patrimony are used to mediate between the seen and the unseen. Metaphysical interdiction is a concept long associated with Native American beliefs and practices. Many cultural objects are considered to be instruments that, in association with other understandings, ensure the continuation of good in our world.

The disruption of burials, the desecration of holy places, and the destruction of the environment are considered part of a negative process that has its roots in a fundamental imbalance between spirit and science.

Native American worldviews are mitigated somewhat by the activities of tribal governments. One southeastern tribe, for example, is considering the disinterment of its historic burials to facilitate construction of a bingo facility. Another tribal nation, curiously enough, publicly displays its own grave goods, making them the centerpieces of its small regional museum. On most issues involving federal historic preservation laws, however, the policies of tribal governments do not differ significantly from the traditional beliefs of their constituencies. Those constituencies, on the whole, still retain a spiritual worldview and still value certain original under-standings and practices.

While tribal governments may recognize the validity of archaeology, this disci-pline, in turn, has never seriously considered Native American spirituality as relevant to its own concepts and practices. This lack of consideration can be understood, given the secular basis of empiricism. Now that the void between spirit and science is narrowing somewhat, Native American spirituality is a concept that must be respected and seriously considered. The participation of tribal historic preservation offices in the issues now before us will continue to ensure that Indian spiritual beliefs will remain important to our mutually inclusive landscape.

Balance

From a full, mutually inclusive consideration of these notions a common sensibility can emerge and with this, of course, a true common ground. I would like to suggest a working model for these considerations, one that we use back home. It's a ceremonial model that holds the potential for wider application.

Balance between spirit and matter is the preoccupation of southeastern cere-monialism. Regulation of weather for crops, protection from illness, and continuity of ethos while allowing for change are the special concerns of our ceremonial leaders.

If we were to extend these considerations further, we could easily transpose them into a recognized need for balance between science and Native American spirituality while ensuring the validity of both. As tribal and professional leaders, these particular considerations have now become our particular responsibilities.

For Native Americans, secular science has already been accepted by tribal govern-ment. Tribal employees now include medical doctors, physical anthropologists, and, of course, archaeologists. In order to create a balance between our shared respon-sibilities, archaeology must also accept the validity of Native American spiritual beliefs and practices, especially with regard to burials and sacred objects.

What is needed at this moment is a return of the sacred. Archaeology must allow sacred considerations to influence its practices. It is not necessary for archae-ology to desecularize in order for Native American spirituality to be included as a significant component of a common ground.

To better understand how to mediate between spirit and science, and when to introduce either or both, an interdisciplinary approach should be developed that would integrate both science and tribal traditions. On the archaeology side of things, this could mean introducing more ethnographic studies at the university level, as well as developing special courses in tribal studies, using Native American elders, traditional leaders, and professionals. For Native Americans, workshops in Indian Country involving special scientific concerns and considerations might be helpful. For both groups, hands-on field experience engendering shared learning situations could also be beneficial. In real terms, balance means parity of esteem, a consideration that cannot reasonably exist without parity of accountability.

Most importantly, a new paradigm needs to be developed, one that includes a sense both of the sacred and the secular. Increasingly, the use of Native American traditional practices in conjunction with traditional scientific approaches is widening the scope of the work as presently conceived, and it appears that a form of holistic archaeology is beginning to emerge. From this new model that we may develop from our common ground, we should expect a code of ethics, one that professional archaeological societies, federal agencies, and tribal governments will further refine and follow. It will be a benchmark of standards and practices for archaeology that embodies a balanced consideration of notions from both science and Native American spiritual sensibilities.

■ ■ ■

The current mandate guarantees a process whereby both archaeology and Native America will change each other forever. How that change may occur, and whom it will benefit, will be determined by our ability to fashion for ourselves a true common ground. For Native America, this must always include a balanced return of the sacred.

INDEX